YAYA HAN's
World of COSPLAY

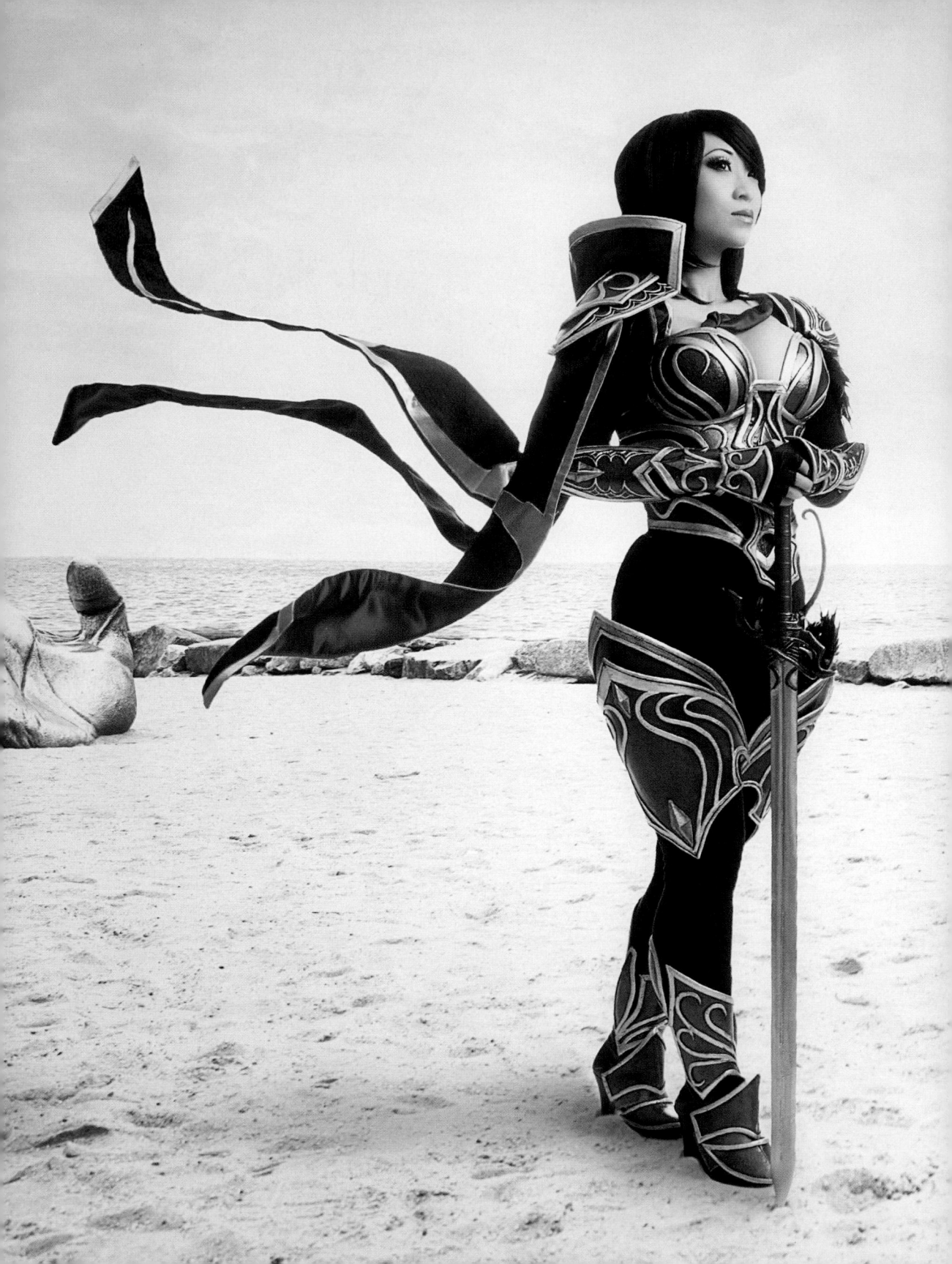

YAYA HAN's

World of COSPLAY

A Guide to Fandom Costume Culture

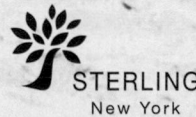

STERLING
New York

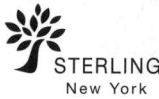

STERLING
New York

An Imprint of Sterling Publishing Co., Inc.
1166 Avenue of the Americas
New York, NY 10036

ISBN 978-1-4549-3265-9

Distributed in Canada by Sterling Publishing Co., Inc.
c/o Canadian Manda Group, 664 Annette Street
Toronto, Ontario M6S 2C8, Canada
Distributed in the United Kingdom by GMC Distribution Services
Castle Place, 166 High Street, Lewes, East Sussex BN7 1XU, England
Distributed in Australia by NewSouth Books
University of New South Wales, Sydney, NSW 2052, Australia

For information about custom editions, special sales, and premium
and corporate purchases, please contact Sterling Special Sales at 800-805-5489
or specialsales@sterlingpublishing.com.

Manufactured in Singapore

2 4 6 8 10 9 7 5 3 1

sterlingpublishing.com

Cover design by Elizabeth Mihaltse Lindy
Front cover photography by Brian Boling
Back cover photography by Kayhettin
Interior design by Shannon Nicole Plunkett

Photography credits on page 231

For all kids, teens, and people
who are searching for their dream.
Keep dreaming, keep creating.

CONTENTS

INTRODUCTION

ivid colors and varied shapes entered my vision whenever I turned my head. I stood against a railing on the second level of the Jacob Javits Convention Center, in the heart of New York City, and marveled at the sea of people below, both in costume and out of it. The shuffle of a thousand bodies mixed with countless voices speaking at once. The music blaring from various loudspeakers filled the air with a continuous roar, as if the building itself had come alive.

I picked out a duo of Disney princesses floating in their shimmering pastel gowns, clutching their skirts as if already late to the ball. Loki, Marvel Comics' beloved antihero, strutted alongside the dames, his golden horns bobbing. A bright blue backpack hung from his shoulder. The Jansport logo clashed against his green-and-black royal attire. A few steps behind him, a group of Batman villains fought to move forward as attendees pressed them back, begging for photos. The Dark Knight himself appeared and walked right past the pack of scoundrels, preoccupied with securing a lanyard around his rubber cowl. No interest in fighting crime today.

People of all ages and walks of life melted into the endless stream, moving with palpable excitement. Familiar and unfamiliar characters tugged at my memory, turning this people-watching moment into a mental game of geek trivia.

There is only one event that can cause such sensory overload and blur the boundaries of fantasy and reality so seamlessly: New York Comic Con.

It was day three, and I was dressed in a red-and-black ensemble—a tight, off-the-shoulder corset with embroidered floral patterns. The garment displayed more cleavage than I would ever feel comfortable showing in everyday situations. Sleek black pants; a short, flowing red cape; and six-inch platform booties completed the outfit. My purple hair was hidden under a voluminous auburn wig, its waves cascading past my shoulders and down my back. A glittering, ruby-red headpiece made entirely of wire and mesh sat atop my head, covered in

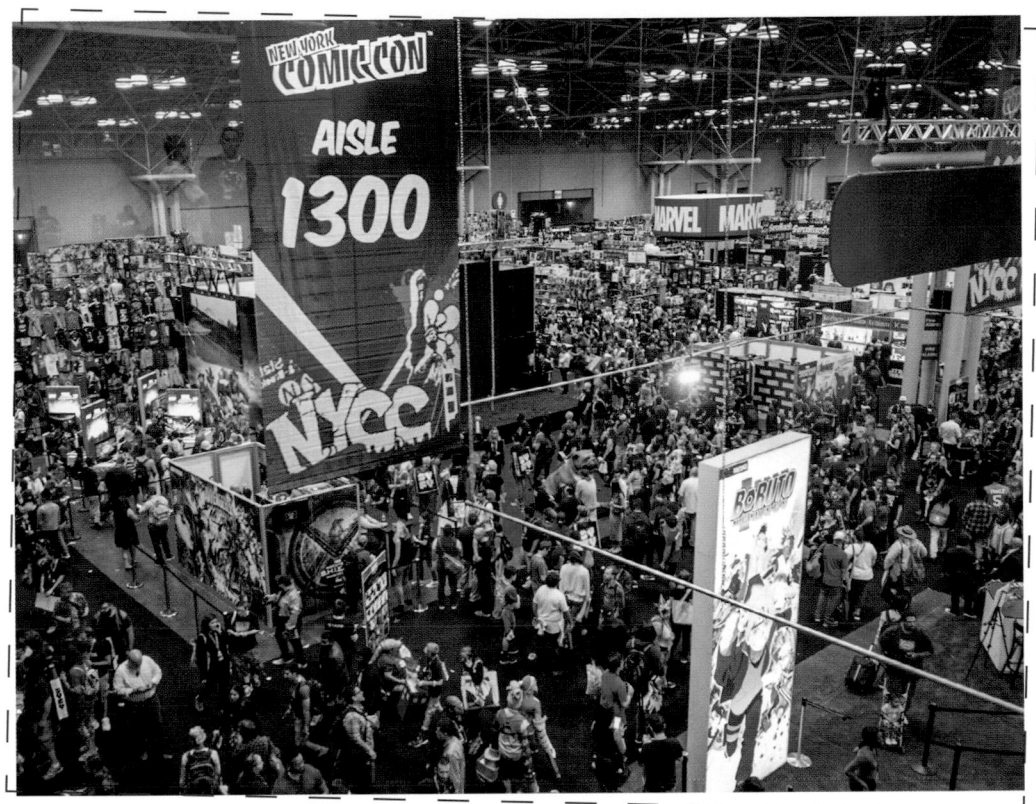

The crowd at New York Comic Con

Swarovski crystals. The jagged edges dripped with long strands of glass beads that perfectly matched my crimson lipstick.

I was a bona fide superhero: far more beautiful, strong, and confident than I felt in my regular life. I was no longer Yaya, a bookish, vertically challenged Chinese girl who grew up on three continents and often felt out of place. Now I was Wanda Maximoff, better known as the Scarlet Witch: a mutant with the ability to alter reality, the daughter of Magneto, and a member of the Avengers. Thanks to cosplay, I could become whoever I wanted. When I caught my reflection in the tall panes of glass lining the hallway, the Scarlet Witch gazed back at me.

I'd re-created Wanda's costume a few weeks earlier to be photographed for a variant cover of Marvel Comics' *Scarlet Witch* stand-alone series. I was about to walk into the Marvel Live studio, to talk on air about the Marvel cosplay covers project, now in its second year of running. Though I had already been on the cover of a Marvel comic issue the year before,

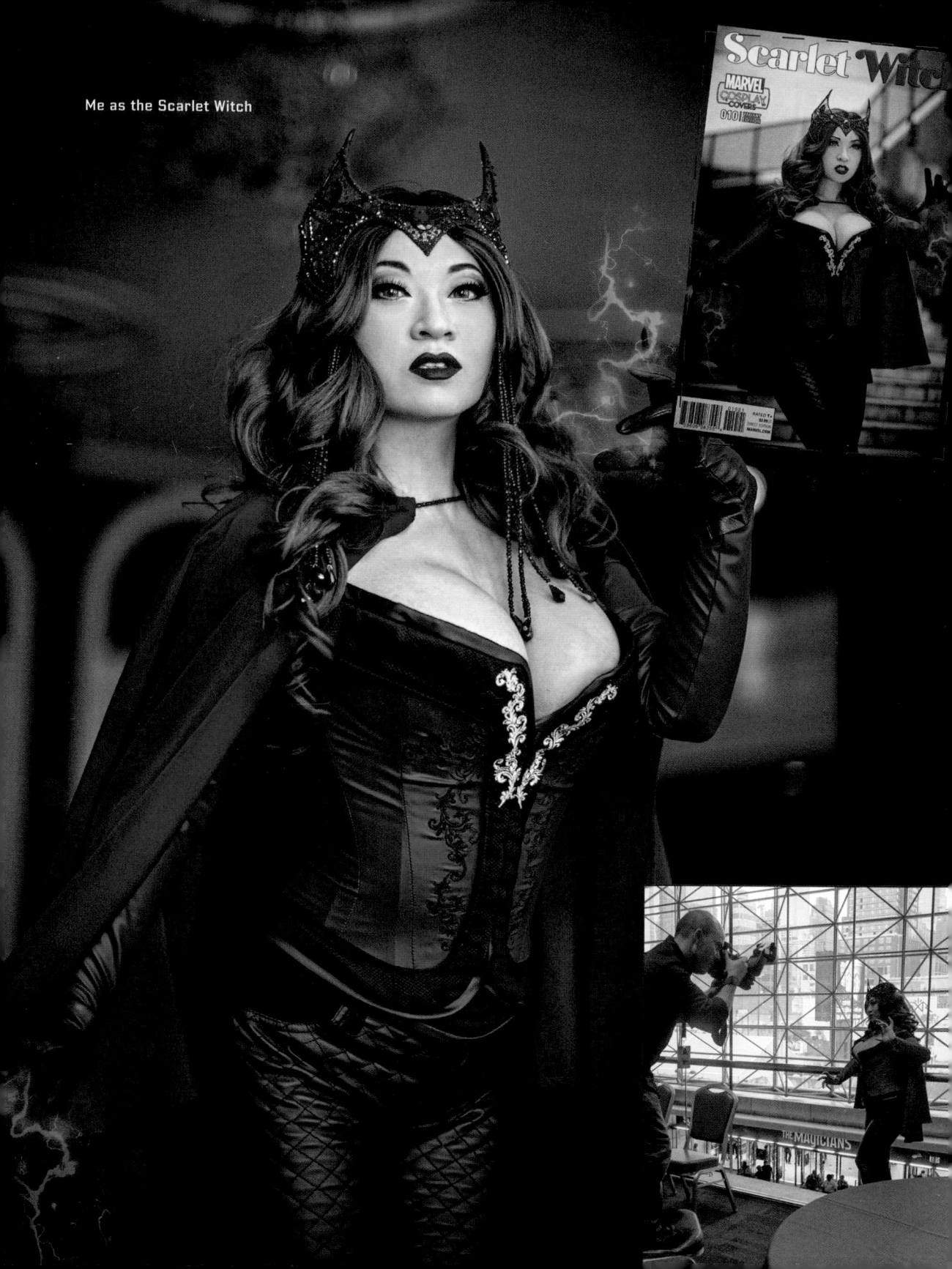

Me as the Scarlet Witch

as Medusa from *The Inhumans*, it was still difficult for me to believe that a major comic book publisher such as Marvel would hire fans—cosplayers—to be featured as official characters on their comic book covers. Such a move would have been unfathomable up until recently.

I felt amazed as I once again reminded myself that cosplay is no longer a niche hobby in the fandom world. There is no shame or stigma attached to it anymore. Cosplay has become a global phenomenon, a lifestyle, and an artistic industry. Cosplay is mainstream.

With one last glance at my superhero attire, I drew in a deep breath and knocked on the door.

— — —

Hello, dear reader, and welcome to the world of cosplay!

There is a good chance that you have heard the term *cosplay* before, either mentioned on a late-night talk show such as *Conan* or in a viral article about video game character lookalikes. You have probably guessed by now that the term *cosplay* is an amalgamation of the words *costume* and *play*. You may have even skimmed through a disjointed Wikipedia entry about it.

People have lots of assumptions about what cosplay is, but in reality, cosplay is an activity that blends fandom, creativity, and entertainment into a unique phenomenon. The layers and nuances of the craft reach far beyond the frivolous idea of dress-up. Cosplay is a lifestyle and a way of being. I have lived and breathed this life for the past twenty years.

In this book, I will share my personal journey through cosplay and offer a comprehensive look into this complex world. We will explore where cosplay came from and why it is considered a form of fan expression, a creative outlet, a social activity, and even a path to self-discovery. We'll also discuss the prestige and pitfalls of cosplay. Finally, we'll look at the current state of the cosplay industry and where it might be headed in the future.

I am thrilled to be your guide on this new and exciting journey. I'm ready to dive in and show you all the vibrant, crazy, beautiful facets of the cosplay phenomenon. It is my hope that by the time you reach the end of this book, you will be fired up and ready to cosplay with me!

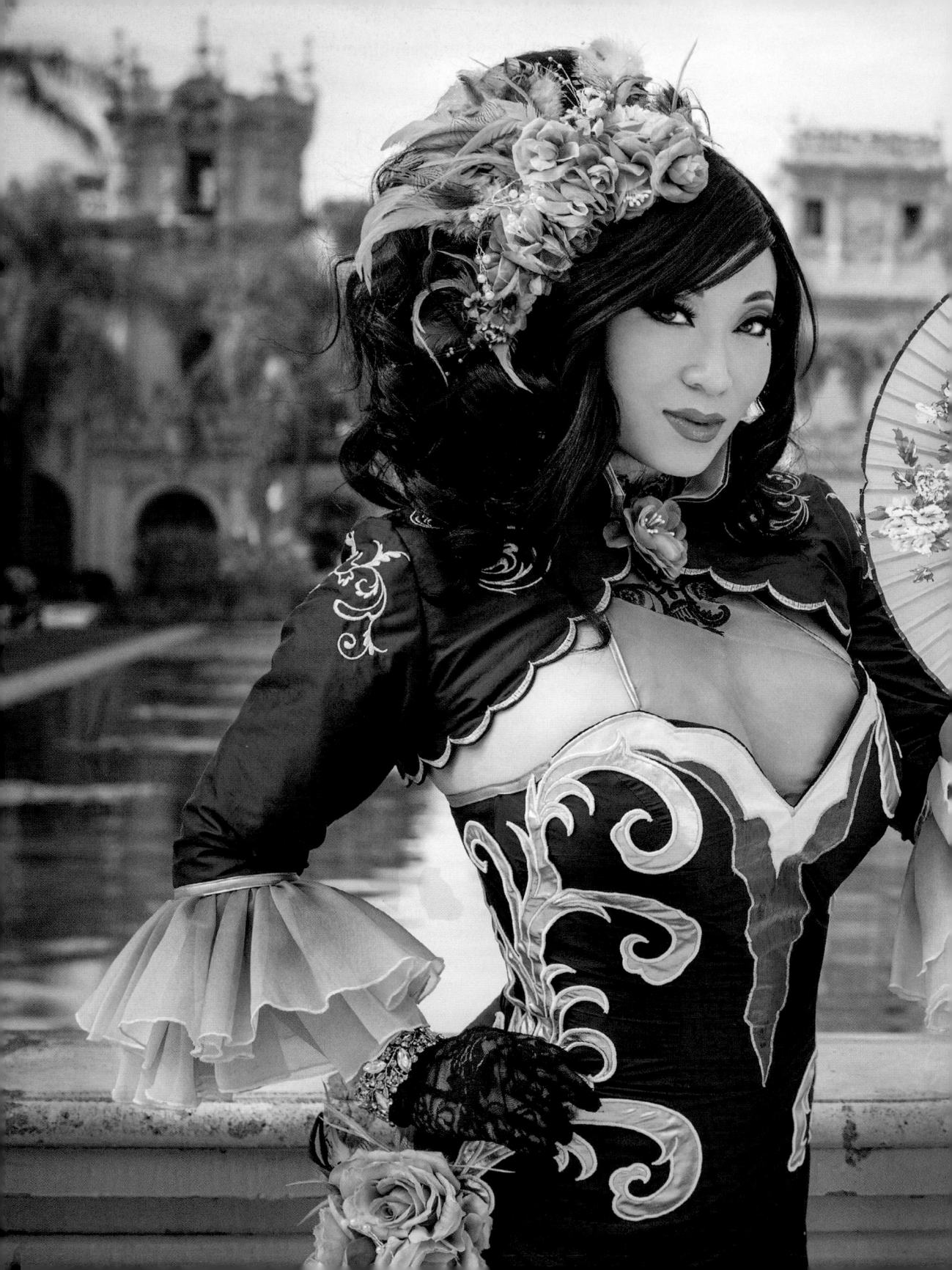

PART ONE

Welcome to the World of Cosplay

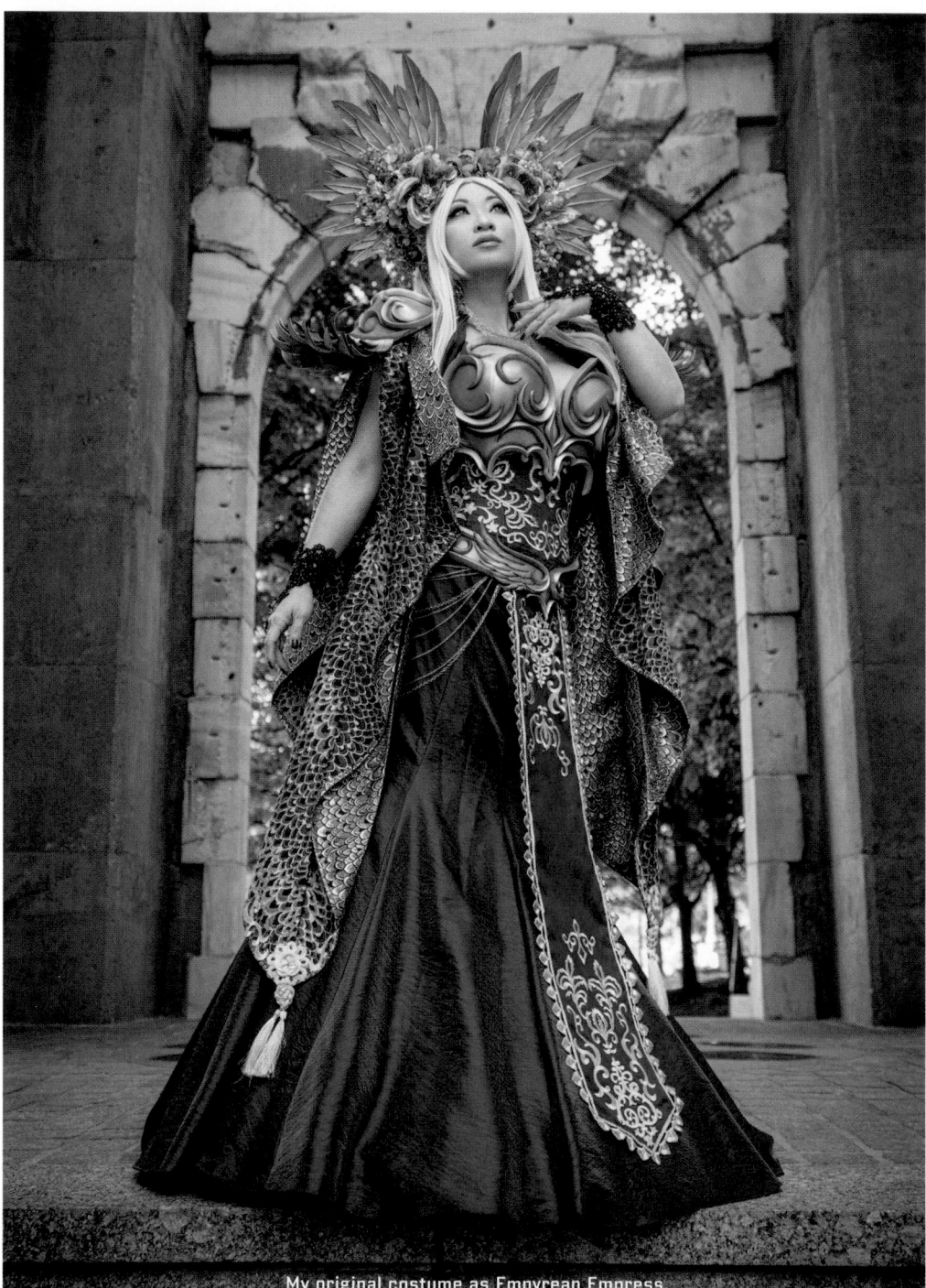

My original costume as Empyrean Empress,
which evolved over time and surpassed my original vision.

CHAPTER 1

What Is Cosplay, and Who Are You?

First, let me introduce myself. My name is Yaya, and cosplay is my full-time job. There's a good chance you've seen my picture on the Internet. Or you may have seen me on network TV, making costumes and judging cosplay competitions. If you've been to a fabric store, you've likely seen the patterns I designed for the McCall's Patterns line or touched samples from my Cosplay by Yaya Han fabric collection, which is now sold in JOANN Fabric and Craft stores across the US.

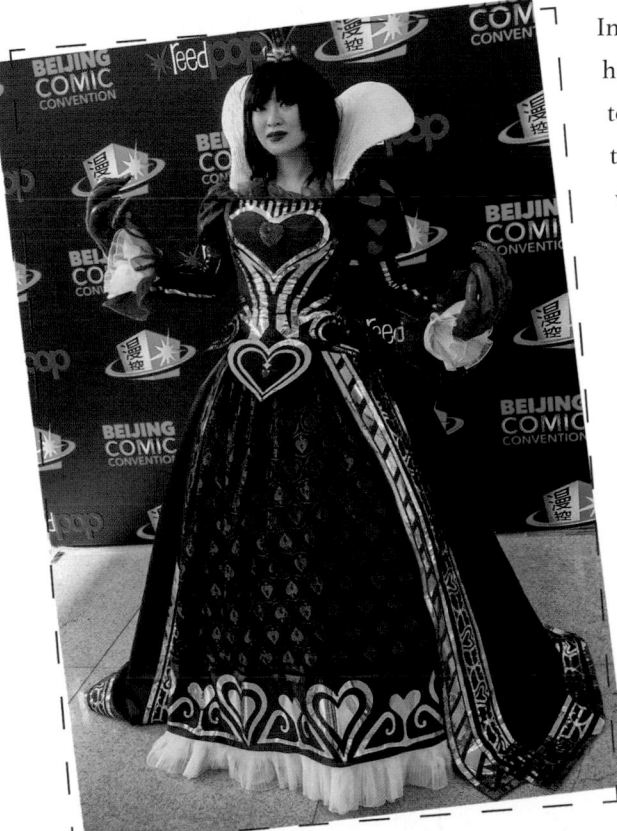

I am what is considered a weekend celebrity. In my everyday life, I'm just a short, purple-haired Asian girl, but I travel all over the world to pop culture conventions to sign autographs, take pictures with fans, and do media interviews. I do what famous actors do at events, but I get invited to these events because I create and wear costumes that allow me to transform into fictional characters.

If you think that sounds like an unusual lifestyle, you're right.

At first glance, cosplay seems very similar to dressing up in a costume on Halloween. Both activities involve wearing outfits for fun. However, there are some big distinctions. Halloween is an annual Western tradition for which people dress up once a year. The costumes are generally mass-produced, and, I dare say, a

My cosplay as the Red Queen

majority of people approach the holiday in a casual, carefree manner. Those who celebrate Halloween aim to have a laugh, enjoy a fun night out, and make nice memories with friends and family.

Cosplay, on the other hand, is not a Western holiday but rather a lifestyle practiced year-round by people all over the world. Cosplayers have a completely different mind-set from casual Halloween celebrators and are fueled by an inner passion inspired by a host of pop culture characters. That passion builds into a desire to become those chosen fictional beings, no matter what it takes. Many "cosplay costumes" require vast amounts of dedication, money, and skill to make, not to mention weeks or months of crafting time.

More than an expensive hobby, cosplay is a lifestyle, because it changes a person on a day-to-day basis. It impacts how you spend your free time. It even changes how you see stories and relate to characters. To this day, I can't watch a movie or play a game without inadvertently analyzing the costume designs on-screen, wondering what materials they are made of and how I could re-create them.

Cosplayers have our craft on the brain every single day.

Sounds kinda extreme, right? There was a time when I was ashamed of the extent of time I spent on cosplay. But now I celebrate it openly and encourage others to celebrate it with me. I can't think of anything else that has brought me as much joy. Growing up in the cosplay/convention scene has shaped me as a person. All my major milestones and life events have a connection to cosplay, including this book. I never would have gotten the chance to write the words you're reading now if I hadn't built a career as a cosplayer. (It also helps that being geeky and cosplaying are considered way cooler now than they used to be.)

Thanks to the thriving fandoms around anime, TV shows, video games, and more, cosplay has enjoyed a dramatic revival in the last fifteen years. Once upon a time, reading comic books or playing video games was regarded as nerdy or uncool, but now the entertainment industry is virtually synonymous with fandom culture and its landscape is dominated by fantasy, sci-fi, and comic book titles. The biggest box office movies are based on fandom properties, featuring the world's most popular movie stars as superheroes. According to Comichron, comic book sales topped $1 billion in 2018. In the same year, global movie box office revenue reached $42 billion as reported by the *Hollywood Reporter*. And, staggeringly, the global video game industry is slated to generate $131 billion in revenue in 2019, according to *Variety*.

On top of everything else, all these movies, comics, and games have inspired countless merchandising options. It's impossible to walk into any store without seeing a *Star Wars* toy or a Batman symbol. Thanks to the popularity of these fandoms, the global toy market reportedly took in $90 billion last year.

Being a geek has become part of the current zeitgeist.

Cosplayers are the very consumers who read these comic books, watch these movies, and collect these toys. But they go one step above other fans by actively creating something inspired by the characters they enjoy. Just as the comic book industry is no longer a niche industry, cosplay is no longer just a hobbyist community. The current landscape of cosplay is full of zeal and promise, with career opportunities, marketing power, and huge forward momentum in commerce.

Cosplay's most notable marriage is with the gaming industry. Video game companies such as Riot Games and CD Projekt Red regularly hire cosplayers to promote their titles at trade shows and tournaments and during marketing campaigns. These projects often extend beyond one-time spokesmodel work into the realms of high-end custom-made costume projects. It has also become fairly common practice for game developers to release turn-around sheets with 360-degree views of their characters, knowing that they may become the subject of a future cosplay. Ubisoft and Gearbox Software do this when they release new installments of their respective *Assassin's Creed* and *Borderlands* franchises, for example.

Blizzard Entertainment, known for its massively successful franchises *Diablo* and *World of Warcraft*, employs cosplayers every year at its annual BlizzCon convention. E3 (Electronic Entertainment Expo), a Los Angeles–based video game conference, bustles with hired cosplayers dressed as characters who will get people's attention and draw crowds around booths. Not only do cosplayers provide an ideal selfie opportunity; their presence creates a memorable experience that, companies hope, will encourage you to buy the game they're promoting.

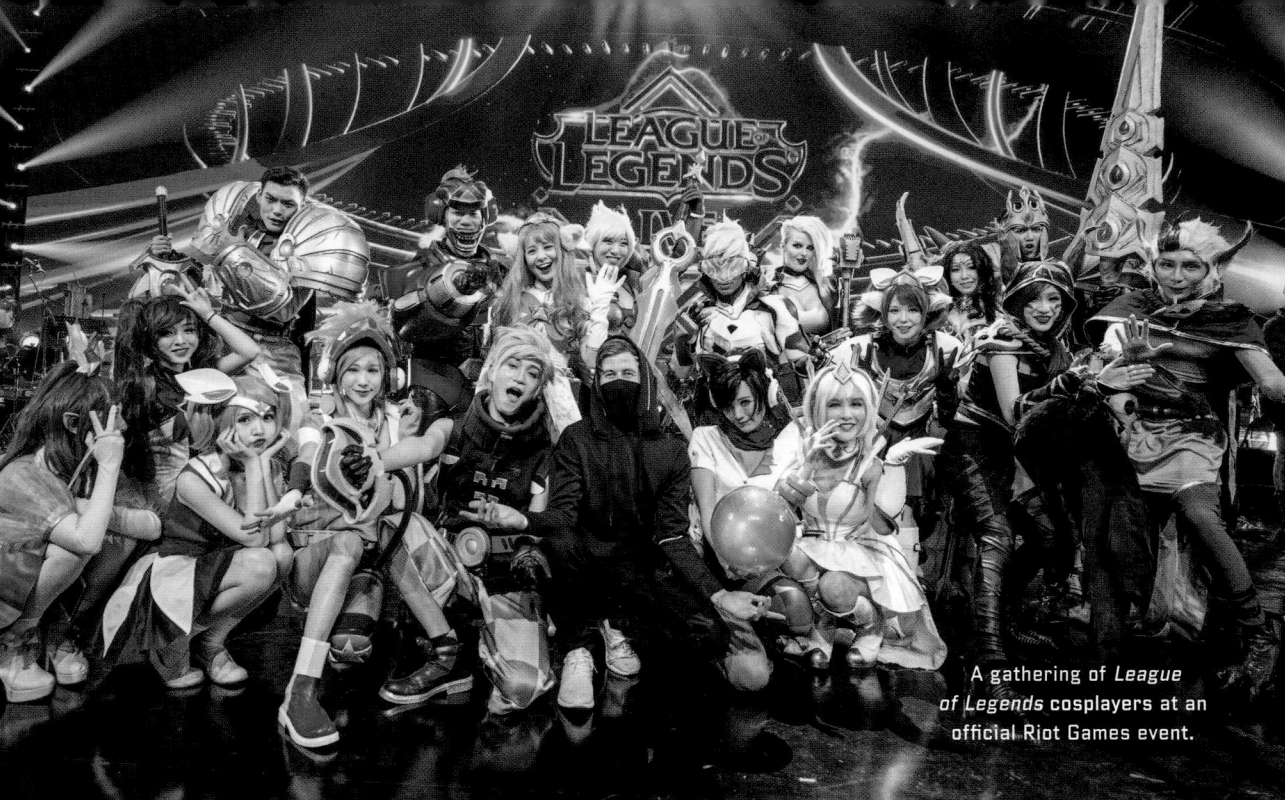

A gathering of *League of Legends* cosplayers at an official Riot Games event.

Twitch, a video streaming platform designed for gamers to monetize video game playthroughs, launched Twitch Creative—a category for artists—in 2015 and heavily marketed it to cosplayers. The developers encouraged costume crafters to broadcast progress on their projects live, offering entertainment and education at the same time. More than 4.5 million people broadcast monthly on Twitch, and while the vast majority are gamers, the close proximity between cosplay and gaming continues to generate a growing interest for creative costume stream sessions.

The comic book industry has also recognized cosplay as an important market. Marvel Comics produces an ongoing cosplay documentary series called Marvel Becoming that highlights a different cosplayer in each episode. In the past, Marvel has also released variant editions of its monthly comics that feature cosplayers on the covers. A lot of comic book artists collaborate with cosplayers for figure modeling and promotional work. Sometimes creators even hire cosplayers to become the face of their titles. In fact, in 2013, I was approached by the comic book publisher Lion Forge to create my own Superhero comic series. Lion Forge even gave me the chance to choose my own superpower and design my costume. The resulting book, *Wonderous 2: The Yaya Han Saga*, told a fun cosplay-centric superhero origin story in eight issues.

There is no denying that cosplay has emerged as a lucrative business, but what really makes the art form special is the sincerity and raw passion of the people within the community. There's a hands-on DIY spirit, and most cosplayers are self-taught (myself included). It's mind-boggling sometimes to look at fan-made cosplay creations that are near-identical replicas of Hollywood costumes. The same thing that takes a team of specialists and state-of-the-art technology to create can be painstakingly re-created by one cosplayer working out of their living room, if they feel motivated enough.

Even on a professional level, cosplayers like me don't generally have a studio or team to make costumes for us. If I didn't make my own costumes, I probably would have lost interest in cosplay a long time ago. I don't get to do it as frequently as I used to due to my hectic schedule, but I am continuously challenged and motivated *because* I am still hands-on in the creative process. There is value and meaning in making the costumes yourself and sharing your progress along the way.

I have been lucky enough to transform my cosplay from a hobby into a business without compromising my key passions. I travel to about twenty-five conventions per year, where I am hired to judge contests, give cosplay panel presentations, and meet fans. In between these trips, I run a cosplay business and design products for my online store. I have a warehouse stocked full of cosplay accessories and thermoplastics and filing cabinets full of cosplay posters that are shipped around the world to fans and sold in convention vendor halls. Ultimately, my business has been so successful that I have been able to expand and hire a small team of employees. As a

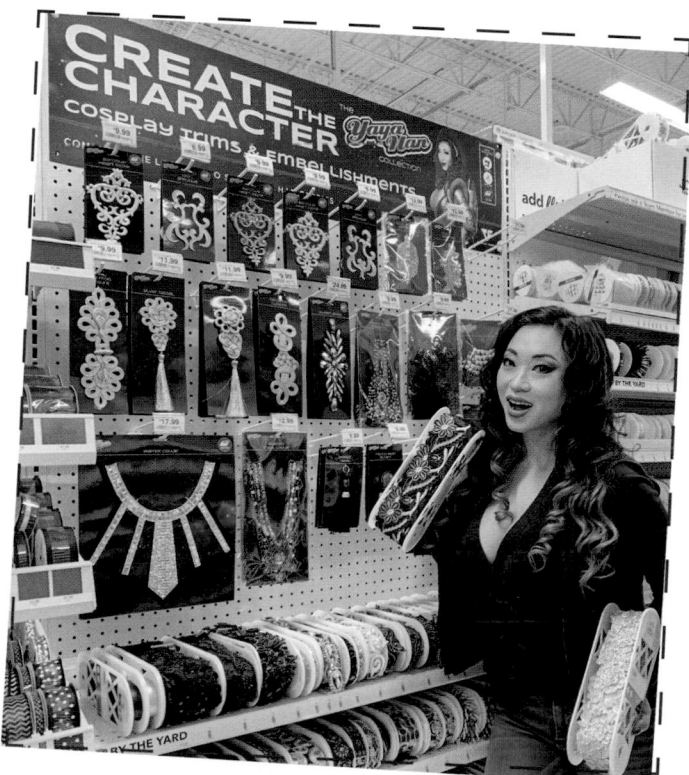

My trims and embellishments line for cosplayers

first-generation immigrant, this is a source of pride for me.

At the moment, what takes up most of my time are my commercial collaborations in the sewing and crafting industry. I have designed more than forty Yaya Han®– branded sewing patterns for McCall's, which are sold worldwide. I also have an ongoing partnership with JOANN Fabric and Craft that keeps me on my toes. Through them, I release two fabric collections per year and maintain a year-round cosplay trims line as well as a new cosplay EVA foam line, all of which are sold in the company's 860+ stores. I am the first cosplayer to successfully enter and navigate the mass retail industry, which has been a huge learning experience as well as a rewarding endeavor. It gives me

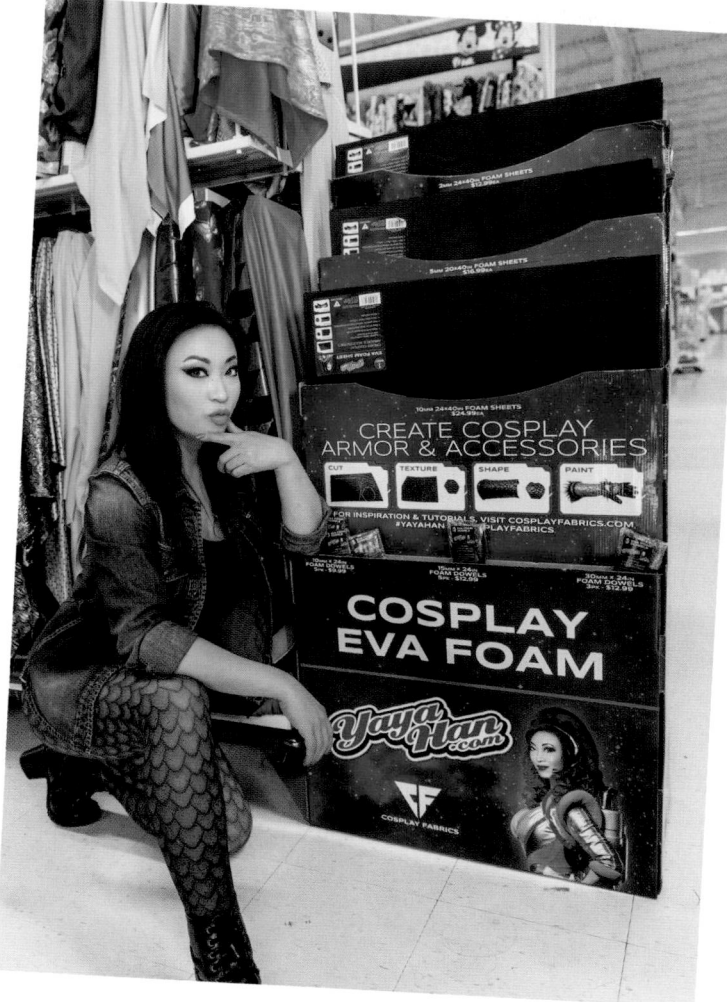

Posing in front of my armor-making EVA foam display at JOANN.

immense delight whenever I meet a cosplayer wearing a costume made using one of my patterns or fabrics, and I love the fact that I get tagged by cosplayers who are working on new projects with my products.

On top of all this, I post daily to a social media following of more than three million people.

I lead a pretty weird life, where the lines are blurred between career and passion. It's a circus that demands my time and energy every single day but also lets me have some unbelievable experiences. I'm usually chasing a deadline or fighting off jet lag, and I can rarely switch off my brain from work for a full day. Despite that, though, I have a fulfilling life that I wouldn't trade for anything.

Whenever I take a step back and look at the current scope of cosplay, one thought runs through my head: *It's about damn time.* The world is finally taking an interest in cosplay and sees it as more than an esoteric hobby some nerdy kids do or a weird fetish practiced by the freakiest of geeks. The public is finally recognizing the value that cosplay brings to fandom culture and, beyond that, to human culture. Every person has a character they relate to, identify with, or just want to be. Cosplay gives people all over the world the chance to become that character, even for just one day. It unlocks the possibilities of actively participating in a fandom instead of just consuming it.

Whether you are a die-hard cosplayer, a newcomer who's just discovered this world, or someone who has not heard of cosplay before, I hope that reading this book will unlock something within you and inspire you to do something you've never previously considered. Maybe it will be to make a costume for the first time, or to step out of your comfort zone and learn a new skill, or to dress up as a character you didn't have the confidence to portray before.

Every cosplayer has that moment of revelation: You can dress up in a costume any time of the year and not just on Halloween. You can be any character. You can make anything. Cosplay has no set rules. It's not a sport. It's the most sincere form of fan expression I have ever encountered and a limitless creative outlet. It is fun and freedom combined.

CHAPTER 2

A Girl Drawing in the Corner

Sometimes I wonder how my life would have turned out if I hadn't discovered cosplay in the summer of 1999. I was on the cusp of becoming an adult and felt quite lost in the world. I had little self-awareness and low self-esteem. Looking back, my discovery of cosplay was the result of many years of searching for kinship and a place where I belonged.

I was born in the early '80s in the city of Xi'an, which was once the ancient capital of China, during the aftermath of the Cultural Revolution. Communism was ingrained in every fiber of the nation, and everything including entertainment was carefully curated, government-approved, and filled with propaganda. While children in America were watching *Star Wars* and reading about the adventures of Spider-Man, I was keeping silkworms as pets and singing old Chinese folk songs in front of my family in the living room.

My grandfather was a decorated military general in World War II, which earned him a highly respected social standing. In his retirement, the government moved him and my grandma from Xi'an, in the north, to a top-notch military housing facility in Guangzhou, in the south, and most of the Han family followed suit by relocating to the city as well. My father was the eldest of five children and was working at the university in Xi'an when he met my mother. She was pursuing a German language degree with the intention to teach, which was quite unusual at the time.

After getting married, my mother wanted to continue her studies, so at three months old, I was flown to Guangzhou to be raised by my

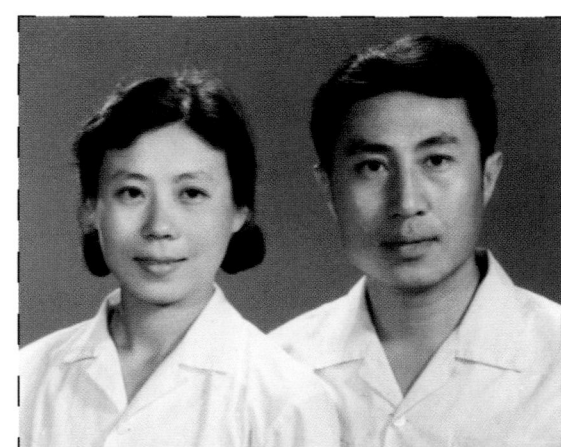

My mom and dad

grandparents, aunts, and a nanny. In China, it was quite common for families to share in the task of childcare, so while my parents remained in Xi'an, the first few years of my life were spent in a large house inside a government-run township where everything was taken care of. We had drivers, cooks, and house staff; these were perks my grandpa earned after fighting for his country. At the time, the one-child-per-family rule was in effect in China, so since I was the only grandchild who lived with the head of the household, I quickly became the family favorite and the darling of the neighborhood. That made my childhood a common Chinese stereotype: I was the spoiled "little golden emperor."

Rowdy, loud, and incredibly confident, I behaved like I owned the township and I bossed my cousins around during playtime. I got in trouble so often that eventually my aunt started locking me in the garden shed to get me to behave. My tomboyishness ensured that I was always covered in bruises and scrapes, but I also loved picking flowers, wearing dresses, and singing. Even at a young age, I had a huge imagination and a sense of adventure.

After three years, my parents brought me back to Xi'an, where I settled into a more regimented routine. We lived in a modest apartment in a concrete building, where studying and school became the focus of my life. By the time I entered middle school, it looked as if my path to becoming an average, hard-working Chinese citizen was laid out.

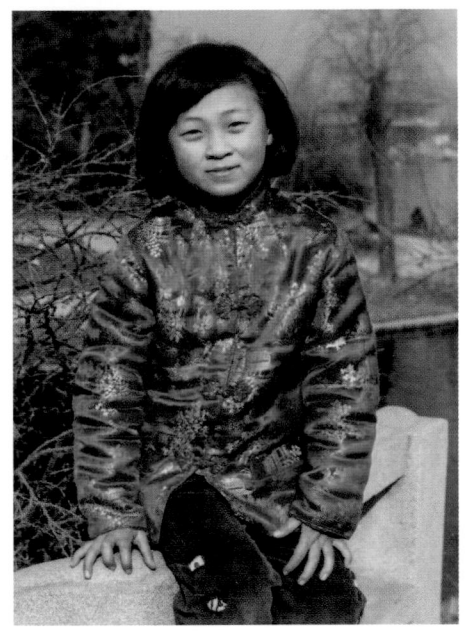

Me as a child in China

Hanging with my cousins (and cake!)

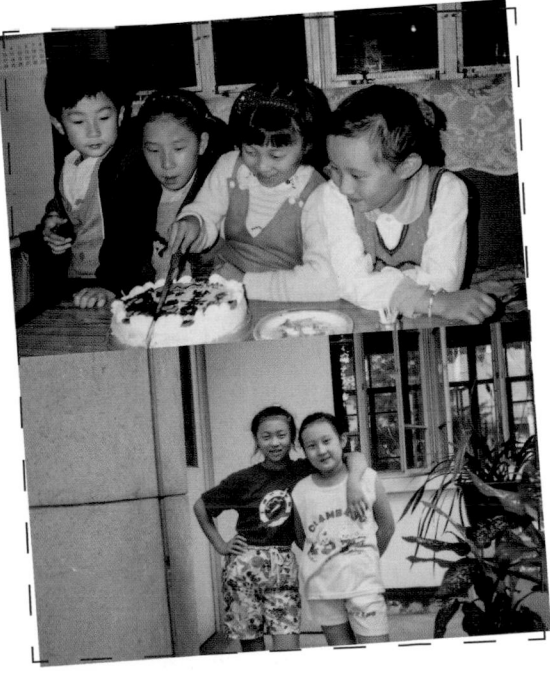

Then my parents divorced.

In a move that could only be described as scandalous at worst and bold at best, my mother left my father and moved to Germany. She had been working as a German teacher at the Xi'an university and became fascinated with Germany after a visit. I was six years old when my mother packed her bags. My father was reserved and quiet and, in typical Chinese fashion, did not talk about the separation or explain to me what had happened. I initially expected that Mama was going to come home soon, but as the months dragged on, I became more rebellious and acted out. I got into fights with classmates, bit people in school, and disobeyed teachers. That didn't go over well in a communist regime, and I was frequently punished.

Eventually, amidst intense feelings of confusion and abandonment, I became withdrawn and quiet. My aggressive side fell away to numbness, and I did what most children of divorce do—seek ways to escape reality. Anime and manga started to become accessible in China in the late '80s, and from the first moment I saw the doe-eyed characters on-screen, I was hooked. The first anime I watched were *Doraemon*, *Astro Boy*, and *Saint Seiya*, followed soon by any broadcast that looked like anime on TV. I begged my father to buy manga books for me, which I devoured each night and every weekend after doing homework. During those years of turmoil, my lifelong love for Japanese animation was formed.

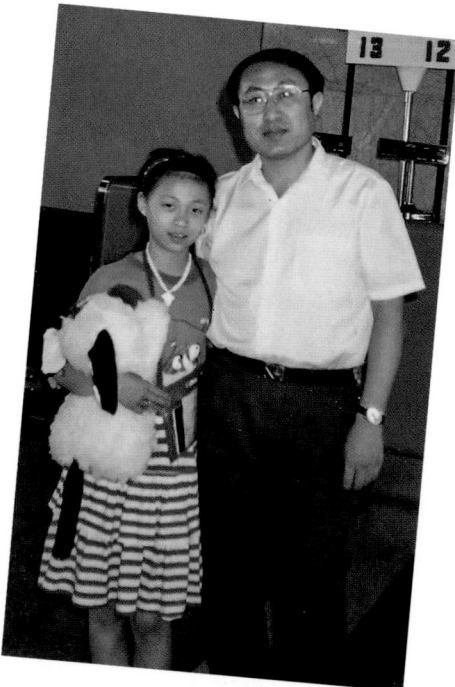

It wasn't until two years later, when my mother flew back to China with a tall, bearded "foreigner man," that I was told the truth. Mama had divorced Baba, married the hairy man, and was living in Germany. I didn't understand until much later that the communist way of life had been suffocating my mother, especially after she saw what freedoms she could have in a Western society. She had to get out. As soon as she could, she came back to get custody of me.

My parents sat me down and asked me where I wanted to live. I was eight years old. Even now, I'm not sure why, but I chose Germany despite never having seen the world outside of China. That choice effectively changed my entire life in one afternoon. A few months later, after all the paperwork was done, I quit school and said

Saying good-bye to Dad when I left China

good-bye to all my friends and family. My father put me on a plane to Frankfurt, and fourteen hours later, I restarted my life in a completely new world, along with a new family, a new language, and a new school.

To say that I had culture shock would be an understatement.

I learned German from the ground up, starting with the alphabet. My school was predominantly white, and I was one of only two Asian students. From the first day on, it was difficult to communicate with my schoolmates and make friends. Not only did I look and behave differently; I also couldn't understand their language. It took six months before I could speak conversational German. Even after that, though, I never got the hang of being social with other kids.

My parents' separation and the transcontinental move solidified my personality as an introverted loner. To say that I didn't get along with Robert, my new stepdad, would be an understatement. In my mind, it was his fault my parents divorced. Moreover, Robert was very open with the fact that he disliked children and only tolerated my presence because of my mom. From the day I stepped foot into their home in Wiesbaden, I knew I did not belong there.

My affinity for Japanese animation only added to my weirdness. During each summer holiday spent in China, I collected manga paperbacks and brought volumes home in overstuffed suitcases. That's how I read all of *Ranma 1/2*, *Revolutionary Girl Utena*, and

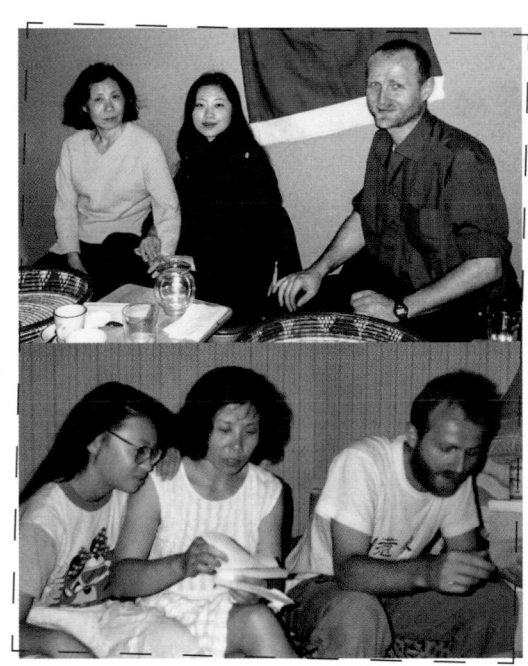

With my mom and stepdad in Germany

Sailor Moon. I scoured whatever scarce anime VHS tapes I could get my hands on—even the really violent ones, like *Ninja Scroll* and *Fist of the North Star*. I hid away in my room to read and watch the treasures I had procured, only coming out for dinner and chores. At school, none of my classmates seemed to understand anime and manga, so I became the four-eyes who read picture books in a weird language. Everywhere I went, my nose was stuck in a manga volume. My parents dismissed my interest in "cartoons" as infantile, and as the years passed and I grew into a teenager, they began to low-key disapprove of it.

Reading manga also inspired me to start drawing. My favorite volume was *RG Veda*, a heartbreaking, dark-fantasy story based on Hindu mythology, by the four-women artist group CLAMP. The ethereal figures draped in jewels and flowing robes took my breath away. I began to redraw my favorite pages. Then I started designing my own original characters. I developed a classic *shoujo*—or "young girl"—manga style. I first drew in pencil, then in ink, and my drawings became increasingly more detailed and polished. I loved drawing intricate hair strands and delicate faces. I became quite skilled at composition and outfit design as well. Art turned into a huge outlet for me, and I replaced the manga volumes I carried everywhere with a sketchbook and pencil case. In school, I stayed to myself and drew manga characters between classes, while my classmates made fun of me for drawing what they referred to as "Barbie figures."

My newly found interest in art was more to the liking of my parents, but they still scoffed at the fact

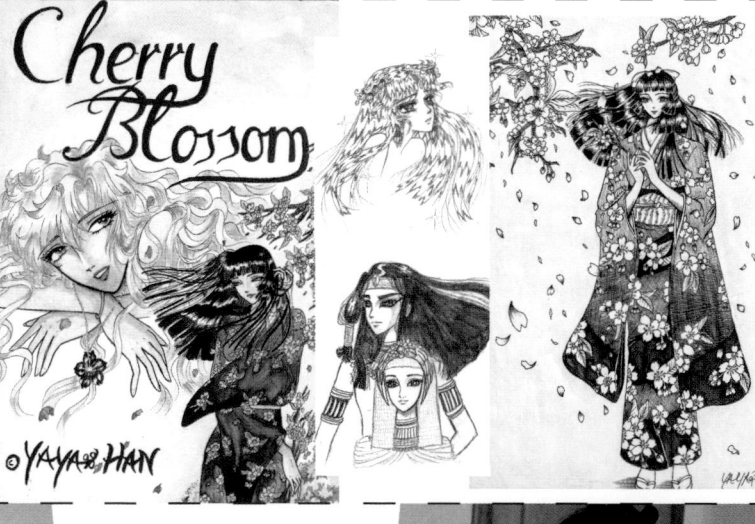

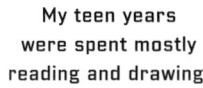

My teen years
were spent mostly
reading and drawing.

that I was drawing manga characters instead of creating "real art." They enrolled me in after-school art classes to foster my burgeoning talents, and while I enjoyed doing anatomical studies in charcoal and landscape paintings in watercolor, I still found myself drawing Japanimation characters deep into the night. It was clear that I wouldn't become a traditional artist. I stopped attending art classes after a couple of years but continued to draw and paint in manga style, eventually teaching myself how to create short stories in sequential art form.

As I stumbled through my teenage years, my feelings of isolation and frustration continued to grow. I never managed to make lasting friendships at school, and all the things I liked doing were solitary. My parents' main interest was traveling, and since I had no friends in the same age group, they were forced to take me with them on trips. This meant that I got to visit cool places such as Egypt, Greece, and Thailand as a young teen, but I always had to tag along with a group of adults. I felt invisible no matter which continent we visited. I was always the girl quietly drawing in the corner of a room.

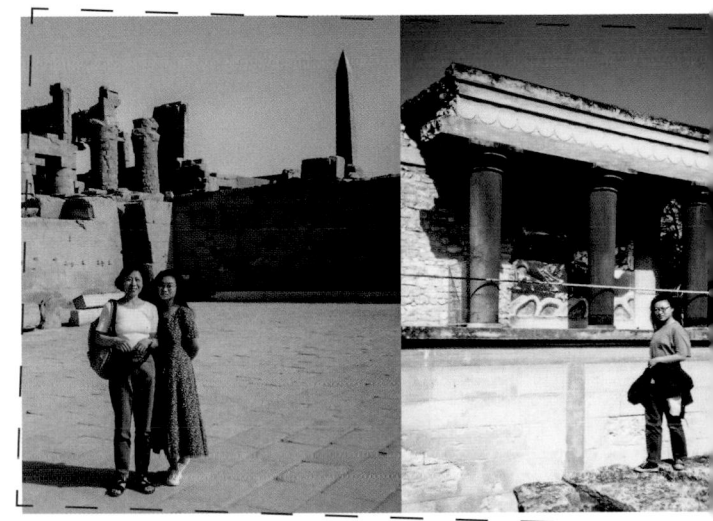

Traveling with Mom to Egypt and Crete

That said, seeing the world at a young age fostered my sense of adventure, and I became especially fascinated by the United States. I often wondered what living there would be like. Pam, a close family friend from America, often shared stories of growing up there. It sounded incredible, with promises of fun and adventure at every turn. She told me about wearing shimmering dresses to prom. Walking through haunted houses with a boy she liked so she could act scared and hold his hand. Putting on musicals and theater performances in high school. Dressing up on Halloween and asking for candy. Her stories sounded exactly like the American movies I watched, and they captivated me.

During my teenage years, I was able to visit the United States twice. My parents took me on a road trip through California at age twelve, and I got to see New York City during another visit at age fifteen. These trips left a huge impression on me and only served to fuel my dream of one day moving to the United States. While I struggled in other aspects of school, I enjoyed learning English, and the language came easy to me—maybe because German was so difficult to learn by comparison.

During many of the quiet moments when I drew, I thought about what I wanted to do with my life once I grew up. My thirst for adventure, fueled by world-skipping anime like *The Vision of Escaflowne* and historical retellings such as *The Rose of Versailles* manga, made me interested in pursuing archeology. That is, until I did a summer internship at a museum and realized how much time I would be spending in the archive rooms doing technical drawings of vases instead of visiting exotic places and excavating ruins.

As my art became more refined and I devoted more time than ever to it, I formed the goal of becoming a professional artist—more specifically, a Disney animator. As much as Japanese animation influenced my art style, I grew up watching and loving Disney movies as well. Unlike anime, an obscure form of animation (in the West) with adult undertones, Disney was considered the pinnacle of cartoon animation. *Snow White and the Seven Dwarfs* even won an Oscar! Everyone respected Disney animators and appreciated their skills, so, in my mind, it was the best job in the world. For a young artist like me, nothing could top making Disney films. And there was only one place where I could pursue that dream—America.

In the year 1998, for the second time, I packed my bags, left my family, and started a new life in a new country. It was completely reckless and irresponsible—and utterly against my parents' wishes. Moving to the United States meant speaking a new language, going to a new school, and adjusting to a completely different culture.

To no one's surprise, the first couple of years were incredibly tough, and I sobered up from my Disney dreams after mere months. I had no idea what it meant for a first-generation immigrant to settle in the United States, from intense money issues to interpersonal relationship difficulties to cultural lifestyle differences. After being hit with unforeseen complications at every turn, I thought of going home, but even in the darkest moments, I could not stand the thought of living in Germany again. I felt so detached from the life I had there; the only thing waiting for me in Wiesbaden was school, followed by a boring, nonartistic job. Despite the challenges, I felt more at ease in the anything-can-happen atmosphere of the United States.

In the end, I gritted my teeth and stayed because I found an open outlet for my nerdy side. Soon after arriving in the USA, I was pleasantly surprised to discover little pockets of anime fan communities all over the country. By today's standards, these communities would be considered miniscule, but their very existence was a revelation to me. There was actually an anime club in my town, where people met up once a week to watch anime, draw fan art, and play video games. I brought my art portfolio to one of the get-togethers and pleaded for a chance to join. Everyone seemed thoroughly impressed with my drawings, and I became a member of the club in 1999. For the first time ever, I felt that I belonged to a community, where people genuinely appreciated my artistic abilities and passion for Japanese animation. No matter how hard everyday life was, I had a little sanctuary where I could retreat to be myself, and that was worth staying for.

However, in 1999, the geeks had definitely not inherited the earth, and having a club didn't mean we could let our freak flags fly openly. Geeks and *otakus*—or nerds—were considered uncool no matter what part of the world you lived in. Most of us separated our fandom activities and daily lives because it was easier than having to explain ourselves to families, schoolmates, or coworkers. Instead, we quietly found camaraderie at anime clubs and conversed with like-minded fans through rudimentary message boards on the Internet. There were only a few conventions across the United States, and they were regarded as precious, near-holy festivals. They offered the rare opportunity for anime fans to come out of our shells and be our true selves.

It was during one of my anime club get-togethers that I learned about Anime Expo, the biggest anime convention in the United States. Only 6,400 people attended Anime Expo in 1999, but to my anime club, that number felt massive. It was the ultimate dream event: an enormous gathering that offered the chance to attend panels and screenings, meet creators flown in from Japan, and even visit a vendor hall dedicated to anime merchandise. My mind boggled at the idea of fans having three whole days to celebrate all things anime and manga. Fellow club members told me stories from past events and showed me photos from previous conventions. I became fascinated by the ones that featured attendees dressed as anime characters. Warriors from *Rurouni Kenshin*. The goddesses from *Ah! My Goddess*. Sailor scouts flanking Sailor Moon. These were real people who looked like the characters I drew, striking poses and smiling at the camera. I couldn't stop looking at them.

This was the first time I saw cosplay in action. Until then, I'd poured all of my love for a series into drawing the characters as nicely as I could, but I never thought about the possibility of actually *becoming* the characters. The mental image of myself dressing up in the same clothes and resembling an anime character sent electricity through my body. It was enticing and daring and a little bit scary all at the same time. Looking at photos of fans just like me, disguised as characters I loved, made a lightbulb go off in my head.

This is what I wanted to do.

So you want to cosplay! That's wonderful, and I have great news for you. There is no better time to get into cosplay than right now. Type "cosplay" into Google and you will instantly be rewarded with an abundance of avenues through which to get started. These options range from mass-produced, ready-made cosplay outfits that can be delivered to your door within days to countless tutorials on every costume-making technique under the sun should you want to make your own cosplay from scratch. The sheer amount of information and resources available today gives newcomers a great foundation to dive right in. But it can also feel overwhelming at times.

When people ask me how they can get into cosplay, they're concerned about sorting through the infinite options of characters, materials, and techniques and how to choose the right project for themselves. Many new cosplayers have expressed to me that they feel intimidated or scared to join the community because it is so well developed and full of brilliant cosplayers already.

Indeed, established and experienced cosplayers bust out one masterpiece after another, and the quality of cosplay outfits these days is mind-boggling, often rivaling the costumes we see in big-budget films. I completely understand that someone who has never made a

costume before could think, *How could I ever reach that level? Why should I even try?* Well, trust me when I say that every cosplayer has had this exact thought— and every cosplayer has to start somewhere.

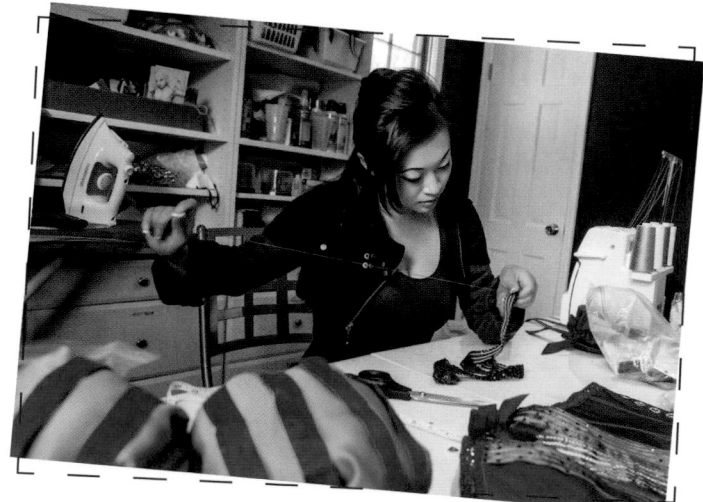

In the advice sections of this book, I will help you build a foundation to get into cosplay crafting and share honest tips on how to navigate this vibrant community.

Let's get started.

Hand-sewing embellishments for a costume

CHOOSING YOUR COSTUME

Think of each costume as an adventure that you're going on with the character.

Find a character you connect with. Connection is key here. Cosplay is a super-fun activity, but it also requires a lot of time, money, and dedication. It's important to choose a character who you feel a genuine connection to. You don't have to be an expert in the source material to cosplay from it, but you should choose someone who sparks a feeling in you. Whether it's the hero you admire, a side character you are curious about, or a villain you love to hate, your passion for the character will drive you to work harder on the costume and make the entire experience more rewarding.

You do not have to look like a character to cosplay them. Cosplay is a transformative process. There should be no physical boundaries to who you can cosplay, regardless of your body type, skin tone, ethnicity, or gender. I explore this topic in greater detail in part 4, The Duality of Cosplay (page 129), but for now, I implore you to not worry one bit about looking like the character you want to cosplay. Whenever I am considering a character to cosplay, I close my eyes and envision myself wearing the costume. If the mental image makes me smile, I know it will be a fun cosplay to work on.

Your cosplay does not have to be 100 percent accurate. Imagery in comic books, movies, and video games is always in motion and perfectly lit for the scene. In real life, your costume won't flow in the wind at the perfect angle, fit flatteringly from every angle, or cascade down your body in exactly the right way. As a pen-and-paper artist, I realized this early on in my cosplay adventures, so I have always taken creative liberties when translating a character design into a costume. While there is significant merit in replicating a costume design as accurately as possible, my advice to newcomers is to focus more on getting the feel of the character across than to make a perfectly replicated costume. In chapter 10, "Going Beyond Re-creations" (page 106), we will explore the various creative ways you can make a character yours and why it can be more fun to put your own artistic spin on a cosplay rather than follow the design 100 percent.

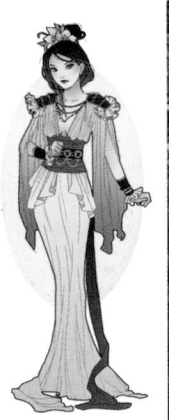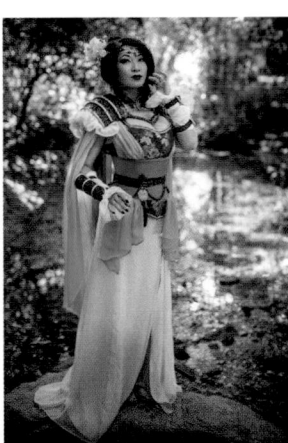

Art Nouveau Mulan design by Hannah Alexander and the finished costume I created.

To buy or to make? You don't have to make your costume in order to cosplay. There are many ready-made costumes out there, and for someone who has never cosplayed before, it might be a good choice to buy a costume and experience what it's like to dress up.

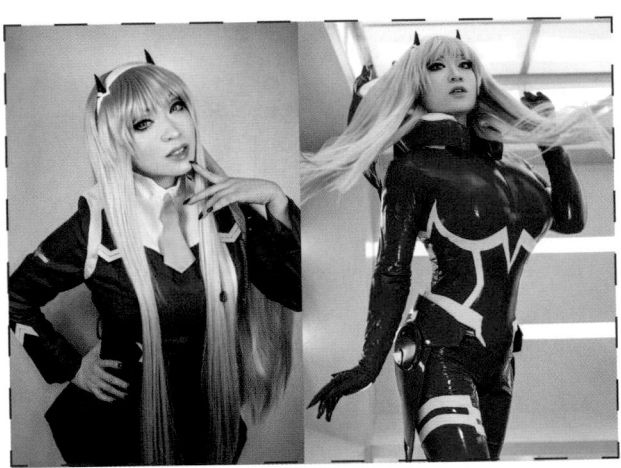

A costume I bought (left) and an alternative costume of the same character that I made (right).

However, by making a costume yourself, you can inject your own interpretation and creativity into the project and have a fuller, more well-rounded cosplay experience. Also consider that you can make one aspect of the costume and buy/commission other components. That way you can divide up the workload and focus on learning one technique per cosplay. For me, the craftsmanship aspect has always been the most interesting, and I'd love for you to experience the unbridled pride of having made your own costume. It's pretty cool.

Give credit where it's due. If someone helped you with a costume, or if you bought a piece for it, please credit the makers in the captions of your photos. Acknowledge the contributors to your project and be honest and transparent with the public. I can't stress enough how important it is to give credit where it is due, especially when you are entering a costume contest that judges on craftsmanship. There is nothing wrong with getting help, after all: It's how we all learn and evolve as creators. Your audience will appreciate the honesty.

PLANNING YOUR COSPLAY

Now that you have chosen your cosplay project, it's time to plan out your costume and gather materials.

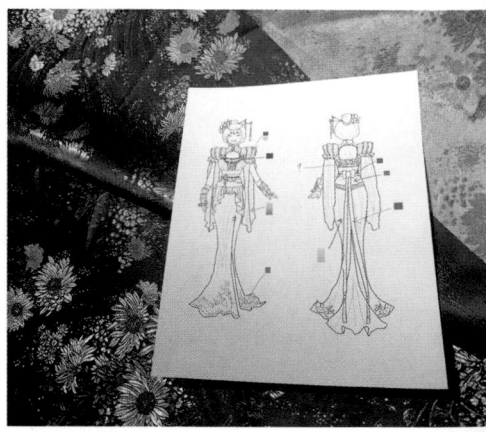

The fabric I chose for Mulan.

Research is really half the battle here, and I will take you through the most important elements in the following steps.

Get into crafting mode. Cosplay is not a cheap hobby, so you should approach each costume as an art project. There are three factors that go into any creative project: **time**, **money**, and **skill**. More often than not, you won't have ample access to all three at once, and that is perfectly okay. By staying organized and focused, you can make up for any deficiencies. For example, if you have a limited budget, you can make up for it by investing time into searching for sales and affordable access to materials. If you have the ability, you can also sink your time into doing more of the hands-on crafting yourself. Take your time, learn the skills, and shop smart.

Gather references. Make a reference folder and collect photos, artwork, and screenshots of the character. I read any articles I can find about how the character and their costume was designed and spend hours online compiling character reference footage, including images and video. Among other things, you'll want to collect front, side, and back views, accessories, and close-ups for makeup and hair. I also suggest looking up other cosplays of your character so you can see how costume components drape and hang in real life and how fabrics and materials look in different lighting. For those who have trouble visualizing an animated design as a real costume, this could be helpful and motivating.

Research techniques and materials. We live in a DIY culture where you can teach yourself how to make anything, and I have never seen this can-do spirit better applied than to cosplay.

Take advantage of the huge array of resources available and relish in the research process. Fabric and craft stores are stocked with more cosplay-centric materials, patterns, and tools than ever. You can find thousands of step-by-step tutorials on YouTube, in PDF form, and in web articles. You can even go to shared makerspaces and take courses on laser cutting and 3-D printing. You don't have to figure everything out by yourself; the community has your back.

Make a shopping list. Almost every technical tutorial tells you what you'll need for the project, so make a list of all the materials and tools. This is your shopping list. Don't forget smaller mundane items, such as paintbrushes, thread, sewing machine needles, and hot glue sticks. More than once I have had to stop in the middle of crafting because I ran out of the right-color thread or paint. Avoid the panic by doing an inventory on crafting products you already own before you go shopping. Bring your materials list and collection of references on shopping trips. I tend to travel a lot and always have a reference folder on my phone in case I come across a shop and want to do some impromptu cosplay shopping.

Shop smart. As I mentioned earlier, it is very possible to cosplay on a budget. You just have to put in more time and research to make up for any lack of funds. My first suggestion is to create a separate e-mail account for mailing lists, then sign up for all the stores you might frequent to get sale notifications and coupon codes. Many craft stores such as JOANN and Michaels hold frequent sales and offer daily discount coupons. These retailers even take competitors' coupons, so start collecting them! Buying general crafting materials such as Velcro, patterns, and acrylic paint in bulk when they are on sale can save you money down the road.

Thrift stores are another great resource for materials. You can cut up sheets and jackets for fabric use, get shoes to cover and customize, or buy clothes to alter into your costumes. My *Final Fantasy X* Lulu costume was made with fifty thrift store belts.

Additionally, research alternative materials and resources. You can make affordable foam look like expensive leather with the right techniques and paint, and there are synthetic versions of fabrics such as silk or wool that cost less than their natural counterparts. Think outside the box when you shop.

Finally, look at tools as investments. Saving up for a quality pair of scissors is worth it because you will use them repeatedly with every project. Buying a heat gun and Dremel multitool will make it much easier to manipulate EVA foam. Investing in good tools can protect your hands and make your work more efficient.

Shop online. Internet retailers can sometimes offer better deals and a more comprehensive assortment of products than physical stores. I often order online when I need items like rhinestones and beads in bulk or when I need specialized items, such as steel corset boning. For crafters living in smaller cities, sometimes the only way to get specialized cosplay

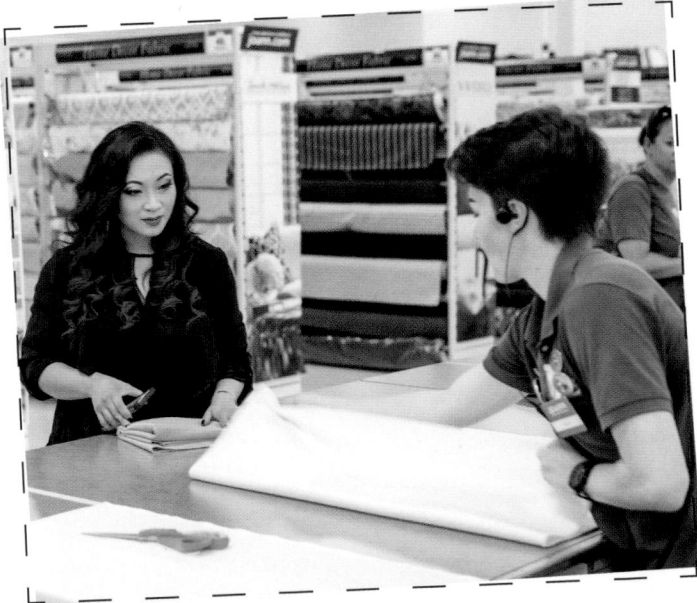

Fabric shopping, usually best done in person

materials is to order them online. The obvious drawback is that you have to wait for shipping (and pay for it), as well as take the risk of buying an item sight unseen. We have all had to deal with the headaches of returning or exchanging an item or chasing down a lost package.

The trick with online shopping is to plan ahead and have a backup plan. Stay organized, refer to your shopping list, and place your orders for materials, wigs, shoes, etc., well in advance. At the same time, look up alternate sources for the items and be prepared in case something goes wrong with your orders.

I strongly prefer buying cosplay materials in person (especially fabrics and trims) because I like to feel the material and see the colors, but for items like shoes, stockings, and wigs, I have my go-to online stores.

See a list of cosplay resources on pages 228–231.

GENERAL WORKING TIPS

Now that your materials have arrived, it's time to start working on your costume!

Pace yourself creatively. Focus on one or two skills you want to learn while making your costume. I have seen first-time cosplayers make some impressive outfits, but based on my experiences (and personal failures), in general I strongly suggest that newcomers start out with a costume design that does

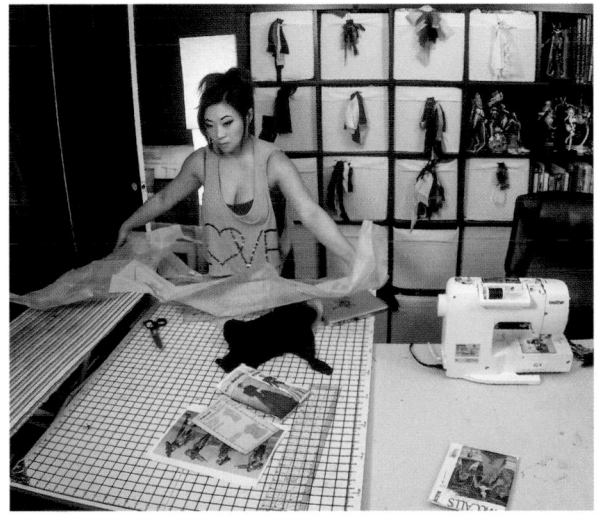

Thinking through the next steps of my sewing process

not overwhelm them creatively. The more techniques a design incorporates, the more there is at stake. Not only does your time commitment and the cost of materials rise, but the likelihood of making a mistake does as well. By focusing on one or two techniques, such as making appliqués or shaping a wooden sword, you can learn skills and make a costume that fills you with pride. After that, each time you take on a new cosplay project you can add a new technique or skill set to your repertoire. It's not dissimilar to leveling up in a video game.

When I first started cosplaying, I only made costumes based on characters with simplistic outfits that could be put together with a limited range of skills. As I learned new techniques and became a more confident crafter, my world of cosplay expanded.

Break down the costume into smaller individual projects. Look at your character's design and make a list of all its components—shirt, pants, shoulder armor, gauntlets, chest armor, belt, shin guards, shoes, etc. Then break down what you need to do to make each piece. By looking at each component of your costume as a separate project, you will feel less overwhelmed by the overall design.

Going back and forth between smaller projects can be very time efficient. Say you built a chest plate out of foam and sealed it with a primer. While the primer is drying, you can look at your to-do list and start working on the gauntlets or shin guards. Instead of tackling the full suit of armor at once, you can check items off the list one by one, making you feel more motivated and accomplished as you go. This has always been the most valuable trick in my arsenal for staying motivated during a costume-making process.

Track your time. Time management is a struggle for most cosplayers, whether they are newcomers or veterans. Every costume is different, and it can be difficult to gauge how much time it will take to make. Crafting tends to shift your perception of time, so it's really helpful to track your time to see how many hours it takes to complete a task. There are plenty of free time-tracking apps available, so download one and try it out. I tend to track by hours, so I'll look back on costumes and remember how many hours it took to make them rather than how many weeks or months.

Remember also that everyone works at different speeds and in different environments, so don't be discouraged if something takes you a while to do. The more

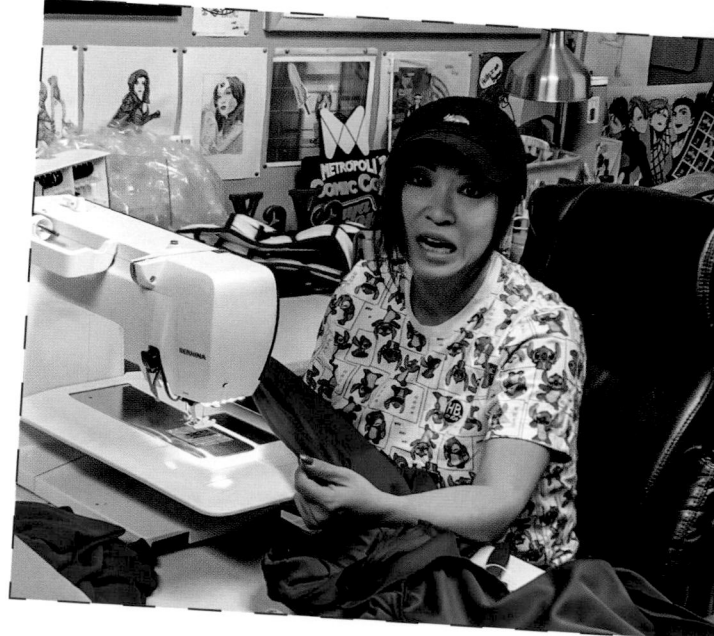

Even after all these years, I still get caught in the rush of con crunch.

you do something, the faster you will become. It's also important to build in extra time for mistakes. You will make mistakes. That is okay. New techniques can require a lot of testing and experimentation, so give yourself time and include those hours in the time tracked for the project. The more you get into the habit of tracking your process, the easier you will be able to gauge the hours required for future projects.

Managing con crunch. In cosplay, a common term that gets thrown around is "con crunch." These are the last few days leading up to the con, during which some cosplayers frantically work to finish a costume. Con crunch can mean pulling all-nighters and even working on a costume during the con itself. This can be very stressful.

You will probably experience con crunch. But you should consider whether it is worth it to rush your costume. If your costume is nearly done and you just have to work efficiently and continually on it to complete all the steps, I would say it's worth it to con crunch. But if you have to rush the costume by skipping steps or taking shortcuts, you should think twice. Sure, it's faster to hot-glue on embellishments instead of sewing them, but will the end result be worth it? If you already spent a lot of money, time, and effort on your costume, wouldn't it be better to finish it in the way you want?

If you feel like you need to take shortcuts, my suggestion is to put the costume aside and enjoy the convention. Take the time you need to finish your cosplay for a later event.

Enjoy the journey. While the goal of cosplay is to eventually wear your costume and become your chosen character, the crafting process can be the most fun and fulfilling aspect of the experience. For many like me, sewing and crafting is deeply therapeutic, just like painting and playing music. Remember that each costume is an adventure; it includes all the problem-solving, experimentation, and emotional ups and downs.

Whether you end up buying the costume or you create it from scratch, these tips will help you get started on your cosplay journey!

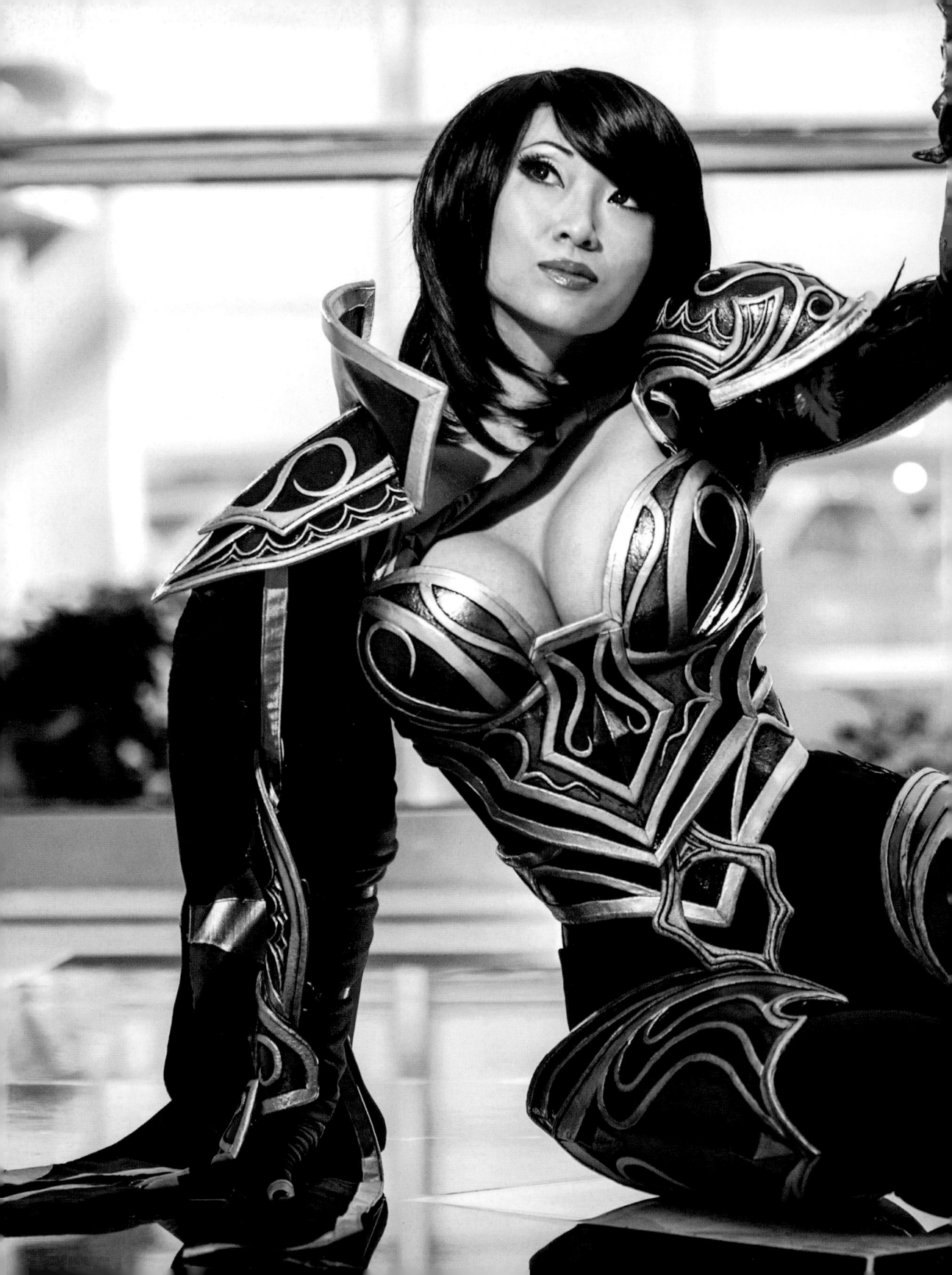

PART TWO

The History of Cosplay

CHAPTER 3

The Boomerang Effect

How Cosplay Bounced from the West to the East and Back

The first time I made a costume, I had no idea what I was doing. The few people in my anime club that cosplayed did so casually, and there were no online resources to learn from at the time. But that didn't matter. I was about to go to my first Anime Expo, and I wanted to dress up in a costume! I had even chosen the character already—Kurama from *Yu Yu Hakusho*, one of my favorite manga series. He's an androgynous, fuchsia-haired demon fox who wears a Chinese qipao and kicks ass with a rose-thorn whip. Kurama is often confused for a girl because he is so pretty, so I thought I could get away with cosplaying him.

There was just one problem: I didn't know how to sew.

Thankfully, a fellow club member kindly offered to show me how to use her sewing machine. I learned to sew two stitches—straight and zigzag— and how to go into reverse to close off the stitch. I went to a fabric store for the first time and bought the cheapest fabric I could find in the approximate colors of Kurama's design. After that, the hardest part was figuring out how to read a sewing pattern, but I followed the instructions as best I could. After a couple of weeks, I had cobbled together my first costume just in time for 1999's Anime Expo.

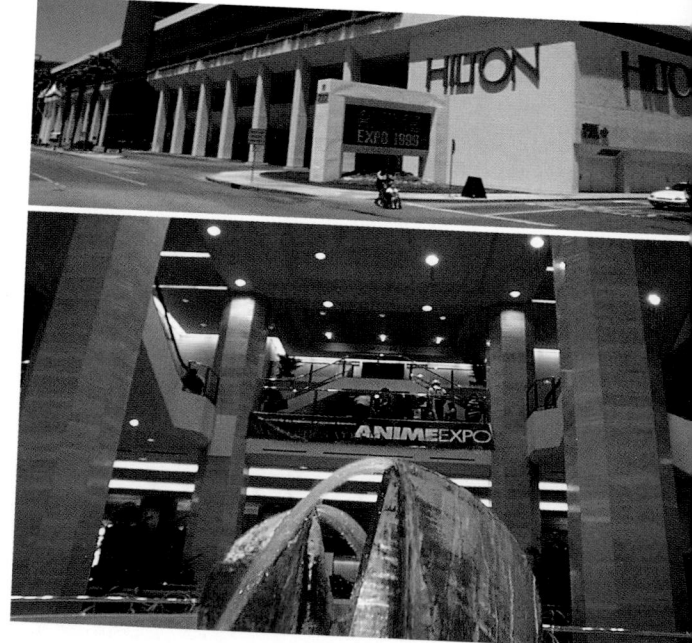

I couldn't find a red wig in time for the convention, so I just let my dark hair hang loose. I didn't wear a stitch of makeup, and I went without Kurama's rose-thorn whip because I couldn't figure out how to make it.

In the end, my Kurama cosplay was unrecognizable, but I will never forget the feeling of putting it on for the first time. It didn't matter that the character was male and that I didn't know how to tweak my silhouette to look more masculine. I didn't care that no one recognized the character or asked me for a photo. I spent an entire day walking around pretending to be a character I

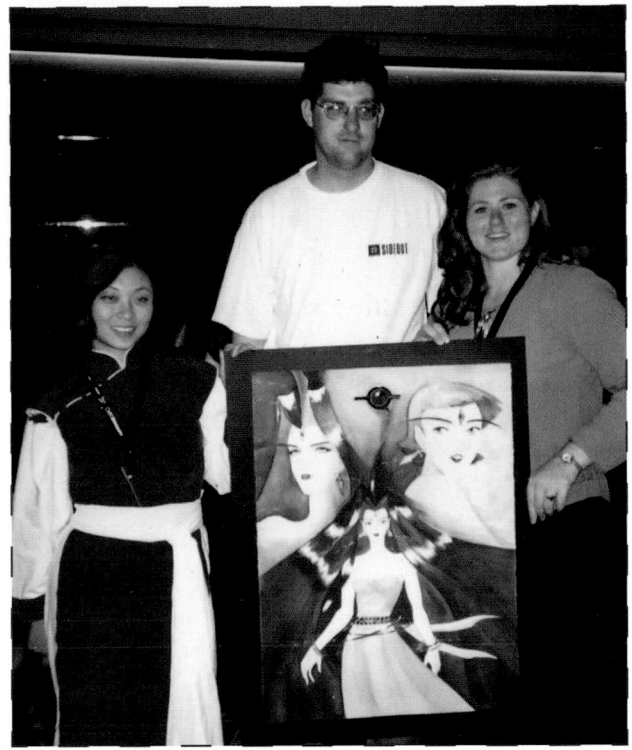

Selling my art at a con in an early cosplay

loved! I was able to wear something on my body that I had created from a pile of fabric and thread! That one cosplay experience was all it took for me to become absolutely fascinated by the process of sewing. My mind swirled with possibilities and the hunger to learn more.

— — —

I didn't know it in 1999, but my introduction to cosplay happened right at the beginning of its modern evolution. That year, I returned home from Anime Expo feeling exhilarated, as if I had discovered a new world that was hidden in plain sight from the rest of society. I had a million questions and wanted nothing more than to find out everything I could about cosplay. How could I make more complex costumes? Where could I go to meet other cosplayers? When would the next anime convention be?

After spending copious amounts of time on Yahoo! and AltaVista, it became clear that answering my questions would be a challenge. The few cosplay web pages I came across were rudimentary hobby blogs, filled with raw HTML coding and pixelated scans of disposable camera photographs. There was no collective listing for geek events or conventions

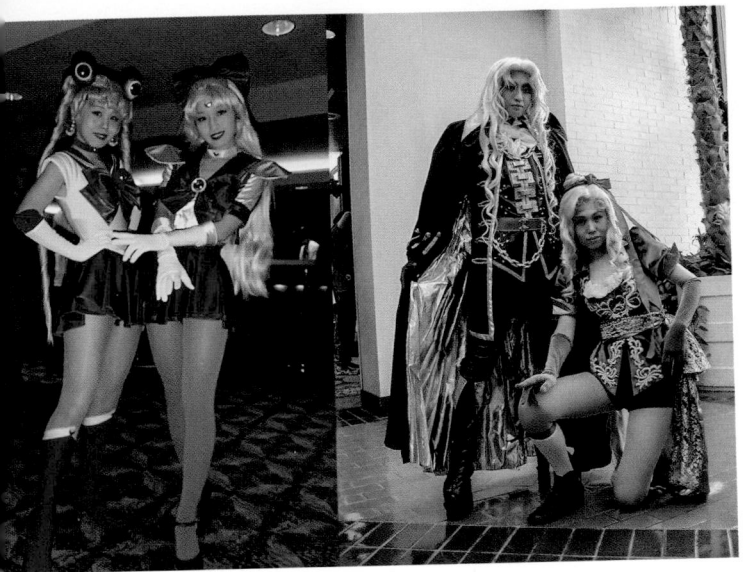

Barbie and Kaie looking amazing
in duo costumes.

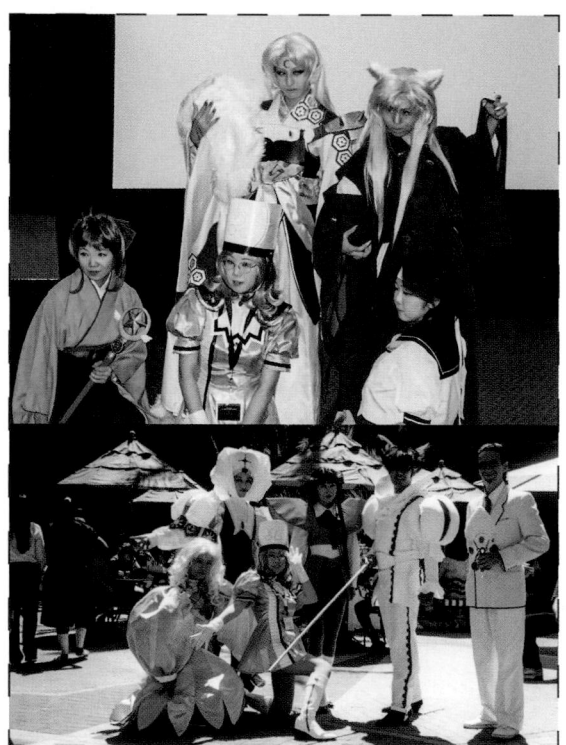

Awesome Japanese cosplayers at Anime Expo.

and only a handful of galleries and reports on past events. And it was near impossible to find resources on making costumes.

Being a newbie cosplayer, it would have been easy to get discouraged at this point, but as with anything that interested me, I was persistent. After all, I had seen what was possible.

During Anime Expo, a group of cosplayers from Japan absolutely stole the show. Every day, they wore different costumes from properties ranging from *Sailor Moon* to *The Five Star Stories*. Each time, this group's outfits looked like they were plucked right from the manga pages. Not only did they have superior costumes, perfect makeup, and perfect hairstyles; they presented themselves with poise and refined elegance as well. At the drop of a hat, they snapped into perfect poses for each character and knew exactly how to stand with one another. I remember wearing my shoddily made Kurama costume, just standing and staring at them in awe. The two who stood out the most were named Barbie and Kaie. I was told by friends that they were theatrical costume designers in Japan who just loved to cosplay and came to Anime Expo every year for fun.

Watching Barbie and Kaie hypnotize the crowd wherever they went was fascinating and made me wonder what the cosplay scene was like in Japan. During my many hours of online searching after the con, I discovered a good number of Japanese websites about cosplay. Without any way to translate them, I blindly clicked links in hopes of landing on a cosplay photo gallery. More than once, these rabbit hole searches led me to adult fetish pages, but eventually I found Barbie and Kaie's photos as well as a ton of other Japanese cosplay galleries. Every page was stunning, featuring beautiful cosplayers in pitch-perfect costumes. I was struck by the high quality of their photos, from the professional settings and lighting to the dynamic composition and posing. The cosplayers exuded the same living-anime-figure charm that I saw in person. I felt pangs of jealousy looking at their smooth, cascading wigs and their costumes' futuristic fabrics. Clearly, the cosplay scene in Japan was far more advanced and developed than that of the United States.

Once again, my mind was filled with questions: Why don't I have access to these materials? How can I make something like that? And how can I possibly compare to these cosplayers?

This curiosity was infuriating. Inspiring. And it gave me the ultimate goal to work toward.

The most burning question on my mind was where the heck cosplay came from. Compared to the level of Japanese cosplay in 1999, the US scene was a tiny hobbyist community still in its infancy, so I was quite surprised to hear from multiple sources that cosplay actually originated in North America. That made no sense to me, so I kept on prodding until I realized that, in fact, two separate costuming communities existed at fandom conventions. There were those who made costumes from Western sci-fi and fantasy fiction and called it "costuming," and those who dressed up as characters from Eastern pop culture and called it "cosplay." Believe it or not, the terminology sparked a lot of heated discussions at the time, mostly over what could be construed as cosplay and how it differed from all other types of costuming. Depending on how each fan discovered the activity, there was even more debate over where convention costuming as an activity originated.

I hope that, by sharing the history of cosplay as I discovered it, I will help you understand how the modern era of cosplay came to be.

It's a pretty incredible story.

The first instance on record of a person wearing a costume at a convention was in 1939, during the first World Science Fiction Convention in New York. A woman named Myrtle R. Douglas made "futuristic costumes" for herself and her romantic partner, Forrest J. Ackerman. The two have been credited as the inventors of fandom costuming ever since.

Over the following decades, subsequent sci-fi conventions began to incorporate costume contests, called masquerades, into their programming, giving attendees a reason to come in

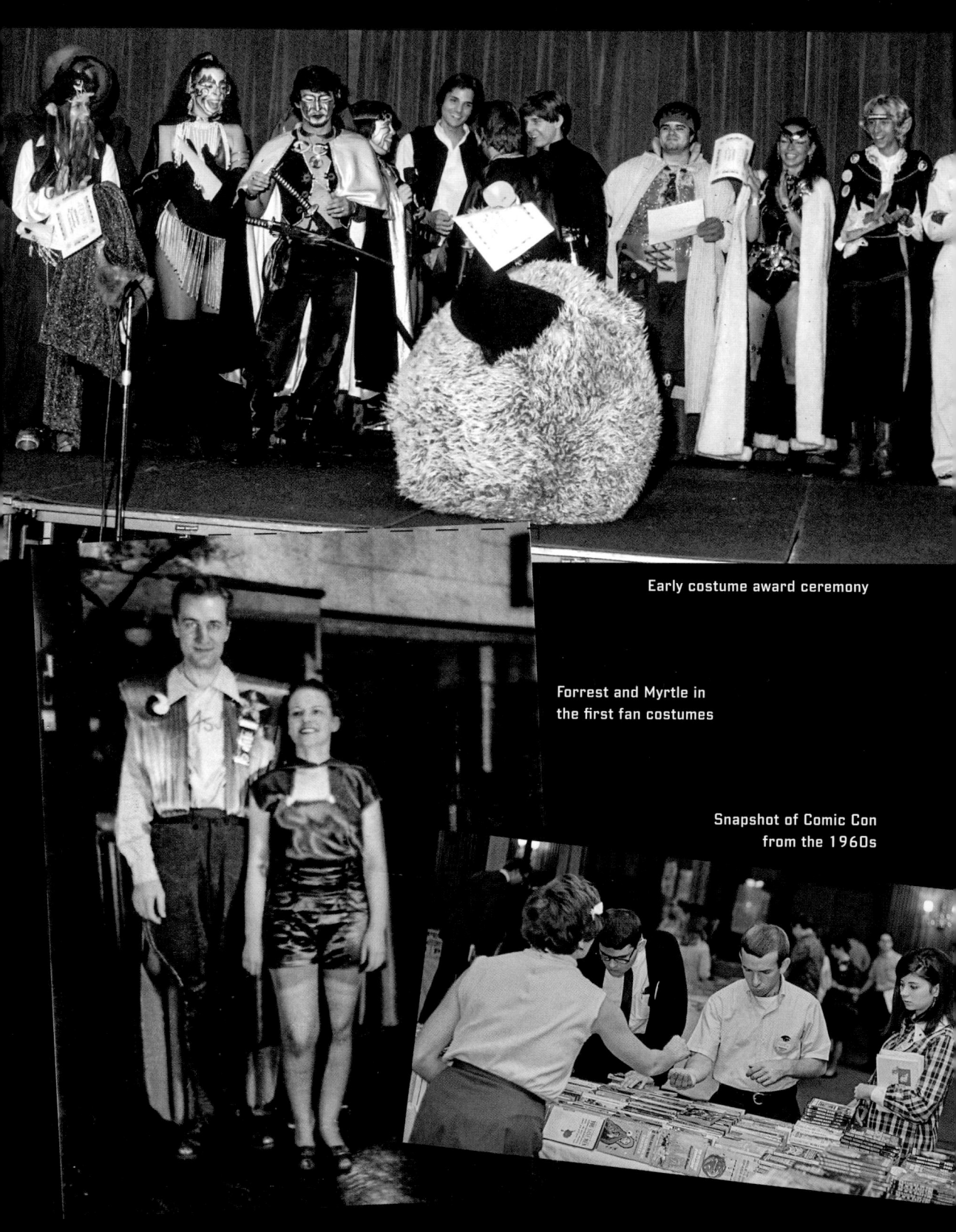

Early costume award ceremony

Forrest and Myrtle in
the first fan costumes

Snapshot of Comic Con
from the 1960s

costume. By the '70s and '80s, fan costuming had become a steady occurrence at conventions, even though it was still practiced by a relatively small community. But then something very interesting happened.

In 1984, Japanese writer Nobuyuki Takahashi attended the same US-based, sci-fi–themed convention as Myrtle R. Douglas, though it had been renamed Worldcon. Upon his return to Japan, Takahashi wrote an article for a magazine about the experience accompanied by images of fans in costume. He referred to what these attendees were doing as "cosplay," an amalgamation of the words *costume* and *play*. Even though the ensembles portrayed in these photos were based on Western science fiction, the activity resonated with the Japanese fandom and soon sparked imitators. Their interpretation had a distinct Eastern pop culture flair, however. People dressed up as characters from anime, manga, and video games, inadvertently creating a new variation of fan costuming.

Cosplay developed into a popular activity in Japan as well as the rest of Asia. By the mid '90s, the increased interest and demand for cosplay content had led to the rise of a focused costuming retail industry in Japan. Cosplay had become a form of entertainment career loosely related to glamour modeling and idol culture an entire decade before geek culture caught on in the West. To this day there are more cosplay-related products available in Japan than anywhere else in the world.

While Japan's cosplay community thrived, the scene in the US was just beginning to develop. Ironically, Americans were growing interested in Japanese cosplay thanks to the anime

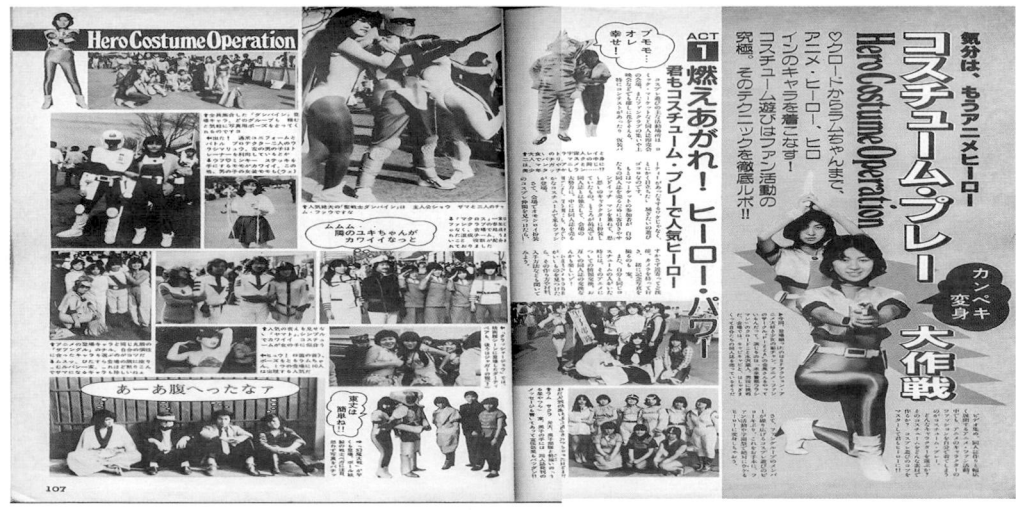

Takahashi's article, where he coined the term cosplay

they found on the shelves of Blockbuster stores as well as in the fan-subtitled VHS tapes that circulated throughout the scene. As more and more anime-themed conventions were formed, such as A-Kon, Otakon, and Anime Expo, fans began to show up dressed as characters from Japanese animation. Overall, the activity was not much different from fan costuming at comic conventions, but the differences in the look and feel of Western sci-fi costumes versus cosplay costumes were glaring. It was like putting copies of *Heavy Metal* magazine next to volumes of *Sailor Moon* manga. Traditional fan costuming cut a wide swath through the sexually charged sci-fi and pulp fiction landscape, which at the time was filled with stories about psychedelic space explorers, barbarian warriors, and barely clothed slave princesses. These characters were mature and adventurous, and that energy came through in fans' costumes.

By comparison, anime characters were positively adorable, with heart-shaped, doe-eyed faces and bright, color-blocked outfits. Even gritty, dark anime like *Akira* or *Battle Angel Alita* featured cute and youthful protagonists. It wasn't a stretch to imagine why younger people, myself included, were attracted to dressing up as these characters.

As such, it wasn't long before a divide appeared on the convention circuit. Old-school sci-fi costumers rarely befriended those in anime garb and largely stuck to their tightly knit communities. The traditional costuming and unconventional cosplay scenes grew and developed alongside each other but always separately. It would take years for the world-wide boom of geek culture to intertwine the two collectives and blur the lines between Eastern- and Western-inspired costuming.

The divide wasn't just a difference in age or interests; it was also a difference in philosophy. Traditional costumers had years to develop a communication network and refine their crafts-manship. The majority approached costuming with maturity and reverence. Meanwhile, when cosplayers first smashed onto the scene, our outfits were made with childish abandon. They appeared amateur. But what cosplayers lacked in experience and grace we made up for with passion and exuberance, unburdened by the weighty rules of traditional costuming that had been established decades prior.

While there are always exceptions, I think most of us who got into cosplay at the turn of the twenty-first century remember it as a carefree time. It's endearing for me to look at old cosplay photos and see how awkward but blissfully happy I was. The only drawbacks to having no rules or restraints were that we also had no guidance and no mentors. There was no community of makers to welcome new cosplayers.

So we had to create our own.

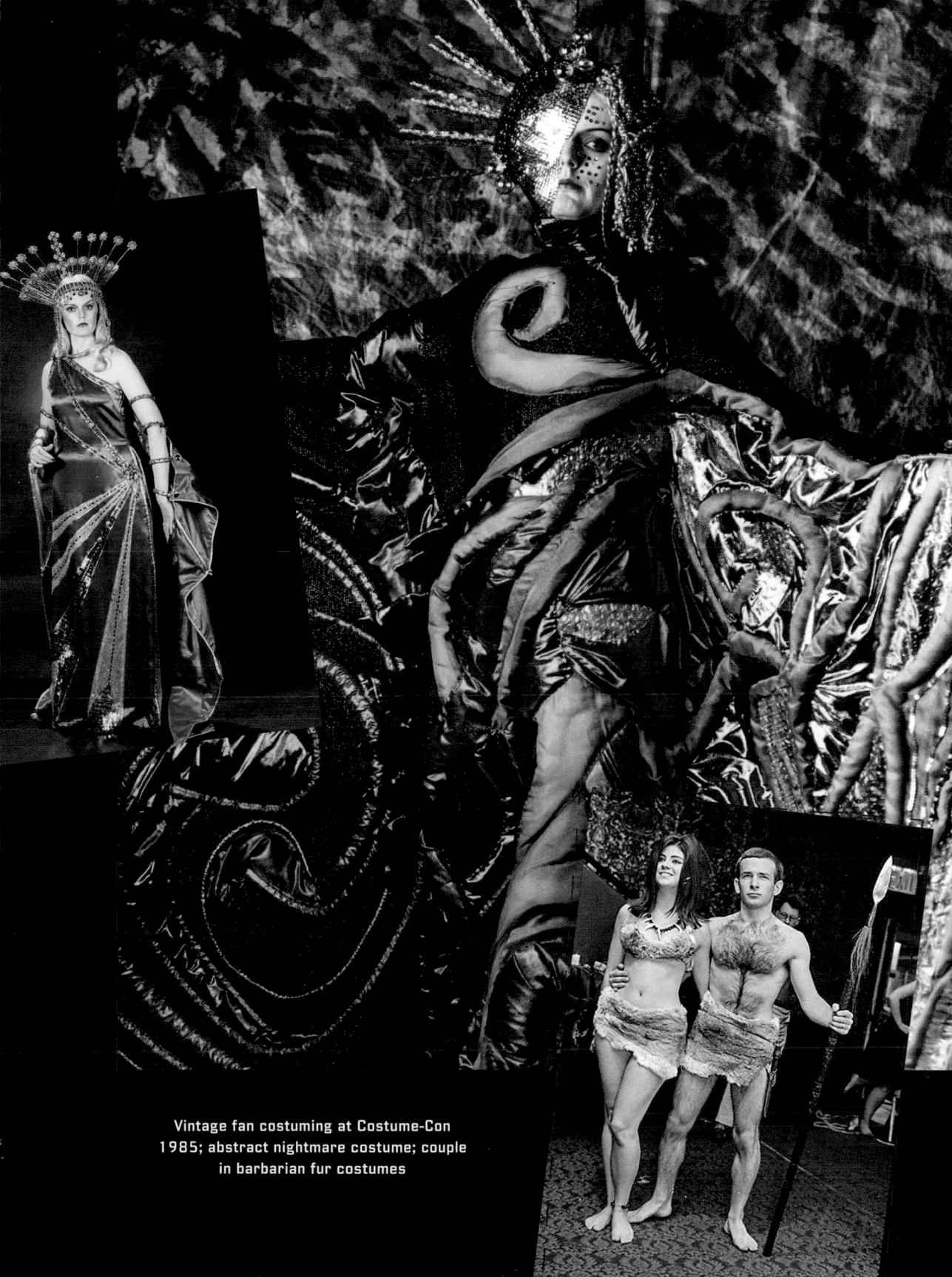

Vintage fan costuming at Costume-Con 1985; abstract nightmare costume; couple in barbarian fur costumes

CHAPTER 4

How Cosplay Saved My Life

After Anime Expo 1999, I joined the only online community focused on cosplay at the time: a Yahoo! mailing list called COSP. It felt like a breakthrough, because I had finally found a way to connect with other cosplayers on a daily basis. COSP was structured around e-mail threads sent to all its members, but since we were all amateur crafters, there was a lot of blind information sharing. Many e-mail conversations were full of outlandish suggestions for techniques and materials for creating certain outfits. At one point there was a lot of hilarious speculation about how anyone could possibly replicate a costume element that defied gravity. None of us knew what we were doing. Still, I was just happy to have found a semblance of community, and it was really nice to have a place to talk about upcoming conventions, look at cosplay photos, and dream about new costumes with other like-minded fans.

Despite getting my feet wet in cosplay, my real-life prospects at the time made it difficult to sustain this new hobby. I had just graduated from high school and was confronted with all the challenges of adulthood. Plus I was still adjusting to life in the United States. I had always planned to attend college, but that became impossible with my fresh-off-the-boat immigrant status. Separated from family by an ocean, I realized that I could only continue to live in the States if I entered the workforce.

My job searches went about as well as you'd expect for a fresh high-school graduate with no work experience, and that first year after graduating was so hard, I almost gave up and moved back to Germany. Thankfully, I found an unconventional way to skim by. It turned out that going to Anime Expo not only introduced me to cosplay; it also gave me a platform to share the fan art that I'd been drawing since I was eleven years old. I had been encouraged by my anime club to display my work at the Anime Expo Art Show, where the public could place silent bids on art pieces throughout the event. To my surprise, all of my pen-and-ink drawings and watercolor paintings sold by the last day of the convention, one of them for the record amount of $400. Back then, that was an insane amount of money to me. In the

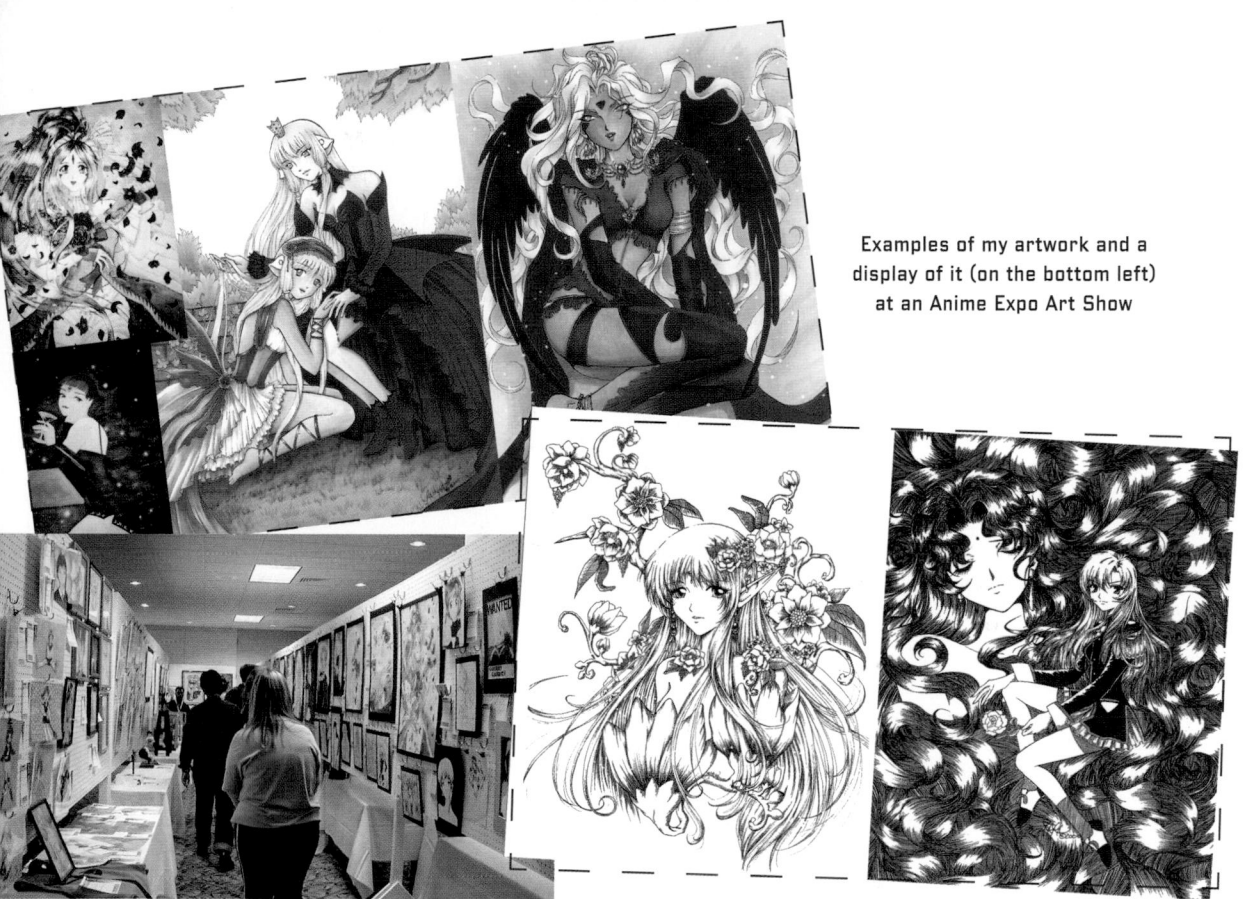

Examples of my artwork and a display of it (on the bottom left) at an Anime Expo Art Show

weeks following, I received numerous commission inquiries. With nothing left to lose, I became a freelance artist.

From 1999 to 2001, I supported myself by drawing and painting anime fan art to sell to clients and at conventions. It was not a glamorous life. I barely made enough money to cover the bills, and there was more than one month where I primarily lived off peanut butter sandwiches and ramen noodles. But I loved drawing, and I loved the freedom of working for myself. Most importantly, this type of work meant that I could go to more anime conventions and learn more about cosplay.

I bought a used sewing machine for forty dollars and found a vintage sewing book at a thrift store. Then I started making trips to the only two fabric stores in town. One of them sold discount fabrics by weight, which is typically a telltale sign of low-quality material. Being broke, I also had to think outside the box and seek materials in unconventional places. I often cut up clothes or curtains from thrift stores to use as costume materials and bought used shoes to form the basis for more involved footwear. I became a coupon warrior

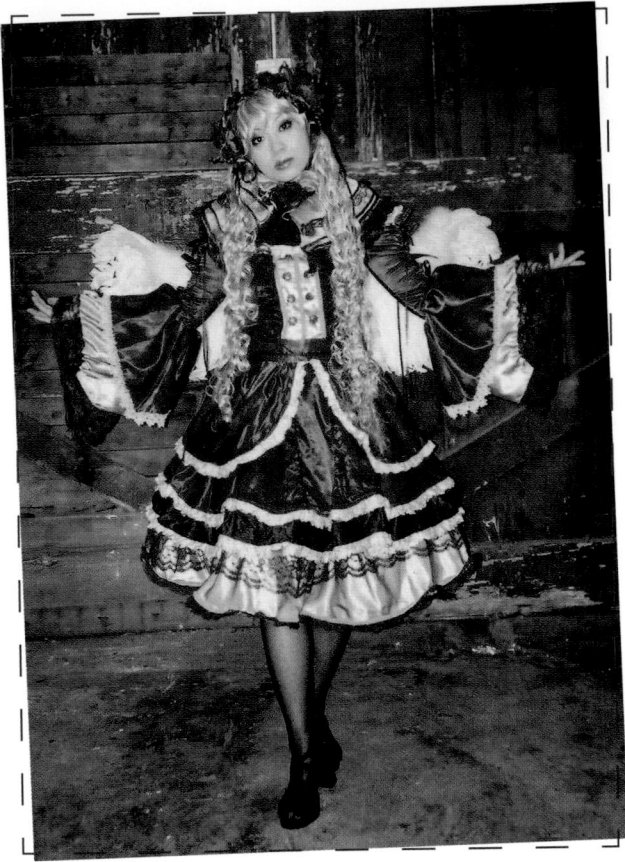

The Myoubi costume I made with
discount Christmas ribbons

at JOANN and Hancock Fabrics stores and was the first in line for sales events and holiday deals. Once I bought a cart full of heavily discounted trims, decorations, and themed fabrics at JOANN the day after Christmas. I used the materials to make a full costume of the character Myoubi from the manga *Alichino*. Another time, I got wind that a JOANN location in a neighboring town was closing, so I rushed over to stock up on materials for several costumes; everything was marked down to 90 percent off. I will never forget buying silky-soft Madonna velvet—usually $24.99 per yard—for $2.50. I had never touched such a luxurious fabric before that day.

However, money was not my only challenge. Finding educational information on how to make costumes was as difficult as finding wigs and fabrics beyond Halloween tinsels and costume satin. The old sewing book's dry terms and outdated lingo weren't exactly helpful, either. Plus most of the questions I posed on COSP went unanswered. Nevertheless, I was determined to figure out the crafting angle of cosplay, and I began to make costumes through trial and error. Crafting my Kurama cosplay had left me with a basic understanding of sewing, so I focused on cosplay outfits that were mostly fabric-based and not overly complicated in design. There was definitely a learning curve, but I soon found that I had an affinity for sewing and that I really enjoyed the problem-solving aspect of costuming. With drawing and painting as my paying job and crafting and sewing as my hobbies, my creative interests went into overdrive.

Eventually, though, the starving-artist lifestyle became too much for me to bear and I started looking for regular employment again. Finally, at the beginning of 2001, I was hired to do low-level data entry at a small technology company in Atlanta. The job itself was boring and repetitive—I literally sat in a cubicle from nine o'clock to five o'clock—but I had a steady paycheck for the first time ever. My salary was meager, but all my bills were covered, and it was such a relief to not have to agonize over money every day. I continued to accept art commissions on the side and used that income to finance my cosplay habit. Finally, I was able to afford nicer fabrics and tools, and I even bought my first brand-new sewing machine.

This is when my creative world opened and I truly began to blossom. With each new costume and convention, I became more invested in cosplay and more confident in myself. I started to take on bigger, more ambitious projects that challenged my craftsmanship skills and pushed me to learn new techniques. All those years of drawing and painting taught me patience and helped me develop a keen eye for details. My costumes became more sophisticated and better constructed, which spurred me to work harder. I sewed in the evenings and on weekends, and I even got up an hour early each weekday morning to sew before going into the office. For each convention I attended, I made three new costumes and would dress up as two to three different characters on each day.

My enthusiasm for cosplay became a borderline obsession because I had nothing else in my life at that time. The move to the United States was more difficult than I ever could have

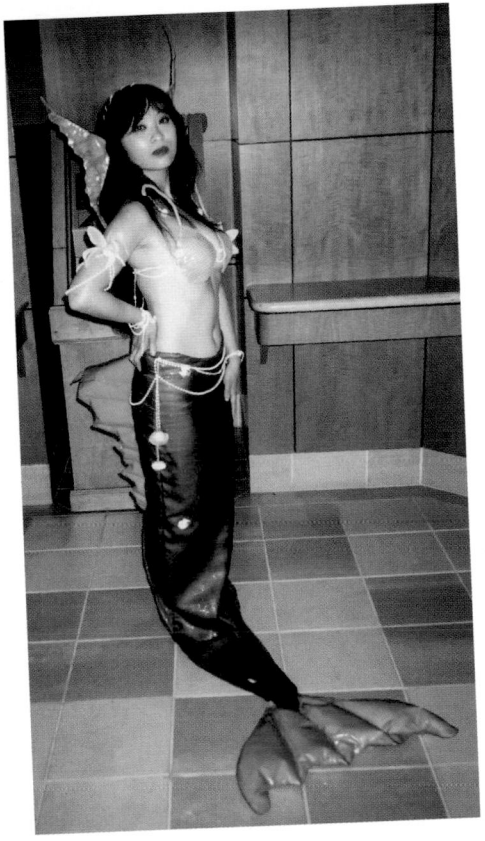

My early cosplay efforts

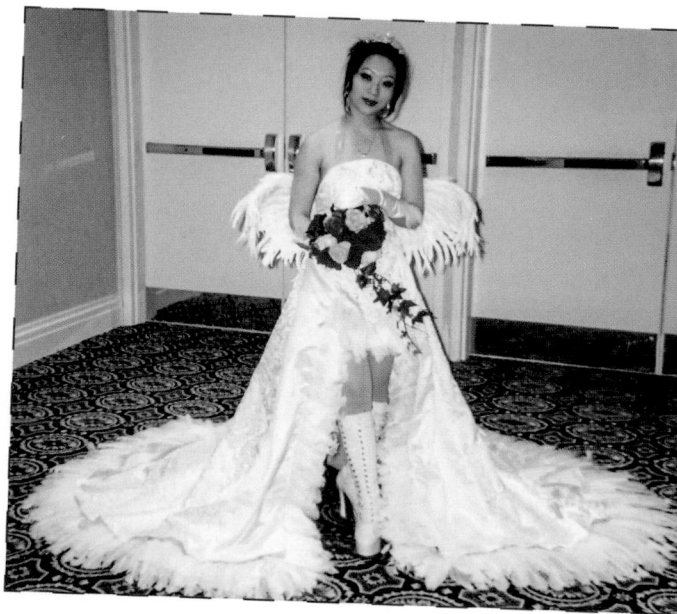

imagined, and it came with compounding problems that affected my daily life for years. I had no prospects for a future in America, but cosplay gave me dreams to chase. It was my only source of happiness during this difficult transition period. It got me out of the house and made me socialize with people. It gave me goals and aspirations, even if they were just to finish a costume by a certain date or learn a new sewing stitch.

Soon enough, I started to enter costume competitions. Every anime convention held a cosplay contest, and its contestants participated by acting out their favorite anime scenes in short skits. Cosplay contests were some of the most well-attended events at cons, often filling the biggest ballrooms and convention halls available, but they were not really taken seriously. They were judged by industry professionals such as artists, writers, and anime voice actors, many of whom did not understand the nuances of costume making. The prizes were donated merchandise from vendors or plaques and paper certificates. For convention organizers, this was a laid-back affair—a way to gather all the costumed attendees and give them an opportunity to geek out. But for those of us who entered the contests, performing onstage in full costume was the final step in truly becoming a character. It was a huge thrill to walk onto a stage with official music from our characters' anime blaring over speakers and thunderous applause coming from the audience. Acting out a scene from a show and inciting laughter from the audience fulfilled a need that we could not get from roaming around the convention halls.

It didn't take long for me to become a frequent competitor at conventions. Sometimes I entered alone, and other times I entered as a part of a group with the cosplayer friends I'd made. We were all pretty engrossed in the hobby at the time and took on each contest with fervor. Not only did we want to represent our characters well onstage; we also wanted to do the source material justice. Preparations would

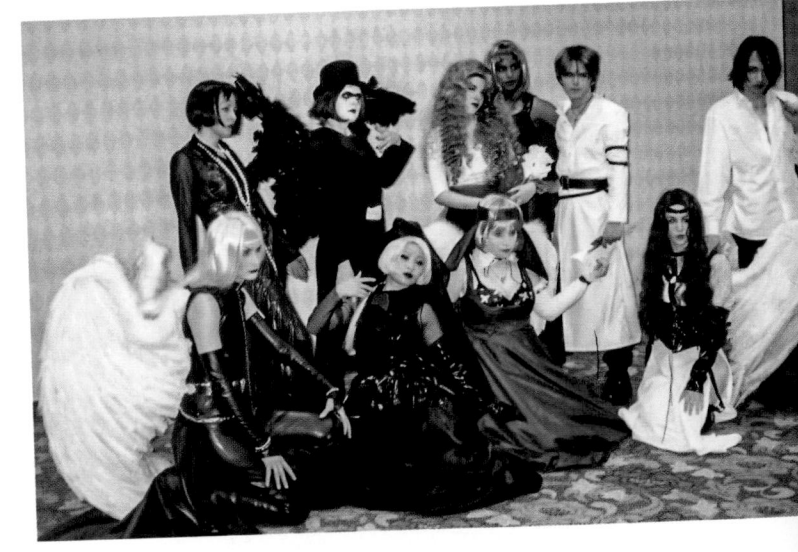

My first Best in Show win with friends cosplaying from *Angel Sanctuary*.

often take months, because I was not only making a full costume but also developing a skit performance that included mixed musical tracks, Japanese rock–inspired choreography, and storytelling elements. Then I had to make sure my group had finished their costumes, round everyone up at the con, and find a place to rehearse, boombox and all.

We really went overboard with our miniature theatrical productions, but it was so much fun and so creatively stimulating. I will never forget the rush I felt when my group won "Best in Show" for the first time at Katsucon 2001. Our skit from the manga *Angel Sanctuary* featured ten cosplayers and went on to spark a trend for expressive, dramatic performances in cosplay contests. Bolstered by this first validation of our efforts, I dove into creating new skit performances. We went on to sweep the convention season with four more "Best in Show" wins that same year, including one at Anime Expo.

In the span of just a couple of years, I became completely engrossed in the cosplay community and fully committed to the activity. I had found my place in the world. There were few tangible rewards and no monetary reason to cosplay, but cosplaying gave me unparalleled joy and excitement. I felt unstoppable when I entered the next phase of the modern cosplay evolution.

Best in Show at Otakon 2000 - X 1999 group

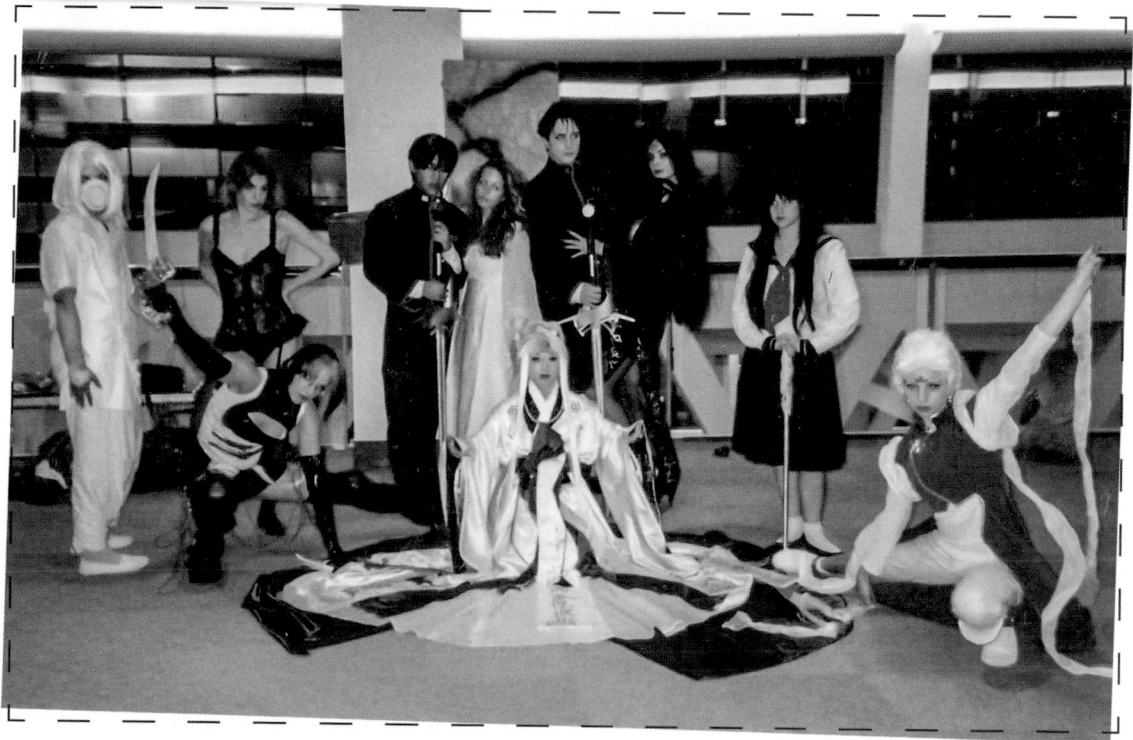

CHAPTER 5

The Fire Fairy

It was May of 2001, and my living room looked like a war zone. I sat in the middle of a carpet, surrounded by sheets of craft foam, a hot-glue gun set on a paper plate, and several bottles of acrylic paint. Piles of fabric in shades of crimson and amber were spread out over every piece of furniture. Bits of pattern paper and loose thread littered the ground, and there was a spill of paint water drying behind me.

I peered at the clock and felt a surge of desperation. It was just past 4:00 a.m. on a Sunday night, and I was scheduled to be at work in five hours (*How did it get so late?*). The entire evening, I had been trying to make a shoulder armor piece, but I could not figure out what material to use. Fabric was too flimsy, and craft foam only curved in one direction. My failed attempts taunted me from where I'd thrown them across the room. I was tired, deeply frustrated, and tempted to give up. My stubbornness won out, though, and I remained hunched on the floor until an idea formed. What if I *sculpted* the shoulder armor, rather than forced a flat material into shape? I reached for a pack of Crayola Model Magic, a children's air-dry clay (the only sculpting material I had on hand) and smooshed it into a dome. It was lumpy and uneven, but it fit and looked more like a shoulder pad than anything else I had made previously. There was hope yet.

That month I was working on my first *big* cosplay project since I had started cosplaying a year and a half ago. It was also my first time designing an original costume: a warrior fairy character dressed in crimson and gold with large wings that spread out like flames. The Fire Fairy costume needed to be beautiful, impressive, and detailed, because I intended to enter a cosplay contest with it. In fact, I had convinced three of my friends to compete as a group of elemental fairies, and they were working away on their costumes, too. Aside from personal pride, I refused to let this costume get the best of me because I didn't want to let my friends down. The original design factor added to the challenges we faced, because our costumes were not from a known anime or manga, so I wasn't sure how the competition judges and audience would react to them. The uncertainty gnawed at me and spurred me to work harder.

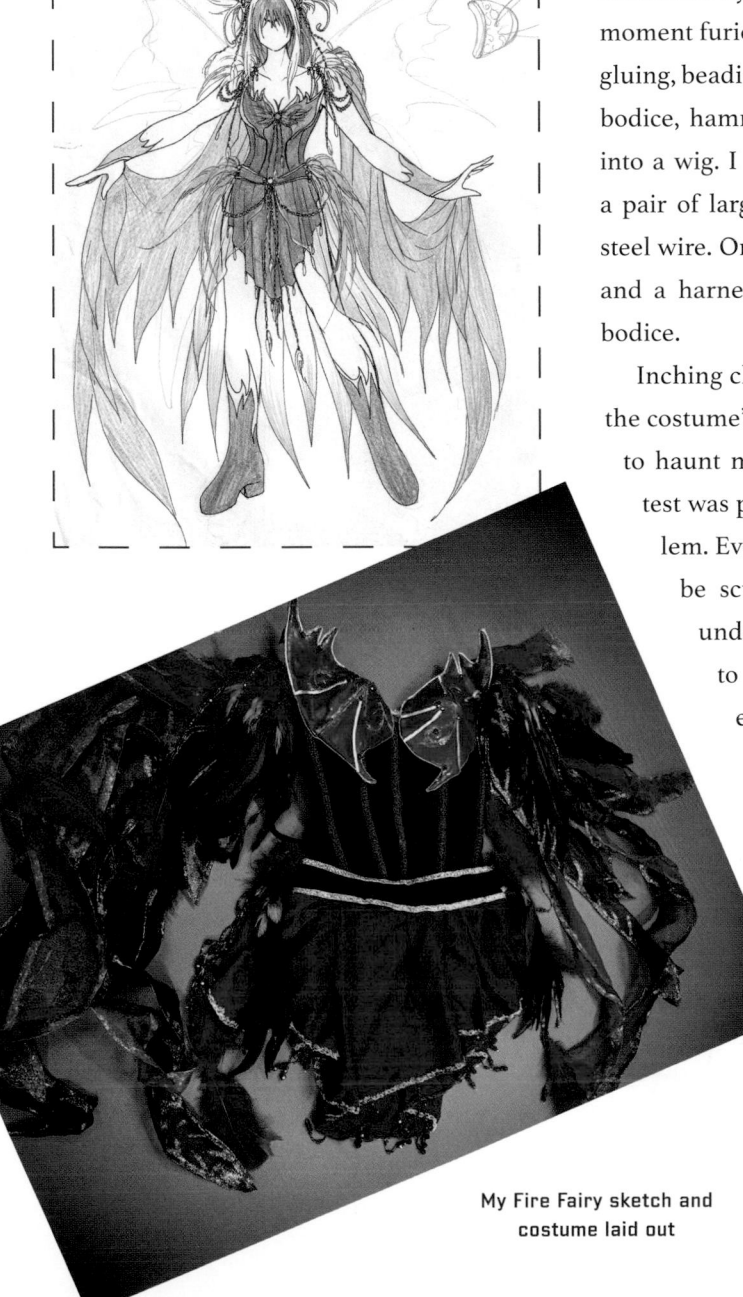

My Fire Fairy sketch and costume laid out

As I entered new creative territory with the Fire Fairy costume, I became deeply consumed by it. For weeks I spent every free moment furiously sketching, cutting, sewing, gluing, beading, and painting. I made a boned bodice, hammered eyelets, and sewed wefts into a wig. I even designed and constructed a pair of large fairy wings using galvanized steel wire. Organza stretched over the frame, and a harness was hidden underneath the bodice.

Inching closer and closer to the deadline, the costume's shoulder pauldrons continued to haunt me. The 5:00 a.m. Model Magic test was promising, but there was a problem. Even though the air-dry clay could be sculpted, it was fragile and tore under light pressure. The pieces had to be reinforced. Unsure of what else to do, I hot-glued craft foam and fabric to them. It looked horrible but gave the pauldrons more stability. At that point I did the only thing I could: I covered up that dumpster fire. I had ordered some long red feathers for the Fire Fairy costume, which I glued on to the entire surface of the shoulders. The result was beyond what

I could have hoped for. Not only did the shoulder armor hold together; it looked really badass, too! Finally, the entire costume was coming together.

Animazement®, an anime convention held in a pretty hotel in Raleigh, North Carolina, was the stage for our Elemental Fairies group. To save money, I chose to cram myself into one hotel room with four other people; it's the only way most young anime fans are able to afford the costs of attending cons. I spent most of Friday checking out the programming and meeting up with friends, decompressing after weeks of hard work.

Then, on Saturday afternoon, my friend Meg and I sat alone in my room, which was littered with clothes and costume pieces. Everyone else was out enjoying the con while she and I were in a frenzy to get ready for the contest. Meg's dress required some last-minute sewing, so I took that on while she added some final embellishments to her Water Fairy wings. I felt pretty good about having completed my fairy costume ahead of the convention . . . until the time came to put it on.

I'd forgotten to create any type of strapping system for my precious shoulder armor! The pieces were ready to be worn, but I had no way to attach them to my body. Panic set in as I stood in the middle of the hotel room. I had worked so hard on the costume and made such a big deal about meeting up on time for the contest, but now I was going to delay the entire group. I looked around for anything to attach the shoulder

Me in the Fire Fairy costume on the con floor and with my fairy group pads with, going as far as unlacing a pair of shoes and attempting to make straps out of shoelaces. It was no use, though. The shoulder pieces were too heavy and kept slipping off.

In true cosplay spirit, I squeezed some fabric glue that Meg had brought directly onto my bare shoulders and pressed on the damn shoulder pieces. It worked. In a flurry of skirts and wings, Meg and I raced down to meet up with the other fairies. Once we were all together, the excitement at seeing everyone's costumes really took over, and we were bombarded with photo requests. Meg was the Water Fairy to my Fire Fairy, and our friends Jenny and Leo looked amazing in their Ice and Dark Fairy costumes.

I felt a thrill when I saw people reacting with awe at the sight of us. I also couldn't stop giggling at the way all four of us had to do a sideways crab walk in order to avoid poking one another with our wings. After a long shuffle with frequent stops and starts, we managed to get to the contest room and sign in for our slot. I'm not sure if it was luck or if the coordinator wanted to end the contest on a flashy note, but our group was scheduled to go on last. It was an unexpected blessing, because we had time to sneak out and practice our skit while the contest began. It was a simple fairy dance set to ethereal music, with spins and movements to highlight our costumes. When the time came for us to take the stage, we kept it short and sweet, focusing on being as elegant as possible. To my amazement, the shoulder pads stayed in place for the entire evening, and the rash I got from ripping them off my shoulders at the end of the night felt well worth the pain.

My fairies and I won "Best Performance" and "Best in Show" that night. It was a perfect weekend and one of my most memorable con experiences to this day. I learned a big lesson as well: Figure out how to attach costume pieces *before* the convention.

— — —

Compared to the quality of today's cosplay costumes, my Fire Fairy was a complete disaster. My skirt had no semblance of shape, the breastplates were hot-glued directly onto the velvet bodice, and the only red boots I could find were '60s platform go-go boots made of blaring-red PVC. At the time, though, it was the single most elaborate ensemble I'd ever created. That costume was a milestone that gave me the confidence and motivation to keep pushing forward.

The cosplay community in the early 2000s was like the Wild West. We didn't have the eyes of the world on us yet, so we felt free and unguarded in our little bubble. There was an air of fearlessness in how we dove into each costume and presented ourselves at cons. The obscurity of cosplay meant that we were open to explore it in all our unrefined, amateur glory.

Many people who got into cosplay in those days picked up sewing first because it was—and still is—the most necessary skill for making costumes. However, unless you had a background in sewing or knew someone who could teach you, the learning curve was steep. The kind of fantastical costumes we made back then didn't correspond much to traditional sewing instructions, and costume-centric

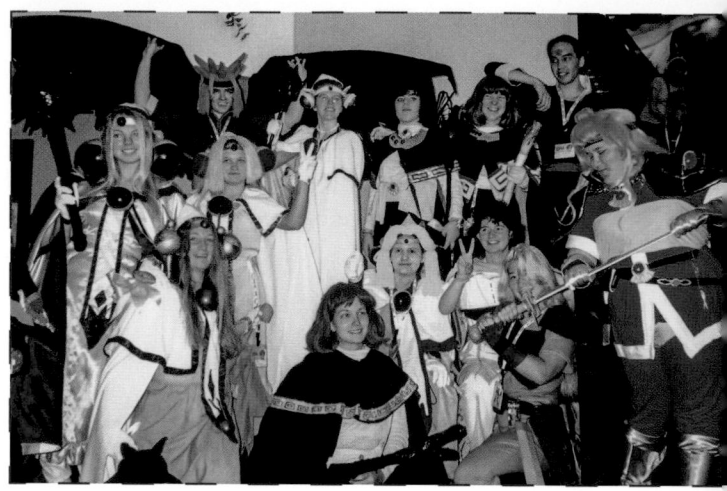

Early cosplayers having fun at a con

patterns were still more than a decade away. I had to teach myself how to piece together fashion patterns, alter them as needed, and cross my fingers that the garment would fit.

There was also a serious lack of fabric and trim choices. Costumes were mostly stitched together out of low-quality shiny satin and cotton because those were the most affordable materials and they came in the most colors. Spandex, PVC, and pleather were specialty items that most fabric stores didn't carry at all. If they did have them, they came in only one or two colors.

Anything outside of sewing was pure experimentation. Cosplayers used a wild array of materials to make armor. These included cardboard, papier-mâché, toilet parts, garbage bins, soda bottles, fiberglass, hot glue, and plumbing piping. Some even used raw sheet metal to make armor, which was dangerous to work with and to wear. Every once in a while some badass costume would appear that was made with advanced materials, such as plastic resin or light-up Electroluminescent (EL) wire, and everyone would gape in amazement, wondering how the heck such a cosplay was even possible.

The lack of tutorials and technical information-sharing was the biggest barrier for cosplayers in the early days of the community. It was very difficult and time-consuming to make tutorials, but more importantly, we didn't have a platform to share what we had discovered just yet. Because none of us knew what we were doing and no one seemed to care (outside of our little cosplay groups), most cosplayers didn't think our unconventional crafting methods were valuable. It didn't even occur to us to document our creation process. I really wish I had taken photos of how my first costumes were made, but this was before the era of smartphones and digital cameras. Photos had to be developed, scanned, and uploaded to be shared.

Without a way to easily share information amongst ourselves, cosplayers would essentially invent the wheel over and over again as they figured out their own solutions to the same problems. Most of us didn't even know about the existence of certain materials and techniques that are now commonly used in costume making. The most poignant example of this is EVA foam, an affordable, flexible, and smooth foam that is currently the most-used material for making armor and props.

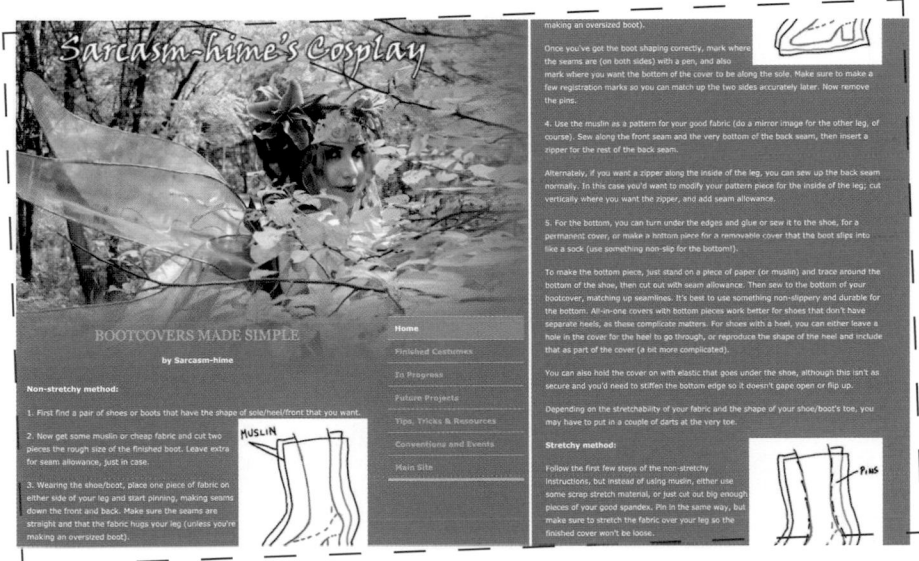

Sarcasm-Hime's old cosplay tutorial for bootcovers

Moreover, some resources simply did not exist in the early days of modern cosplay. Take wigs for example. Walk through any anime convention today and you'll see a few vendors selling wigs in every style and color. Back then, though, we could only choose between low-quality Halloween wigs and expensive wigs made from human hair. It was difficult to find them in person or online. Plus the color and style range was tiny. Wigs were a major source of headache for all cosplayers.

Despite all these setbacks, I made it work. A lack of materials and instructions forced me and other cosplayers to innovate and find unconventional ways to be creative. The thrill of trying something new was addictive to me, even when I made mistakes or failed completely. The moment of triumph when I learned a skill or discovered a new technique was indescribable. There were no stakes at hand, so I could just craft and experiment for myself.

However, the next few years would prove to be more complicated.

CHAPTER 6

The Growing Pains of a Fringe Culture

One night, when I was about twelve or thirteen, my parents hosted a dinner party. I sat in a chair off to the side of the living room, drawing like always, while the adults talked and mingled around me. I kept hearing this melodic laugh. It belonged to a tall woman with long, curly red hair. She had a magnetic quality, commanding the attention of the room with the way she talked and moved. At some point that evening, my mom came over, put her arm around me, and pointed to the woman. She said, "Look there. Isn't Brigitte beautiful? That's what a beautiful woman looks like. You and I are not. We are ordinary. And that's okay."

She gave me a hug and left me to my drawing.

We all go through our own ugly duckling phase, but when I say that I grew up feeling plain and average, I don't mean it was just the way I felt; I was told to accept it as a fact. Living in Germany (in the land of blond and blue-eyed Anglo-Saxons), I did look different from almost everyone else. Every time I saw myself in the mirror, I would pick out the same flaws. I thought my face was too flat, my nose was too wide, and my eyes protruded too much. It also didn't

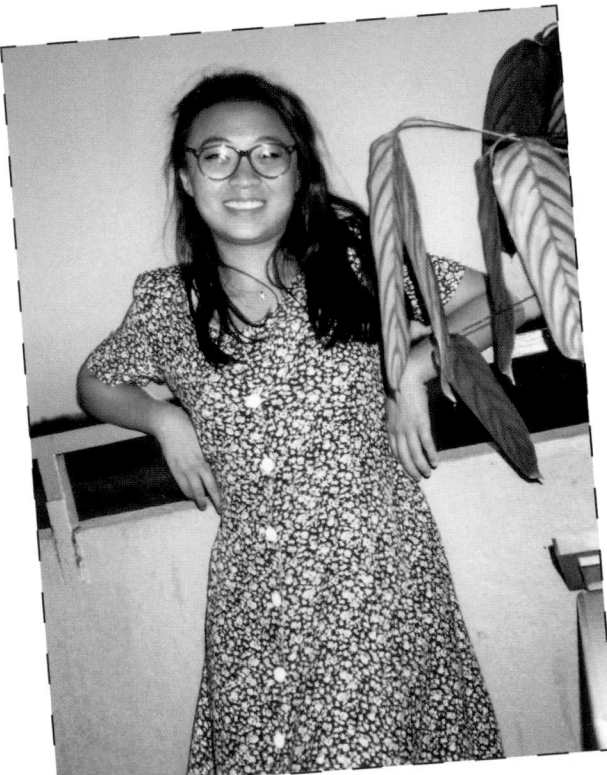

The awkward teen years

help that I stopped growing past five feet two inches tall at age eleven. After every summer holiday, on the first day of school, my classmates would pat my head and jokingly ask, "Did you shrink again?"

I know now that my mother was projecting her own insecurities on me that night. Her words were intended to protect me from future disappointments. Maybe it had something to do with her childhood, growing up in a communist regime where every person is conditioned to see themselves as the same, but she truly never thought of herself as beautiful.

She is wrong. My mother is gorgeous.

When I started cosplaying, I still felt like an ordinary, moon-faced girl. However, as I fell into the craft, I got utterly swept up by it. Not only did crafting and sewing make me happy, but the ability to dress up and transform into someone else was intoxicating. Then, when I looked at photos of myself in costumes like the Fire Fairy, I could see traits that I found attractive, or even dazzling.

One of my cosplay friends, with whom I frequently competed, was in school studying photography. She was the first person who asked me to do photoshoots in costume, partially for her class projects. That was my first experience with professional cosplay photography. We staged

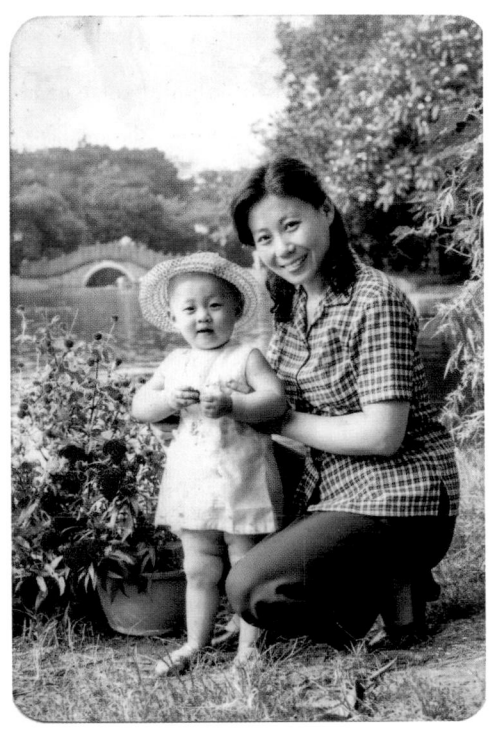

Me as a baby with my mom

little photoshoots in her living room and even occasionally ventured out to local parks, where she snapped pictures of me from every angle. Posing for the camera gave me the same feeling of exhilaration as when I immersed myself into a character while performing during a cosplay contest. I had no idea how to do makeup, so after each photoshoot I would look at photos of myself and figure out how I could improve. Slowly, I learned to apply makeup that flattered my features and even enhanced my cosplays. Through trial and error, I figured out what posing angles looked most graceful. The combination of cosplay and photography made me feel beautiful for the first time in my life.

At the same time as I was discovering new things about myself, the world of cosplay was beginning to blossom as well. In the early 2000s, only a few photographers and reporters documented the anime convention scene. The most well-known convention coverage website was called A Fan's View, and it was run by hobbyist photographer Kevin Lillard. Not only did Kevin photograph the guests of honor and cover panels at the anime events he visited; he also documented costume contests and dedicated multiple pages to hallway snapshots and casual photos of cosplayers. He was the first convention photographer to ever take my picture in cosplay. Kevin provided same-day coverage, uploading photos and writing up reports late into the night. Then he would get up early the next day to shoot more. In the era of dial-up Internet, that required unbelievable dedication.

Lionel Lum was another highly respected anime convention reporter. He ran a website called Usagichan Company that was sleek and modern, featuring comprehensive and well-curated event coverage. Most importantly, though, Lionel took some of the nicest cosplay photos in the American scene at the time. His photos had a magazine portrait quality to them that not only showcased the costumes we were wearing but also captured the spirit of cosplay and brought our characters to life.

For the budding cosplay community, these event coverage websites were a lifeline. After every convention, cosplayers around the nation would race home to their computers and wait for A Fan's View to update. If you missed out on a con, you would go to Usagichan Company to see who'd finished a new costume. My first click was always on the cosplay contest winners page to see which costumes competed and won top honors. In 2001, I ended up on a lot of winners pages, and it was a thrill each time I saw my photo.

As my collection of costumes and photos grew, I decided to make a website for myself. I wanted to emulate the Japanese cosplayers I admired, and many of them had sleek web galleries dedicated to their outfits. At the time, the most common way to create a website was to hand-code it in HTML. We were still years away from social media platforms such as Facebook and website builders such as WordPress. I'd learned basic HTML after making a simple Yahoo! GeoCities page for my fan artwork, but coding a cosplay website is a lot more involved. Thankfully, Meg, my Water Fairy friend, showed me how to use a website coding program called Adobe Dreamweaver and helped me create a decent-looking portfolio site called Angelic Star. (Let's not dwell on the name, okay?)

Having a website meant that I had become one of the first cosplayers in the United States with a consistent Internet presence. My nicer-than-average photos and frequent award wins were making waves already, so with the addition of a website, I started to gain notoriety within

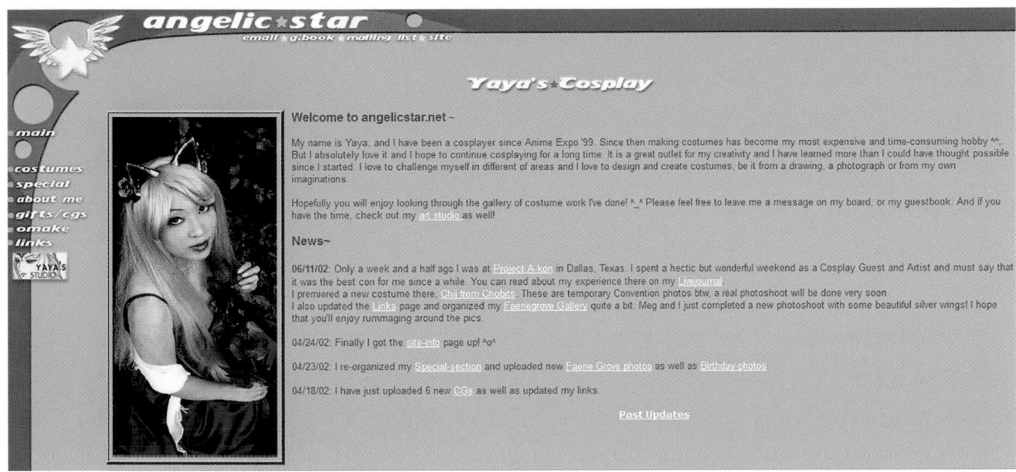

angelic★star

email ★ g.book ★ mailing list ★ site

Yaya's Cosplay

main
costumes
special
about me
gifts/cgs
omake
links
YAYA'S STUDIO

Welcome to angelicstar.net ~

My name is Yaya, and I have been a cosplayer since Anime Expo '99. Since then making costumes has become my most expensive and time-consuming hobby ^^;
But I absolutely love it and I hope to continue cosplaying for a long time. It is a great outlet for my creativity and I have learned more than I could have thought possible
since I started. I love to challenge myself in different of areas and I love to design and create costumes, be it from a drawing, a photograph or from my own
imaginations.

Hopefully you will enjoy looking through the gallery of costume work I've done! ^_^ Please feel free to leave me a message on my board, or my guestbook. And if you
have the time, check out my ad studio as well!

News~

06/11/02: Only a week and a half ago I was at Project A-kon in Dallas, Texas. I spent a hectic but wonderful weekend as a Cosplay Guest and Artist and must say that
it was the best con for me since a while. You can read about my experience there on my Livejournal.
I premiered a new costume there, Chi from Chobits. These are temporary Convention photos btw, a real photoshoot will be done very soon.
I also updated the Links page and organized my Faeriegrove Gallery quite a bit. Meg and I just completed a new photoshoot with some beautiful silver wings! I hope
that you'll enjoy rummaging around the pics.

04/24/02: Finally I got the gifts-info page up! ^o^

04/23/02: I re-organized my Special-section and uploaded new Faene Grove photos as well as Birthday-photos

04/18/02: I have just uploaded 6 new CGs as well as updated my links.

Past Updates

My old cosplay website

the community. I received a rapid influx of e-mails with inquiries about how I made specific costumes, started getting more comments on my photos, and was alerted to increased mentions of my name in forums. An anime convention flew me across the country to appear as a guest in fall 2001, which raised a lot of eyebrows. Inviting a cosplayer to be a con guest was pretty much unheard of at the time, and I had only burst onto the scene two years prior. My hobby career's momentum snowballed from there, as I received more and more requests to partake in convention programming. I judged the cosplay contest at Otakon 2002, the second-biggest anime con in the country. I taught panels on cosplay at conventions from Georgia to California. By 2005 I had become a regular cosplay guest on the American anime convention scene.

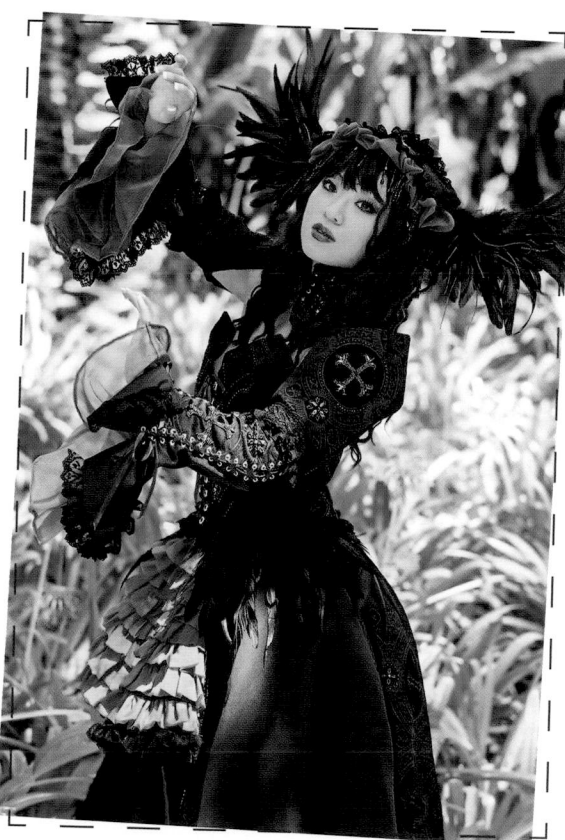

Posing in a purple Gothic Lolita costume I made

For the first time in my life, I was popular. My work was featured on every cosplay website imaginable. When I walked through convention halls, I heard my name whispered. People paid attention when I talked, praised me for my skills, and even complimented my attractiveness. For a young woman who was always overlooked and ignored, this kind of attention was jarring. At the same time, I got to experience all the drawbacks that come with popularity: jealousy, rumors, and gossip. It started with snide remarks, inside jokes, and passive-aggressive comments. As the years went on, the criticism became broader, condemning not only the quality of my costumes but also my persona. I definitely was not equipped to handle that kind of scrutiny and often approached the situations aggressively or put my foot in my mouth. It was . . . messy.

I was not the only one being criticized, though. At the time, whenever a cosplayer received a guest invitation to a convention or was featured in a major media outlet, there were discussions focused on whether they deserved the opportunity or whether their costumes were good enough. There were countless forum threads about "attention-whoring" and cosplaying for the sake of garnering popularity. Self-promotion was viewed as immoral and selfish. Even though cosplay community sites had finally given cosplayers the opportunity to share crafting tips and tutorials, a lot of cosplayers were very secretive about their costume projects and did not like to share their methods, as if it would be like giving away a magic trick. I can't speak about the whole landscape of fan costuming, but at least within circles of Eastern-influenced cosplayers, there was an air of closed-mindedness and elitism.

It wasn't until years later that I saw the bigger picture. The amateur mentality of the cosplay scene cemented it as a hobby, and everyone within the community was on an equal playing field as fans. In the 2000s, cosplay was a fringe culture, and in the early stages of any fringe culture (such as hipster culture), there is a sense that your community is unique and different from the rest of the world. It might even be shunned by the rest of the world, so you want to protect it, keep it pure, and preserve its authenticity. However, as fringe cultures become more popular and mainstream, pushback from within the community is inevitable. As the pool of members grows bigger, there is more concern over how and *who* is representing the community and more scrutiny over individuals potentially polluting the waters with their personal agendas. Individuals who are placed above the equal playing field are denounced, because other cosplayers don't want the power of influence to be taken from the collective. The question of who deserves what kind of recognition is entirely human and resonates through all facets of our society. It calls on people's basic insecurities and can cause smaller subcultures like cosplay to take on a high school mentality.

The quest to keep cosplay authentic, combined with the obscurity of the activity itself, had an unfortunate side effect: It was not easy to normalize cosplay to loved ones. I was lucky in that regard, since my family was thousands of miles away and had no say over my cosplay activity regardless of whether or not they supported it. However, in those years, a large percentage of cosplayers faced disapproval from their family and friends.

The misconceptions were vast. The most popular video games, such as *Mortal Kombat*, were violent. Anime was as much known for kids' shows like *Pokémon* as it was for adult-themed hentai such as *La Blue Girl*. Even family-friendly shows such as *Sailor Moon* included microskirts and plunging dresses (on the villains) in their character designs. Comic book heroes were grotesquely muscular and clad in body-clinging spandex. Kids and teenagers had a hard time explaining why they wanted to dress up as these characters or what they got out of going to a convention. The idea of dressing up for a convention was iffy enough, but actually spending money and time on making these costumes was considered a meaningless waste. Many people were forced by their parents to stop cosplaying or received enough pushback from them that they lost the motivation to continue. Even adults with successful careers who cosplayed on the side as a hobby spoke of it with a feeling of unease. It was as if even they had to keep it secret from their family. Over the years I have talked to many cosplayers who told me of these unfortunate situations, and I can't help but wonder how many left the community before they could experience all of its good parts.

I didn't let the barrage of negativity drive me out, but there were many times when I wanted to quit. I took periodic breaks from cons and making costumes, the longest being six months, but I always came back. A big reason I did was because of my fiancé, Brian, who I met while cosplaying at Dragon Con. From the start of our relationship, we shared the same burning passion for all things geeky. Brian would take me out for drives or drag me to play mini golf (which I intensely dislike) just to get my mind off stressful matters. Even when I felt like the world was against me, I always had Brian's unwavering support. Aside from giving me the opportunity to find the love of my life, cosplay was also the first place where I made lifelong friends. The value in going to cons and dressing up with them always outweighed the drama.

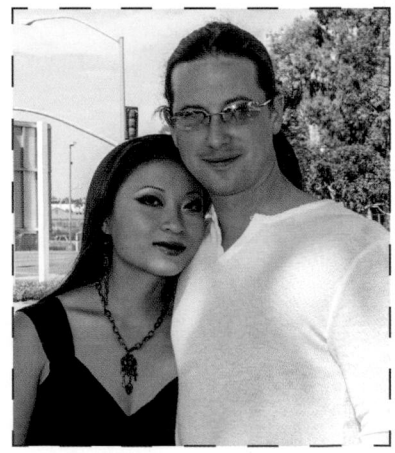

Me and my fiancé, Brian

Lastly, I think the creative process itself kept me from leaving the cosplay community. I could never go a long time without starting a new costume. Whenever I was sewing or crafting, I would lose myself in hours upon hours of beadwork or let the rhythmic noise of the sewing machine drown out my thoughts. Making costumes was and still is healing for me. Even though I had to learn some tough life lessons, I remember the good things the most.

Toward the end of the 2000s, cosplay had transformed into a vibrant creative community. A lot of this was thanks to the growing influence of geek culture, of course. During this decade, comic books started to get adapted into movies, kicking off a new golden era of sci-fi and fantasy entertainment. *X-Men* dropped in 2000. After that, Sam Raimi's *Spider-Man* released in 2002 and was followed by Christopher Nolan's *Batman Begins* in 2005. By the time Tony Stark assembled his first Iron Man suit in a cave in 2008 and the Marvel Cinematic Universe was created, the world's opinion on superhero movies had changed completely.

At the same time that the market for superhero movies was growing in the West, manga and anime

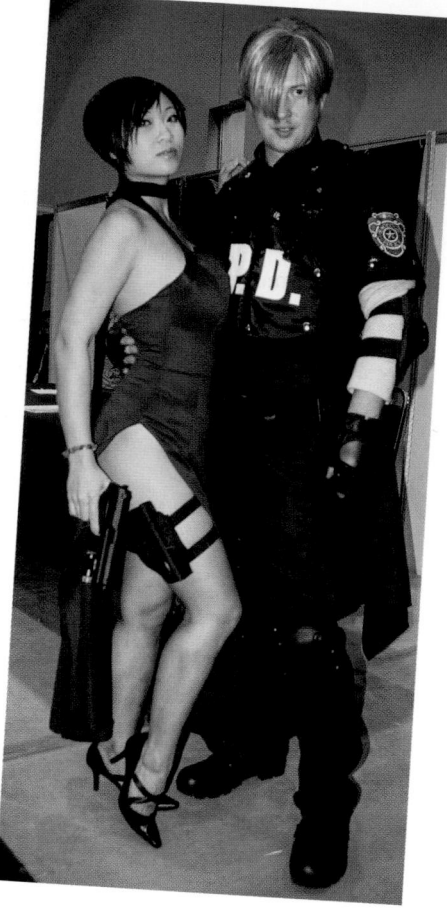

Brian and I cosplaying as *Resident Evil* characters.

were becoming more accessible to Americans as well. Major book chains carried wall-to-wall manga displays, anime films were widely released on DVD, and streaming platforms such as Crunchyroll began to simulcast anime at the same time it aired in Japan. Slowly, the stigma of being a nerd crumbled.

Remember how, when I first started cosplaying, there was a distinct line between Western sci-fi costumers and Asian pop culture–influenced cosplayers? As I mentioned earlier, it was at this point that these communities started to intertwine. Western costumers were exposed to more anime and video games, and cosplayers started to make costumes from Western comic books. Cons that used to be focused on either Western *or* Eastern pop culture introduced broader programming that covered more genres and invited more people to come dressed up in whatever costumes they wanted.

Outside of cons, cosplayers were able to interact and meet on a growing number of online forums and websites, essentially enjoying the hobby year-round. American Cosplay Paradise—now ACParadise or ACP—was the first community website created for cosplay, fully outfitted with free memberships and profile pages where photos could be uploaded and collected into costume galleries. I was the thirteenth person to sign up for ACP, and the site grew to host over 100,000 members in a few years. Community hubs such as Cosplay Lab and cosplay.com sprang up, giving cosplayers multiple platforms on which to connect with one another, share their work, and exchange knowledge. Before social media, cosplay lived on these community sites.

Whenever someone discovered a new technique or material, it spread like wildfire throughout the community and forum pages. The first cosplay tutorials were created and shared this way. Years before the trend of cosplay how-to books, a cosplayer by the name of Amethyst Angel wrote a book on making armor. Due to the difficulties in accessible self-publishing at the time, it never reached wide circulation, but she definitely inspired many cosplayers to try their hands at making armor and props, contributing to the growth of the cosplay scene.

With the rise of eBay® (and online shopping outlets in general), a whole new market of materials became available to cosplayers. As long as you were willing to wait six to eight weeks, you could get wigs in more colors and styles from sellers in Asia than you could from American retailers. eBay also gave cosplayers the option to buy ready-made costumes, which was completely revolutionary at the time. I was shocked when I first saw ready-made anime costume listings. Every year, more and more cosplay components became available through online shopping.

I look back on that period as the *Renaissance* era of cosplay. Despite the growing pains we experienced as individuals and as a community, it was an exciting, adventurous time where beautiful things were created for the sake of creating. None of us could have foreseen that cosplay would evolve into a viable career path. It was unfathomable, even in our wildest dreams. The lack of commercial pressure gave us a sense of boundless artistic freedom. Spending $500 to $1,000 on materials and devoting three hundred hours to making a costume was a labor of love, a matter of pride, and a personal challenge. We created our own stakes and pushed past them simply because we could.

There was a rebellious spirit throughout the 2000s in art, music, and pop culture. Cosplay was a part of that. The community was far from perfect, but you cannot deny that it was passionate, tenacious, and persistent. Those who held on continued to innovate and open doors for others until, finally, the dam broke and geeks took over the world.

YAYA'S ADVICE ──
SEWING AND ARMOR,
AKA THE PILLARS OF COSPLAY

In the realm of cosplay, the two pillars of costume making are sewing and crafting armor. In this chapter, I will go over the basics and give you some tips and tricks for mastering both sets of skills. At the end of the book is a resource list (page 228), which includes more educational materials.

Please know that you do not have to master all these techniques or invest in all these tools and materials in order to join the cosplay community. I'd look at this as a way to open your eyes to new ideas, so hopefully you can find the right techniques for you.

INTRODUCTION TO SEWING

Sewing is the backbone of costume making. Every costume requires sewn aspects because it is the most efficient way to form fabric to the human body. Whether you make a robot costume or a full suit of knight's armor, the ensemble will include sewn components such as undersuits, capes, belts, and accessories. Materials such as latex that are glued with contact cement still benefit from sewing skills like patterning and seam-finishing. Even when you buy ready-made clothing pieces as a part of your costume, alterations and tweaks often have to be made.

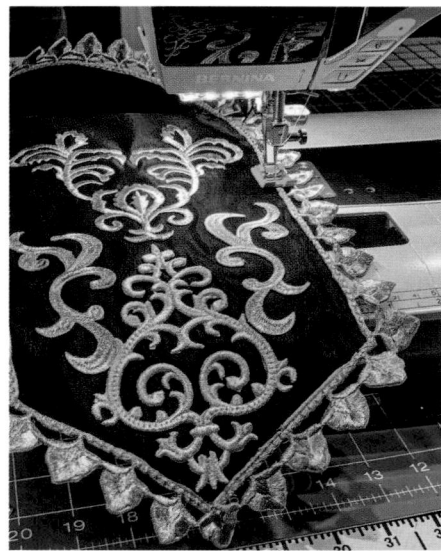

Close-up of a costume in mid-creation

The bottom line is that learning how to sew will not only be helpful to all of your cosplaying endeavors; it will also really open up your world creatively. Sewing has traditionally been viewed as a feminine task, but cosplay has expanded society's outlook on it. Today's sewing industry offers tools and machines that are more sleek and futuristic in design and function. Anyone can sew—you just need the right tools and to follow some basic steps.

Important Sewing Tools and Supplies

Sewing Machine: Buy a sewing machine. I have talked to far too many people who said they were afraid or intimidated by sewing machines. Don't be. They are there to help you make costumes faster and easier. These days, entry-level machines start at $99 and can be easily found online and in fabric stores. If you're unsure which machine is the right one for you, borrow one from a friend or relative, if you can. You can also try out different machines at some brick-and-mortar stores.

For your first sewing projects, you probably won't need more than a straight stitch, a zigzag stitch, and maybe a simple overlock stitch to finish your seams. If I could learn how to sew on a used forty-dollar machine, so can you.

Fabric Scissors: This is the next tool to invest in. A huge part of sewing is cutting fabric. You need a strong and sharp pair of scissors to protect your hands and make your cut pieces more precise. I didn't have good sewing scissors for the first few years I was making costumes because I was too cheap to buy them, and I really regret it.

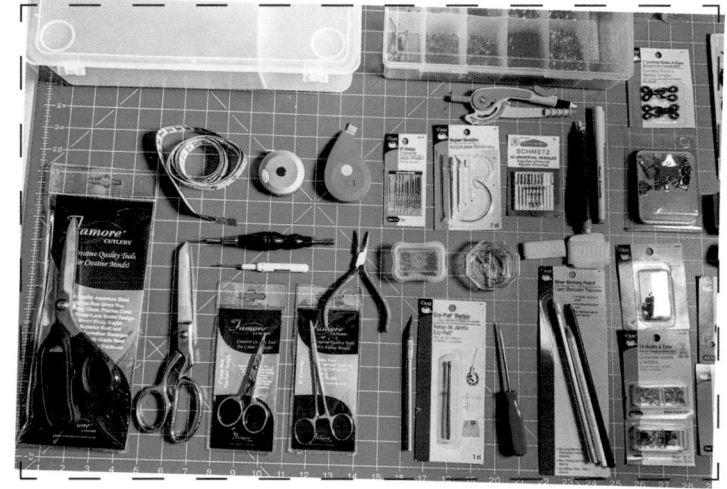

Important note: Do not cut any materials other than textiles with your fabric scissors—no paper, no foam, no boning. Quality steel scissors can be disassembled so that a pro can sharpen the blades. If you take care of your scissors, they will last a lifetime.

Seam Ripper (or small, sharp scissors): This is arguably the single most important tool in a cloth fabricator's arsenal. You will soon realize that you cannot sew without unpicking your seams from time to time. I depend on my seam ripper so much that I keep multiple pairs around just to have one within arm's length at all times. It's an amazing and indispensable tool.

Pins and Sewing Needles: Thin steel pins hold your garment and pattern pieces together without damaging the fabric. Even with a sewing machine, you will need to use a hand-sewing needle from time to time in order to attach buttons or finish a delicate seam. Buy a set of sewing needles in multiple sizes. Use a magnetic pin wheel or wand to pick up pins that are lying around. You do not want to step on sharp objects or risk a pet swallowing them.

Sewing Clips: These little plastic clips can be used instead of sewing pins to hold pieces together until you sew them. They are helpful for elastic and slippery fabrics, as well as for nonwoven materials like PVC leather, in which a pin would leave a lasting hole.

Marking Tools: Depending on your preference and fabric, use chalk pens or fabric markers with disappearing ink that fades when exposed to light, water, or heat from an iron. Always test your marker on a fabric scrap to make sure it leaves no permanent trace.

Measuring Tape (and Ruler): Regular sixty-inch measuring tape or retractable tape will suffice. A transparent ruler will also be very helpful.

Iron: Every pattern instruction includes the words *press seam open*, which means ironing down the seam you sewed to make it lie flat. I always sew near my ironing board because I frequently have to iron seams open or iron hems. The difference an iron makes in assembling a costume, or taking care of any garment, is astounding.

Pattern Paper: This tool is indispensable for drafting your own patterns or copying a commercial pattern that you want to preserve instead of cut up.

Dress Form: Cosplay costumes are usually very close fitting, so an adjustable dress form or a mannequin that has your measurements will be very helpful. A dress form can also be used to drape fabric without using patterns or to display your costumes for photos. These days, custom-size dress forms are available for purchase. Alternatively, you can pad out a dress form with foam to better match your shape (which is what I do). You can even create your own duct tape dress form with tutorials found online.

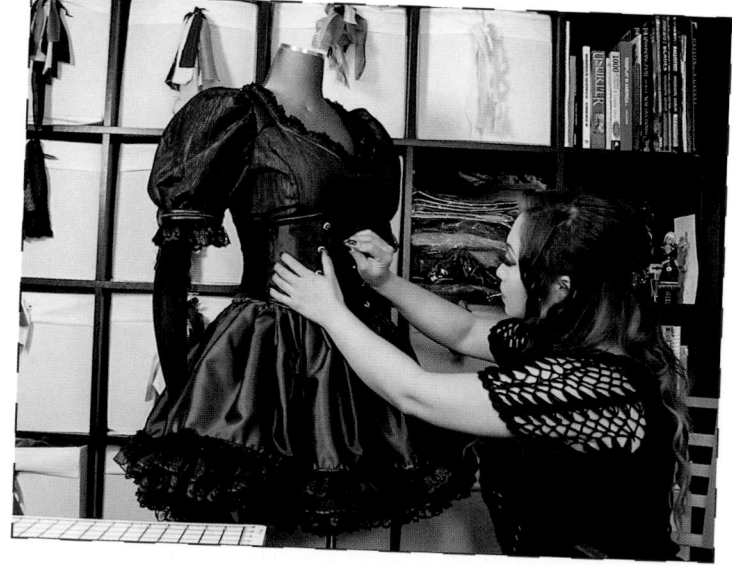

Working on a costume on my dress form

Basic Sewing Tips

I like sewing because it's clean and can be done almost anywhere—even in a cramped space. In the following section I will give you some tips that have helped me tremendously in my sewing projects. Think about sewing a garment like putting together a puzzle. So much about sewing is practice, patience, and planning.

Measure yourself. The first thing you should do is measure yourself and note down a few basic measurements, such as bust/chest, waist, and hips. More often than not, your body will not fit neatly into a sizing chart. That is fine as long as you know where to make adjustments! Commercial sewing patterns include instructions on how to measure yourself and how to alter the patterns to fit your body.

Use sewing patterns. I learned how to sew by following commercial patterns. Nowadays, an endless variety of patterns are available. Look for patterns that share the same seams and shapes as your costumes, and collect a set of basic patterns, like a pair of pants, a fitted dress, a shirt, and a jacket. Patterns give you a basic blueprint to follow, but you can always alter details like sleeves or collars. Read the instructions and look up any unfamiliar lingo. Also remember that there are tons of tutorials out there for specific stitches and sewing techniques.

Pattern sizes are different than dress sizes, so here is where your measurements come in handy. Compare your measurements to the sizing chart printed on the back of the pattern. This will tell you how much fabric to buy.

Choose the right fabric. Think about what kind of fabric your character would wear, what type of garment you need, and how much movement you want to have. Does the fabric need to flow or drape? Does it need to stretch? You don't have to become an expert in textiles, but basic information on fabric is easy to look up and will really help. Learn to distinguish the different weaves (plain, twill, satin, or nonwoven fabrics like jersey) and different materials (cotton, polyester, wool, or silk) and how they behave. I recommend buying fabrics in person so you can feel them and see them up close. If you are in a store with fluorescent lighting, take the bolt

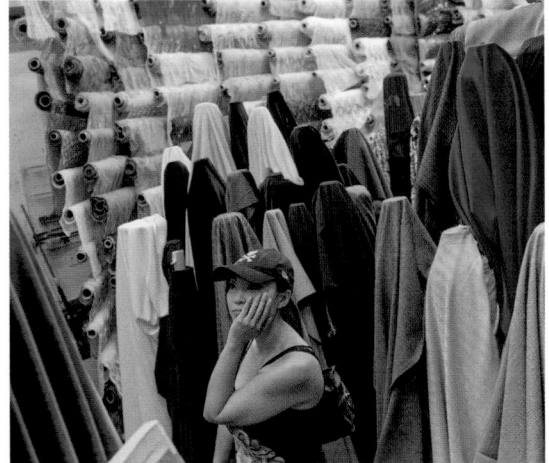

Feeling overwhelmed while fabric shopping

near a window and look at the color in natural lighting. You can also take photos of a fabric with and without the flash to see how it reacts to lighting.

If you must buy fabric online, sight unseen, plan in advance and order swatches. All online fabric stores offer swatches or samples in some manner.

Make a mock-up. Before cutting up your precious fashion (or final) fabric, sew a test piece out of a cheap material like muslin (raw, unbleached cotton broadcloth) or a fabric with a similar drape and weight as your fashion fabric. Try it on for a fitting and make alterations to the pattern if necessary. This is very useful for complicated patterns with many seams, or whenever you try something new, as there will be no fear of messing up! You can cut the mock-up at the seams and trace it on paper to get your final pattern.

Embrace unconventional materials. Cosplay often entails working with unconventional materials, such as leather, neoprene, upholstery, PVC leather, heavy spandex, and rubber-coated fabrics. Here are some tips for sewing these types of materials:

- Use the right sewing machine needle. There are not only different thicknesses in needles but also different finishes and tips. Use a leather needle for leather or PVC leather.
- Use a nonstick sewing foot or a walking foot to make the fabric flow through your machine more evenly. These keep slippery materials from getting stuck or sliding all over the place as you sew.
- Alternatively, place pattern paper or parchment paper on top of your fabric before you feed it under the sewing foot.
- Most machines can handle more than you'd think. Keep your sewing machine oiled and go slow. As I've already mentioned, always test on a fabric scrap.

Use closures and attachments. Artists and character designers are not always experts in sewing, so sometimes fictional characters have costumes that don't have apparent closures. Alternatively, sometimes the way their costume parts are visibly attached wouldn't make sense in real life. It's worth researching what kind of closures, such as invisible zippers, hook-and-loop fasteners such as Velcro, eyelets and lacing, snaps, hook and eyes, etc., are out there. I like to make as many detachable costume parts as possible for easier transportation and cleaning.

Dye your fabric. Sometimes you can't find your fabric in the right color. Luckily, you can buy dyes for natural fibers like cotton, wool, and silk, as well as for synthetic fabrics like polyester. Always do a test and note down the type and weight of fabric you are trying to dye. Follow the instructions and know that sometimes one pass of dye will not be enough. It's an artistic process, so have fun with it.

Elemental's Merida Dye Plan
6.5 yds silk Georgette

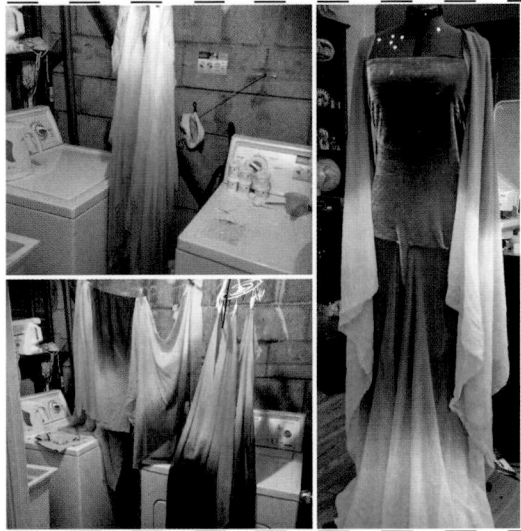

Gathered dress at mid thigh, radial gradient

45" width

Make gradient more green than yellow

39" cutting line on fold for circle skirt (4.3yds total)

Sleeves will be free draped

45" width

Radial gradient on bias

36" or whatever is left halved

The process of dyeing fabric for a costume

Embellishments

This is my favorite part of sewing! There are tons of ways to add details and designs to your costumes. Here are some of the most commonly used techniques.

Painting: Fabric paint or watered-down acrylic ink is the most straight-forward way to apply decorative patterns to your fabric. Because most

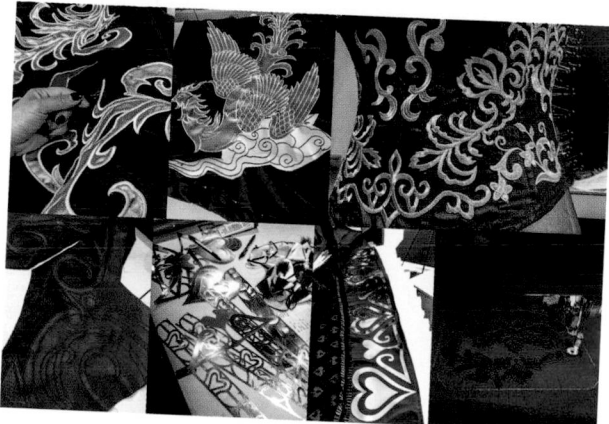

Examples of embellishments including appliqué, embroidery, and heat-transfer vinyl

paints stiffen the fabric and can leave visible brushstrokes, use these materials on smaller areas. An airbrush or a fabric spray paint can easily create gradients or be used to visually weather your garments.

Appliqué: With this technique, you bond one layer of fabric to another to create a design or pattern. Most of the time, you can do this with an iron-on adhesive such as Heat n Bond® or appliqué sheets. With a regular sewing machine, you can use a freehand satin stitch (a very small zigzag stitch) to seal the edges of the design.

Embroidery: This is a traditional way to add quality designs and motives to fabrics that is especially useful for historic or fantasy designs. Hand embroidery can be very time-consuming but gives an amazing effect. You can also save up for a programmable embroidery machine or buy a sewing machine that has embroidery module add-ons if you want to apply this technique to multiple projects.

Heat-transfer vinyl: This is a modern way to apply logos, letters, or elaborate designs to your fabric, inspired by the T-shirt industry. Cut out the vinyl foil with scissors, a utility knife, or a programmable cutting machine (aka a plotter), and iron it onto the fabric. There are special kinds of vinyl for stretch fabrics and ones that imitate different materials (with a metallic or velvety finish, for example).

The good thing about sewing and embellishment techniques is that a lot of information is already available. From your grandmother's sewing bible to copious online tutorials and videos to Facebook Groups devoted to couture sewing techniques—everything you need to learn to start your next project is out there. The lingo and the range of options can be overwhelming, so start with a simple-looking pattern that doesn't have too many details. Challenge yourself by learning one new technique at a time.

INTRODUCTION TO ARMOR AND PROP MAKING

Beyond fabric-based costumes, the cosplay landscape is full of armor and prop-heavy designs. From futuristic mechanical robots and humanoid aliens to high-fantasy warriors wielding outlandish weapons, the spectrum for armor and prop making is impossibly wide. Unlike sewing—a tried-and-true set of creative techniques that have been passed down for centuries—armor designs can be brought to life through countless methods. I will go over the most effective,

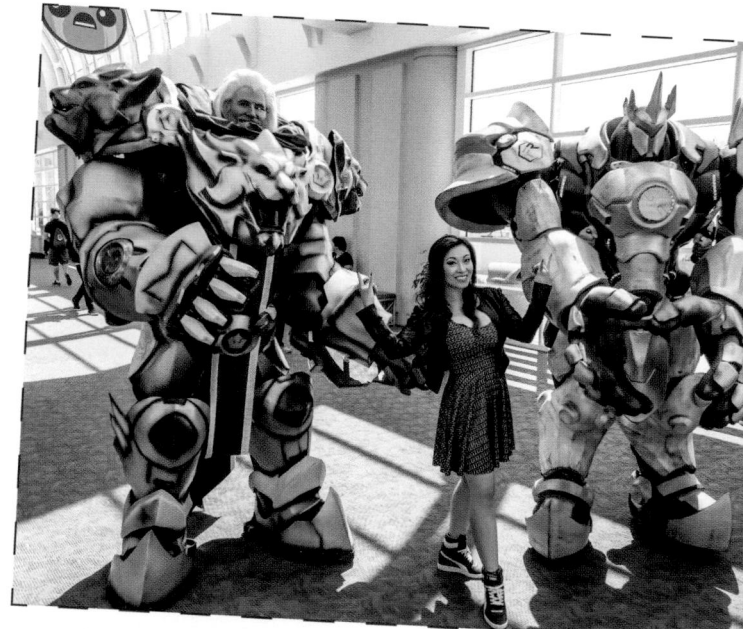

Being dwarfed by two *Overwatch* cosplayers at a con

affordable, and easily applicable techniques that give you a well-rounded understanding of how armor and props are made by the majority of people in this community.

Aesthetics: Cosplay armor is all about the look. There are exceptions, but 99 percent of the time, armor designs in fiction and media will not be realistic in terms of mobility, proportions, and range of movement. Characters are designed to look badass, and the functionality of their armored outfit is secondary.

Proportions: Characters designed for video games and animation often do not have the proportions of a human. Consider altering pieces or shifting their sizing to fit your proportions in order to create a suit that accommodates your needs and flatters your body. The most convincing armor costumes look effortless and recall the proportions of the original character designs.

Tip: The right inner structure can help. Wear an undersuit with foam padding to imitate muscles or strap yourself into a corset or waist cincher and attach the armor parts directly to the garment.

Durability: The reality is that fabric can rip or be easily ruined. Foam and plastic can be crushed or can melt at high heat. As you learn to use these materials, you will understand how much they can be manipulated. It's worth it to go through some extra steps—such as using the right glue for your materials or sealing and priming the pieces multiple times—to make sure your costume is durable and can be worn again and again. Especially with armor and props, it's all too easy for people to bump into your cosplay on a convention floor or for your outfit to be damaged during transport. You don't want your hard work to go to waste.

Weight: The lighter, the better. Even if your costume's armor doesn't have full-body coverage, you'd be surprised how heavy parts of your outfit can feel after a while. This is especially true of anything you wear that is attached to your head or limbs. Consider the materials you choose and the size of the

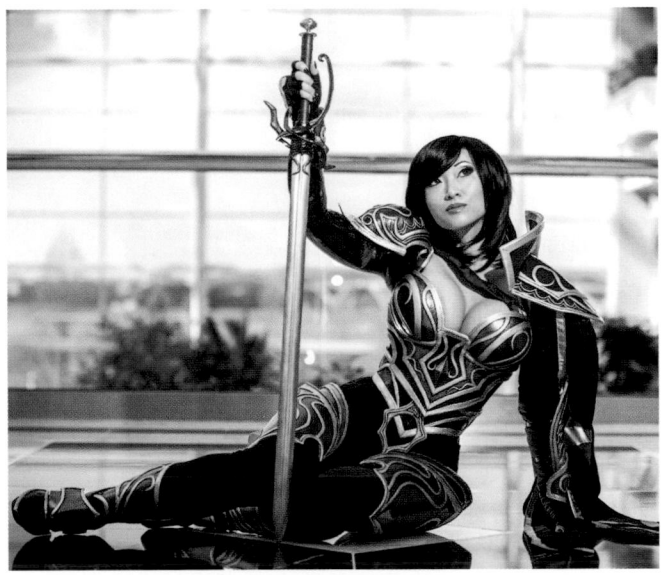

Posing in the Nightraven Fiora costume I made, complete with prop sword.

pieces. Bonus points if you make detachable pieces that can be removed when you need a break.

Safety: Conventions usually have a form of weapons check and a peace-bonding guideline, or a method of marking a prop as inspected by attaching a noticeable tag to it, because real weapons are not allowed inside events. Some props can look very realistic, so it's important for any cosplayer to be responsible and have their props inspected.

You can probably see now that armor and prop costumes require a bit more thought and consideration. It's in your best interest as a creative to make your work as comfortable as possible, last as long as possible, and look as convincing as possible. Now we can finally talk about the different steps of armor and prop making. Crafting is not as rigid and structured as sewing is in its process, so please know that these are just suggestions.

Commonly Used Materials for Armor and Props

The following three materials can be manipulated through heat. They can also be cut and sanded or filled in, sealed, and painted.

EVA Foam: EVA stands for ethylene-vinyl acetate and is a closed-cell flexible foam. Also called high-density (HD) foam, it is emerging as the leading material for making cosplay armor and props thanks to its affordability, versatility, and high availability. Nowadays, companies make EVA foam specifically for costume crafting and there is a variety of foam products available online. In 2019, I released a cosplay EVA foam product line through JOANN with the intention of giving cosplayers easier access to this important material by having it available in local neighborhood stores.

Choosing the right thickness and density of EVA foam depends on your crafting project, but the most commonly used thicknesses

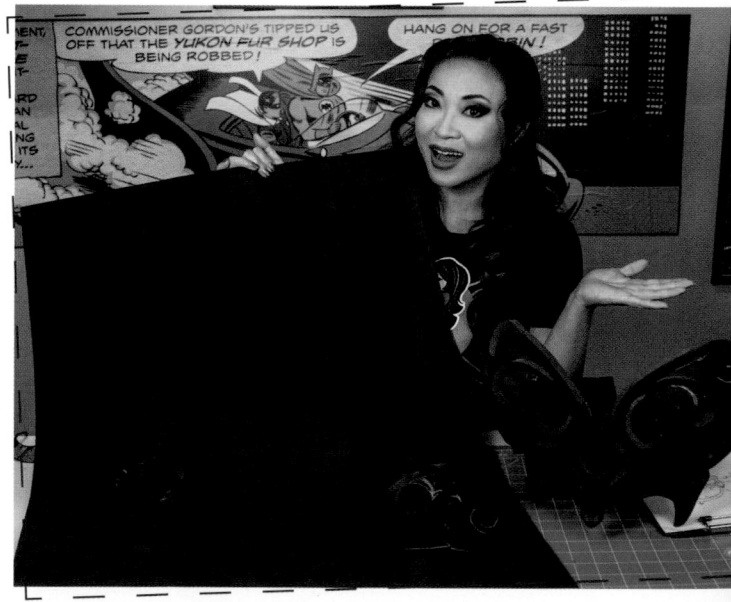

Showing EVA foam in it's sheet form against a chest piece and shoulder pads I made.

are 2-millimeter, 5-millimeter, and 10-millimeter. Do not use cheap alternatives like camping mattresses. The fumes from these materials can be toxic when you use heat on them!

Foam Clay: To add 3-D details to your foam, you can use **foam clay**. This ultra-lightweight nontoxic modelling clay is air-drying and has a foamlike texture when cured.

Thermoplastics: Worbla, Wonderflex, Cosplayflex, and TerraFlex are all thermoplastics. Thermoplastic is a composite material made of plastic that is very malleable when activated with a heat gun or hot water, allowing you to mold it into different shapes. At room temperature, thermoplastic is rigid and durable—more so than foam (although it is heavier than foam as well). It comes in thin sheets and when you heat it up, the material will stick to itself, so it is easy to layer multiple pieces for stability or to add details. The great thing about thermoplastic is that it is non-

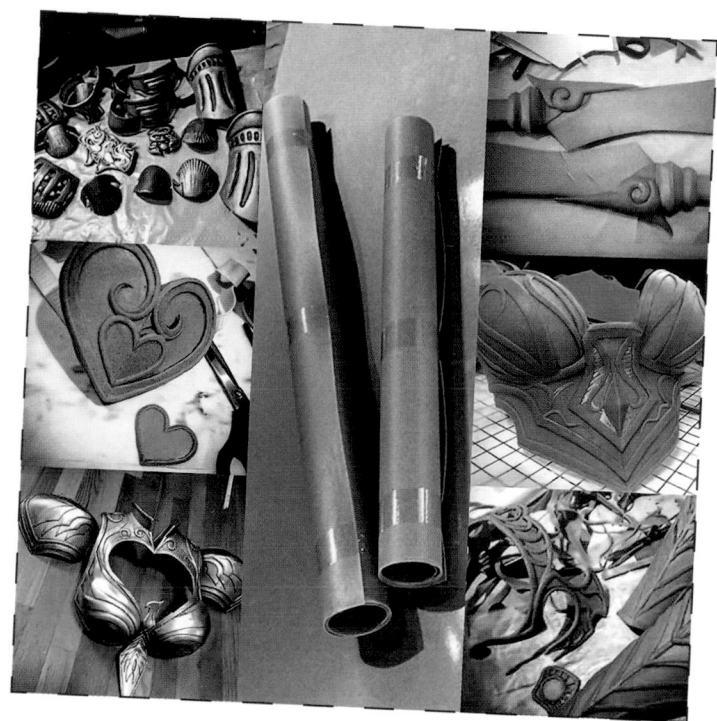

Raw Worbla and examples
of armor pieces made from it

toxic. You can use these materials in conjunction with EVA foam (as a stabilizer) or on their own to create complex and organic shapes as well as detailed and filigreed designs.

Another form of thermoplastic comes in pellet form (two well-known brands are Friendly Plastic or Worbla's Deco Art). You can heat up the pellets in hot water and then sculpt them like modeling clay. The pellets are best suited for smaller designs like emblems and pendants. They also stick to other thermoplastics while hot.

PVC: Polyvinyl chloride (PVC) boards are most commonly used for signs and displays. For years, cosplayers have used sheets of PVC to make armor because of its rigid structure and smooth finish. This material is a lot heavier than foam and can be harder to cut and shape than thermoplastic, but its durability is undeniable. Sintra is the most well-known and easily accessible brand of PVC, and you'll find many cosplay tutorials and resources by searching for it online.

Additional Armor- and Prop-Making Materials

PVC Pipe: It's amazing what you can make out of PVC pipe. Examples include sword handles, staffs, wing frames, oversize costume frames, and even homemade stilts. Hardware stores carry PVC pipe in the plumbing department and offer a great variety of circumferences.

Insulation Foam: Also known as extruded polystyrene (XPS) foam, this is the large, lightweight yet rigid sheet of foam board you can find at hardware stores. It is used to insulate houses, but it's also often used to build large props and armor parts because it is cheap and very light. However, this foam is also rather brittle and requires a hard coating. I recommend using insulation foam for the base of a large prop and stabilizing it with a thermoplastic or resin coating.

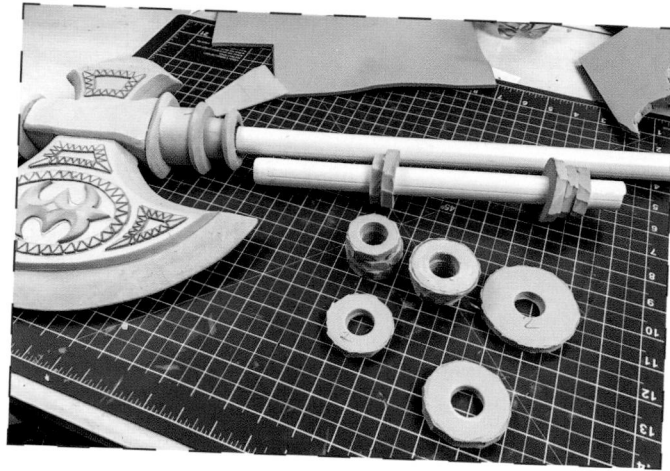

PVC pipe being used in a prop ax

Wood: Wood is a classic material choice for props—especially swords. Woodworking is a great skill for cosplay, and there is no shortage of information and tools, but the material can be heavy and the tools can be expensive. Small pieces like wooden dowels can be used to stabilize props and craft sword pommels/grips or can become a base for staves and lances. Make use of a relative's or friend's workshop and experience if you can.

Molding/Casting: Another classic and reliable way to create movie-quality props. Molding and casting are especially useful if you want to create multiple identical pieces, like decorative gems or horns. The company Smooth-On offers every sculpting, modeling, and casting material under the sun, as well as educational step-by-step guidelines. This method of crafting can be a little more expensive than others, but it offers so many advantages if you put your mind to it. Always make sure to read the instructions, ventilate your work space, and wear protective gear when working with chemicals.

3-D Printing: 3-D printing is emerging as a new, modern way to create costumes. It has arguably changed the game because you can create every piece imaginable from scratch and re-create them as often as you want. 3-D printing has a steep learning curve, and you need to gain digital art skills to create the graphic files first, although you can also buy and download template files of many popular designs. The printer itself is also an investment, but the technology is evolving fast and printers can now be attained for as little as a few hundred dollars. Still, you can't expect a 3-D printer to spit out a wearable costume. You have to do a lot of cleanup and finishing work on printed pieces. Moreover, printers only have

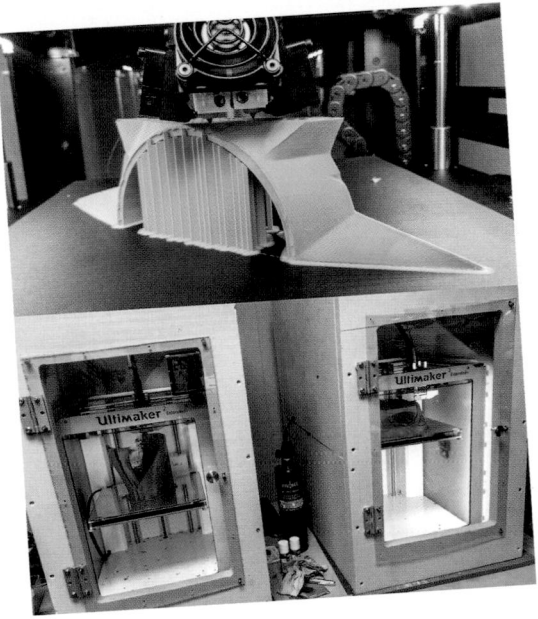

A 3-D printer in action

so much space. This means that if you were to make a helmet, for example, you would have to print it in parts and combine the pieces, so there are still practical skills involved.

Patterning Armor

Duct Tape Patterning Method: For many cosplayers, the easiest way to make patterns is by using duct tape. Wrap whichever body part (an arm, your torso, etc.) you want to make a pattern for in saran wrap. Then apply strips of duct tape around the area to make a shell, so to speak. You can also use masking tape to do this, but it's not as durable as duct tape.

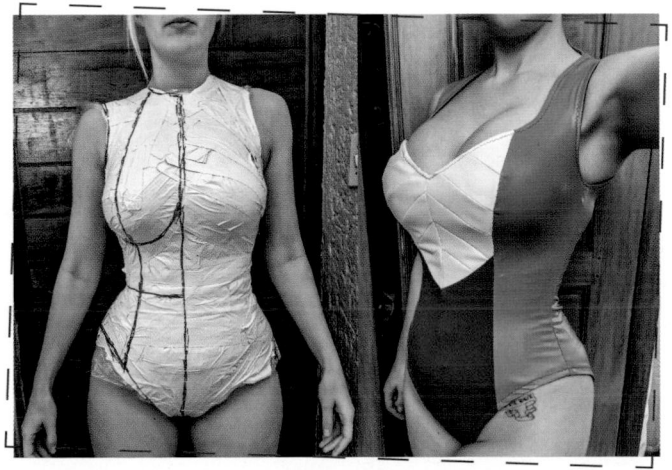

A cosplayer's duct tape pattern versus the finished bodysuit

Once you have encased your body part in duct tape, you can draw the armor piece on the shell and then carefully cut the tape open to remove it from your body. Finally, you flatten the tape and transfer the design onto paper, labeling each piece.

Patterning by Measuring and Tracing: For more complicated or larger pieces that sit away from your body, measure and graft the pattern on paper or experiment with scrap foam or poster board. Sometimes I will draw out an armor template based on my measurements simply because the piece will sit on a part of my body that I can't easily reach. A basic understanding of sewing patterns can help you add seams and darts, which will help you shape the two-dimensional pieces to fit your body.

Some people also pattern digitally by scanning and enlarging reference art to match the size they need. They trace the lines or use the shape as a guide to create a template that can be printed.

Pepakura Designer: This is a program that allows you to create a 3-D template and print it out on paper in numbered pieces. You then glue the paper pieces together to make the 3-D shape. This tool is fantastic for those who are patient and need some guidance with sculpting multidimensional shapes. You can cover the parts in resin, papier-mâché, and other materials.

Once you have a template for your armor piece, transfer it by tracing the shape onto whatever material you are using, whether it be a sheet of foam or thermoplastic.

Don't be discouraged if you can't get the hang of patterning the first time. These days, there are so many resources for patterns and templates. Head over to the resources list on page 128.

THE MOST IMPORTANT CRAFTING TOOLS AND SUPPLIES

Cutting Tools: A utility or hobby knife (X-Acto® knife) with sharp, replaceable blades is your basic tool for cutting foam and all sorts of plastic. A pair of cheap scissors that are not your fabric scissors will come in handy as well. Always wear protective gloves when you use a sharp blade. If you cut and carve a lot of insulation foam, invest in a heat cutter, which melts through foam like a hot knife through butter. Wood and other hard materials need to be cut with a saw.

Safety tip: Always wear protective gloves when you use a sharp blade, and be sure to cut on a commercial cutting mat. Safely dispose of dull blades by following the manufacturer's instructions.

Glue: Just like fabric clothing, a suit of armor will need to be put together from multiple pieces to achieve a nice 3-D shape. Contact cement is a versatile adhesive that works with many different materials. Super glue and hot glue can be used to quickly attach details and decorations or to fix a broken prop. Many thermoplastics like Worbla are self-adhesive. The solvent in some glues can eat plastics and insulation foam, so make sure to do a test and use an adhesive that is compatible with your material (e.g., foam-safe glue).

Safety tip: Work in a well-ventilated area and consider wearing a respirator, because the fumes can cause headaches and pose a risk to your health.

Sanding Tools, Fillers, and Primers: You can use these materials to make a base piece look more polished and to ready it for painting. Foam is great because it can be sanded easily with a handheld Dremel rotary tool or a sanding belt. It can even be sanded by hand with sandpaper. Other materials must be filled in with acrylic filler from a hardware store to achieve a smooth surface. After leveling the surface, you then need to seal the raw material with a primer to help it better absorb paint. Primer can be wood glue, flexible latex spray like Plasti Dip, artist-grade acrylic primer, or even self-levelling resin like Epsilon PRO.

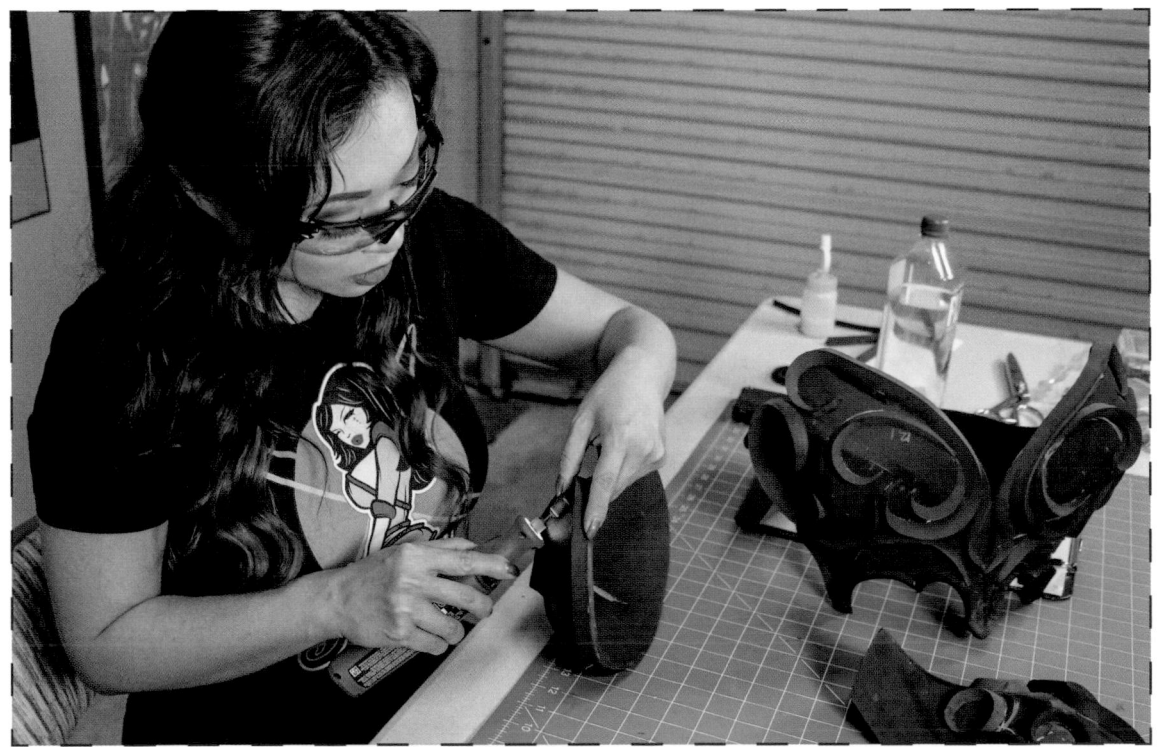

Working with a Dremel tool to sand a piece of armor

Read up on the best and safest filling and priming methods for the material you're using and for the kind of prop you're trying to make.

Safety tip: When sanding, always wear safety glasses and a respiratory mask. Do not work in an enclosed space like a bedroom, and always vacuum or sweep up loose particles at the end of a sanding session.

Paint and Painting Tools: A lot of armor designs have a metallic finish, and once upon a time, I thought I would have to make armor out of metal if I wanted to achieve that look. Thankfully, these days there are a wide variety of ways you can create various finishes, from painting techniques to sealing methods. Acrylic paint is the most versatile paint for props and armor. It can be applied with a paintbrush or watered down and then dabbed or sprayed on for effect. Spray paint is a quick and easy way to achieve an even coating. An airbrush comes in handy if you do a lot of painting. With a little practice, it will help you produce flawless gradients, shading, and metallic surfaces.

No matter which painting tool you use, learn how to add shades and highlights to make

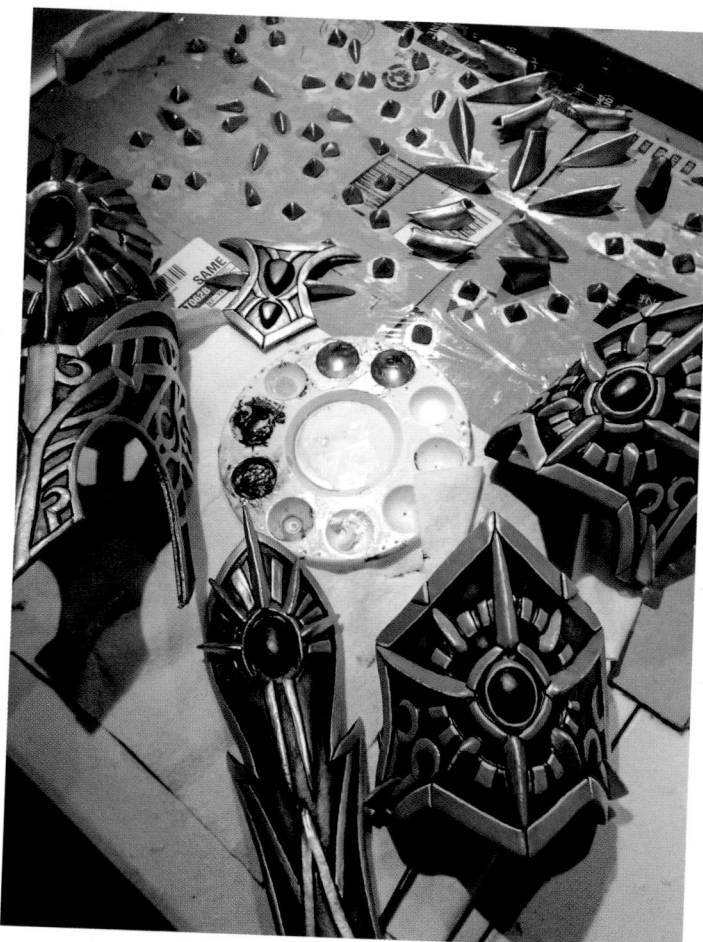

Armor painting in progress

your armor pop in photos. You can also add battle damage for a more realistic look. Apply a coating of clear varnish for durability and to give your paint a shiny finish if needed.

Attachment: This is a step in the process that often gets overlooked, but it is so important. I tend to favor elastic straps for armor attachments, and I cover them with matching fabric and a stretch stitch. I use buckles or heavy-duty snaps for the closure, and the elastic allows some give while I move. I also like using hook-and-loop fasteners and magnets for attachments. There are many other ways to attach armor, and it's fun to try out different methods.

— — —

Whether you choose to pursue sewing or armor making, these tips will help you along the way. Beyond these two areas, there are many other fun and fulfilling costuming techniques used in cosplay, such as wig styling, millinery, and jewelry making. Enjoy researching and trying out new techniques. Above all else, let your curiosity guide you on your cosplay adventure!

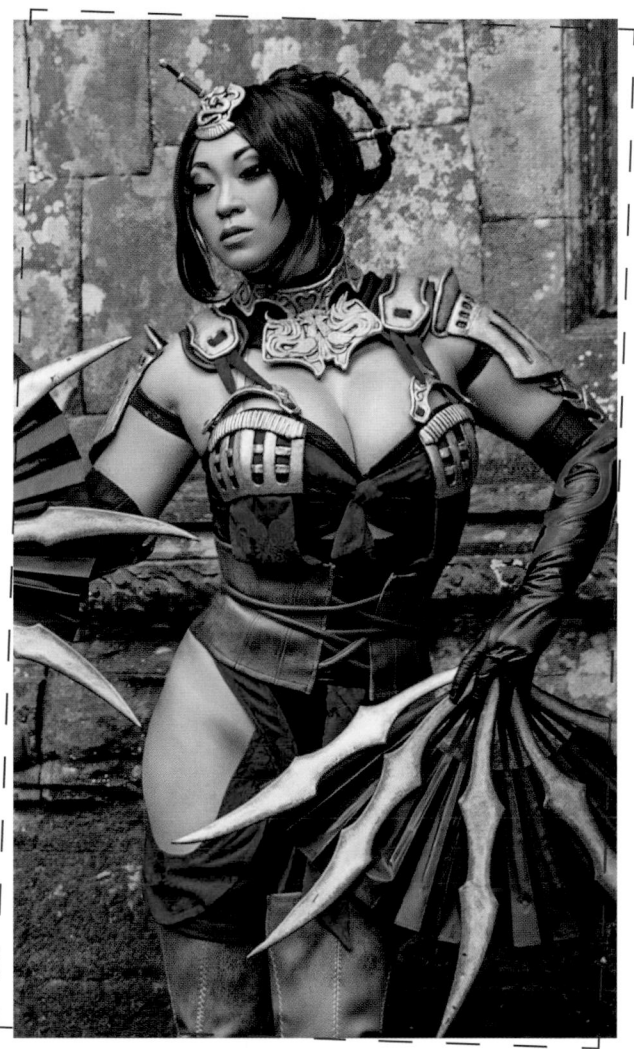

My Kitana costume had many small pieces that were attached with snaps and hook-and-eye closures.

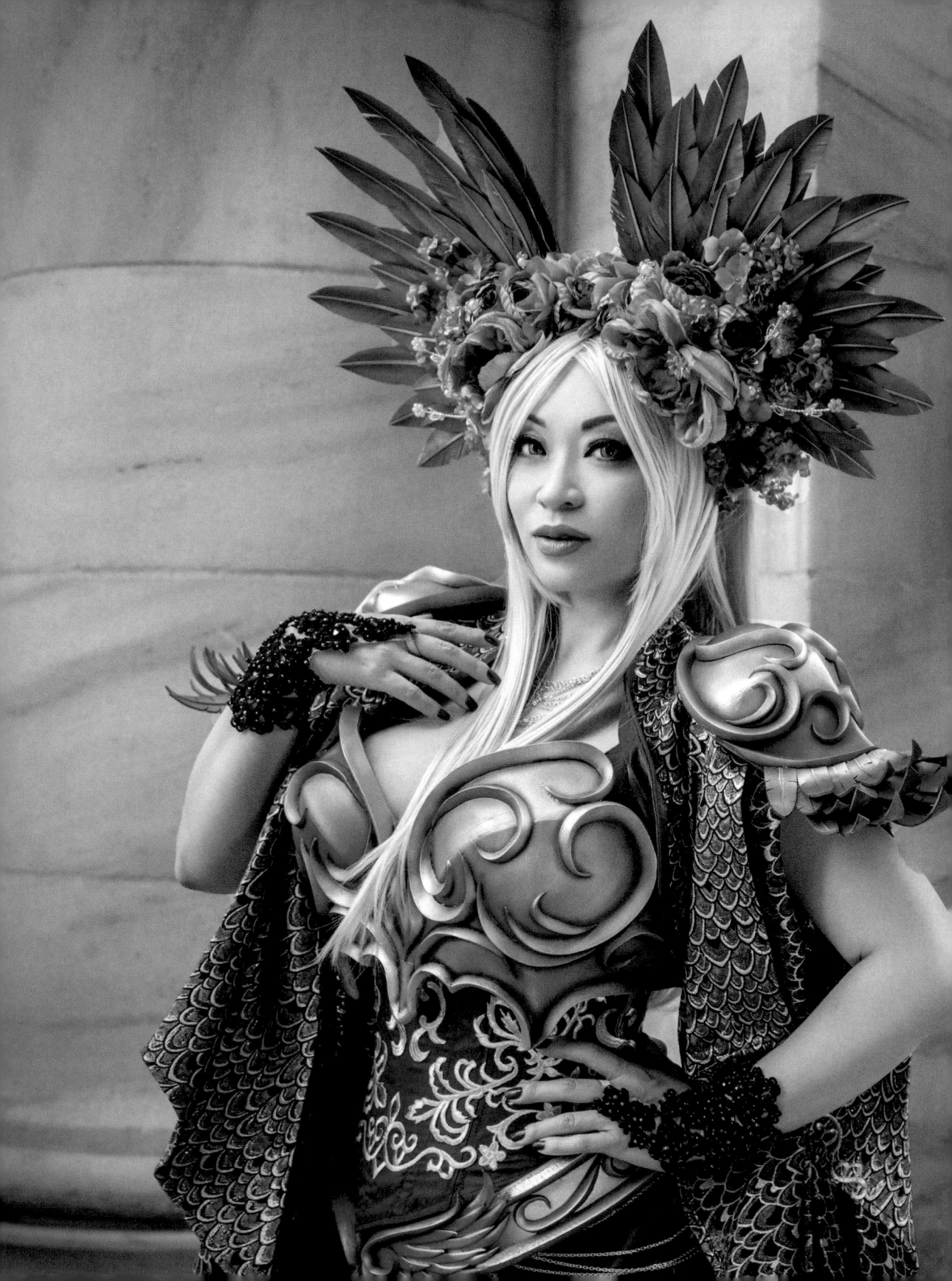

PART THREE

The Creative Expression of Cosplay

CHAPTER 7

Conventions

Where Cosplay Comes to Life

In a packed, dimly lit ballroom at San Diego Comic-Con, I sat in a pale lavender dress, holding a dragon. All eyes were trained on the huge stage, where the cast of *Game of Thrones* sat and chatted about filming the TV show. Jason Momoa told a joke, and the entire room erupted in laughter.

The year was 2011, and HBO had aired the first season of *Game of Thrones* a few months prior. The entire world had Westeros fever. I was very familiar with the Seven Kingdoms, as I had been an avid reader of the A Song of Ice and Fire series since I was a teenager. Daenerys Targaryen was my favorite character, and on that day at Comic-Con, I was dressed up as her. I'd made a full costume based on descriptions of the dress she wore in the book while in Qarth. That meant including a key feature: the exposed right breast. To meet the convention dress code, I'd strapped on a sculpted version of one of Dany's three dragons, Rhaegal, to cover myself (a clever modesty solution if I may say so).

Purple contact lenses and a silvery-blond wig with complicated braids and small jingling bells completed my Khaleesi look. The dragon was made of artificial stone and resin, so it was not all that comfortable to wear. I'd also had to explain why it was in my suitcase to the TSA agents at the airport, but it was so worth it; I was on cloud nine. Earlier that day I'd been able to meet George R. R. Martin during a signing at a booth. I walked up in my Dany costume and he signed my dragon. Then he asked me to come to the *Game of Thrones* panel, so of course I did.

After an hour of banter and stories from the set, the panel concluded. As everyone clapped and got up to leave, I made my way through the crowd to the front of the room and called to George. He waved at me to come backstage. The only reason I was able to get past the two gigantic security guards at the curtains was that I was accompanied by a friend who was also a staff photographer for the con. I remember tripping over the giant cables on the floor and breaking one of my sandals, but somehow I managed to get onto the stage. All of a sudden, I was face-to-face with the entire cast of the TV show, dressed as the Mother of Dragons. In rapid succession, I met and took pictures with Jason Momoa, Lena Headey, and Nikolaj Coster-Waldau. As if George hadn't been gracious enough already, he then introduced me to Emilia Clark, who plays Daenerys on the show and is even more beautiful in person. All of the actors were an absolute delight, and I am so grateful for this once-in-a-lifetime experience. An experience that could only have happened at a con.

— — —

We live in an exciting time. Geeks have inherited the earth, and cosplay, our once obscure, weird hobby, has gone mainstream. There are so many ways to enjoy cosplay now that, depending on your interest, each person can have a completely unique experience. Some cosplayers love to perform onstage. Others are drawn to the storytelling power of photography and center all their projects around cosplay photoshoots. Others still are devoted to building costumes and sharing their progress through videos or livestreamed

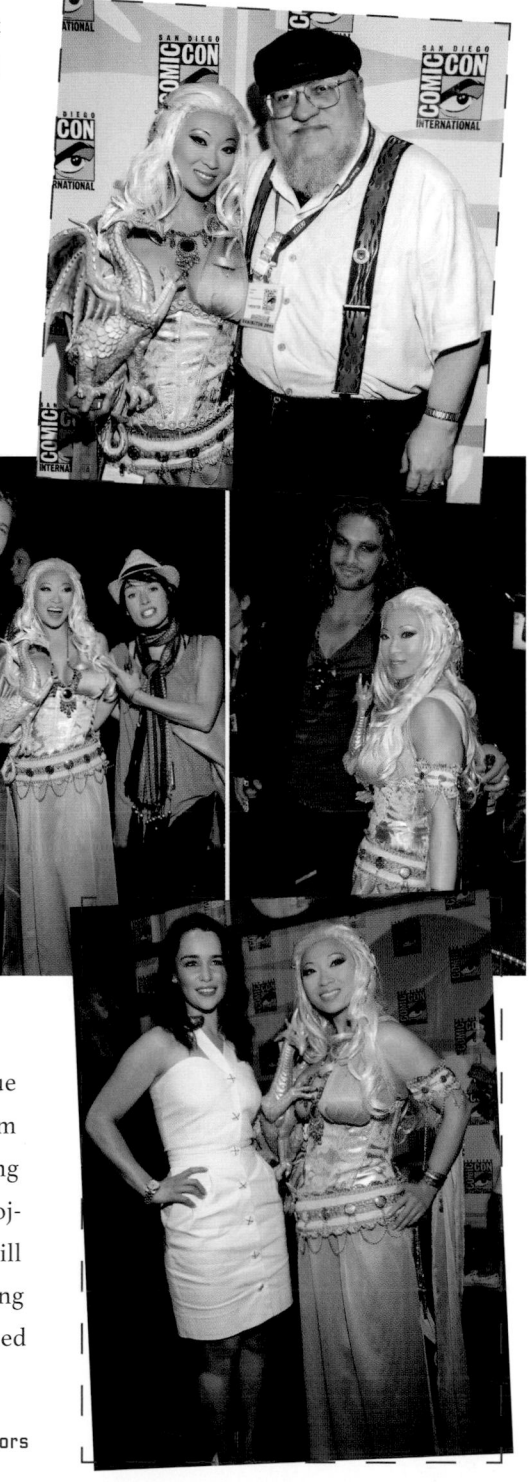

Cosplaying as Daenerys Targaryen and meeting George R. R. Martin, Emilia Clark, and other *GoT* actors

crafting sessions. In the following pages, I will explore the different avenues cosplayers use to express themselves.

I am convinced the global culture of cosplay could never have existed without fandom cons. As geek culture has gained significance, conventions have become a billion-dollar global business. Fancons.com shows that on any given weekend, there are as many as thirty fandom conventions in the United States and over fourteen hundred per year in North America. Worldwide, the number of comic cons, anime cons, video game conferences, and pop culture expos rank in the tens of thousands. The typical fandom con runs two to three days, although there are one-day shows as well as four-day events. Some, such as San Diego Comic-Con and Atlanta's Dragon Con, are big enough to stimulate the economy of an entire city. Con programming includes panel presentations, guest Q and As, screenings, concerts, contests, and more. The schedule is often so jam-packed that attendees have to download an event app to keep up and plan their day. There is usually a dealer hall and artist alley, where geeky merchandise is offered, but the main draw for most attendees is the celebrity guests. The invitees range from local artists, voice actors, and writers all the way to the biggest A-list Hollywood stars and legendary creators in the world. For many fans, cons are the only place where they can potentially meet their icons in real life. They are willing to stand in line for hours for that chance.

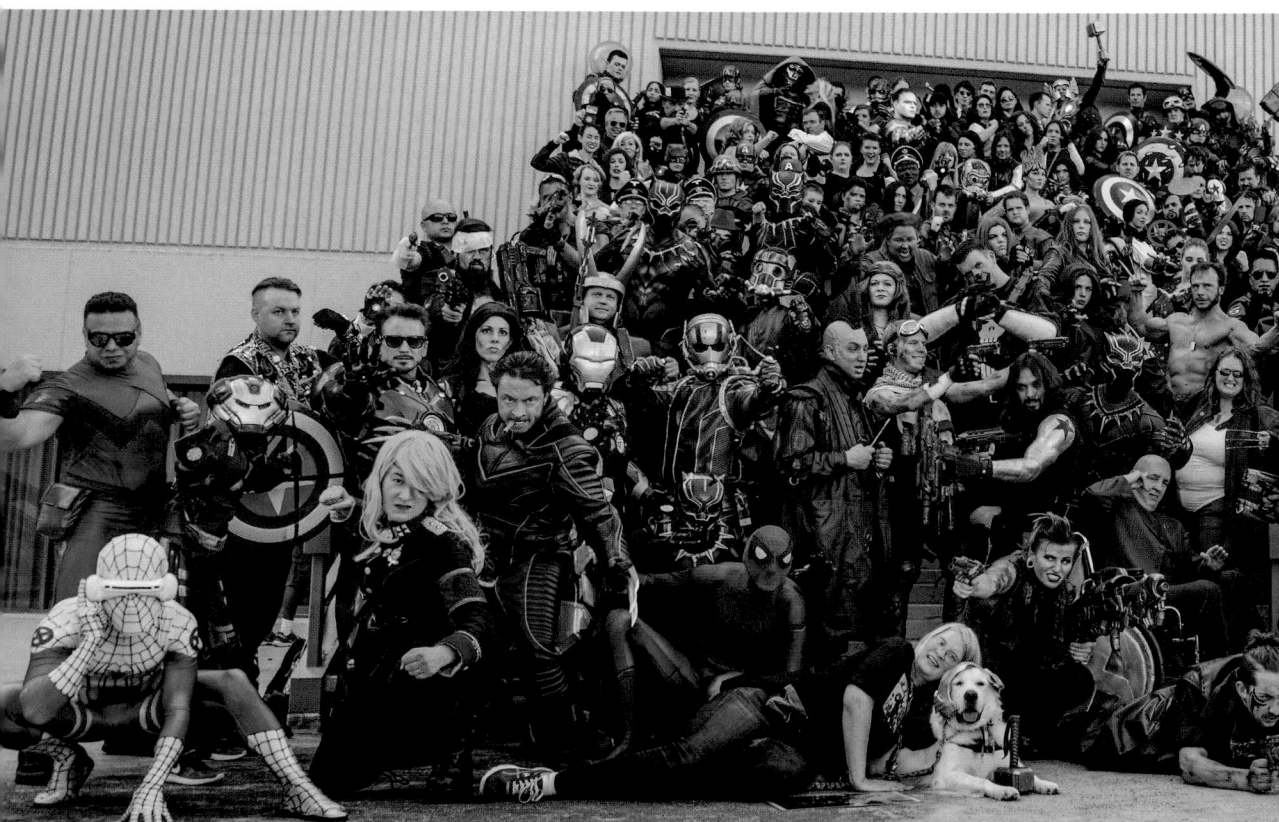

At every single convention, people dress up in costumes. There are big group meetups, photoshoots, panels, and other activities that will keep a cosplayer busy all weekend long. Virtually every media article about a fandom con highlights images of people cosplaying. The phenomenon of cosplay has become such an intrinsic part of conventions that some people view cosplayers as the face of a fandom.

We are certainly in your face—cosplayers are basically walking art projects, loudly proclaiming their passions to the world. When I'm at a con wearing a costume I made, it not only tells people across the room what fandom I'm into; it also shows that the fandom inspired me to do hours of handiwork on a costume. Cosplay is an instant icebreaker and creates unique and unexpected experiences. I've run into characters from the same comic series and gotten pulled into hilarious banter and impromptu photoshoots. I've been saved by cosplayers in times of need when something on my costume broke, and in turn I have given out countless safety pins and fixed parts on strangers' outfits. Cosplayers take care of one another. I've made little kids light up when I dressed as their favorite Disney character or superhero. Conversely, I've also been completely bowled over by cuteness at the sight of little kids wearing costumes. I will never forget the little girl who tugged on my hand while I was dressed as Sue Storm from the Fantastic Four and asked, "Can you turn invisible?"

I answered, "Yes, but not right now. I don't want to scare everyone." She hugged me, and we took a picture together.

These magical moments are what make cosplay unique. Conventions create opportunities for interactions with other fans who love the same shows and characters—interactions that you can't have anywhere else. It is also a place where you can truly become a character onstage in front of a live audience. That's the magic of the costume contest.

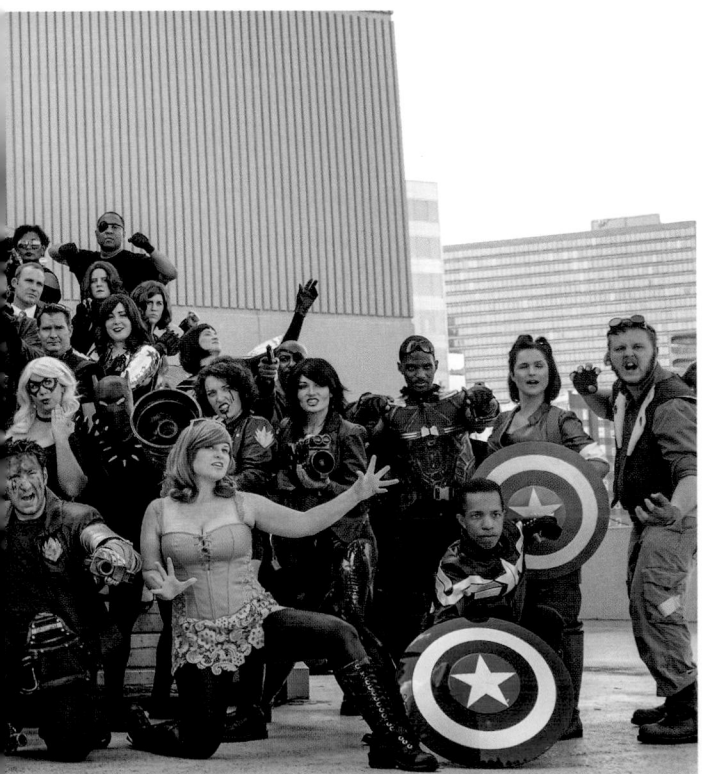

Huge gathering of Marvel cosplayers—only at a con

Costume contests have been the ultimate gathering spot for cosplayers since fandom cons were formed. For the attendees, it is an exciting and entertaining variety show that features fans just like them. It's an exciting way to see the skills and talents of cosplayers onstage. Whether or not the fans like to craft cosplay themselves, watching a costume contest can be very fun. You never know which character will come onstage next or what they will do. Some put on dramatic and action-packed performances, create comedic skits full of inside jokes and puns, or simply wow the room with their elaborate costumes. One contest can be awe-inspiring, laugh-inducing, and tear-jerking all within the span of an hour or two. It is a spectacle.

For cosplayers who enter contests, it can be a huge investment of money and time—not to mention an emotional journey. Many competitors plan far in advance,

Team Australia performing their winning skit at the World Cosplay Summit—action in armor.

spending months creating their costumes and developing a stage performance. For some of the biggest contests, entrants also build sets and props, create special effects, organize costume changes, and record their own audio tracks. The effort that goes into competing can be staggering.

That doesn't mean that every cosplayer competes, though. The competitive aspect of cosplay is actually a commonly debated topic in the community. Despite the fact that cosplay contests have been around since the beginning and every fandom convention has at least one, the opinions on competitions and their validity vary. A huge portion of cosplayers fundamentally dislike the idea of competition. For them, cosplay should be for fun, so placing cosplayers next to one another and deciding who is better than who is off-putting. They also might feel that the pressure of competing is too much to bear on top of the complicated process of making costumes. A lot of newcomers are hesitant to enter any contests, because they don't think their skills are good enough. They look at the past winners and don't believe that they could win anything even if they tried. Indeed, a large number of cosplayers devote months to making the most elaborate outfits imaginable but don't ever enter any contests.

So why do some people choose to enter contests? What do they get out of it? Let me share my own experiences first. By now, you are familiar with my awkward early years of going to cons. You also know that at the beginning, I devoted most of my energy and time to entering cosplay competitions (they were called masquerades back then). I did this because, besides the fact that they were the only cosplay-related programming we had, the prospect of combining craftsmanship and stage performance was the ultimate cosplay experience for me. Making a costume for a competition challenged me to better my skills and focus on perfecting the details of my construction. Forming a group taught me communication and organizational skills, because I had to coordinate with my teammates and motivate them along the way. Choreographing a skit made me think of ways to bring the character to life onstage.

Competition pushed me outside of my comfort zone and stimulated me creatively, in both crafting and theatrical terms. For those one or two minutes onstage, I could freely act out as the character I was cosplaying, and that was addictive. I was competing against myself more than against the other entrants. Some of my first good friends in cosplay were competitors I met backstage. I remember feeling a strong sense of camaraderie because we were all into the same weird thing, and the hours we waited to go onstage were full of chatter and laughter. Awards weren't really good reasons for entering, because the prizes were just random anime DVDs or paper certificates, so for us, contests were more like variety shows in which we all performed for the audience.

At the time, cosplay contests were laid back and didn't have the public pressure they do now. But those early years set the foundation for the spirit of competitive cosplay, which has not changed to this day. Without entering competitions, I'm not sure I would have developed such a deep, lasting passion for cosplay or gained the skills and experience I needed to turn it into a career. The discipline and work ethic I learned during my competitive years has also helped me in everyday life. Since 2001, I have judged hundreds of cosplay contests all over the world and seen the development of cosplay's competitive side firsthand. I consider the growth to be very positive overall.

That said, there were a lot of hiccups along the way.

When cosplay contests evolved and became more complex stage events, some cons had a harder time than others in adapting. I think organizers started to pay attention to their costume contests because they were a valuable promotional tool—a bigger contest drew bigger crowds and more media attention. Events began offering more prestigious prizes such as large amounts of cash, oversize trophies, sewing machines, electronics, and even vacation trips. They used the grander cosplay contests to hype up the con during marketing campaigns. However, not every organization behind those big contests understood the needs of people who entered or how to choose the winners.

For years, a panel of judges (usually industry guests who were not familiar with the process of costume making) watched the entrants along with the audience from a spot near the stage and chose their favorites during an intermission. Craftsmanship judging sessions, where judges could meet contestants in a one-on-one setting and see their costumes up close, used to be incredibly rare. I remember getting craftsmanship judging sessions at Anime Expo 2001 and Otakon 2001 and feeling pleasantly surprised by the opportunities to showcase the details of my costume to the judges directly. Craftsmanship judging (or prejudging) sessions require more effort and time for all parties, but they are absolutely vital. Otherwise, there is no fair way to determine the most deserving winners of a competition. Judges need to see the construction details of costumes close-up and to understand the thought processes behind them. In the past, some cosplay contests were reminiscent of flashy Halloween contests at Las Vegas nightclubs, where the biggest and showiest costume that got the loudest audience reaction usually won.

Things started to change once bigger conventions began involving cosplayers as judges and staff. They were mostly previous contest winners who had craftsmanship experience and knew the process the contestants were going through. I stopped competing partially because I was asked to help judge contests I had previously won and I realized how much

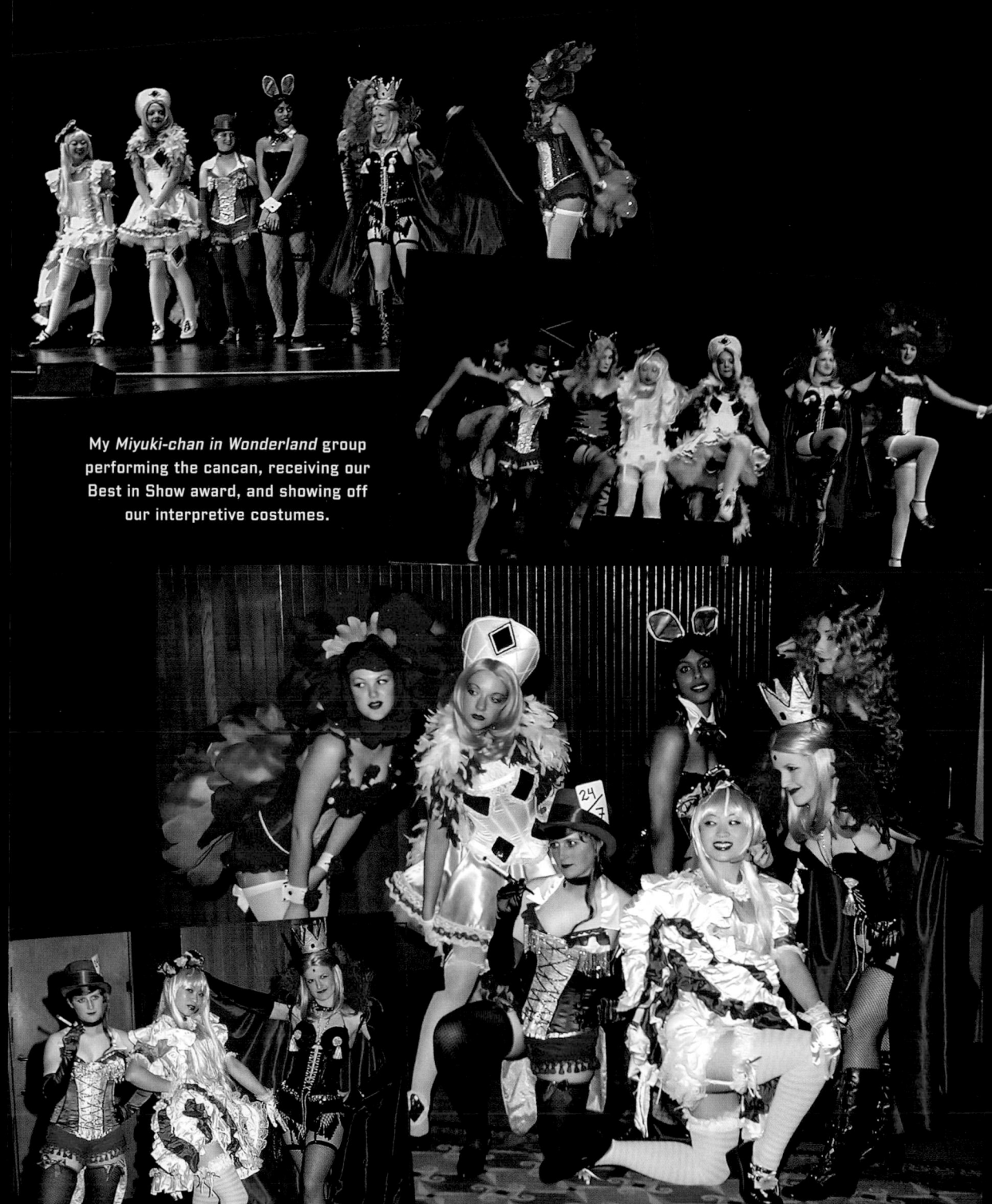

My *Miyuki-chan in Wonderland* group performing the cancan, receiving our Best in Show award, and showing off our interpretive costumes.

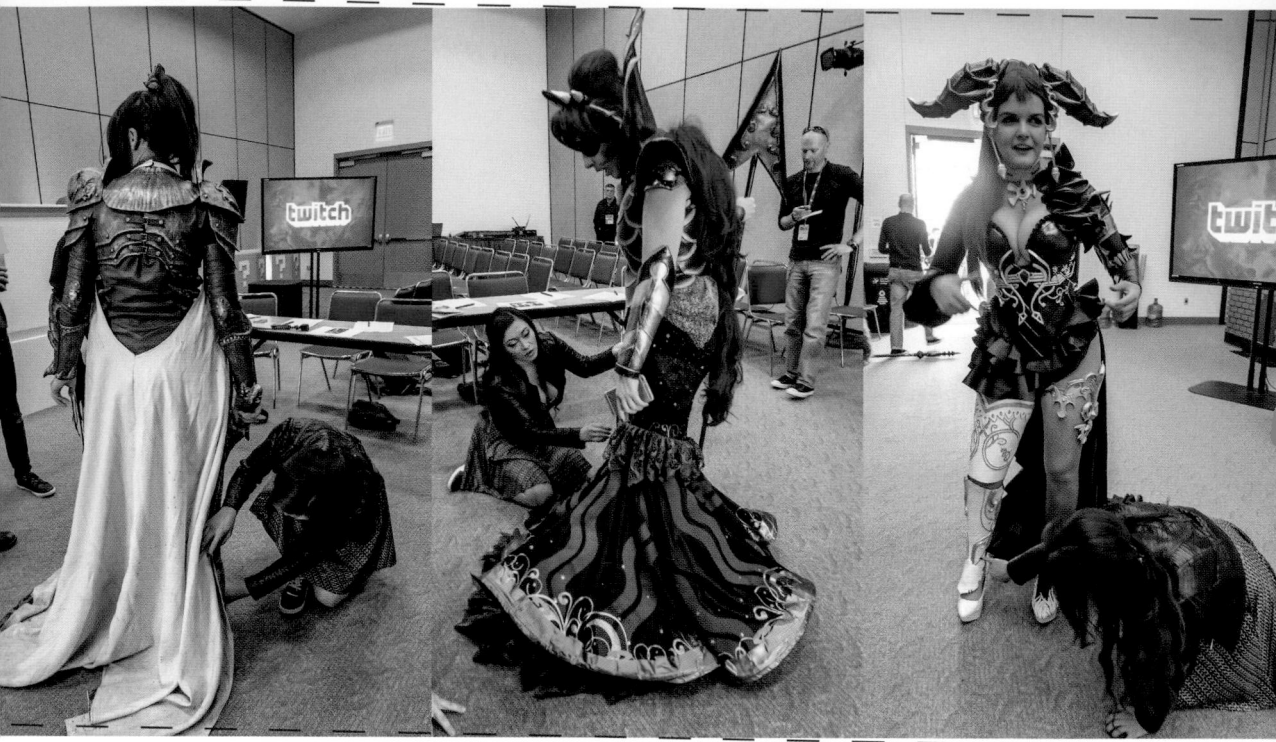

Craftsmanship judging requires close-up looks at all aspects of a costume.

I liked being on the other side of the curtain. It was not only fun to have one-on-one inter-actions with the contestants before they went onstage; I also felt a strong responsibility to reward efforts in an objective manner and choose winners regardless of audience reaction. The combination of cosplay judges and craftsmanship judging sessions gave more prece-dence to entries that were well-rounded in both construction and performance. Ultimately, that helped raise the overall quality of entries. Involving cosplayer judges also gave conven-tion organizers a direct line to feedback from the community. That made them more aware of contestants' needs, such as access to a changing area, water, chairs, and more.

Convention organizers had to learn that it is a big commitment for cosplayers to enter a contest. If the experience is not enjoyable, cosplayers might have a hard time finding rea-sons to enter again. Competitors devote weeks, if not months, to work on their entries, and they spend most of their time at the convention preparing for the contest. Collectively, the contestants put on a stage show that can last for hours. No other con programming requires as much work from paying attendees. In all of my years of judging, I have been a strong advocate for cons recognizing entrants as the stars of their cosplay contests and supporting them with everything they need. A big cash-prize contest is indeed awesome media bait, but it should be accompanied with strong organization, careful planning, and an understanding of the cosplayers' needs.

Our society thrives on competition. We see it amped up in reality TV shows and game shows with high stakes and big rewards. We love a spectacle, with all the excitement of watching extraordinary people pitting their skills and creations against one another. Similarly, when a cosplay competition has a $10,000 prize, a trip to another country, or even a world title on the line, it can cause entrants to feel self-doubt. Costumes are very personal and meaningful projects, so if you lose in a contest with your best costume, it can make you feel invalidated. It's not a good feeling, and I have certainly had my losses to cope with. Given the mental energy and the amount of time preparing for a competition takes, it's understandable if someone would rather spend their precious con hours doing something else.

Some organizations have tuned into the entertainment value of competitive cosplay and raised its prestige by hosting multilevel international contests. The World Cosplay Summit (WCS) was the first example of this. Launched in 2003, this competition is held in Japan each August. The WCS can be described as the Olympics of cosplay because contestants from from all over the globe attend and compete. Each of forty countries hosts preliminaries and chooses a duo to represent their country at the finals in Japan. The contestants must not only make stunning costumes but also create a dynamic performance onstage. If selected by their country, they are flown to Japan. There, in addition to competing onstage for a number of titles and prizes, they spend a week doing parades, interviews, and PR events.

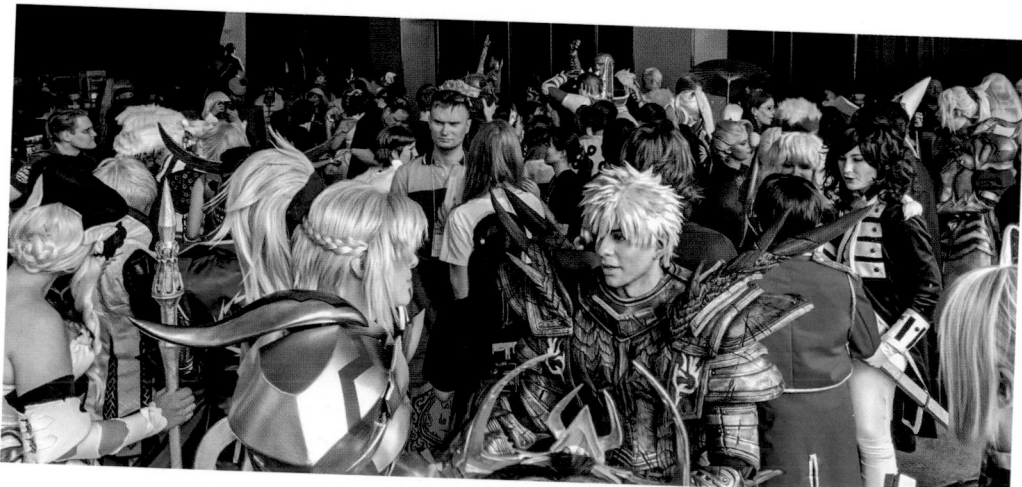

WCS contestants waiting in a hall to go onstage

The European Cosplay Gathering (ECG) is another long-standing international contest. It selects cosplayers from all over Europe to compete at the finals held in Paris during the annual Japan Expo®. As with WCS, those hoping to represent their nations at the ECG must first win their local event's selection rounds with great performances and costumes.

Yet another example of an international competition is the C2E2 Crown Championships of Cosplay. This purely craftsmanship-based contest hosts competitors from more than ten countries and offers cash prizes as part of the Chicago Comic & Entertainment Expo. Representatives from all over the world come to Chicago every spring to compete for the title of world champion, traveling from as far as Indonesia, Australia, and Switzerland.

These types of international contests all have one factor in common: They treat the competitors as performers rather than attendees. They pay for the regional winners' expenses and travel to the finals, involve them in media opportunities, and sometimes offer judging positions to winners from previous years. These organizers understand that, in order to put on a spectacular competition, they must attract talent with more than just cash prizes. For

Cosplay contests: huge WCS stage in Japan full of cosplayers; award ceremony at ECG in Paris; finalists on the Crown stage in Chicago

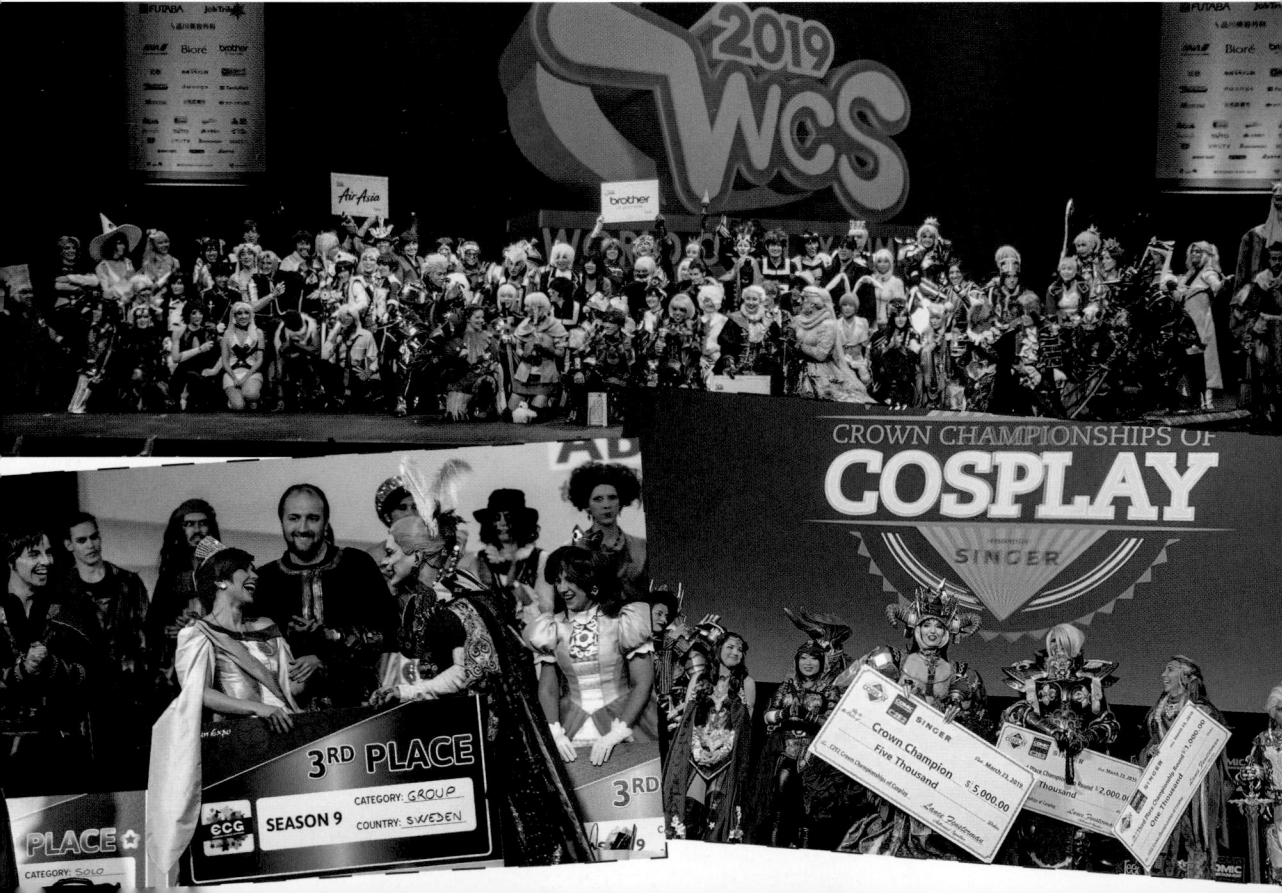

cosplayers, it is more meaningful to compete for the title of a regional winner because they get to represent their community; it's recognition for their hard work, which has lasting effects. To me, the best part of international contests is the cultural exchange between cosplayers from opposite ends of the earth. Some cosplayers have made lifelong friends on these trips or even found love along the way. They bring back new techniques, materials, and ideas to their local communities. Through these international competitions, the world of cosplay becomes more tightly knit and accessible to everyone.

For me, contests have a valid place in the world of cosplay because there are so many benefits to entering a contest that go beyond winning awards. I also think it's possible to keep the spirit of competition positive rather than combative. It's necessary to do so, since the competitive aspect is one of the most visible parts of cosplay. Just like e-sports tournaments are shedding light on the world of gaming, cosplay contests are making headlines and gathering the interest of the masses.

I think it's important to remember that competition is not always about whose costume is best; rather, it's about who put the most effort into a project out of the pool of entries and who deserves the most recognition for those efforts. Sometimes it is also about who meets the requirements of that particular contest, especially those with specific rules. Winning is just the icing on top of the cake. Not winning an award doesn't mean a costume is bad and should not diminish anyone's self-worth.

Cosplay competitions are not for everyone, but they are a great way for cosplayers to challenge themselves and have exciting new experiences. I hope that after reading this chapter, you might feel inspired to enter a contest!

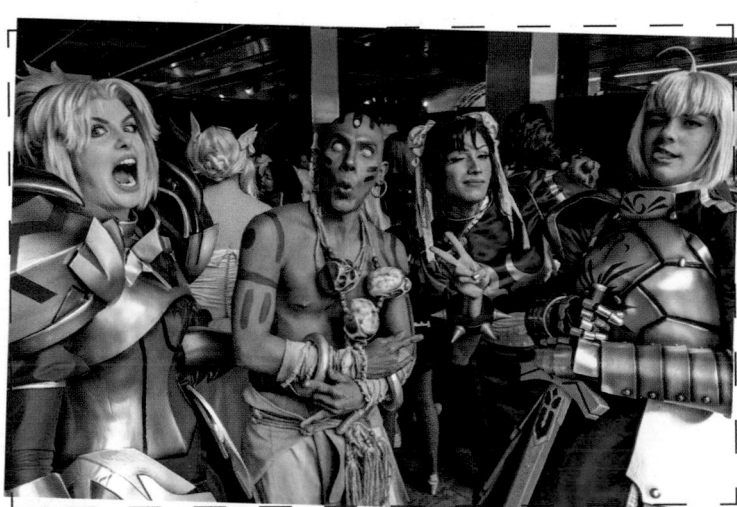

Cosplayers from different countries goofing off

CHAPTER 8

The Cosplay Guest

From Attendee to Attraction

Standing on the center of the stage, the lights illuminating me were blinding. I couldn't see the crowd, but I heard the whoops and cheers. I concentrated on one spot in the sea of darkness surrounding me, waiting for the music to begin.

I was Sheryl Nome, the Galactic Fairy and the most beloved idol singer on the planet—at least in the anime series *Macross Frontier*. My hair was a cascading mix of soft pink and blond curls. I wore a sleeveless purple dress that pooled on the floor in waves of chiffon. Atop my head sat a flower crown in matching shades of mauve. As the music cued me in, I began to sing. The opening song from the series, "Lion," is a catchy pop number that swells in emotion. The song is entirely in Japanese, which I didn't speak at the time, and I had spent months learning the lyrics phonetically and practicing the song to a karaoke track.

I tried to calm the shake in my microphone hand by moving around the stage and focusing on the next line in the song until the instrumental break came on. It was time. Praying that I wouldn't accidentally drop the mic, I grabbed the side of my dress, pulled at the Velcro holding it together, and unveiled Sheryl's iconic opening-sequence outfit from underneath the chiffon. The crowd broke out in thunderous applause (cosplayers love a quick change), and I managed to finish the song without forgetting the lyrics or falling down. Phew!

The year was 2008, and I was a cosplay guest at the Grand Cosplay Ball in London. It was my first European guest appearance (a huge personal milestone), and to this day it is one of the most unforgettable cosplay events I've attended. For one evening, an old theater venue called The Clapham Grand was transformed into a glamorous fantasy ball with music and performances throughout the night. The setting was enchanting and reminiscent of the masquerade ball in the movie *Labyrinth*, except that the Cosplay Ball had a geeky twist to it. Hundreds of cosplayers from all over Europe fluttered around the dance floor, dressed in their finest evening garb as characters from anime, video games, and movies. I counted at least ten different nationalities amongst the people I met and at one point I marveled at the fact that I conversed with attendees in English, German, and Chinese (all within the same hour!). Standing in the theater looking at all these cosplayers from different walks of life, I realized how much cosplay could bring people together and how valuable and rare that is.

— — —

For many years, cosplay was considered purely a fan activity amongst attendees at conventions. At some point, though, it became apparent that cosplaying was not just something fans did while enjoying the various offered programming—it was the entire reason some people came to cons. A large percentage of costumed attendees did not spend much time in the vendor halls, panels, or screening rooms. Instead, they hung out for hours in the hallways, atriums, and surrounding areas, taking photos and chatting with one another. Conventions held near parks and at pretty locations attracted cosplayers in droves. Group gatherings

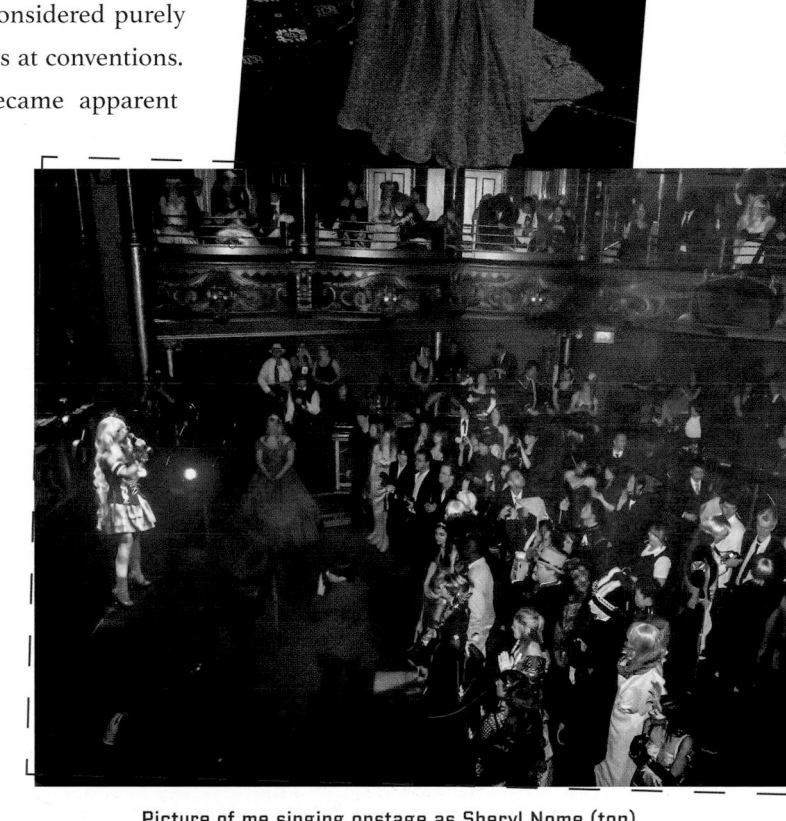

Picture of me singing onstage as Sheryl Nome (top)
Performing at the Grand Cosplay Ball in London (bottom)

became bigger and bigger, overtaking entire areas of the convention and stopping traffic for long periods of time. Media outlets that covered fandom events focused more and more on cosplay each year, including big media sites such as CNN, MTV, and *Entertainment Weekly*.

As convention organizers started to realize that cosplay was a draw, they recognized that having cosplayers show up was a great way to advertise the con. They also recognized that they needed more cosplay-related programming to cater to interested attendees, so cosplay-specific panels and workshops started appearing on their schedules. Panels used to be reserved for guests and industry professionals to teach their craft, discuss their work, or talk about various aspects of the fandom industry. As cosplay gathered steam in the 2000s, some events sanctioned fan-run cosplay panels, which were quite rare at the time. I did my first panel at AniMagic near the end of 2001 on how to embellish costumes, which basically entailed passing pieces around the room and explaining the techniques I used. The

majority of early cosplay panels were devoted to craftsmanship-related topics, such as Sewing 101 or Cosplay 101. People who came to them were mainly curious con attendees who had never cosplayed before and wanted advice on how to start.

While these ideas were progressive, the entire fandom con scene was still young and struggling to find its footing in the early 2000s. Anime and comic cons were not rolling in money yet. In fact, some of the biggest cons were run by nonprofit organizations. It was expensive to put on a convention and fly guests over from Japan or other countries, and many events had to rely on volunteer staff to help put on a successful show. When cosplayers first got involved in official fan convention programming, it

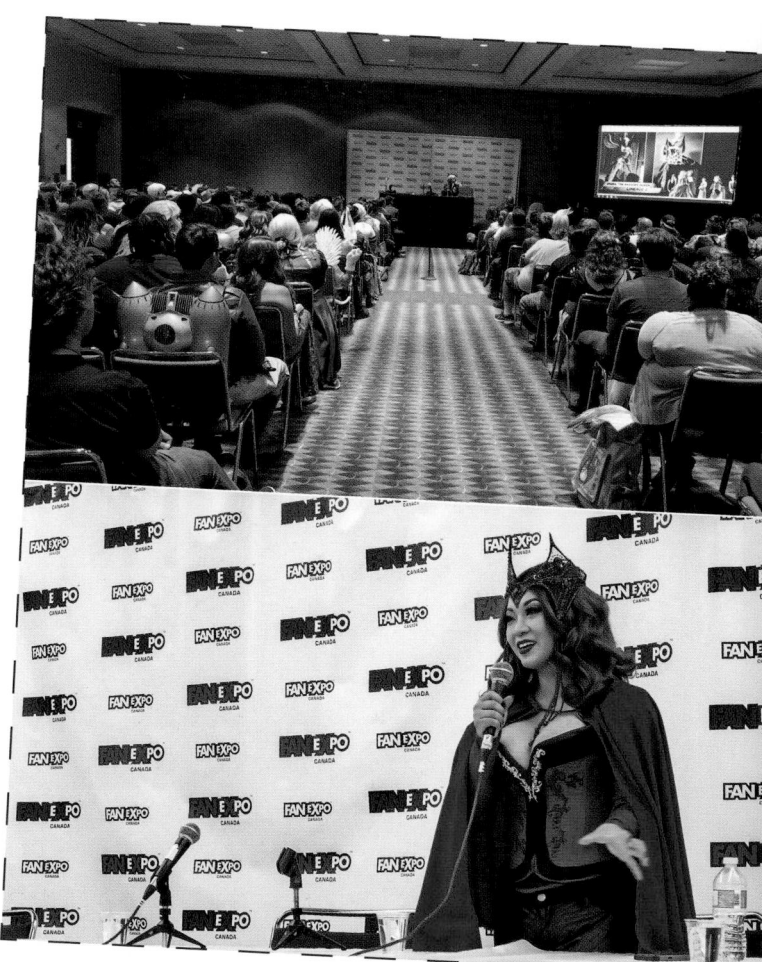

Speaking at cosplay panels

was a new and untested concept. As such, it should come as no surprise that we were asked to participate in voluntary positions as well. Costume contest judges and panelists were generally compensated with a free ticket for that day or a complimentary weekend badge.

Things got more complicated when select conventions began to invite cosplayers as guests.

Traditionally, the title of official con guest was reserved for actors, artists, writers, voice actors . . . You know, people working in the entertainment industry. When conventions started to give the title to cosplayers, who were considered fans rather than professionals, it turned the entire system upside down. It wasn't unthinkable for cosplayers to hold positions such as panelists or judges, but as soon as someone was announced as a guest, the entire cosplay community exploded into debate. It didn't matter how many awards a cosplayer had under their belt or how excellent their craftsmanship was: the word *guest* was incendiary. Why does a fan who has not worked in the industry deserve to be a guest? Why select a cosplayer from the ranks and put them on a pedestal? Why actively highlight the distinction between "popular cosplayers" and "everyone else" when there was already enough high school–level drama in the community? These questions fueled countless pages of forum threads and LiveJournal posts.

I already put forth my theory of fringe cultures feeling the need to protect the authenticity of their communities. However, what made the misconceptions worse was that most people had no clue what it meant to be a cosplay guest. Even though cosplayers like me were billed as such, we were on a completely different tier than industry professional guests. Our guest titles were largely empty gestures that did not change the type of work we did at cons. We still ran panels and judged contests. The guest title didn't assure any special treatment beyond that of a volunteer, either. We were not paid for our time, we didn't have access to the green room, we weren't allocated lunch breaks, and we often did not even get travel or hotel expenses reimbursed.

That said, the title itself was powerful. By giving us a spot on the guest list, conventions officially recognized fans in an official forum for the first time. It was the perfect bargaining chip. When cosplayers were listed in the same program book under, say, legendary *Final Fantasy* artist/writer Yoshitaka Amano or actors from *Star Trek* and *Star Wars*, they got a feeling of prestige from being in the same pool as actual industry guests. It didn't matter how many hours we were asked to work or that we were treated differently than all other guests; for many of us, the title of guest was a tangible credential and a milestone to strive toward. It was more than enough compensation for a whole weekend of work.

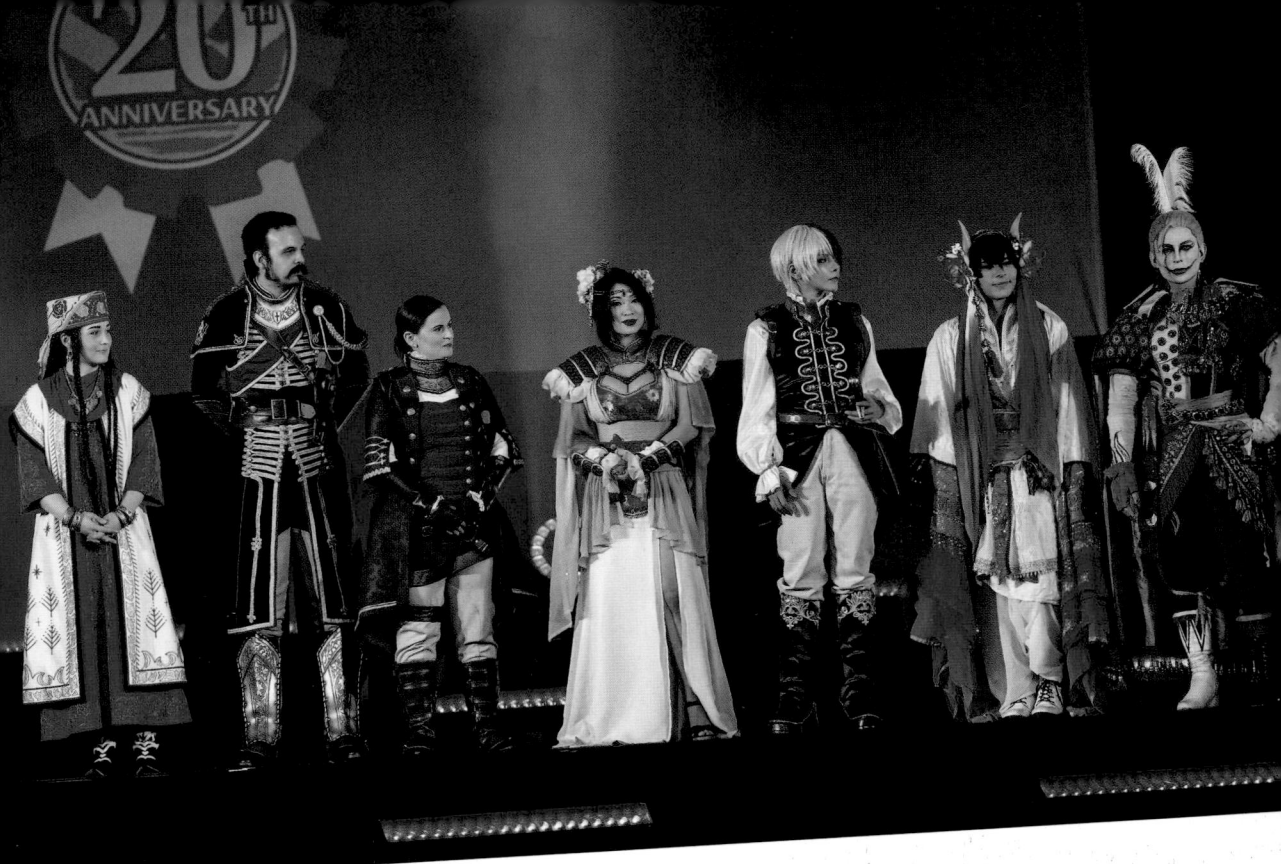

Standing onstage with other cosplayers as
we're announced as judges for the ECG contest

For the better part of the decade, I hosted panels and judged competitions at conventions as a cosplay guest in return for a weekend badge. I hosted as many as six hourly panels over a period of three days and gave most of my Saturdays to judging contests. I did it all while wearing costumes every day. The first con that invited me, AniMagic 2001, actually flew me from Georgia to California, booked a hotel room for me, and treated me like a proper guest the entire weekend. That gave me a rough idea of what to expect when I was invited to be a convention guest. And also made me acutely aware of how little most cons valued me when none of those amenities were available. Every once in a while, a convention would surprise me by offering to pay for my travel, or at least give me a spot to sleep in a staff room.

Despite not getting paid, what made me accept guest invitations again and again was the feeling of finally contributing to the cosplay scene in a profound way. Sure, I enjoyed seeing my picture in the program books and wearing my guest badge, but it felt even better to have a purpose. I really loved having a platform to share my thoughts in panels. I also liked being able to use my experience as a competitive cosplayer to judge contests objectively and fairly. Being behind the scenes and carrying out tasks made me feel accepted and wanted. At every con, I got to see friends, meet new people, and strengthen the sense that I'd found my place in the world.

Then came a new milestone: international convention invitations and autograph signings.

The first time I was invited to a convention outside of the US was in 2006, when I received a request to appear at a comic convention in Mexico. It was such an honor to be asked that I made a new costume of Psylocke from *X-Men* to match the theme of the event. I couldn't believe that someone wanted me to be a guest so much that they were willing to pay for all of my expenses—they even let me bring along my fiancé, Brian. It was an amazing trip. I not only received an overwhelmingly enthusiastic welcome from the crowds; I was also treated like a VIP guest by the organization. They gave Brian and I access to their green room, provided a translator and security staff, and even took us out to dinner every night. Compared to how I rushed around on my own from one programming event to the next at American cons, the event in Mexico truly made me feel like a guest. I was still not getting paid a dime, but the experience was vali-

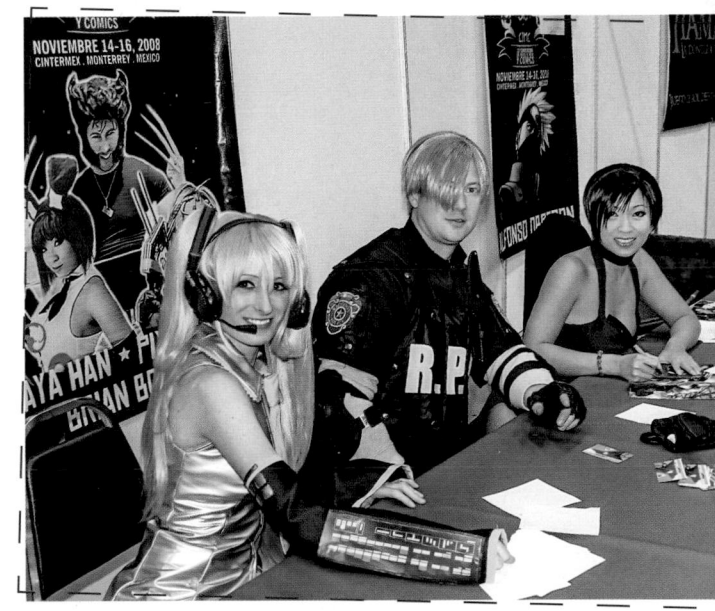

Signing autographs at a con in Mexico

dating because I realized I had true value to bring to events like these. People wanted to see me and learn what I had to offer in terms of knowledge and experience, and having me at a con translated to ticket sales for the organizers.

One of the new events I did in Mexico was an autograph session. In the past, I had often lined up for the chance to meet a manga artist or voice actor. Now I got to experience what it was like for others to do the same in order to meet me. I remember practicing different versions of autograph signatures until one looked right, all the while feeling stunned that people wanted me to scribble my name on a piece of paper. Another new discovery was that, instead of wanting to take a photo *of* me, which is rather normal to a cosplayer, attendees wanted to take photos *with* me. That's when I really felt like a celebrity.

When organizers on other continents started inviting me, I got really nervous. I wondered if cosplayers in other countries would even know who I was. My worries turned out to be unfounded, though. Every person I spoke to at these cons, whether in Italy, Switzerland, or England, seemed to have a story of how they had heard of me and how much my costumes inspired them. It was humbling.

Year by year, I added more countries to my international cosplay experience. Events abroad gave me creative confidence, but now I had an added feeling of responsibility to live up to the expectations of the public. That emotion tapped into the same desire to make an audience happy that musicians, comedians, and actors feel. I knew from the start that these cons were not just paid vacations but a job I was hired to do. I tried to be punctual, professional, and competent. The farther I traveled, the harder I was willing to work.

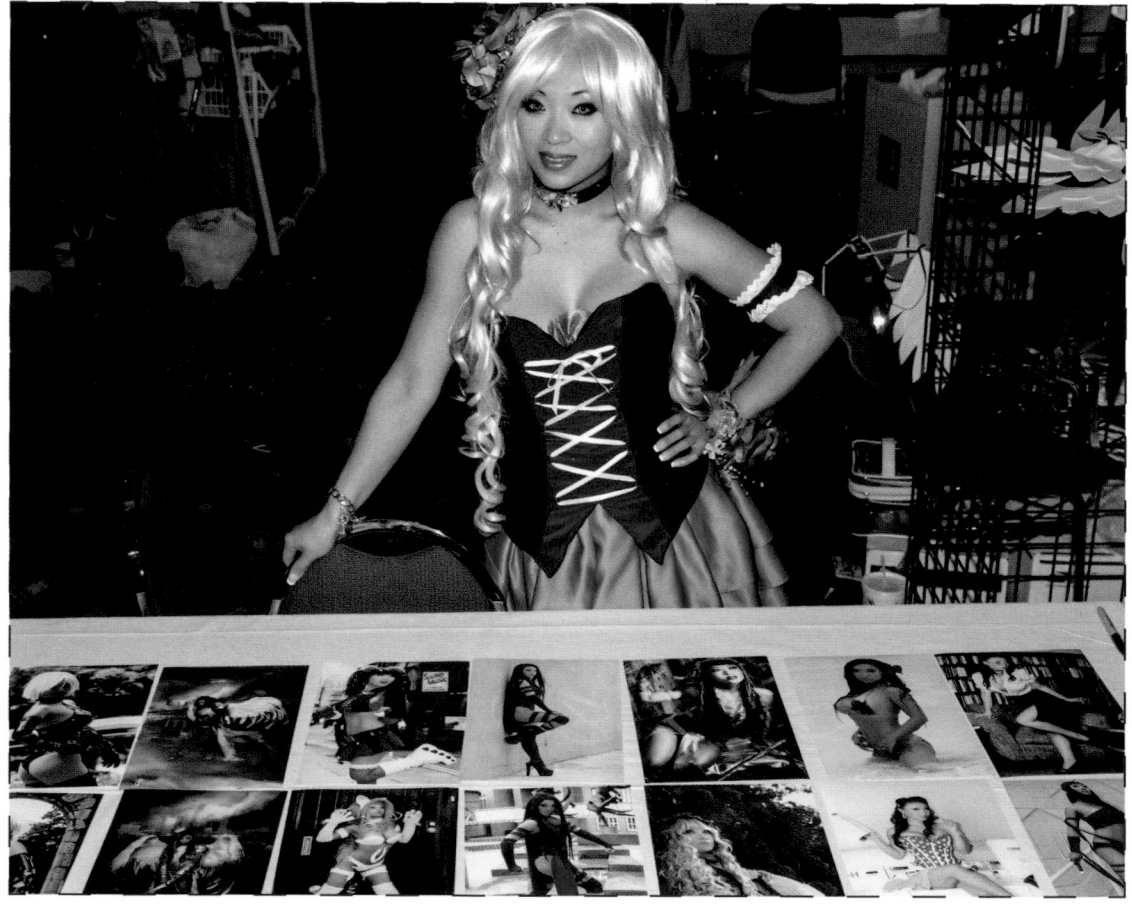

Cosplaying in front of a table of my prints at a con

Back home in America, the community's response to the widening scope of cosplay guest appearances became even more polarized, in part because of the practices of signing autographs and selling prints. Nothing caused more of a controversy than signed cosplay prints. I started to offer these because people I met at events kept bringing me photos to autograph that they had printed out from my website. The print quality was horrible due to the compressed pixels, and I wanted to offer nice-looking photos instead. As someone who sold fan art prints for years at artist alleys, the idea of cosplay prints wasn't that farfetched to me—it was like fan art in photography form. The rest of the cosplay community did not agree, though. I was completely demolished for the audacity to offer prints and was labeled a sellout, as were other cosplayers in similar positions. Nevertheless, there was a small but steady demand for printed cosplay photos, and I sold a few at every con. It felt good to take in some small form of income, and I saw it as a reinforcement to keep going whenever the criticism became really overwhelming.

The evolution of the cosplay guest is very indicative of the mental hurdles the community had to overcome on its journey to commercialization. In hindsight, so many taboo topics in the cosplay community were unspoken symptoms of fear and uncertainty for the future. Today, selling prints is a very common and accepted practice in cosplay. It's easier to understand why cosplayers get more special treatment in foreign countries, too. Organizers who spend a lot of money to fly someone in might feel more inclined to make sure they are fed and taken care of so that their guest can fulfill their part of the agreement. And, of course, they want to show cultural hospitality to anyone who visits their country.

The concept of the fan-guest is a lot more familiar now. In the age of self-made fame, conventions frequently invite fan artists, YouTube stars, and other personalities who started out as fans or amateurs. Cosplay has become a guest category for the majority of cons in North America and other parts of the world. Most conventions have at least one or more cosplay guests to round out their judging panels and participate in cosplay-related programming activities.

Even now, though, the life of a traveling cosplayer is often not as glamorous as you think. Long hours, jet lag, lost luggage, and more are all parts of this lifestyle. However, every time I visit a new country, I see it as another opportunity to learn about the local fandom cultures. Even if I don't speak the same language as the locals, we find ways to communicate with one another, because cosplayers are bound by the same passion. I have met some of my best friends only because I was able to go to international cons as a guest. For most of us, the chance to travel and represent the cosplay community is an honor and a responsibility we cherish.

This rocky road has been worth traveling. In the end, recognizing cosplayers as guests is a positive thing. When a convention invites cosplayers who have experiences and knowledge to share as guests and who hosts activities such as cosplay panels, contests, and photoshoots, it recognizes cosplay as an important part of fandom. It attracts a loyal group of attendees and grows the local cosplay community. Without the bright costumes and personalities of cosplayers, convention halls just wouldn't be the same today.

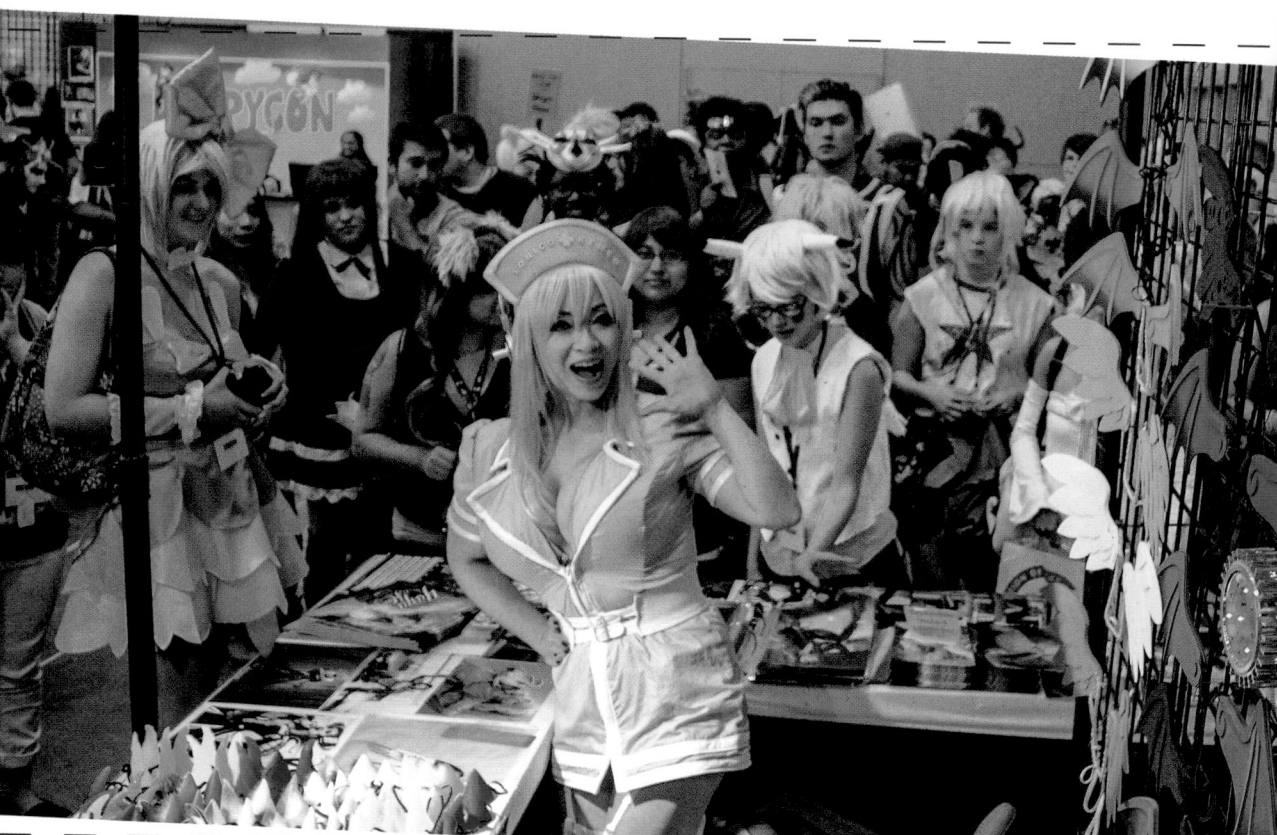

Saying hello to my fans at a con booth.

CHAPTER 9

Cosplay in Focus

Photography and Social Media

A long-standing inside joke in the cosplay community is that all cosplayers are hopeless attention-seekers. After all, we don't go through all the trouble of making costumes and dressing up just to prance around in our living rooms. We expect to be stopped for photos whenever we go out in costume. We want people to take photos of us.

At conventions, cosplayers are the only people aside from celebrities who are constantly stopped for photos. Actually, walking around in a big flashy costume is probably the closest thing to a celebrity experience that any of us can ever have. You have a crowd following your every move. You're blinded by flashes going off all around you. You hear the constant clicking of cameras in your ears. It is an undeniable thrill and an adrenaline rush. Some costumes can attract so much attention that the wearer is stuck in one spot for hours, causing hallways to become clogged with onlookers and people clamoring for photos.

I think the desire for attention in cosplay comes from the same place that spurs people to dress in eye-catchingly fashionable outfits or go into acting, stage performance, and music: It's a way to express yourself. Cosplay comes with added excitement over a shared passion and a desire to belong to a community. Sure, it can feel awesome to pose for a circle of flashing cameras, but nonstop photo requests can also become tiring after a few hours. The convention environment is usually too hectic and crowded for nice and clean costume photos. Typically, there isn't a lot of time to share your thoughts behind a project, either.

That's where the Internet comes in. Today, the cosplay community thrives online as much as it does at conventions through two key elements: cosplay photography and social media.

Photography is such a vital part of cosplay that many consider it the final step in the cosplay process. Whether it's a mirror selfie, a cell phone snapshot, or a professional photoshoot, seeing yourself dressed up as a character in a photo can really complete your transformation.

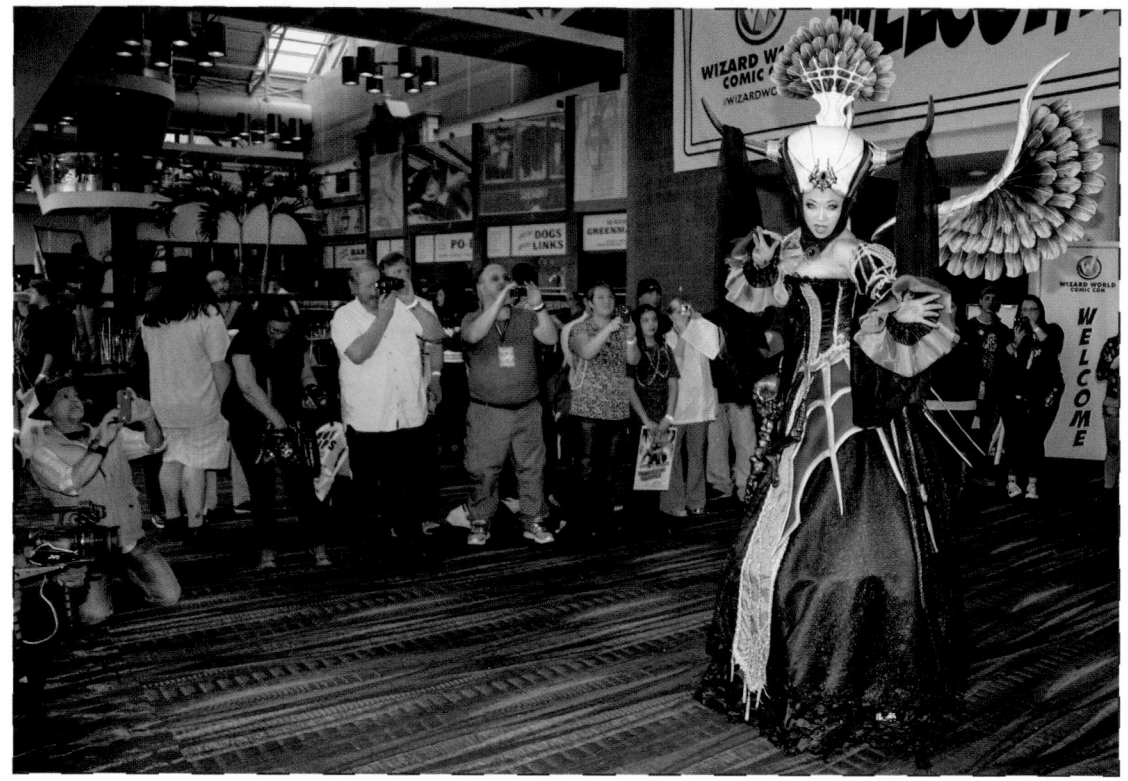

Posing on stilts dressed as Banshee Queen Enira

The first cosplay photos in the USA were mainly taken on disposable cameras in dimly lit convention hallways. Back in the late '90s and early 2000s, very few people had technical know-how or access to professional photography equipment. While photography was established as an art form already, most of us newbie cosplayers thought it was something only professional models did. The idea of setting up photoshoots with people in homemade costumes was unheard of.

When it came to posing, none of us really knew what we were doing, either. Kids these days grow up with Instagram models as their posing inspirations, but in those early years we didn't know how important good posture was for posing or that varying angles create distinctly different photos. Click through old convention reports on sites like Usagichan and you'll see cosplayers (myself included) standing with arms dangling and shoulders slouching or throwing up a peace sign while grinning widely at the camera. You could see that we had a blast, but we didn't know how to get into character yet.

Slowly, inspired by the professional Japanese cosplay photos we shared with one another, American cosplayers got into photography. As I mentioned before, my first cosplay photoshoots were done with a friend who studied photography. That's how most early shoots were accomplished. Either a cosplayer knew someone with decent camera equipment or had connections to a fashion photographer. Either way, it was all pure, unpaid, creative experimentation. The way cosplayers were photographed mirrored the way we made costumes. We were unburdened by commercial

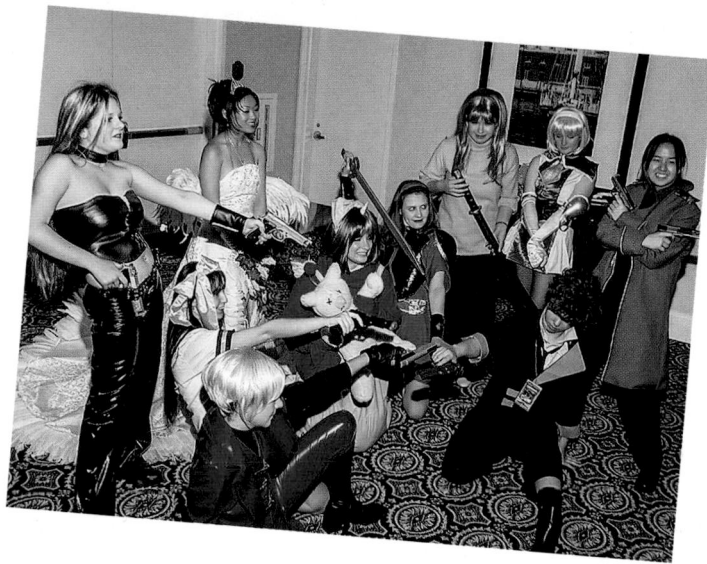

An early photo of me and other cosplayers doing amateur poses

pressure and free to explore artistically. In those days, I really enjoyed doing photoshoots and met a number of professional photographers. Most of them really seemed to enjoy shooting cosplayers because it was so much more interesting and creative than their usual assignments. Because cosplay was still unknown at the time, there were no money-making opportunities with cosplay photos, so we worked on a TFP, or time for prints, basis. TFP trades your time in front of the camera for usage rights of the photoshoot images.

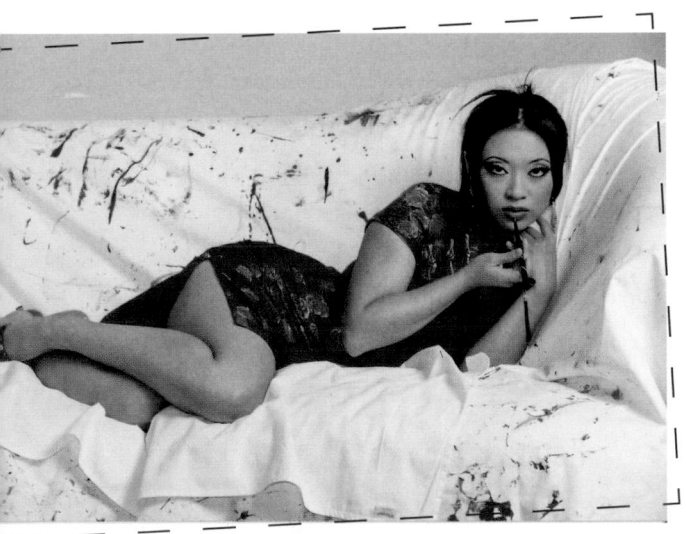

An early modeling shot

As time went on, digital cameras became more and more affordable, which really helped cosplay photography evolve. By the mid-2000s, single-lens reflex (SLR) digital cameras such as the Canon EOS Rebel series started showing up at more fandom cons as well as during cosplay photoshoots. The lower price point and decent functionality of these SLR cameras gave amateurs the incentive to pick up some gear and learn how to take photos with cosplay in mind. People who were already going to cons could try out

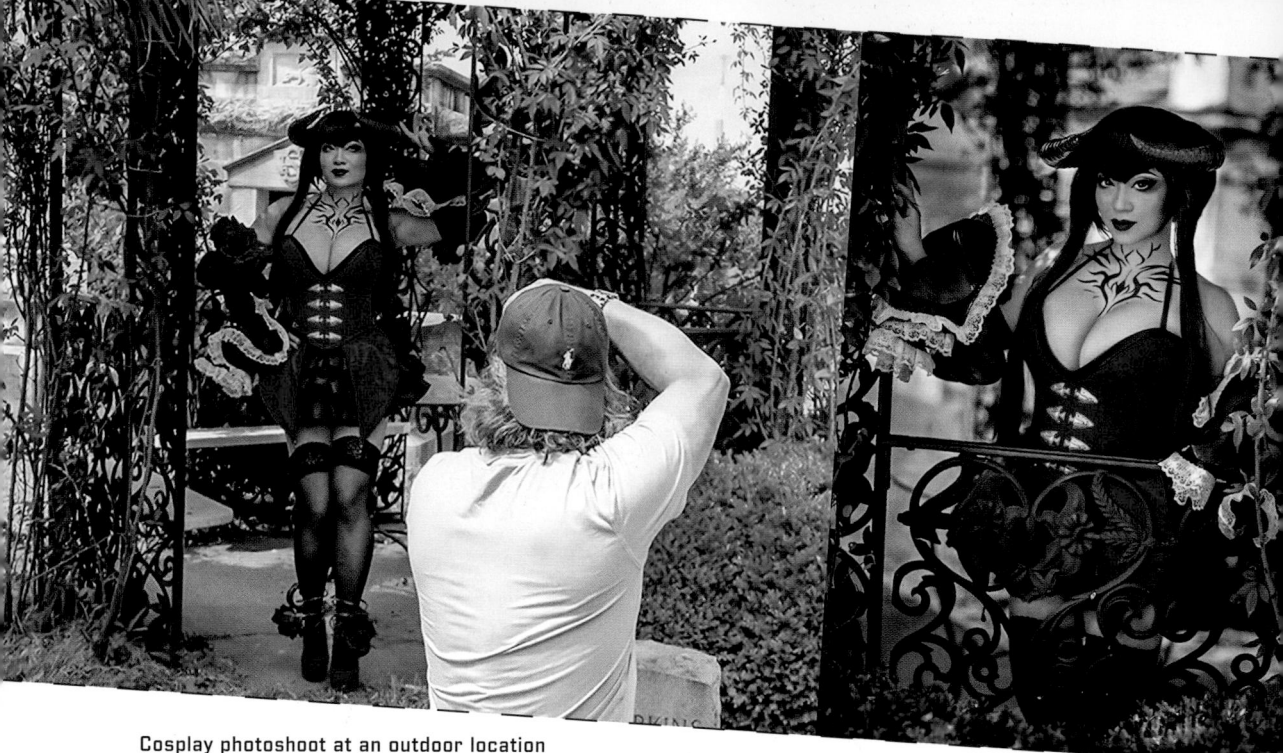

Cosplay photoshoot at an outdoor location

photography in a fun setting amongst like-minded fans. As long as photographers were polite and respectful, cosplayers were happy to pose for them since they also wanted to collect images of the costumes they had worked so hard on. Just as people became hungry for costume-making information, photography became a point of interest in the cosplay community.

Most of my photos were posted to my personal website, but I also shared select cosplay photos to community websites such as cosplay.com, Cosplay Lab, and ACParadise. Eventually, photography groups and sub-communities were formed within the cosplay community as well. These groups planned more opportunities for on-location and studio photoshoots away from conventions. Whether they were organized by cosplayers, photographers, or the new sub-community groups, these outings gave people a chance to create nice photos in pretty settings, like in a park or on the beach, where they were not restricted by hectic convention schedules. These types of gatherings continue today.

Before social media, one platform that really made an impact in cosplay was DeviantArt, which was the biggest art-sharing website in the 2000s. For reference, DeviantArt had more than thirty million annual visitors by the year 2008. While the site was primarily made for artists to share their drawings and paintings, cosplayers started to make profiles on it as well. I created my DeviantArt profile in 2006 and placed my very best photos in the gallery, curating a collection of cosplay works of which I was proudest. DeviantArt used an award system called

Daily Deviations that showcased selected user uploads on the site's heavily visited front page. This award system created the first opportunity for me to see cosplay photos featured alongside artwork created by working professional artists. Having an art website recognize cosplay in such a way was incredible. It also made DeviantArt one of the first places where cosplay photos reached an audience outside of the cosplay community. A lot of people visited DeviantArt as fans of pop culture titles looking for artwork of the characters they liked. Instead, they found people dressed up as the characters and were introduced to cosplay that way.

Cosplay photography in its current iteration was truly born from grassroots efforts and community peers inspiring one another. The same DIY mind-set that leads cosplayers to

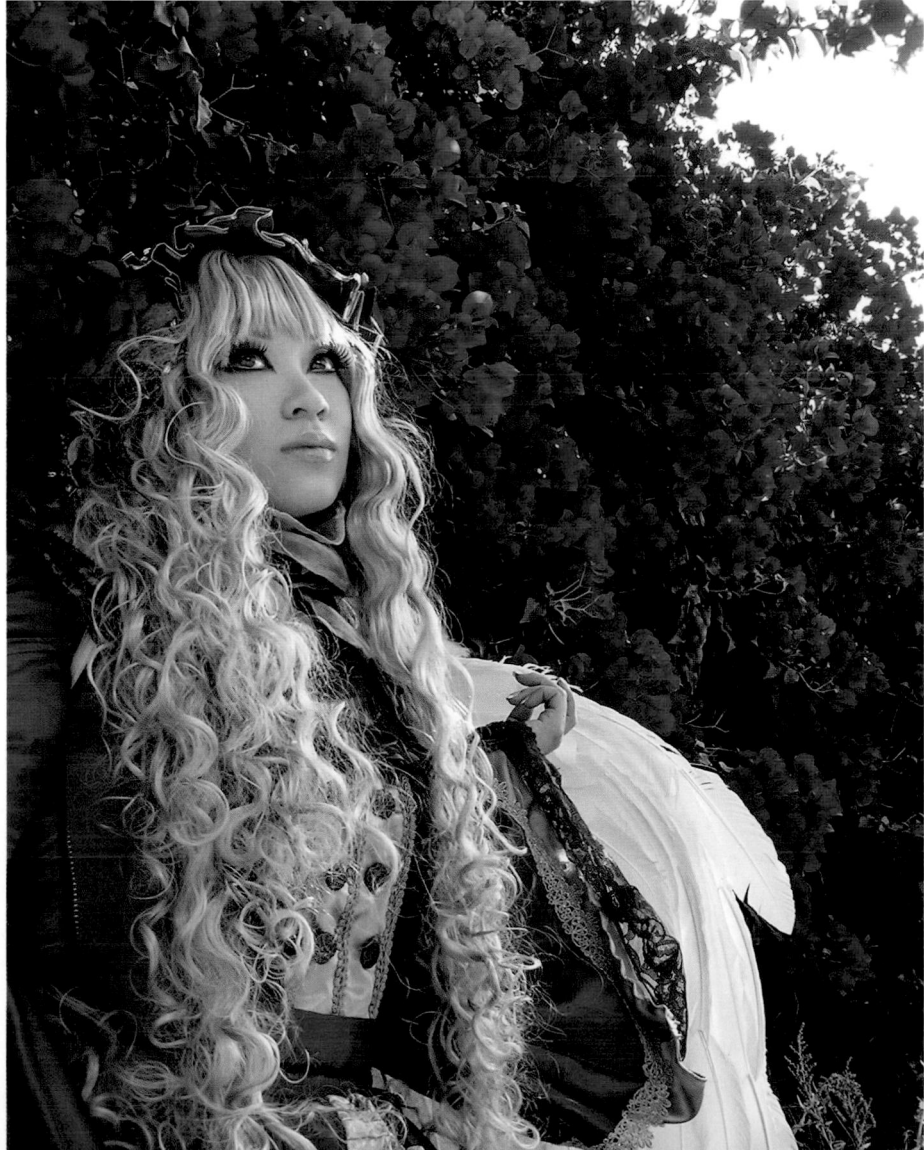

The first cosplay photo Brian took of me

master skills like sewing, prop making, and makeup applications lends itself well to learning photography and post-processing. In 2009, Brian picked up a digital camera for the first time and snapped some pictures of me during a cosplay shoot I was doing with another photographer. I loved Brian's photos more than the professional shots from that day because I was so comfortable around him and because he knew me so well, he got expressions from me that no one else could. Brian discovered from that experience that he really liked taking photos, so we invested in some decent equipment and have done photoshoots together ever since.

Each year, more cosplayers around the world learn how to capture and edit their own photos, really taking the creative process into their own hands. Some have built home studios and backdrops in order to do photoshoots with self-timers and tripods.

The advantage of cosplayers doing their own photoshoots is two-fold. For one, cosplayers don't have to wait for the availability of a professional photographer; they can create photo

Epic cosplay photos with blue flames in front of a cathedral and as Phoenix in flames content whenever inspiration strikes. Secondly, they also own the photos and don't have to worry about licensing rights from photographers or how the pictures might be distributed.

That said, collaborating with professional photographers is still the most common way for cosplayers to get photos. These shoots can produce incredible results that you can't achieve on your own.

By combining the skills of a costume maker, a model, and a photo creator, the quality of some cosplay photography nowadays is comparable to high-fashion magazine photoshoots. It can involve sweeping and epic shots, dynamic action poses, storytelling editorials, and glamorous portraits. Productions also include elaborate elements such as backdrops, pyrotechnics, and stunts. The photo-editing process often incorporates special effects, CGI, and composites. Cosplayers and photographers are continuously pushing the envelope in terms of what is technically achievable, and they are doing it with the fervent passion for which fans are known.

Taking photography a step further, one of the fastest-growing trends in cosplay is videography. Around 2010, a videographer named Ackson Lee burst onto the cosplay scene with stylized cosplay videos filmed at conventions. Using a Steadicam and a body rig, he captured cosplayers in well-composed slow-motion shots and edited them masterfully to catchy music. His videos showed not only the craftsmanship of the costumes but also the vibrancy and fun of conventions and the characters brought to life by cosplayers. Sometimes upbeat and fun, sometimes wistful and dreamy, Ackson's captivating videos soon reached millions of views on YouTube. People began anticipating new video releases after every convention he visited. Other videographers began

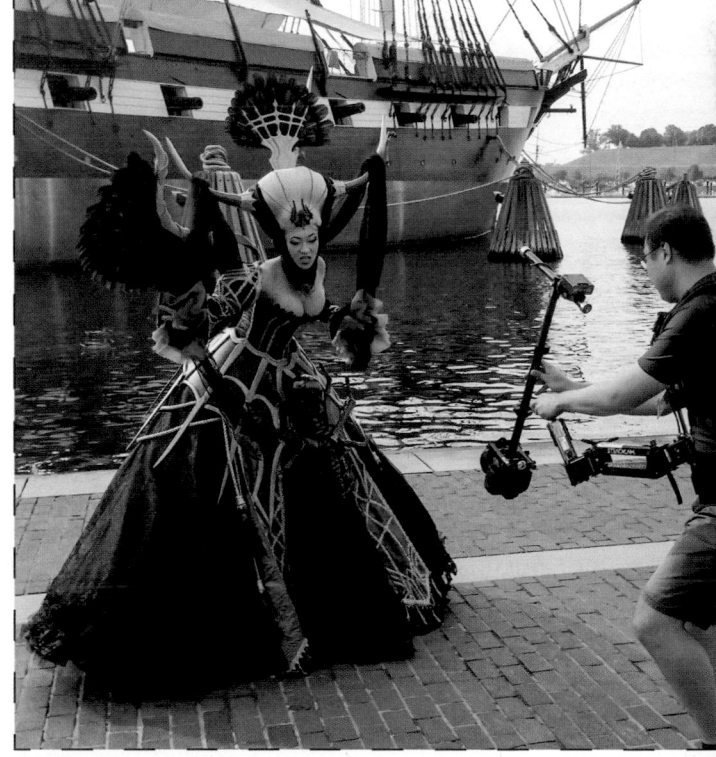

Being filmed in my Enira costume by MLZ Studios

to emulate his style and filmed cosplayers at events. However, instead of being secretive about his methods, Ackson openly shared his techniques and equipment. He actively encouraged people to give videography a shot. YouTubers like MLZ Studios, Rescue the Princess!, and Sneaky Zebra developed their own unique videography styles and are now highly respected artists in the community. Thanks to his focus on camaraderie and sharing, Ackson helped create a whole videography community in the cosplay scene that allows us to enjoy many cosplay music videos today.

While photography, conventions, and costume standards improved steadily throughout the 2000s, what really pushed cosplay over into the mainstream was social media. Social media has had an irreversible impact on our global society as a whole, but it was especially vital for a young and visual trend–driven community such as cosplay. Social media changed how cosplay was perceived by the rest of the world, and it also completely revamped how cosplayers create, interact, and express themselves.

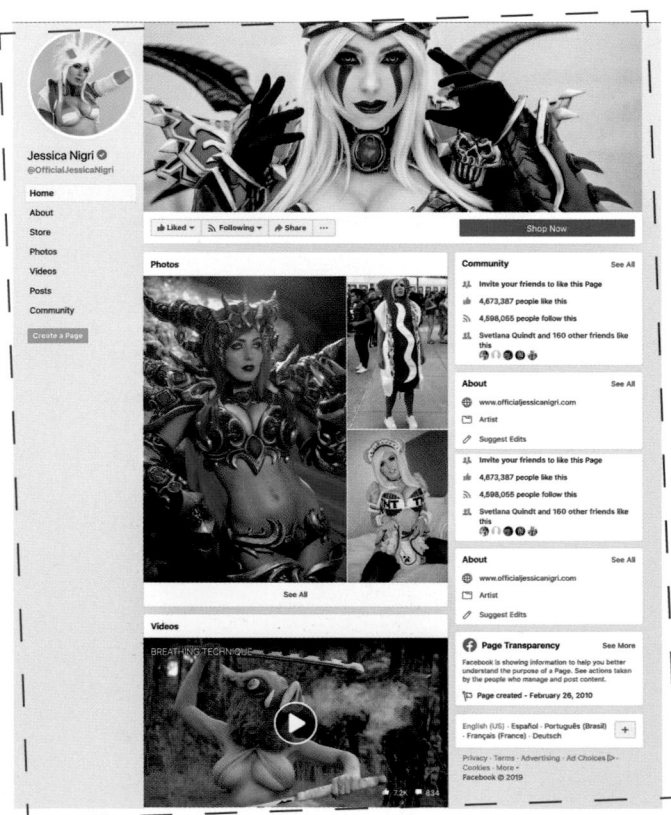

Cosplayer Jessica Nigri's public social media page

The biggest push forward was around 2010, when Facebook introduced Facebook Pages, a new social profile designed for public brands and figures. It was perfect for cosplay. Unlike a personal Facebook profile, where friends could mutually agree to see and follow one another's posts, Pages' one-way, subscription-based format allowed brands, artists, and creatives to curate an audience and to develop a public persona that could reach an unlimited number of people at once. In addition, many cosplayers prefer to keep a separation between their personal lives and cosplay personas, so it made more sense to showcase their work on Pages rather than accept friend requests from strangers on their personal profiles. One by one, cosplayers moved their cosplay content from personal Facebook profiles over to Pages and began to openly market themselves to an audience. This was a big deal at the time.

Another growing pain of the cosplay community was the tendency to criticize people who wanted to become professional cosplayers. A lot of people scoffed at cosplayers who created public Pages as if they were brands. However, even with that stigma in mind, in the new world of social media there was no more suitable platform for cosplayers than Facebook Pages. Once enough people switched over and proved that the public had no issue liking and following cosplay pages, the uproar subsided. Before long, other social media platforms such as Twitter, YouTube, Instagram, and Snapchat became popular in the cosplay community as well. These days, most cosplayers are active on at least two or three platforms.

Aside from changing how cosplayers could present themselves to the world, social media also opened up the global cosplay scene. Cosplayers from different countries could now curate an international following no matter the size of their local fandom scene. Even in remote countries such as Norway and South Africa, where the fandom scene was still developing, cosplayers could reach thousands of fans on a daily basis. Not being limited to a localized customer base meant that for the first time ever, cosplayers could enter the world of cosplaying with a career in mind and promote themselves as professionals from day one.

Social media has also changed the way cosplayers make costumes. Before the social media boom, cosplayers strived to finish new costumes in time for conventions. You built your entire calendar and cosplay to-do list around event dates, which is why the term *con crunch* is so common amongst members of the community. The utmost priority was given to finishing and wearing costumes at cons, because that's where it all happened—the socialization, the networking, the press coverage, the chance for winning awards, and more. These kinds of experiences could occur only at events.

However, after the online community developed around social media, cosplayers had more flexibility to create and post content anytime they wanted. With an Internet audience, they could build a schedule that suited their lifestyle, post about cosplay anytime during the year, and make costumes independent from convention planning.

That doesn't mean the pressure is off, though. In some ways, an online audience puts even more pressure on creators to create content on a regular basis in order to keep their Internet profiles relevant and interesting. Nowadays, the time we used to spend worrying about con crunch is spent worrying about our social media numbers and keeping up with the ever-shifting algorithms.

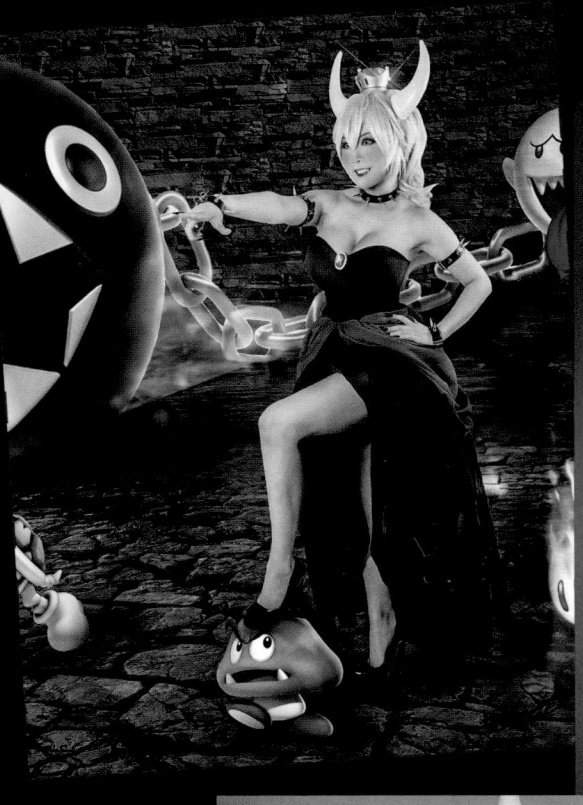

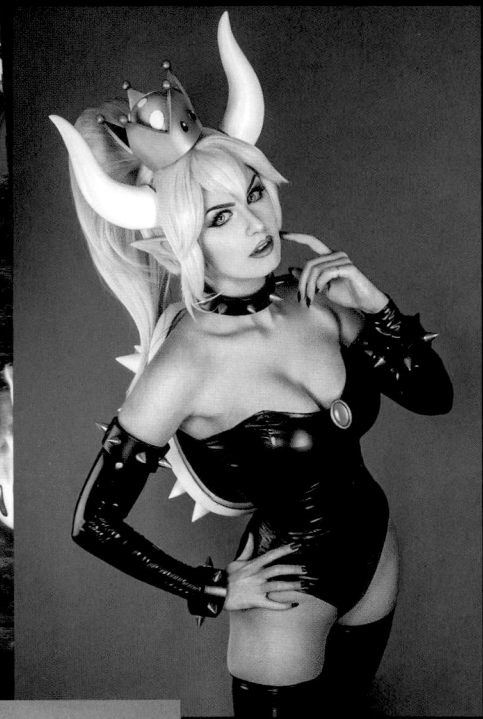

Cosplayers'
renditions of
Bowsette

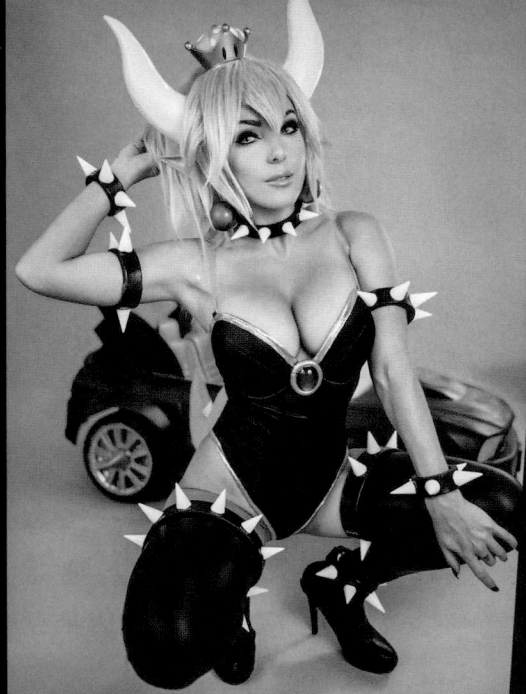

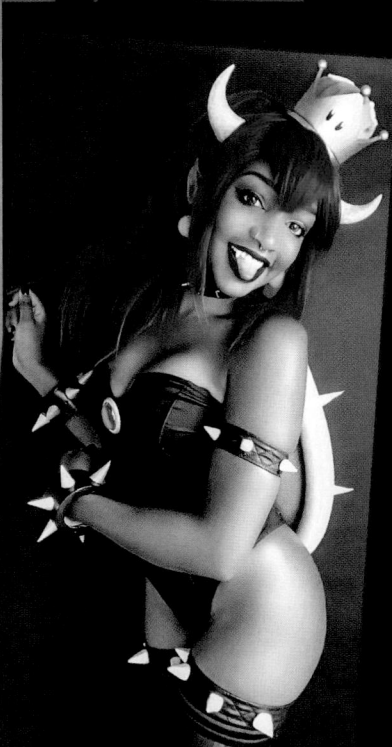

The fast-moving social media landscape has also put many cosplaying fans under pressure to chase the hype train, which means that many people try to cosplay characters as soon as the concept for a new movie or game is revealed to the public. Big announcements for popular franchises such as *Overwatch*, *League of Legends*, the Marvel Cinematic Universe, and *Star Wars* often spawn a race to see who can cosplay a new character first, because the first cosplay posts are more likely to go viral while the hype is hot. Even memes can catch on with the cosplay community and lead to new trends, such as with Nintendo's announcement of a new item, the Super Crown, in the Switch version of *Super Mario Bros. U*. The Super Crown turns Toadette into a Princess Peach–like character called Peachette, and it spawned a viral Twitter joke about a potential Bowsette in late 2018 (a mash-up of the characters Bowser and Princess Peach).

When it comes to the hype train, most of the time I believe that fans who cosplay as new characters do it out of a genuine sense of excitement. Just as fan artists will quickly post a sketch of a newly announced character on their social media, cosplayers will often feel an overwhelming desire to become that character and thus make their costume as quickly as possible. I was so swept up by the announcement of the *Assassin's Creed Chronicles: China* game that I made Shao Jun's costume within a week based on one teaser image alone. It's still one of my fondest cosplay memories to date. Sometimes you just have to throw other plans out the window and make the cosplay that consumes you.

Other times, jumping on a new character's costume is a calculated move and is less fan-driven. That is completely valid as well. In recent years, it has become an

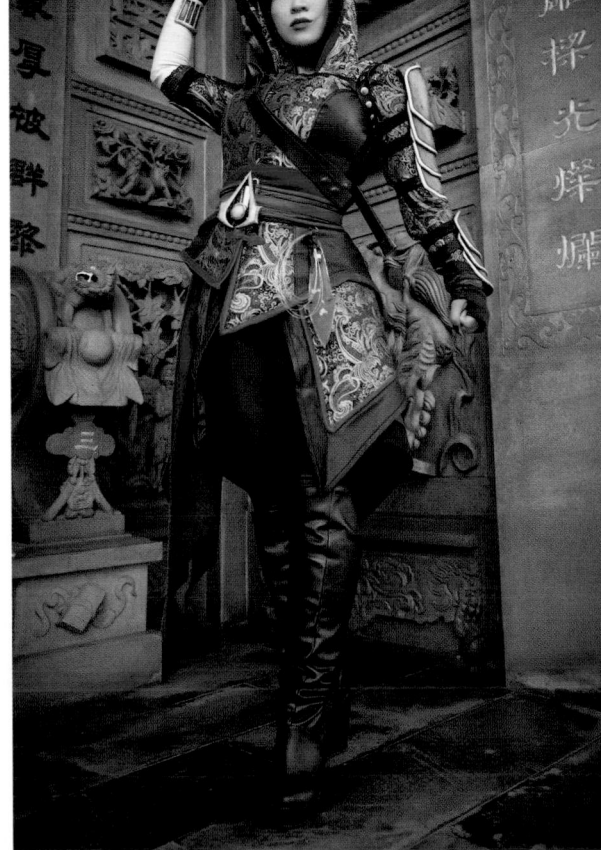

My cosplay of Shao Jun from *Assassin's Creed*

unspoken goal within the cosplay community to post content that can potentially go viral, and posting the first cosplay photos of a character after a big announcement certainly qualifies as potentially viral content.

In general, cosplay makes for great viral content because the photos and videos are often so highly stylized, colorful, and stimulating. Not only can cosplay photos and videos generate a lot of likes, comments, and shares on social media; they also frequently circulate on forums such as Reddit and on big viral content–sharing sites such as BuzzFeed. Cosplay transformations and makeup videos are especially popular, as well as oversize costume builds and clever mash-ups (like Bowsette). Viral content has helped a number of cosplayers garner a fanbase and make an income.

Beware, though: Viral cosplay content can be beneficial to your profile, but it can also be damaging, so choose your projects with care. If a post goes viral, it can reach a huge number of random people with many different opinions on the costume, your looks, and your words. There can be wonderfully positive but also extremely negative comments. You have little to no control over where viral content gets shared, so the audience you reach might not be the one you wanted. It is also hard to gauge what will go viral and what won't, so if you repeatedly spend time and effort making costumes based on popularity and not your personal interest, it can lead you to burn out on the entire hobby.

Social media tends to bait us with high-engagement content and instant gratification. When you get a lot of reaction to a post, it makes you feel validated and accepted. It also makes you want to create more posts like the ones that work. When a post does not perform well or gets low likes and few comments, it can be equally defeating and depressing. It can make you feel disappointed in yourself. What we have to keep in mind is that social media tends to skew engagement toward certain types of posts and that it is only a communication tool, not the golden standard by which to judge anyone's work. Lack of engagement on a post does not invalidate your hard work—the love you have for a costume and the joy you felt while creating it are what matter.

One of the most positive things to come out of social media is the ability to share educational content. Whether it's sharing costume progress photos on Facebook, uploading crafting tutorials on YouTube, or streaming costume-making sessions live on Twitch, cosplayers have found ways to connect with peers and fans through their crafting abilities. While cosplay photography can be used to showcase the finished costume project in stunning ways, creators can use Internet platforms to share valuable content on their works in progress. These posts can show details, go behind the scenes, and take audiences on a journey. Fans can follow along as cosplayers make a costume and get to know their thought processes and what lessons they learned along the way.

A decade ago, most cosplayers didn't even think of documenting their crafting progress, and there was no easy way to share knowledge or monetize their work. Compared to that time, we really are blessed to have so many resources at our fingertips now.

Whether you are a professional cosplayer, are aspiring to go pro, or just want to enjoy cosplay as a hobby, social media can be an invaluable tool and an amazing source for inspiration. Cosplay has always been about community, and the Internet has helped us connect, learn new skills, express ourselves in different ways, and share our passions with the world—even if we don't speak the same language. Thanks to social media, cosplay is truly a global phenomenon.

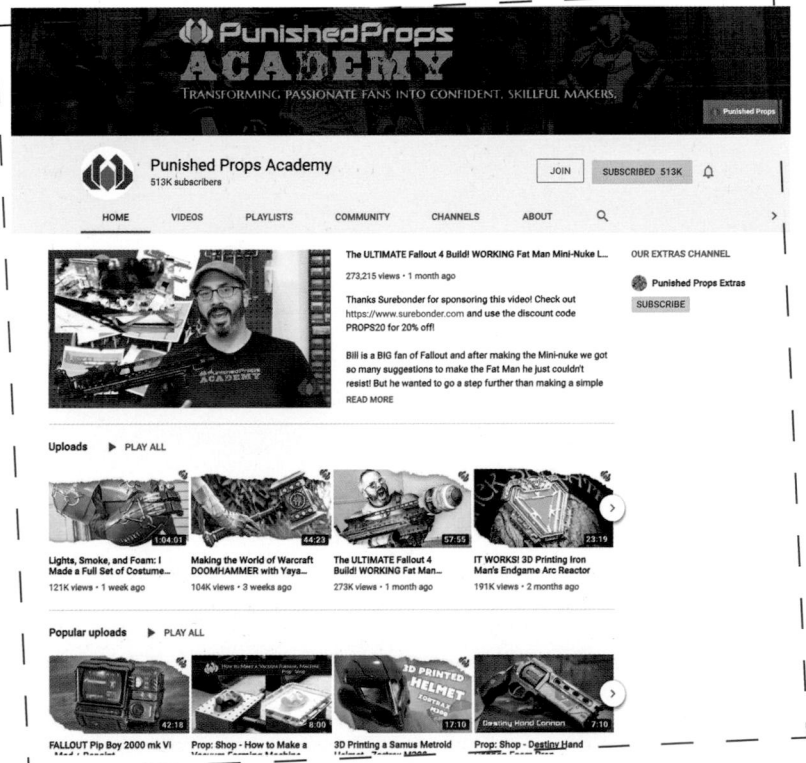

Punished Props Academy's educational site

CHAPTER 10

Going Beyond Re-creations

Trends in Cosplay

People always ask me, "What is your favorite costume?" As someone with more than 380 of them, that's a hard question to answer. Each costume has a deeply personal meaning to me and memories attached to it. I also love the freedom to cosplay a villain one day, a warrior the next, and a princess in a cupcake dress the day after. That said, my fanbase does seem to associate me with Chun-Li from *Street Fighter* more than any other character I have cosplayed, and I consider her one of my top favorite costumes.

I grew up with the *Street Fighter* arcade games, so I was button-mashing opponents into the dust with Chun-Li at a young age. She was my favorite character because I felt a strong connection to her Chinese heritage and loved her "Yatta!" victory pose. For a long time, she was on my to-cosplay list. Finally, in 2011, I was ready to make her iconic blue outfit. I bought the white wrestling boots for the costume, but then I saw a work of fan art that fit my aesthetic so beautifully, it caused me to place a new costume at the top of my project list.

The illustration was of an Art Nouveau–inspired Chun-Li. It was drawn by artist Kim Razvan Courtney and posted on DeviantArt. I was immediately drawn to the intricate swirling adornments, multilayered skirts and flower-covered hair buns. I loved the cute and ornate boots, the way Razvan had changed Chun-Li's white belt into a waist cincher, and how she had hung beads down Chun-Li's signature spiked wrist guards. It was such a charming design and stylish translation of Chun-Li that I became obsessed with the idea of making it. I e-mailed the artist to ask for permission to cosplay her version of Chun-Li, and she kindly granted it.

After that, I started furiously gathering materials. I acquired everything from silk taffeta to chiffon and bought as many jewelry dangles as I could. Over two weeks in the early months of 2012, I created the full costume, patterning it from scratch as well as doing freehand embroidery and beading. The first time I tried it on, it was so cute that I couldn't stop smiling.

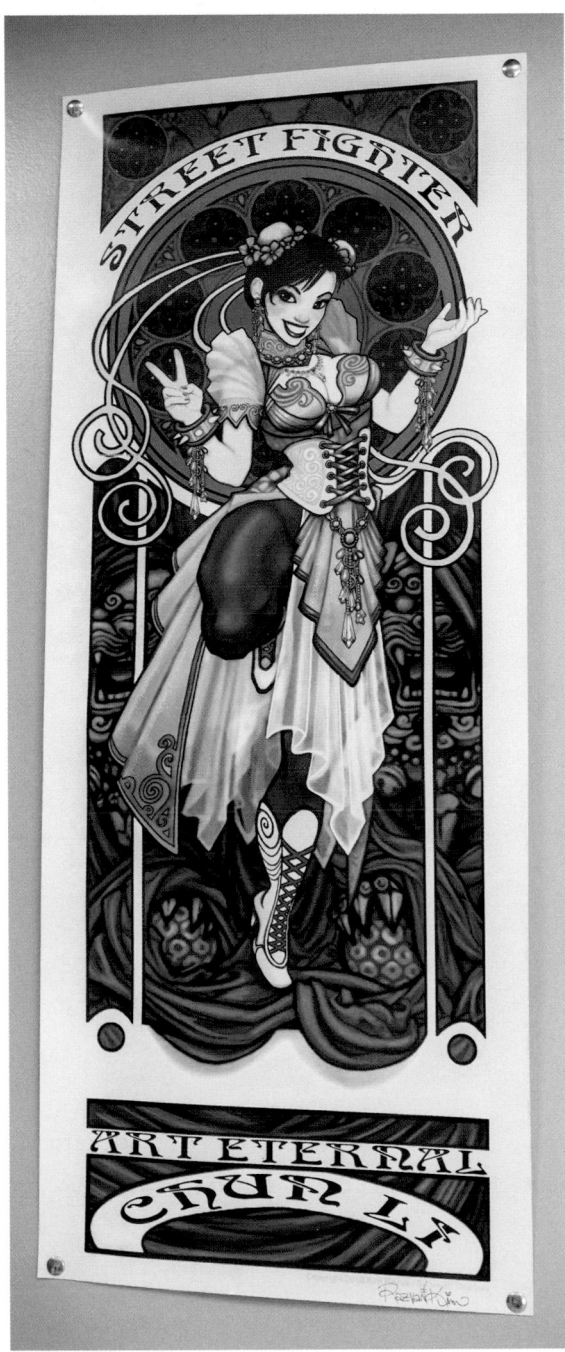

Illustrator Kim Razvan Courtney's
Art Nouveau rendering of Chun-Li

However, when it came to wearing the costume to a convention for the first time, I distinctly remember feeling nervous. I didn't know if people would comprehend my Chun-Li cosplay because it looked so different from the outfits that she wore in the video games. There were recognizable components, such as the hair buns and white boots, but overall my outfit was far removed from any official design. I wondered if *Street Fighter* fans would accept my unorthodox portrayal of this beloved character.

My worries were unfounded. As soon as I stepped out onto the convention floor, I was bombarded with photo requests that never seemed to end. Countless people called out "Hey, Chun-Li!" to me before asking for selfies and photos with me in which I assumed fighting stances. Online, I received hundreds of enthusiastic comments on every picture I posted. Not only did they praise the quality of the costume; they also talked about how much I resembled Chun-Li. The fangirl in me was so flattered. In subsequent years, I wore this Chun-Li cosplay to so many events due to popular demand that the costume is close to being retired because of wear and tear.

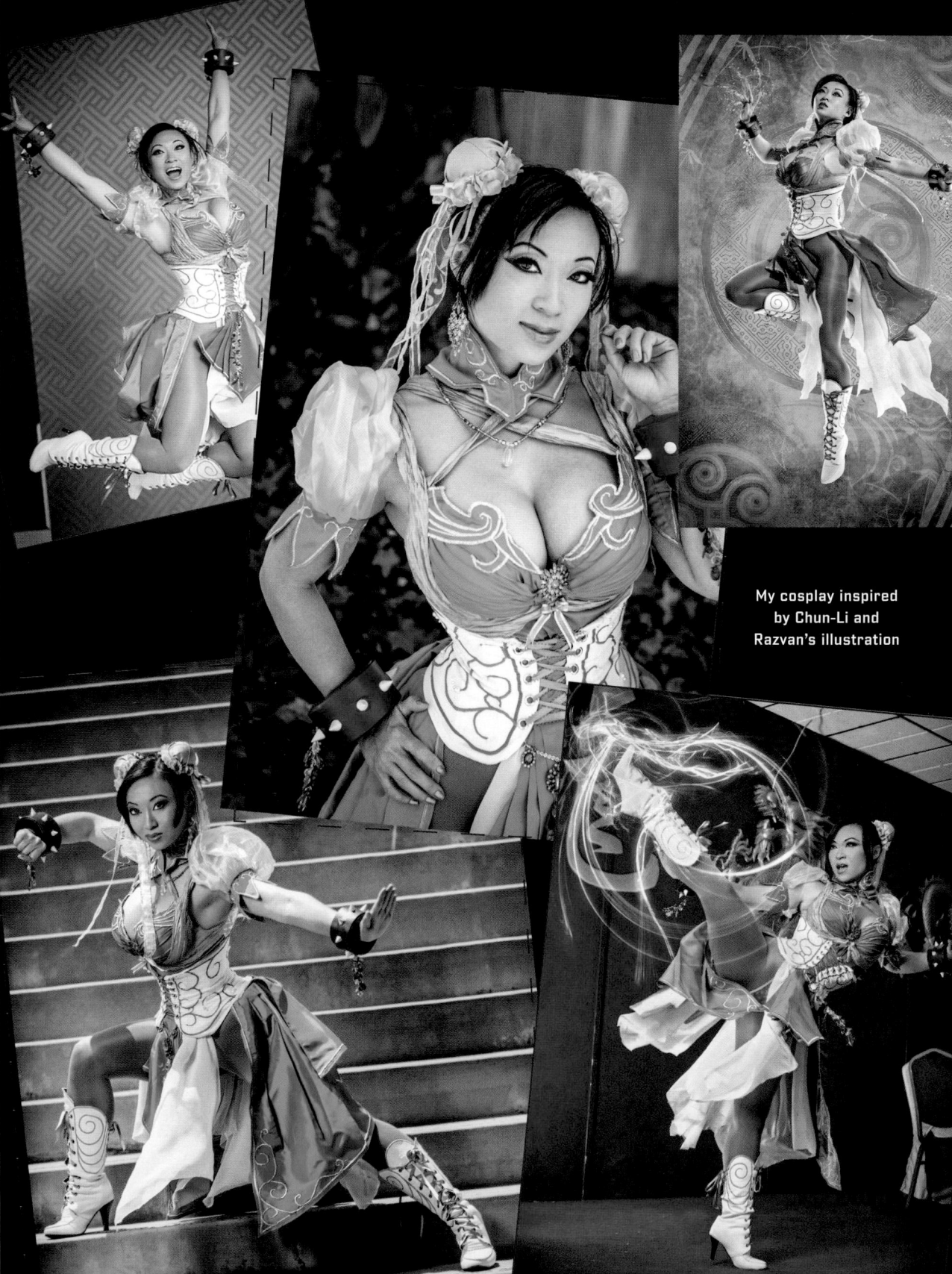

My cosplay inspired
by Chun-Li and
Razvan's illustration

The funny thing is that despite so many people considering Chun-Li my most successful cosplay, I've never dressed up in an outfit inspired by an official design of the character. The costume I'm best known for is a non-canon fan design. *Canon* is a term used in fandom to describe materials that are officially accepted as part of the story, while *non-canon* encompasses fan art, fan fiction, and other derivative fan works. Fan-made creations can either complement or elaborate on the original source material, or at times contradict it.

Inherently, cosplay developed as an art of replication, where the goal is to resemble a fictional character. By that definition, the more accurate your costume is to the character's design, the more respect you show the source material and its creators. Chun-Li was an unfamiliar experience for me, because up until that point, I had subscribed to that line of thinking and had mostly cosplayed canon designs because of it. That's because the first time I changed up a character design significantly . . . it didn't go over well.

About ten years before I high-kicked in hair buns, my friends and I entered the masquerade costume contest at Anime Expo 2001 as a group. We cosplayed characters from *Miyuki-chan in Wonderland*, a manga series that was a comedic parody of *Alice's Adventures in Wonderland* with lesbian overtones; in every story, female characters tried to seduce Miyuki-chan. Earlier that year, Baz Luhrmann's *Moulin Rouge* had released alongside the (undisputable) best music video of 2001: the film's rendition of "Lady Marmalade" by Christina Aguilera, P!nk, Lil' Kim, and Mýa. Seeing a parallel between *Miyuki-chan* and *Moulin Rouge*, we decided to create a *Miyuki-chan* dance skit set to "Lady Marmalade" and gave our costumes *Moulin Rouge*–inspired twists—you know, garter belts, sequins, tassels, bustles, and ruffled cancan skirts . . . the whole cat's meow. We sashayed onstage, we danced the cancan, and we won the contest. It was awesome.

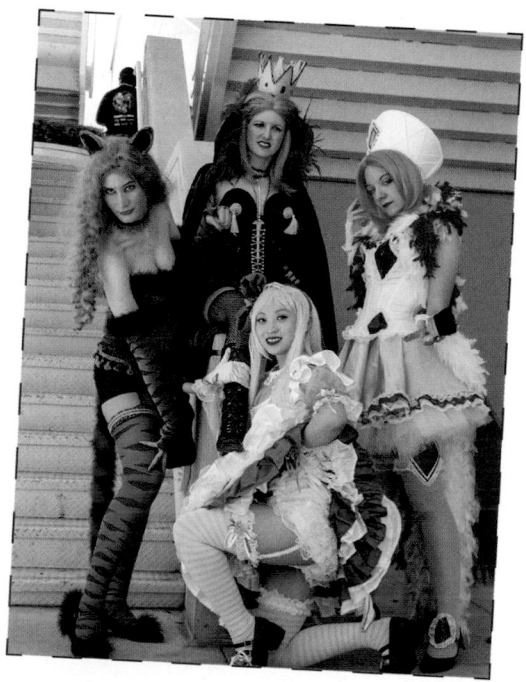

However, the celebration after our victory was dampened by the barrage of blame our group received from people who said we were not being accurate to the *Miyuki-chan* designs and that we had oversexualized our costumes.

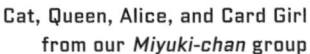

Cat, Queen, Alice, and Card Girl
from our *Miyuki-chan* group

What hurt me most were the accusations that we had also disrespected the characters and CLAMP, the creators of the manga. I have been a huge CLAMP fan since my childhood; I owned the *Miyuki-chan* manga books as well as the anime VHS, so I knew the characters well. My teammates and I put a lot of effort into our costumes and focused on making sure we stayed true to the essence of each character even as we altered their designs. To be told that we disrespected the series with our cosplays was the worst thing someone could say to a fan.

From that point on, I largely stuck to faithful re-creations of canon designs for my costume projects and stopped thinking about alternate themes. I still had a penchant for choosing patterned fabrics even if the reference called for solids or adding embellishments and detailing where it felt right, but those changes were minor and complemented the designs; they did not alter them in a fundamental way. Without realizing it, I had imposed a rule on myself to be as authentic and accurate as possible with every cosplay I made. It wasn't until I fell in love with Razvan's brilliant Chun-Li redesign that I was compelled to break that rule. Looking back, I probably missed out on some fun in those years.

For many cosplayers, striving for accuracy is the sincerest way to pay homage to a character and thus is the ultimate goal in the costume creation process. The importance of accuracy sets cosplay apart from casual dress-up or Halloween costuming. It is what drives us to put more effort into crafting and to devote ourselves to learning new skills. It has also helped propel our community forward as a respectable branch of fandom. That said, though, as I learned through personal experience, the perception that accuracy is the golden rule of cosplay can also limit creativity, diminish artistic freedom, and lead to exclusion or even elitism.

From a craftsmanship standpoint, the challenge of making a costume that replicates a character design down to the smallest details is tremendous. However, cosplayers with enough knowledge and financial means can re-create live-action film and TV costumes using the same materials, tools, and techniques as the originals. Today's user-focused technology gives individuals access to screen printing, dye sublimation, computerized embroidery, 3-D printing, laser cutting, vacuum forming, CNC (computer numerical control) milling, and other costume-making resources that were previously available only to industry professionals. The caveats are that some materials are only commercially available in certain countries and that many cosplayers don't have the disposable income to use certain techniques or tools. While the effort of re-creating an entire costuming department's project by yourself is extremely admirable, we must face the fact that technological advances have created a precedent for screen accuracy that is achievable only to those with a certain degree of privilege.

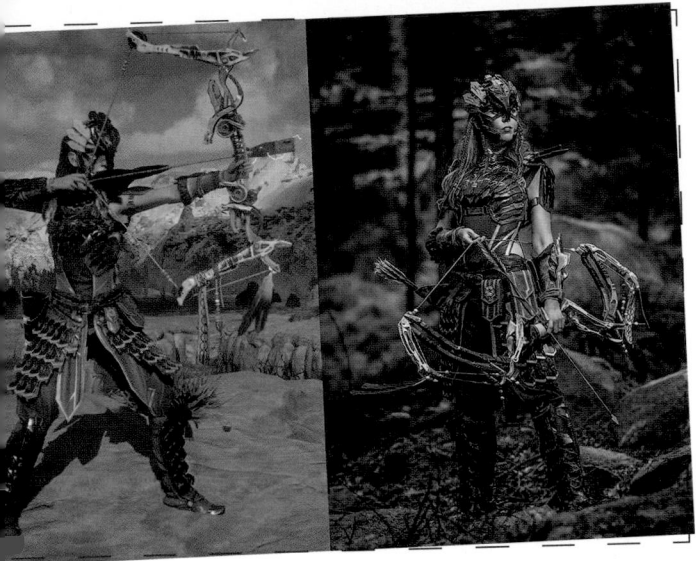
Side by side of Kamui Cosplay's super accurate Monster Hunter costume

At the same time, character designs have also become more complex and detailed. High-definition video and hyper-realistic video game renderings have left a lot less room for interpretation and turned up the pressure for accuracy in replicating not only the costume designs but also the physical appearances of the characters. Using makeup, wigs, contacts, and even prosthetics at times, cosplayers can change their features in the same ways that drag queens and Hollywood actors can transform into unrecognizable personas. You can also use padding, corsets, foam chest pieces, or muscle suits to change your body shape. For most cosplayers, accuracy means going through extra efforts to match their appearance to their chosen character's design as closely as possible. These elements of transformation have always been some of my favorite parts about dressing up, but when the goal is to look like an existing person (such as an actor playing a comic book hero) or a fictional character with distinctly rendered features, inevitably some cosplayers will be considered by many to be more successful than others based on their natural appearance. Lookalikes have always been a part of human culture—just consider the longevity of the celebrity impersonation industry. With the right costume, cosplayers with natural resemblances to famous actors can enhance their portrayals to uncanny levels of perfection.

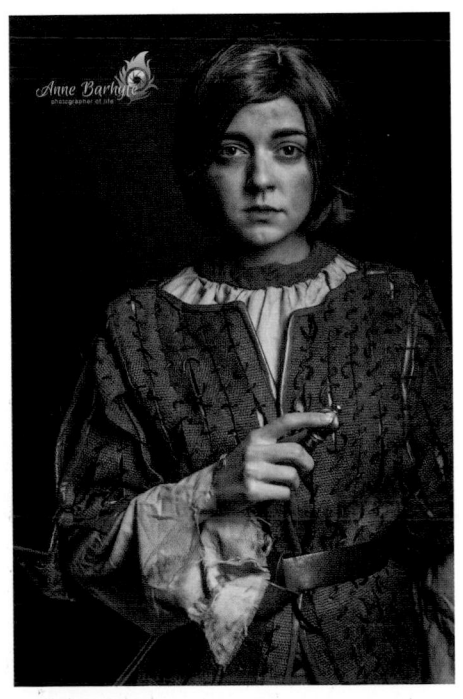
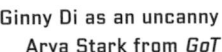
Ginny Di as an uncanny Arya Stark from *GoT*

What does that mean for the rest of the community? As the standards for screen accuracy continue to rise, the struggle to meet them becomes greater as well. These days, it seems to be harder for people to separate the costume from the individual behind it. An all-too-common mind-set amongst cosplayers and the public is that unless someone goes through extreme lengths to re-create a costume design accurately, they are not a good cosplayer. Many still think that if you deviate from the source material, your costume is mediocre, half-assed, or downright disrespectful. Others believe that cosplayers with the "wrong" body type or skin tone are not good representations of their chosen characters. These narrow-minded thoughts foster elitism in a community that should be welcoming to all. The pressure to be accurate plays on our insecurities as makers and as fans. Ultimately, that stress can alienate even the most experienced makers—not to mention inexperienced newcomers and cosplayers from marginalized groups.

I'm not here to disparage cosplayers who work hard to achieve screen accuracy. Rather, I want us to remember that everyone has different means at their disposal and can approach cosplay however they want. I am a strong advocate for the idea that anyone can cosplay regardless of their ethnicity, height, body shape, gender, or skin tone. Don't let the pressure to achieve accuracy make you hesitant to cosplay a character, even if your skin tone or body shape is different from that individual's. Don't be afraid to change a design to suit your taste or to work with more affordable materials than those used to craft the original costume. Remember that cosplay is a personal form of expression. If there is an ultimate goal to the art form, it should be your enjoyment.

Thankfully, cosplayers have always been some of the most creative and innovative fans in any fandom, so there are many different ways you can enjoy cosplay today. The landscape of cosplay is vast and vibrant; it's full of fun trends and personalized costumes made with humor and whimsy.

For example, there are a lot of hilarious mash-up costumes, where cosplayers take a character from one fandom and combine their design with that of a character from another fandom. The practice has resulted in costumes like Ironpool, where Deadpool is combined with Iron Man, and mecha (humanoid mobile robots) designs from *Mobile Suit Gundam* that are augmented with elements from *Sailor Moon* costumes. Mash-ups can draw from properties of different artistic mediums, and there is no limit to their creativity and cleverness. There have even been some truly iconic fast-food chain versions of pop culture characters, such as Taco Belle and the McVengers.

Another incredibly popular cosplay trend is to take characters from their canon settings and reimagine what their outfits would look like in a different storytelling universe. Taking

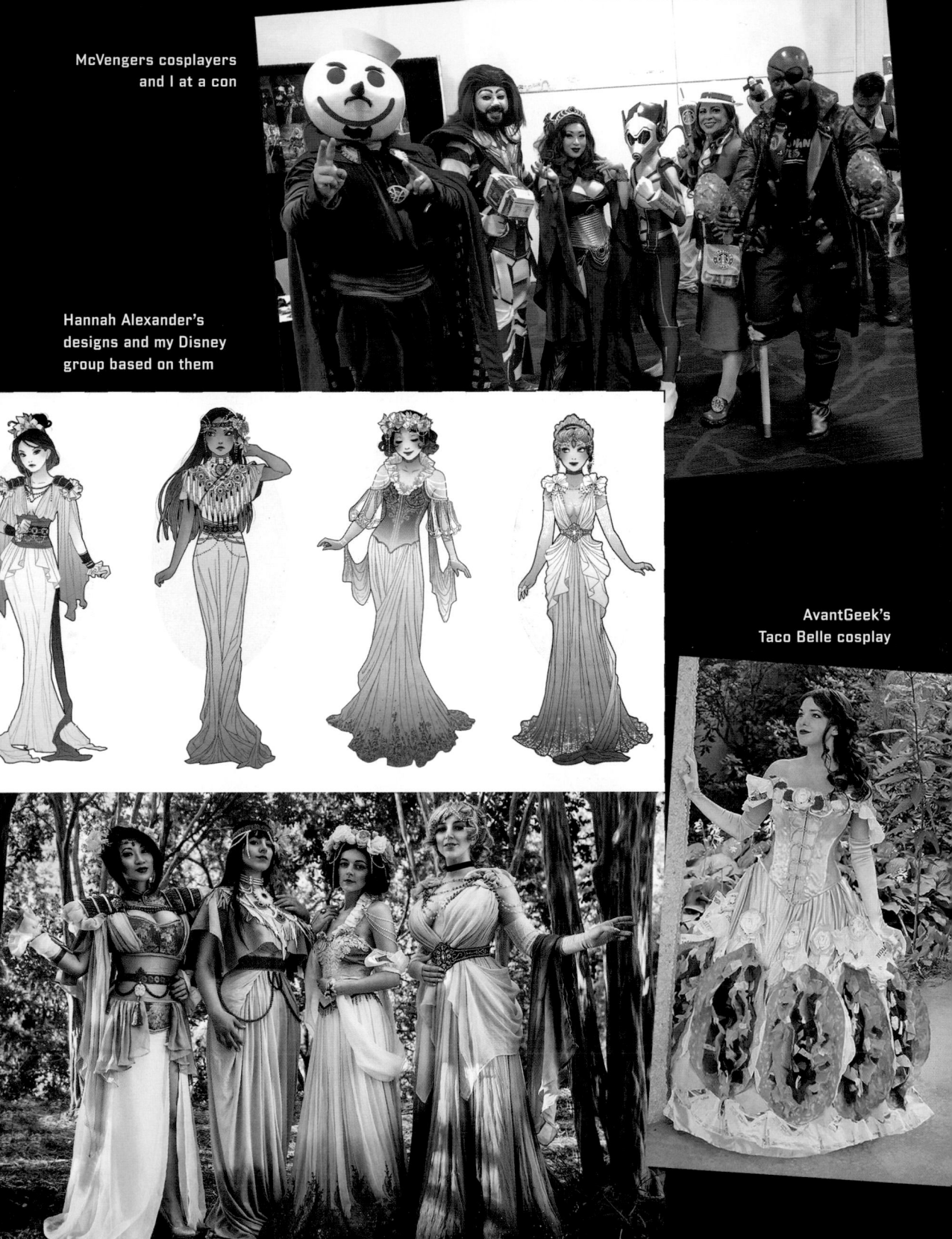

McVengers cosplayers and I at a con

Hannah Alexander's designs and my Disney group based on them

AvantGeek's Taco Belle cosplay

influence from fan fiction writers and fan artists who have done this, these alternative universe (AU) cosplays include Disney princesses reimagined as battle-ready tribal warriors, *Gotham Crusaders* characters outfitted in steampunk gear, and *Star Wars* characters brought back to life as zombies. These costumes can be lighthearted, meticulously thought out, or both. Either way, these costumes are often paired with the additional challenge of coming up with an original design. For example, a cosplayer working on a steampunk Batman costume would have to think about what the Dark Knight would look like if he lived in a steam-powered Victorian era. The cosplayer would then have to change distinguishing elements of Batman's costume and prop elements to fit the theme.

Yet another trend that has swept across cosplay is humanized animal cosplay, or *gijinka*. In Japanese, *gijinka* means "anthropomorphism," and in cosplay, it refers to the practice of taking a nonhuman character such as a Pokémon or a pony from *My Little Pony* and creating a costume that gives that character a more humanlike form. Most gijinka cosplayers reimagine an animal character as a human being but include recognizable animal characteristics in their costumes. With *Zootopia*, for example, cosplayers portraying Lt. Judy Hopps the rabbit and Nick Wilde

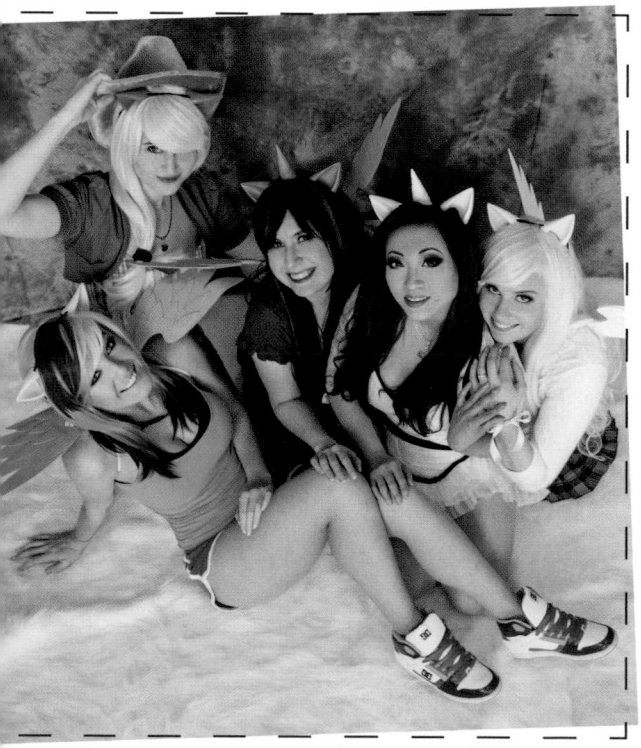

the fox are usually dressed in human clothes but have animal ears and tails. By comparison, if you see a straightforward re-creation of a nonhuman character, such as a giant Pikachu or a round, huggable, and fuzzy Totoro (think sports team mascot), that's usually called—you guessed it—a mascot cosplay. Gijinka cosplay is all about imagination and translation and can apply to inanimate objects as well; there are a lot of video game console gijinka cosplays for some reason. With the gijinka style, you are compelled to make changes to a character's design, so the process of creating such a costume can be an incredibly fun and freeing experience for those who feel burdened by the pressure of accuracy.

My friends and I in Pony Gijinka costumes

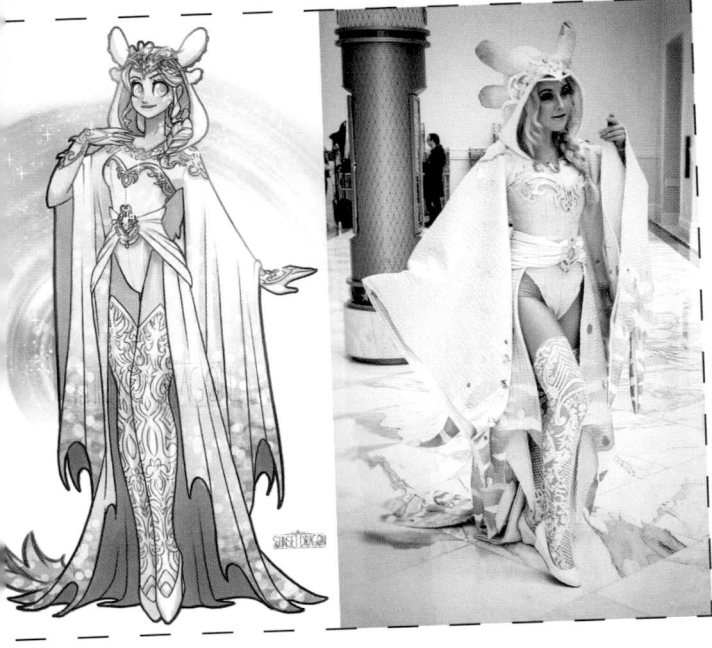

Side by side of Sunset Dragon in her Lightfury cosplay

For cosplayers who prefer to follow a design illustration rather than creating a wholly original design, there is plenty of inspiration to be drawn from fan art. The excellence of non-canon AU fan art is what broadened many cosplayers' minds to consider stylized costumes in the first place. A lot of fan artists openly welcome cosplayers to make costumes based on their artwork, and some have even built a brand for themselves by redesigning characters for cosplay. Hannah Alexander, Zach Fischer, and NoFlutter became known in the cosplay scene for their unique art styles and common penchant for designing original costumes for existing characters. Their artwork is not only beautiful; each piece has a design quality to it that calls out to makers. All three artists are highly regarded, and their designs are frequently cosplayed by people around the world. Other artists like Sunset Dragon and Gladzy Kei are cosplayers

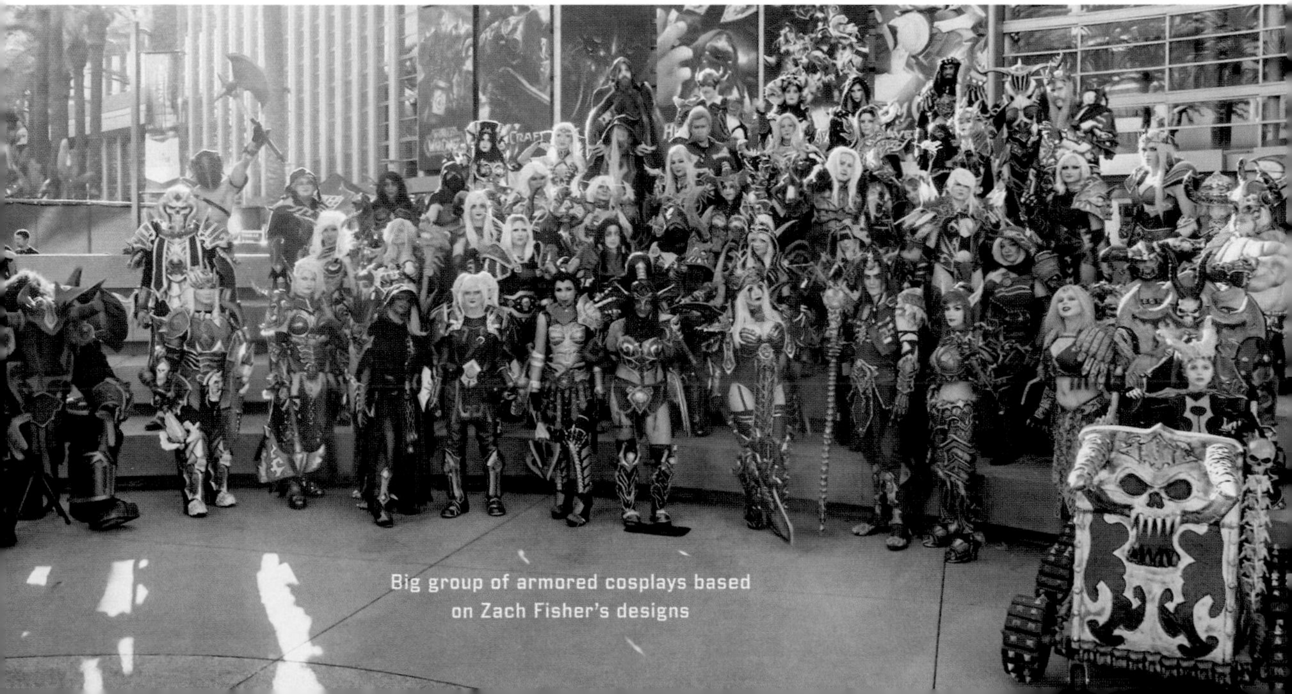

Big group of armored cosplays based on Zach Fisher's designs

themselves; they use their dual knowledge of design and crafting to create fashionable design illustrations and intricate costumes to accompany them.

These elaborate artworks and clever mash-ups may have broken the ice for redesigns, but there are no rules or guidelines to limit how you personalize your cosplay. Plenty of cosplayers enjoy creating their own original adaptions and freestyle themes. Whether they put their characters in bunny suits, streetwear fashion, swimsuits, or pinup lingerie,

Gladzy's *Overwatch* redesigns and the cosplay group

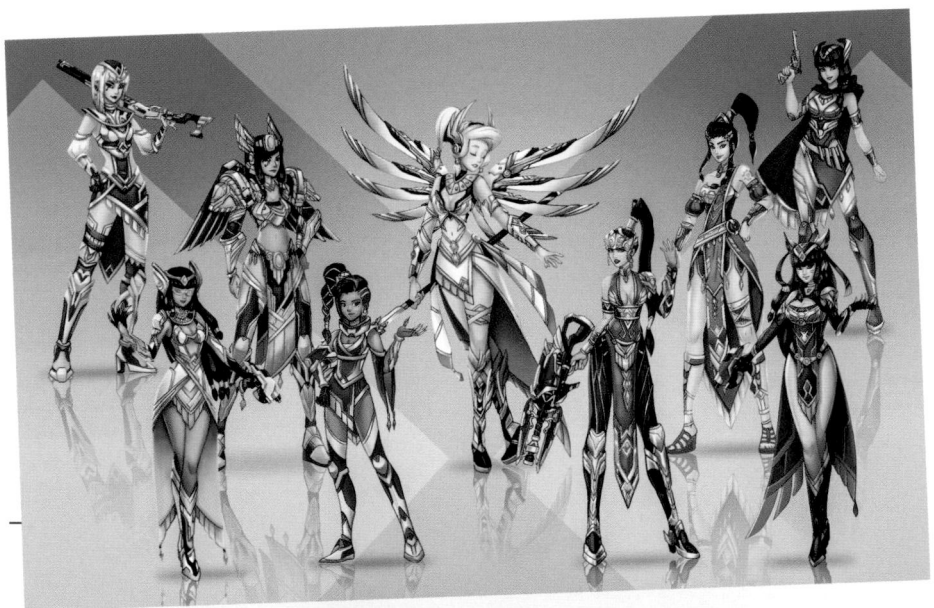

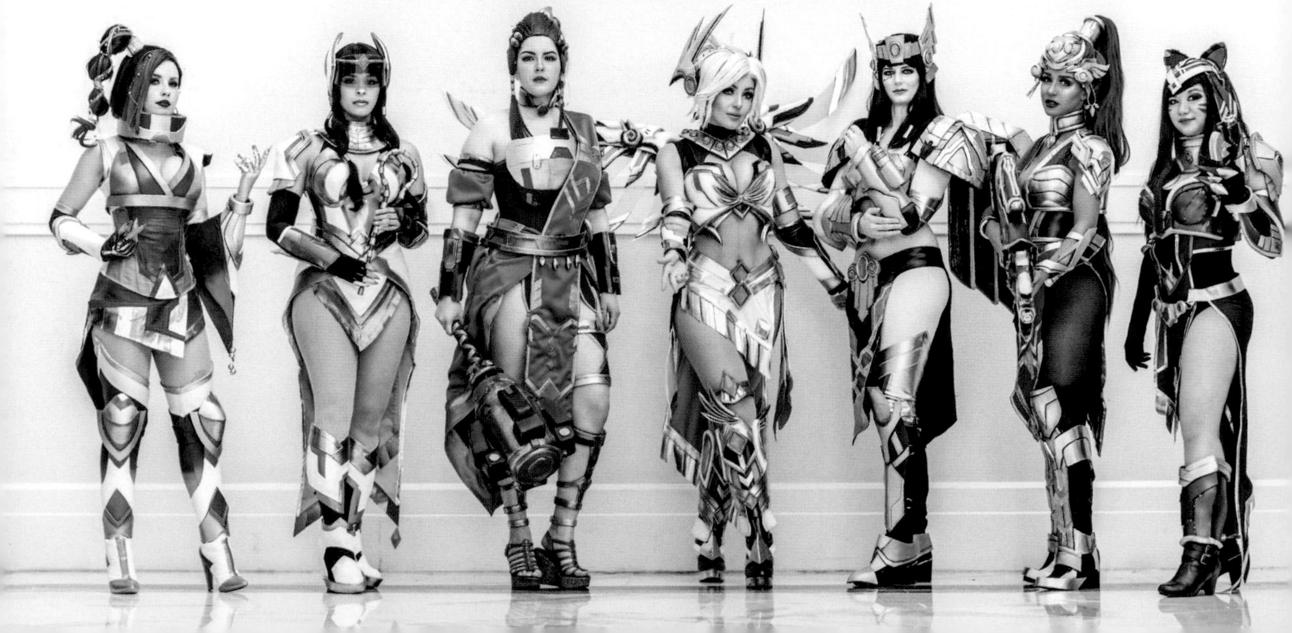

cosplayers have reimagined fictional characters in all these ways and then some. There are no specific categories you have to follow and no checklists you have to mark off if you want to adapt a costume. That is the beauty of it. Terms like the ones we just discussed can help us understand the different trends and styles of cosplay that are out there, but in the end you can dream up and make whatever you want.

I think there are a few reasons why so many people now customize their cosplay. For one, the community is huge and global. Between the number of people who cosplay, how incredibly easy it is to buy costumes, and how popular it is to cosplay some characters, there is an understandable desire to make your costume stand out as one of a kind. Crafting a fan-designed outfit can be refreshing and can make you feel more unique. It can also function as a way of wish fulfillment if, for example, you have an idea for an outfit that you think would look great on a certain character from a show. Lastly, as we've previously discussed, by making your cosplay an original interpretation of a character, there is less pressure to be 100-percent accurate to the character's standard design. Instead, you can inject some artistic freedom, creativity, and personal style into the costume.

One trend I have not yet mentioned is *genderbending*, which requires a more nuanced approach for discussion. In cosplay, to genderbend means to redesign a character's costume to fit a different gender. Other terms you might hear are *genderswapping* or *Rule 63*, the latter of which is a Rule of the Internet that states that for every fictional character, there exists a counterpart in the opposite gender. Overwhelmingly, genderbending applies to women who dress up as female versions of male characters by redesigning masculine costumes to emphasize the female form. For example, one could take a pantsuit worn by a male figure skater from the anime *Yuri!!! On Ice* and turn it into a female skating dress. The same character is being cosplayed, but they are being presented in a different light.

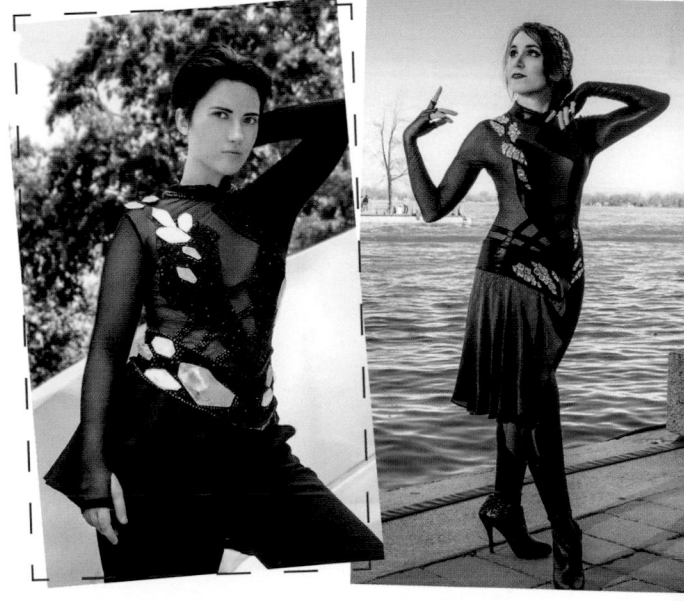

Male and female renditions of the character
Yuri Katsuki, a figure skater.

It is not hard to understand why so many women are drawn to genderbending. Most major protagonists in pop culture, from comic books and video games to anime, are male. In an industry that has been dominated by men for decades, most heroes and villains are created by men for men, period. Female characters are not only harder to come by in fandoms, but many of them are not designed to be realistic or relatable. Often, women feel compelled to dress up as male characters simply because they are their favorites.

Similarly, just as women like to imagine themselves as male characters, some male cosplayers also pick their favorite female characters and reimagine them as men. Some female-to-male genderbends are meant to be satirical, such as with burly, bearded Disney princesses. Others are queer-positive and celebrate gender fluidity. Either way, genderbending can be empowering and freeing.

You don't have to change a character's gender to cosplay them. Regardless of the character's gender relative to the cosplayer's, many cosplayers dress up as characters as they are originally portrayed simply because they like them. When a cosplayer takes the time and effort to emulate the perceived gender of the character, it is usually referred to as *crossplay*. Whereas Rule 63 cosplayers redesign the character to be another gender, crossplayers aim to preserve the authenticity of the character's gender and might elect to tweak their own bodies a bit to achieve greater accuracy.

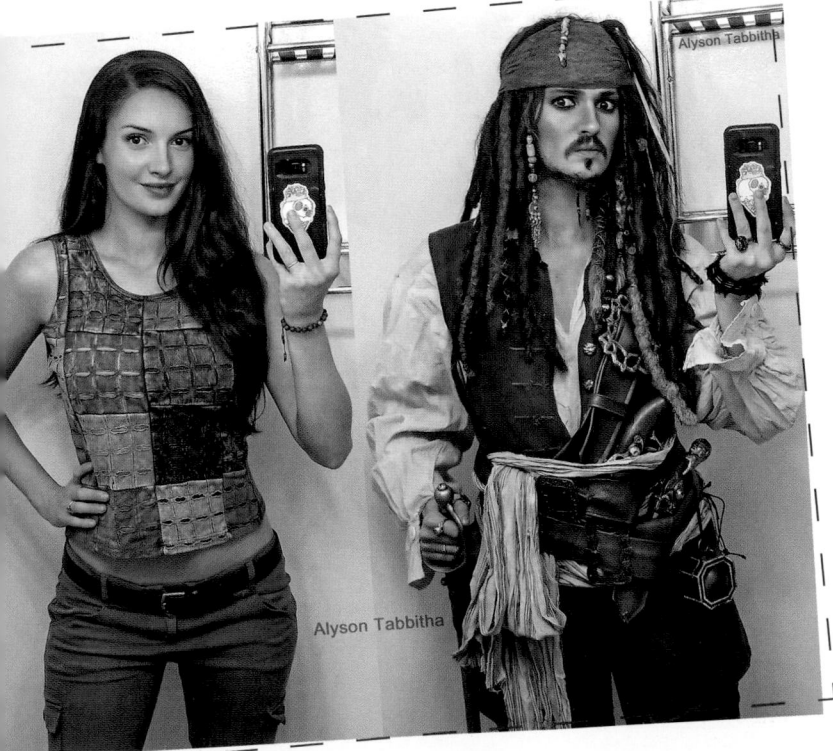

The term crossplay was generated fairly early on in the cosplay community. In fact, I remember learning about it soon after I started cosplaying in 1999. In those early days, crossplay was mostly used to describe men who dressed up as female characters. It may be easy to see a connection to the word *crossdressing*. Nowadays, crossplay also includes

Alyson Tabbitha cosplaying as Jack Sparrow.

a sizable cosplay subculture in which women emulate male characters to very convincing results by using chest binding, padding (in the waist), face taping, and contouring makeup. The transformations are astonishing at times. For example, cosplayer Alyson Tabbitha cosplayed Jack Sparrow from *Pirates of the Caribbean* and altered her features to look stunningly similar to the original actor's. However, just as it's more important to have fun making your cosplay than it is to make it wholly accurate to the source material, you can alter your features to crossplay as more or as little as you like—your comfort comes first.

For some people, dressing up as characters from different genders is a way to explore their own gender identity. Whereas in real life it might be difficult to find occasions to change your perceived gender appearance without judgment, conventions and cosplay offer a relatively safe space for people to become whoever they want, even if it's just for a day. That doesn't mean the cosplay community is devoid of social stigmas such as homophobia, but in a fandom setting where others are portraying superheroes, aliens, and mythical beings, it can be more comfortable for someone to experiment with cosplaying characters of different genders. As our understanding of gender identity continues to evolve, it is important that we foster an open and welcoming environment for all, including LGBTQ+, nonbinary, and transgender cosplayers.

Cosplay may have started out with the replication of costume designs, but it has evolved far beyond that into a vast field full of artistic freedom and creativity. Besides redesigns of existing characters, many cosplayers enjoy making original costume designs of creatures such as fawns, fairies, and mermaids. My Retro Space Girl is an original character I created more than a decade ago and who I still make new costumes for. There was a time when a lot of people were hesitant to consider original costumes as cosplay, but thankfully they are now widely accepted as part of the art form.

Still, you might be asking yourself where cosplay ends and when it becomes something else—especially since there is so much crossover and influence between cosplay and fashion, theater, live-action role playing, and historical costuming. I think that any inspiration can be turned into a costume and that what you want to call it is up to you. Cosplay would not exist if people didn't have all these different fun and weird ideas and were compelled to make them into real, wearable outfits. It also would not be nearly as exciting if everyone looked and dressed the same. As such, I hope that in the future we won't feel bound by terminology or limited by categories. Cosplay is an art form that is meant to be explored, and the diversity and variety is what propels our community to continue growing. The most important thing is that people have fun doing it.

HOW TO NAVIGATE CONVENTIONS AND PHOTOSHOOTS

Conventions and photoshoots are two great ways to experience cosplay. They allow you to show off your skills and your love of a character in the most intense ways. The thought of going out in public can be intimidating to beginners, though, so here's my best advice on how to smoothly sail through your first events and endeavors in costume!

YAYA'S CONVENTION SURVIVAL GUIDE

Figure out event logistics. People travel from around the world to attend conventions, so approach your con trip like any other vacation. Find out where the con is held and how to get there in costume. How far is your hotel from the convention center, and can you walk a lot in your costume? Is your outfit comfortable and safe to wear outside given the weather conditions? Some costumes are too painful, heavy, or hot to be worn all day, so schedule your day accordingly and consider a simpler costume to change into at night.

Safely transport your costume. If you travel by plane or public transport, you'll need to fit your costume(s) in a small space. Making any long props, such as swords and staffs, collapsible will make them a lot easier to transport in a suitcase. Keep your fabric costumes and accessories in a garment bag so they stay protected and organized. That will also keep small items from getting lost. Styled wigs should be kept on foam heads or padded with paper. A good rule of thumb is to put all delicate costume pieces that are not sharp or weaponlike into your carry-on suitcase. There, you can keep an eye on them at all times. Make a packing list of costume items and bring reference images to the convention so you know how the pieces fit together.

Carry a costume repair kit. This kit should contain thread and needle, scissors,

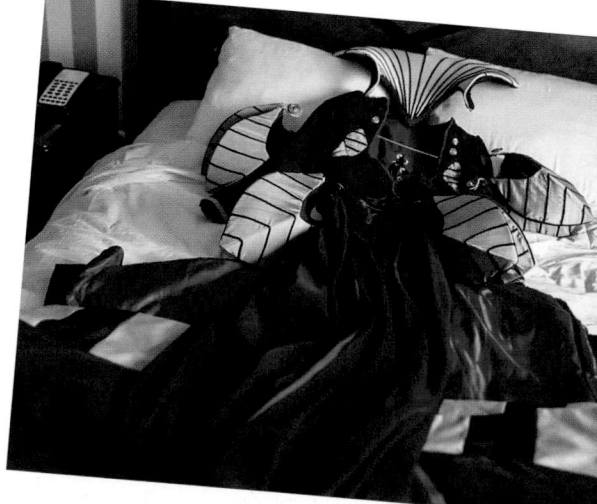

My Carmilla costume laid out in preparation of getting dressed.

super glue, safety pins, duct tape, possibly paint, and whatever else you think could be used to repair your costume just in case something happens to it. Unpack your costume as soon as you arrive at your destination and make sure all your costume pieces survived the journey. Hang up what can be hung, and consider ironing your costume before you're meant to wear it.

Manage your time. When scheduling photoshoots, gatherings, or meetups, give yourself plenty of time to get into costume. Especially with a new cosplay, give yourself thirty extra minutes to prepare beyond your initial estimate, just in case there is a mishap. Don't pack your schedule, and allow yourself lots of time to get to that one panel you really want to see. Time flies at cons, and you want to enjoy the experience of being in costume as much as you can!

Practice a few poses. Before you strut out of your hotel room in your new costume, consider preparing a few poses for photo requests. Most characters have signature poses that will make them more recognizable. Look at yourself in a mirror to find out which poses and angles look awesome and show off your costume best! I recommend having three poses ready for each costume. That way you won't feel put on the spot when a great photographer asks for a mini photoshoot.

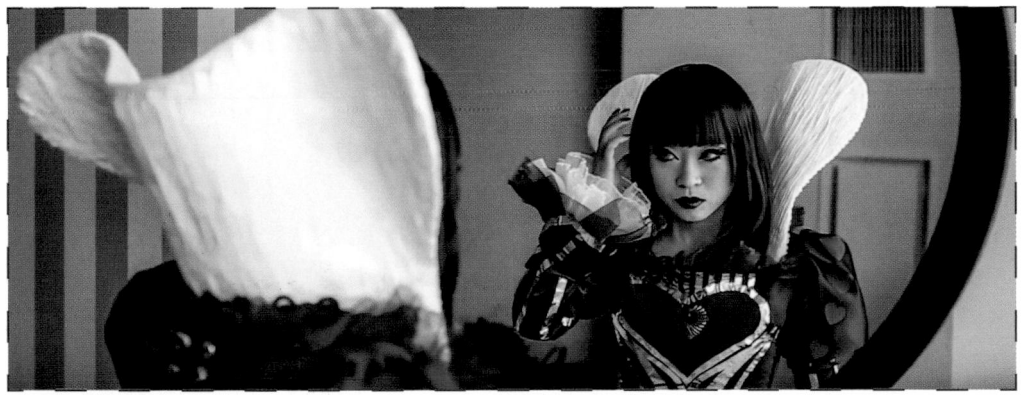

Final double check to make sure my costume is perfect before leaving my hotel room.

Attain a trusty handler. Let's face it: The majority of the coolest and most badass costumes are big, cumbersome, painful to wear, and not entirely practical. Having a friend help you out for a few hours by playing costume handler can make your cosplaying experience a thousand times more enjoyable. Don't hesitate to ask for help if you know your vision will be obscured, you'll be carrying a giant prop while wearing large armor pieces, your hands will be stuck inside paws or claws, or you'll be encumbered in any other way.

That said, be sure to return the favor and help out your friend when they need a costume handler, too—and maybe treat them to dinner for assisting you!

Prioritize safety. While 99.99 percent of the time, the interactions you have at conventions are positive and fun, cons are public settings with lots of people, so anything can happen. Walking in groups can be more fun and is safer. This is especially true at conventions held in downtown areas of big cities, where you may have to walk a few blocks after dark. If you find yourself in an unpleasant or uncomfortable situation, do not engage; simply walk away. Then find security staff and report the incident. In the fan community, we watch out for one another!

Pace yourself! This is my mantra for all conventions. Come to the event with a game plan, and keep your group informed. If you must party, choose one night to do so, and get some sleep on the other nights. Keep yourself hydrated, and eat! Bring a change of clothes and know when you need to get out of costume. Have fun and pace yourself so you can enjoy all days of the event!

Practice photo etiquette. If you show up to a con in cosplay, people will want to take a photo of you or with you. Embrace these photo requests, because they'll make you feel special! They show that someone loves your costume or the character you're dressed as so much that they want to take a moment out of their busy con day to capture you on camera. However, keep in mind that there are unwritten rules for interactions with photographers (and any con attendees with phone cameras).

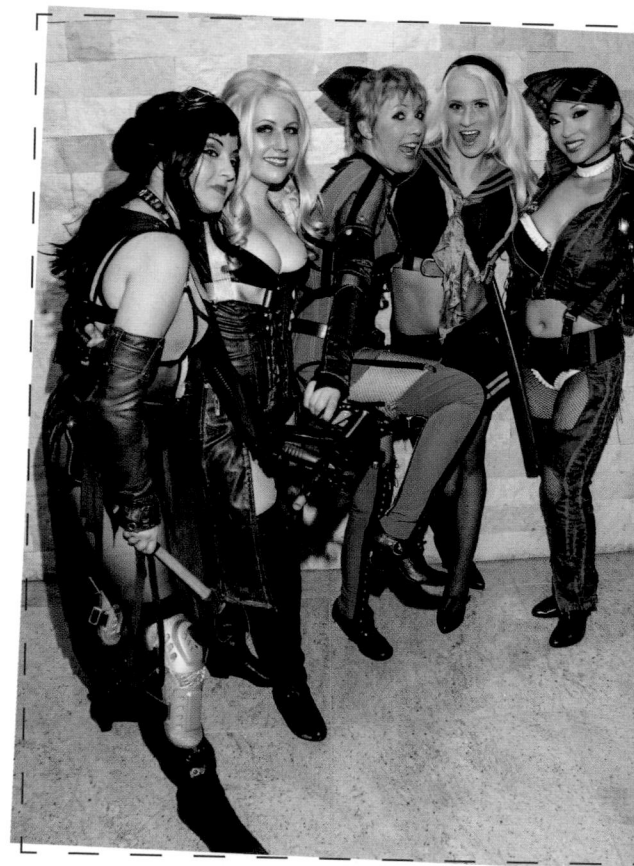

Group of *Sucker Punch* cosplayers laughing

When someone stops you for a photo, they should give you a moment to put down your bag, adjust your costume, and strike a pose. Cons are crowded, so use common sense and put your belongings between you and the photographer, in a place where you can see them.

Don't block passageways. If snapping a photo isn't practical in the middle of a hallway, some photographers may ask you to step outside for a mini photoshoot. After taking your photo, they will often show you the pictures on the camera's screen. Don't be too shy to tell them if you aren't happy with the poses or the angles; it's okay to ask to try again. Afterward be sure to exchange contact info and ask them where you'll be able to find the pictures later. Many cosplayers prepare little business cards, or "coscards," with their social media handles on them. Thank them and enjoy the rest of your con.

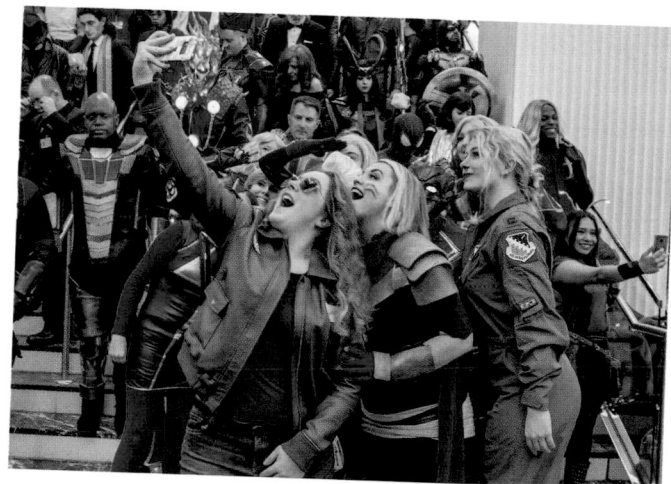

A bunch of Captain Marvels taking a selfie

Say no. Cosplayers are often bombarded with photo requests. Every once in a great while, it is okay to say no. When you need a break, you're eating, you're on the phone, or you're heading to the bathroom, don't let anyone pressure you into having your photo taken. Stay polite, but be firm. This also applies when someone puts their arm around you for a photo without asking or poses you in a way that you don't like. You have every right to decline a photo request if the situation makes you feel stressed out or uncomfortable. Cosplaying at a convention should be for your own enjoyment.

— — —

Conventions are great fun and the best way to connect with fellow nerds. Attending a con in costume for the first time is a mind-blowing experience, and it can really help boost your confidence.

To really showcase your costume, however, you'll need good photos. Those are hard to get in busy and dimly lit con halls. I've found that some of my costumes are so cumbersome, it's better for me to save them for a photoshoot outside the confines of a convention. Cosplay shoots are great opportunities for you to collaborate with another artist to create lasting images of your cosplays!

YAYA'S TIPS FOR PHOTOSHOOTS

Find a photographer. Even if you are a newbie cosplayer, it's possible to work with experienced photographers who will challenge you to level up your game. You can hire a professional for money, but many photographers will also work on a TFP basis if your costume inspires them. Some of the most amazing cosplay photography is done by amateur photographers who shoot purely as a hobby, just like many of their models cosplay primarily for fun.

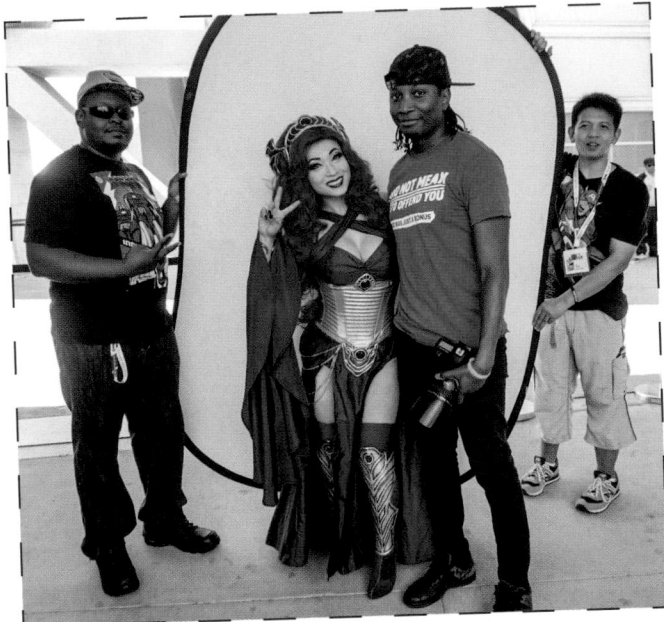

Posing with my photographers after doing a shoot

The easiest way for a cosplayer to find a photographer is through social media. Follow cosplay photographers whose style you like. You can also join local cosplay groups and convention groups on Facebook. Many of these groups will let you post requests where you can say that you are looking for a photographer to shoot a costume. There are threads and even entire groups dedicated solely to matching cosplayers with photographers or organizing local photoshoot events. Don't be shy—message photographers from your area! For best results, send your prospective photographer a picture of the costume you want to shoot. Bonus points if you already have a visual concept or a shooting location in mind that is in line with the photographer's style. That might get them excited to work with you.

Find a location. Photo studios are a safe place to experiment, but unless you create your own home studio, renting a studio will require a budget. The lighting setup for studio photography takes some experience as well. Outside of Asia, most rental studios aren't equipped for cosplayers and don't offer fancy backgrounds and props. Outdoor and on-location shoots, on the other hand, are mostly free and offer an endless variety of backgrounds for any costume.

Always check out the location before you meet up for the photoshoot. You may not need permission to shoot in open spaces like public parks, but make sure you won't bother anyone while you're there. If in doubt, find out who owns or runs the place and ask permission to shoot there for a noncommercial art project. Do not trespass on private property and never put yourself at risk for a photo.

Take pictures of the location so you can share them with your photographer. Is there a changing area nearby, or will you travel to the location in full costume? Can you shoot there at all times of the day? For soft, natural lighting, golden hours in the morning and evening are great because the sun is not blindingly bright.

Plan before the shoot. Jot down some photo ideas. These can be as detailed as you want; you could create a visual storyboard with shots from your cosplay's source material that you'd like to re-create. They can also be as simple as a bulleted wish list. Taking compositional inspiration from other sources like movie screenshots or magazine ads can help you visualize your ideas for the shoot. Share a few reference images of your character and discuss how you'd like to portray them. Keep in mind that your photographer may not know the source material, but understanding your character and the world they're from will help them envision the perfect setup that brings out your character's personality.

Communication between photographers and cosplayers should be open. Look at the shoot as a collaboration; you both want to get something out of it, so both parties should contribute their ideas to the shoot.

Prep on the day of the shoot. Give yourself plenty of time to get ready so you can show up to your chosen location on time and in full costume. Bring a handler to help with your costume and to assist the photographer if needed. I always bring a friend when I meet with a photographer for the first time, too. Not only is it more fun, but it also makes me feel safer working with someone I don't yet know. Just make sure to tell the photographer who you'll bring along and discuss their

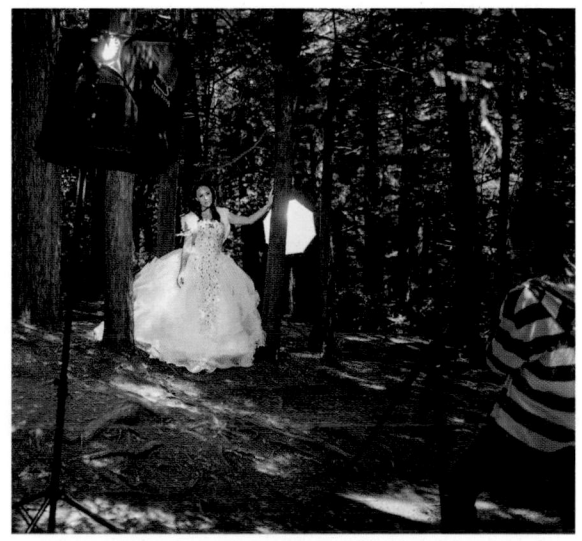

Behind the scenes at a whimsical cosplay shoot

role(s) during the shoot. A friend who is also a cosplayer is more likely to notice when something about your costume or makeup isn't right. If they can help with those elements, the photographer can focus on the technical aspects of the photoshoot.

During the shoot, reference your list of shots to make sure you get the ones you want to take home, but allow yourself to be inspired by the location and the photographer's posing instructions as well! Be mindful of your surroundings and leave the place like you found it so you don't ruin it for other visitors.

Communicate afterward. Your photographer should be upstanding and honest with you about the editing process. Make sure you understand what their editing style is like and what the timeline for editing will be. Cosplayers, you should know that you may not get dozens of photos out of a shoot. Sometimes three or four is enough! Editing is part of the artistic process, and it takes time and inspiration. If you want to be involved in choosing the photos to edit, ask your photographer if they are okay with sharing a preview of the raw photos. You should have a say in what photos get shared publicly, though.

When you post photos online after the shoot, always give credit to the photographer. Tag their social media profiles or put a link to their portfolio in your photo description so that other people in the community can find them and share their work. Photographers should give the same treatment to cosplayers when posting photos from the shoot as well. We all benefit from giving credit, and it is a sign of respect.

Work out photo rights. In the US, the photographer has the photo rights to any pictures taken by them. However, cosplay is a joint artistic effort, and I encourage photographers to share photo rights with their cosplaying subjects. Make sure to talk about image usage rights and photo rights before the shoots.

If you'd like to monetize photos from a shoot, you must get prior approval from the photographer. They should also get your permission to release and use the images, so talk to each other as collaborators. When I use photos for merchandise, such as prints or a calendar, I pay a licensing fee to photographers for the image usage as a thank-you for their contribution. A written agreement, no matter how simple, will protect both you and the photographer.

— — —

Remember, you can always get an affordable camera and put it in the hands of someone you trust! You don't need a professional photographer to practice posing, and it may be fun to develop your skills together.

If you do go for a collaborative photoshoot, I hope you have a lot of fun with it! Photoshoots are my favorite way to explore the characters I cosplay. To me, a good cosplay photo does more than make me feel pretty or badass. Of course, I want each photo to showcase the costume, especially if it has been painstakingly handmade, but above all, I aim to evoke the essence of the character I'm cosplaying and create a photo that tells a story. My cosplay photos capture a happy moment in time, and they will remind me of the experience long after I've worn out the costume. Creating images is another part of the cosplay adventure that is not to be missed.

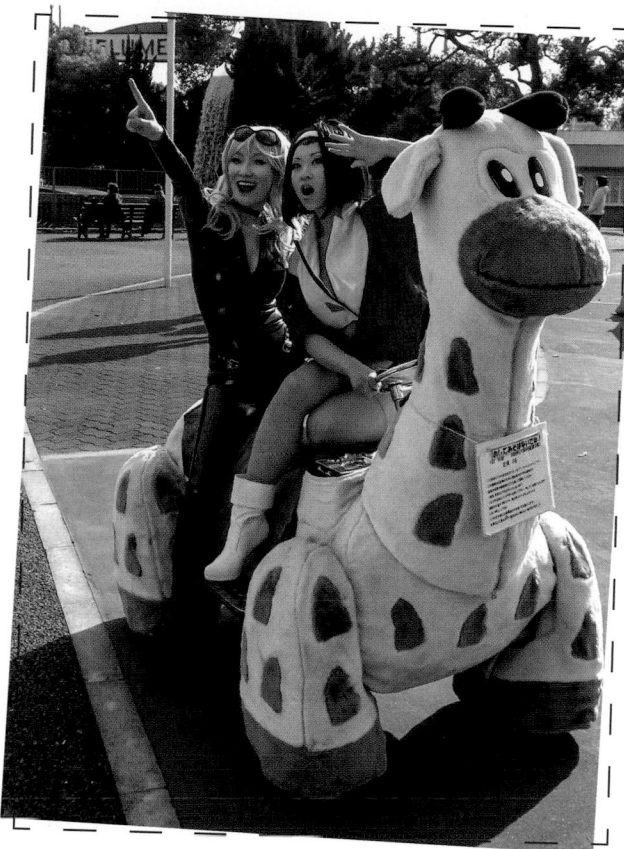

My friend and I sitting on a Giraffe plushie in Japan during a photoshoot

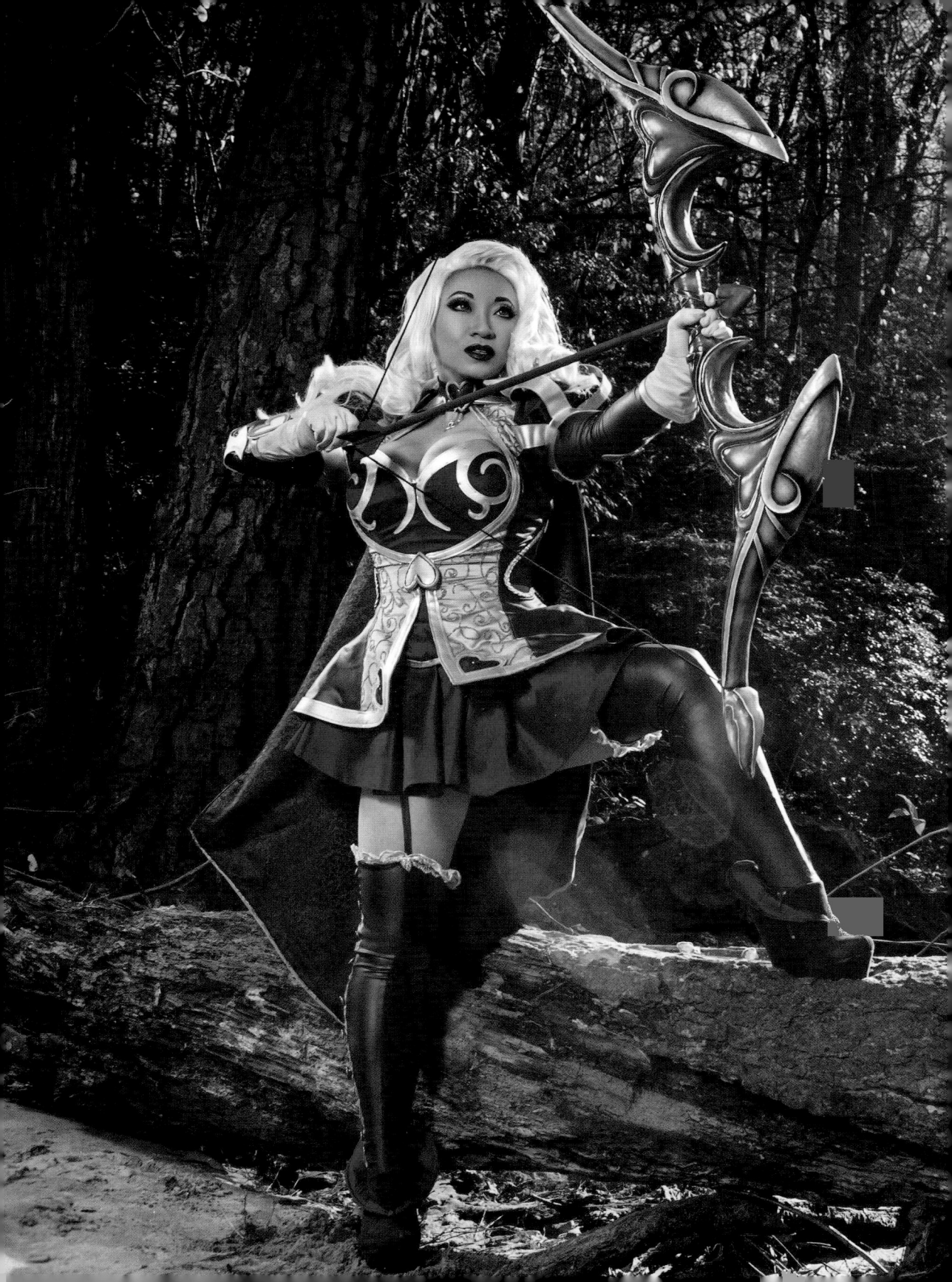

The Duality
of Cosplay

Negativity in Cosplay

Can't We All Get Along?

The first time I received a negative comment on a costume, it was because I wore the wrong type of shoes. They suggested that I was lazy and had done a half-assed job on the costume. The next time I received criticism, I was told that I was too short and did not have the right facial structure for the character I was cosplaying. The time after that, I was called a slut because my costume had a rip-away skirt and I'd worn garters underneath (this was for the *Moulin Rouge*–inspired *Miyuki-chan in Wonderland* skit).

It may come as a surprise to hear about negativity in a community where everyone plays elaborate games of dress-up. However, after twenty years of cosplaying, I could fill a book with all the unkind comments people have said about me. Many other cosplayers could, too. It's easy to view cosplay as a fun escape from the real world with its ultra geeky premise, but

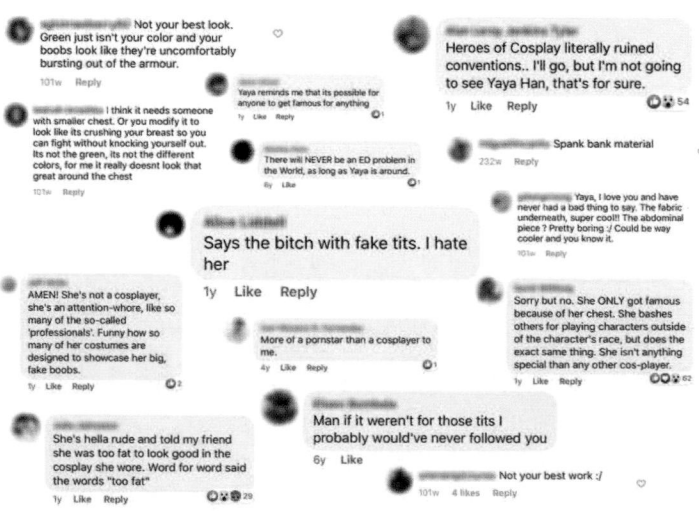

Just a few comments I have received over the years . . .

we are not free from real-world issues. In the next few chapters, I will talk about why negativity exists in the cosplay community and how you can deal with it.

The very nature of cosplay makes it vulnerable to criticism. Just like art, music, and writing, when you create something it becomes open to judgment regardless of whether you want it to or not. Creators know that this comes with the territory of sharing their work, but cosplay has an added caveat: *You* are the final product. As cosplayers, we not only put our crafting abilities to the test; we present *ourselves* as part of the finished costume as well. Our faces, bodies, skin tones, and ethnicities are open to judgment along with the quality of our costumes. Because we are dressed up as these larger-than-life fictional characters, it can be easy to forget that cosplayers are real people with real feelings behind their disguises.

In the first few years that I cosplayed, I got super upset over negative comments. It got to the point where I would break down in tears in front of my computer. I couldn't understand why someone would go out of their way to hurt me. What did I ever do to them? They didn't even know me. Sometimes I would reply to comments on my photos in my defense, explaining why my shoes were not accurate or why I didn't wear a better wig. However, that only made things worse. My replies seemed to spur the critics on, and the subsequent comments would spiral out of control, into nasty expletives. Every time, my adrenaline would kick in and my heart would start beating rapidly. Feelings of hurt, anger, indignation, and dread all swirled together as I refreshed the screen and awaited the next reply—no . . . attack. My entire body would heat up while a cold shiver shot up my spine. The pounding in my ears would become so loud that I couldn't hear anything else.

It took a long time for me to understand that what I was encountering again and again was a form of abusive online behavior. There are some folks who are rude enough to make nasty comments to a cosplayer's face, but most of the time such criticism happens anonymously—or at least behind an online username or persona. In the cosplay and fandom world, we call this behavior *trolling*, and it has become a blanket term for all acts of negative commenting. Trolls are haters for no reason. Their purpose is to leave shitty comments that make you feel bad. There's no way to control them because they do it for fun and to anyone and everyone.

At least, that's what we tell ourselves.

"Don't feed the trolls" is a common saying amongst cosplayers. The implication is that ignoring the comments can solve all our problems. However, as I can tell you from personal experience, seeing those comments at all still takes a mental toll on you.

Let's be real here: We can't blame trolls for everything. The criticism we face as cosplayers is multilayered. It comes not only from trolls but also the general public and even from members of the cosplay community itself. These commenters single out factors such as not looking like a character, having the "wrong" body type for a cosplay, or wearing a costume that is not accurate enough. These kinds of remarks often stem from ignorance and misconceptions, and they are left in reply to cosplayers' social media posts with little regard for how they affect the people on the receiving end. In particular, being told you are the wrong race or gender to cosplay a character is deeply personal and painful because they are physical attributes that you can't do anything about.

With that in mind, I won't say "don't feed the trolls" to you. Rather, I want to explore the reasons behind these negative behaviors and then talk about how we can combat them within the cosplay community.

What drives most cosplayers is the desire to dress up as characters who inspire them. These characters usually originate from established pop culture titles. Many are created as mythical beings—they are gods, aliens, or super humans in peak physical shape with perfect facial features. In other words, they are a fantasy. Moreover, some of these characters have become significant beyond the works in which they're featured; they're cultural icons beloved by millions and familiar figures we grew up watching. At their best, some of them have helped us through dark times in our personal lives and continue to inspire us every day.

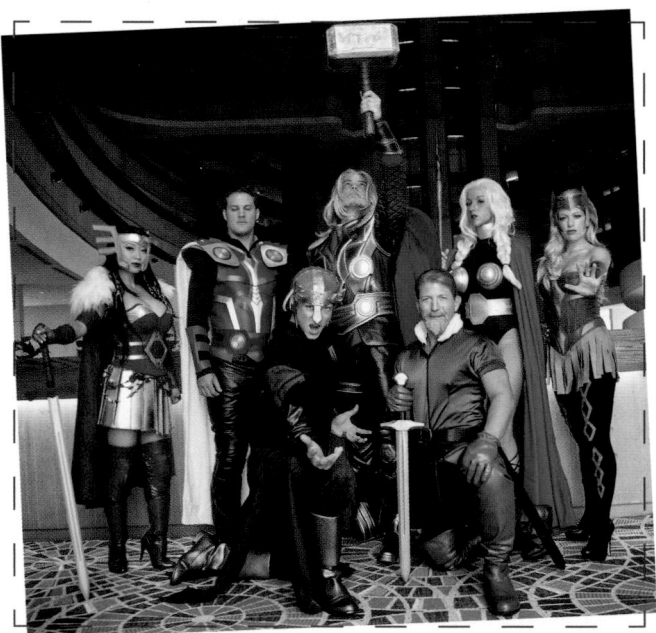

Group picture of Asgardians

It is completely normal for fans to develop feelings of ownership over a character. Hardcore fans know everything about their favorite characters, from their backstories to their motivations and their favorite foods. Of course, these fans also have an idealized image of what their favorite characters look like.

It is impossible to expect an average person to meet the standards of appearance set by digitally created characters. However, since cosplayers choose to emulate characters with such looks, I think it's easier to compare them to the original designs and point out differences. In some cases fans even feel as though they are defending the character's representation when they see a cosplayer's portrayal that doesn't match their internal idealized vision.

"You don't look like Wonder Woman" translates to "You don't represent Wonder Woman as I see her in my mind."

That is a comment I received, by the way. Word for word. While I definitely do not look like the traditional depiction of Wonder Woman in her statuesque and European-influenced Amazonian glory, at the time I was cosplaying the *Ame-Comi Girls* variation of her character. This look came from a line of collectible figures that drew design influence from Japanese anime. Not only was I criticized for being the "wrong" ethnicity to cosplay Wonder Woman; I was also criticized for wearing a costume the commenters thought was inaccurate but which actually reflected the fact that they had not seen the *Ame-Comi* design before.

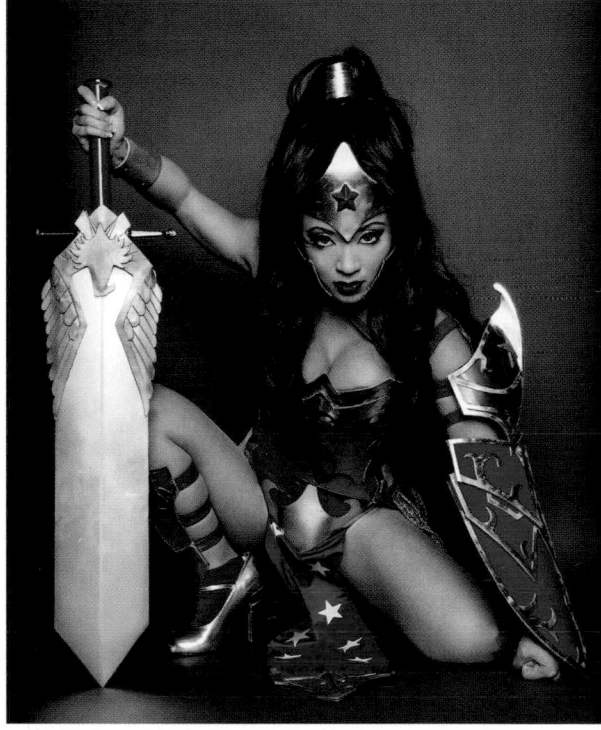

Cosplaying as Ame-Comi Wonder Woman

This brings me to my next point: accuracy. As I previously discussed in chapter 10, "Going Beyond Re-creations," there is a misconception that cosplay is all about accuracy and that the end goal is to replicate a costume and a character's look as closely as possible. The pressure to achieve such accuracy can hinder cosplayers more than help them, and 100-percent screen-accurate costumes sometimes require materials and tools that not everyone can access.

However, on a fundamental level, what does accuracy even mean in cosplay? Even if we only look at official canon character designs, there are endless versions and variations for many fictional characters. DC Comics' Batman, for example, has been depicted with dozens of different costumes throughout the years. They range from color-blocked spandex (Adam West) to a nipple-centric rubber suit (George Clooney) and even full-on metal tank-like armor (Ben Affleck). Beyond movies and television, there is the Square Enix Play Arts Kai figurine version of Batman, the design from the *Batman Ninja* animation that imagines Batman as a samurai, and the *Batman: Return of Bruce Wayne* comic series in which Batman is depicted as a historical figure throughout various time periods. None of this even gets into the fact that more and more cosplayers are now creating their own original designs and AU versions of characters.

Accuracy is in the eye of the beholder. Live-action film costume designs offer some clearer guidance than comics or animation when it comes to materials and how the final product could look in the real world, but you don't have to use the same exact materials or techniques to create the same look as the design you're taking as inspiration. One of my greatest joys as a cosplay contest judge is talking to contestants about the creative ways in which they make their costumes. I marvel at the ways they manipulate mundane materials such as foam to look like metal and papier-mâché to look like plastic. When it comes to translating a drawn design into a real, wearable garment, costumes embody a wide variety of interpretations. Different viewers might see the same anime, comic book, or video character designs and interpret them in entirely different ways because such designs are more abstract. Part of the fun of cosplay is that one character can inspire a hundred differently executed costumes that employ unique materials and crafting techniques. There is no right or wrong way to make a costume, and you can't enforce your perception of a character on to another person.

I'm here to remind us all that cosplay is a personal form of expression. It is not about who you look like but rather who you want to be. There is no difference between wearing a Captain America™ T-shirt or dressing up as Captain America; both fans are expressing their admiration for the character.

As cosplay continues to grow and expand, we need to keep an open mind and think of the new people joining our community. They are the most vulnerable to negativity. There are a few long-standing serious issues that have tested the cosplay community time and time again, so let's take a closer look at some of them and talk about how we can address the issues to make the cosplay community better.

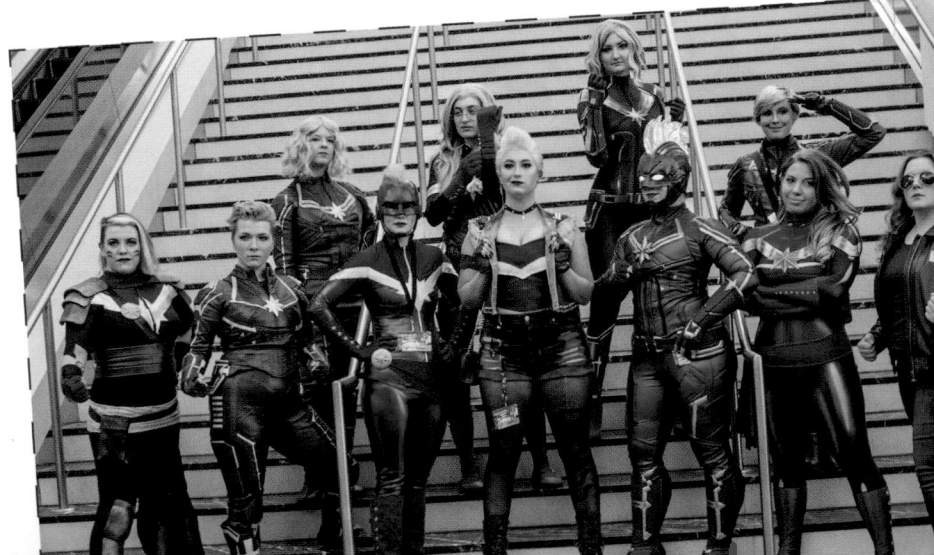

Group of Captain Marvel cosplayers with variations in their costume interpretations

CHAPTER 12

The Cosplay Body Issue

Why All Shapes Should Be Welcome

It was the last night of one of my favorite conventions. I was dressed in a red vinyl leotard with a cutout in the front that exposed my belly button, nude fishnet stockings à la Folies Bergère, and shiny red stiletto heels. A pair of fuzzy bunny ears sat on top of my fuchsia wig,

and there was a matching ball of floof sewn to the back of my bodysuit. I looked the part of an anime *Playboy* bunny because I was cosplaying the classic magical girl Misty May, a character from the 1980s anime *Otaku no Video*.

It was 2008, and I'd been working hard to build up my cosplay business, traveling to cons around the country as a cosplay guest. Cosplay had become a job for me, so I had a hard time reconciling where the work stopped and the fun began at conventions. However, I was looking forward to a weekend of just hanging out at this particular event.

The location of interconnected hotels made it easy for attendees to change in and out of costume. I loved being able to put on an outfit, walk out of my room, and be at the con without ever having to leave the hotel premises. In the evenings, long after the exhibit halls closed, the convention would turn into a costume party. Clad in my cute bunny ensemble, I was eager to enjoy the last night of the con with other costumed friends. At the main con hotel, a group of us were standing around a few sofa chairs in the open atrium. The space was filled

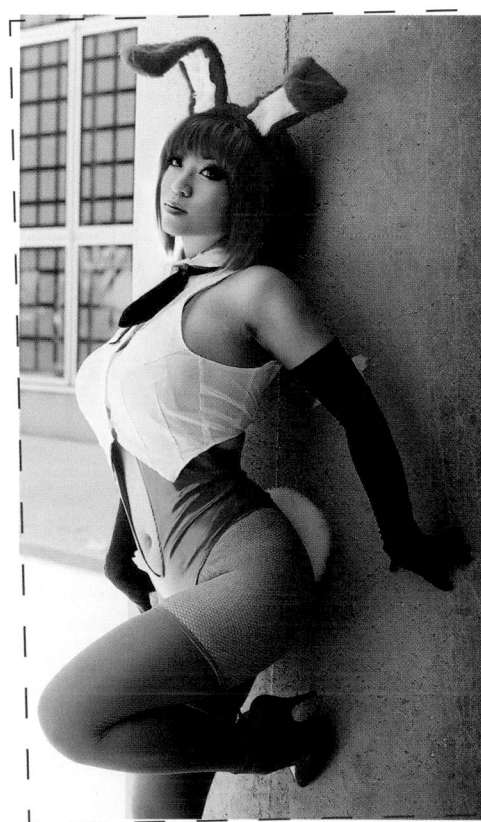

My Misty May cosplay

with fellow cosplayers and attendees who were enjoying their evening just like we were. I was talking to my friend James, a six-foot-three well-built guy, when a man I didn't know kneeled down to talk to another friend in the sofa chair in front of us.

Then, all of a sudden, the stranger turned to me, wrapped both his arms around my butt, and put his face between my legs.

For a second, no one moved. I was in complete shock as I looked down at the man's bald head pressed against my body. I did not remember pushing him off me, but I must have, because the next thing I heard was James telling him in a stern voice, "You need to leave. Now."

And he did. He vanished into the crowd, leaving me stunned in a roaring hall of people.

— — —

I wish I could say that this is the only time someone touched me inappropriately while I was in costume. However, it is not. This particular incident sticks out in my mind, though, even a decade later. I prided myself on being a sensible person. My costume, revealing as it was, had more coverage than a bathing suit. I wore it in the evening, long after families with kids had left the convention location. I made sure to walk around with a group rather than by myself, and we were in a space full of people who were also wearing costumes. On top of all this, I was already a well-known figure in the cosplay community, so I thought my recognizability gave me an additional layer of protection.

I thought I was in a safe environment.

This incident happened when I least expected it. For a while, I questioned if I'd brought it upon myself. Should I not have dressed as Misty May? Should I have known that the late-night environment meant alcohol and lowered inhibitions? Should I have been more aware of the people around me and fended him off before he could grab me?

Of course, the answer to all these questions is no.

If you are a parent, please do not put this book down and forbid your child from cosplaying. I do not share my story in order to scare anyone off from cosplay. Rather, I want to be honest about all aspects of the community, good and bad, so we can talk about why things happen and how you can deal with uncomfortable situations. By and large, cosplay is a very safe and positive activity, but the same passion that brings out the best in people can also make some of them forget common sense.

What happened to me is part of a deep-rooted problem that I call *The Cosplay Body Issue*. In simple terms, some people think that because you are cosplaying, your body does not belong to you. As such, it is free to be judged, criticized, and even touched without permission.

Cosplayers embody the characters they dress up as and create a buzz of excitement when someone sees them in the flesh, because to the viewer, their favorite character is walking through the convention halls rather than an actual person. That perception, combined with the party-like atmosphere of a convention environment, can inspire a fantastical feeling in some people that makes them think they can disregard normal etiquette and ignore societal standards. Over the years, as conventions became bigger, incidents like mine became more apparent, but the community did not ignore these issues. We wrote about our experiences. We condemned people like the man who groped me. We raised awareness with a clear message: Cosplay does not equal consent.

In 2012, after years of speaking up, the Cosplay Is Not Consent movement was born. It started with cosplayers holding up handwritten signs at cons and making blog posts. Then it evolved into viral memes, web articles, and media interviews. In 2014, New York Comic Con implemented the Cosplay =/= Consent clause into its official rules and posted large anti-harassment signs throughout the event. Since then, hundreds of fandom cons in North America and other parts of the world have adapted similar policies, reminding attendees to treat cosplayers with respect and common courtesy. They also define the repercussions of inappropriate behavior. While harassment has not yet been eradicated, the awareness and support from official events has helped to reduce the amount of it that goes on at conventions.

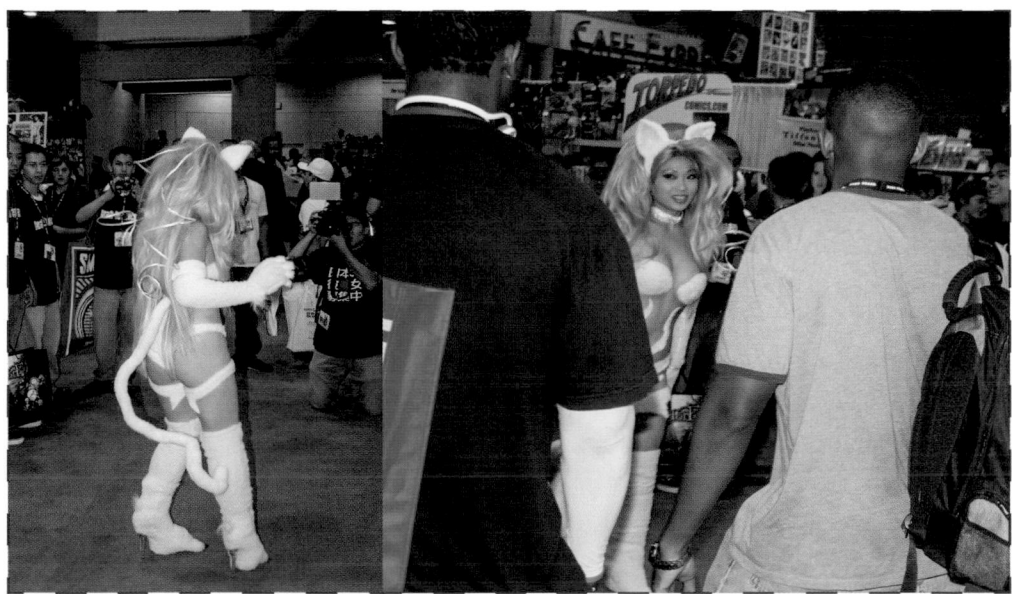

Walking around SDCC as Felicia from *Darkstalkers*.

Sexual harassment within cosplay is not limited to convention halls, though. A lot of it happens online.

People are a lot bolder behind a computer screen, and it's nearly impossible to regulate Internet comments. Conventions have security staff on site, visible Cosplay =/= Consent signage, and clearly spelled-out anti-harassment rules. If you touch someone at a convention, you will be removed from the premises and banned from the event and you could face potential legal penalties. On the Internet, there are no real consequences for people who make disparaging comments, which leaves more openings for bad behavior.

In the modern age of social media platforms, inappropriate sexual comments are rampant. I have had to deal with sexual comments more than any other kind of criticism. They come in all forms imaginable, ranging from attempts to be clever to making lewd suggestions, being crude, or simply making downright pornographic statements. I've gotten comments that go into great detail about my body and what the commenter would like to do to me.

What I find most perplexing about this phenomenon is the complete disconnect between the commenter and the person on the receiving end. A lot of men leave sexual comments and think they are paying cosplayers a compliment by doing so. It's as if they believe we should feel flattered by their words. Their mentality is that we asked for it. We chose to wear revealing costumes. We chose to pose in provocative ways. We chose to cosplay a character that is a man-eater in the show. By choosing to use sex appeal, we have lost the right to be treated with common courtesy or dignity. And if you're a cosplayer who's being paid to portray these characters, whether you were hired by a company or you posted a shoot for your Patreon supporters, then some people feel even more entitled.

All too quickly, this type of criticism can devolve into slut shaming, which is when a person is said to be inviting harassment because of the way they dress or act.

"Whore."

"Bitch."

"Slut."

Those are just a handful of the words I've had to block from my Facebook page throughout the years. Slut shaming is not focused on the content put forth but on the person creating the content. The judgment is made on the cosplayer's character, motivation, and sense of decency. It is character assassination, and it can come from both men and women. When I get comments like "I wish you would stop sexualizing everything" or "Typical Yaya, another tits-out costume," it hurts a lot more to see that a woman left it.

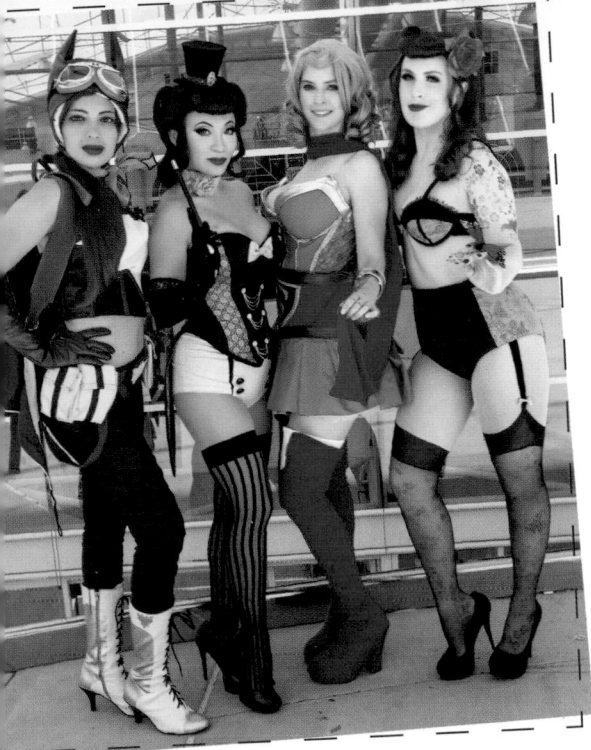

Group of DC Comics *Bombshells* cosplayers

You'd think that women would understand one another and want to build one another up, but oftentimes, women are harder on one another in regard to what they consider inappropriate or obscene. Maybe it is because they assume a female cosplayer who uses sex appeal is degrading themselves (and therefore all women). Perhaps it is because society has convinced them of what is deemed "too sexy." Either way, the anti-lewd cosplay issue is more often than not perpetuated by women.

This is poignant because cosplay has become one of the few industries in the world where women dominate. The most well-known and successful cosplayers are women. They have more likes, more followers, and more brand power. It's not just that there are more female cosplayers; women are shared more, photographed more, and featured by media outlets more often than men. A good portion of the most visible cosplay content depicts attractive young women in tantalizing costumes.

But that exposure comes with a price.

It's not just sexual harassment that cosplayers deal with; they're faced with more general judgment of their bodies as well. One of the most pervasive forms of harassment in the cosplay community is body shaming. Like slut shaming, it primarily happens on the Internet and is thus

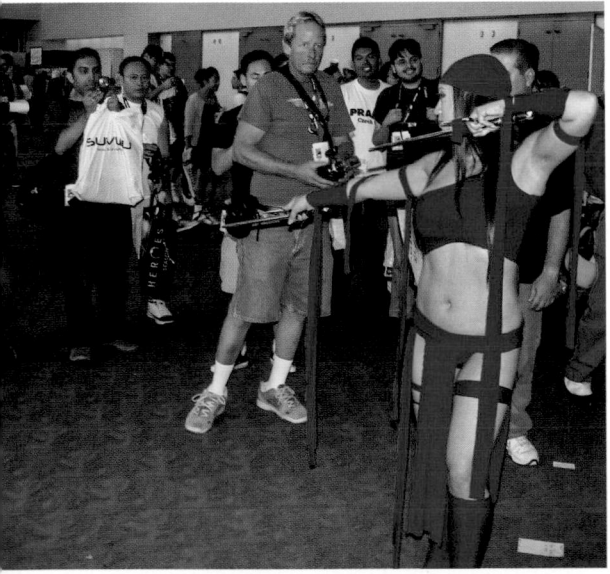

Posing for photos in my Elektra cosplay

hard to fight head-on. It may not sound as severe or damaging as getting touched in person, but body shaming is another form of harassment. The mind-set that leads someone to think it's okay to grab cosplayers also gives them the incentive to body shame them. Women at large are overwhelmingly affected by all types of body shaming, and it's a problem that has become more unyielding and toxic over the years.

The most transparent form of body shaming is fat shaming. Plus-size cosplayers are routinely accused of ruining a character. They are mocked as "fun house mirror versions" of the characters they cosplay or are called heinous things for simply having the body they do. What's worst about fat shaming in particular is that because society in general undeniably looks down upon plus-size people, it has become normalized to not only mock them online but in person and in the media as well. Even though we know that it is not morally right to make fun of someone's body, the unspoken mentality is that being overweight is abnormal and something to be ashamed of. Within the landscape of cosplay, with the unreasonably high expectations placed on cosplayers to resemble the characters they portray, fat shaming is so common that it's often treated like a joke instead of a hurtful offense.

A big part of the problem is that people do not consider what plus-size cosplayers go through to even be in our community. To start, there are not a lot of overweight characters in pop culture. Titles tend to feature characters with slim, fit body types at the center while relegating overweight characters to being sidekicks, villains, or comedic relief. Such stereotyping might make it harder for cosplayers to find inspiration in those characters, especially if they are already insecure about their bodies. As a result, many plus-size cosplayers end up inevitably cosplaying someone who isn't their body type, such as the hero of a series, and they have to do so with the knowledge that as soon as they put on the costume, they'll be perceived as inaccurate to someone in the community.

Beyond the mental hurdles plus-size cosplayers have to go through, when it comes to physically creating costumes, cosplayers are at a disadvantage if they are above a certain size. There are a limited number of plus-size sewing patterns, armor templates, and tutorials available. It's inherently difficult to figure out how to make a costume, but imagine having no usable instructions or blueprints to help get you started! Even if you do manage to construct your costume, if you decide to buy extra components such as boots or gloves, you'll find a limited selection of articles available in larger sizes. There is a booming market of mass-produced and ready-to-wear costumes as well as a larger number of geek-centric clothing collections. However, the available size ranges of both these types of products is often limited, too.

Imagine working your way through all of these barriers only to be met with ridicule. Plus-size cosplayers deserve our admiration and support for overcoming all of the barriers they face and for adding more diversity to the fandom, rather than being on the receiving end of lame jokes.

On the opposite end of the spectrum, thin cosplayers are also shamed for how they look. In sum, these comments create a never-ending cycle of body shaming where if you're plus-size then you're rudely told to lose weight, but if you appear too thin for someone's taste you are told to eat a burger or are accused of being too obsessive about exercising.

If we want to make the cosplay community more welcoming and accessible, we need to show that all types of cosplay and all kinds of bodies are accepted. Thankfully, the body positivity movement has been embraced by many cosplayers in recent years and we are making strides in raising awareness on the issue. At many conventions, you can attend panel discussions about body positivity, women in cosplay, and diversity in cosplay. Cosplayers frequently write online articles to deliver the message that cosplay is for everyone. Many also share memes about welcoming all body types. There are community websites for plus-size cosplayers, as well as Facebook Groups and Pages celebrating plus-size cosplay. Hashtags such as #PlusSizeCosplay and #CosplayAnyway can be found across various social media platforms such as Instagram and Twitter.

Aside from curtailing the shaming of women for how they choose to dress or how their bodies look, we should also recognize the sources of inspiration for cosplayers and accept that sexuality is ingrained in fandom culture as a whole.

Most comic books, video games, and films depict male protagonists as strong and powerful, while women are shown as more sensual and sexually pleasing. The entertainment industry has always been dominated by heterosexual/cisgender white men, and it shows in the kind of characters we traditionally see in media. Many female characters designed by men appear as femme fatales, man-eating vamps who ensnare male victims with their sexual charms, ditzy blond damsels who need to be saved by men, or any number of age-old sexist tropes that have been discussed, analyzed, and called out countless times.

That said, a female character can be both sexy and empowering. *Tomb Raider*'s Lara Croft is a perfect example of a feminist icon who is also a heterosexual male's sexual fantasy. The film character Jessica Rabbit from *Who Framed Roger Rabbit* was created specifically to subvert the tropes that are often built into the personalities of sexualized characters. With her exaggerated and curvaceous animated figure, clad in a sequin dress that's barely there and crooning to a bar full of men, Jessica Rabbit initially appears to be the ultimate male fantasy. As the movie goes on, though, we find out that she is a devoted wife in love with a rabbit because he makes her laugh. She's a woman with agency who's capable of saving the male characters in the story. In the film she even points out that her appearance leads to assumptions and certain negative perceptions, with the brilliant line "I'm not bad. I'm just drawn that way."

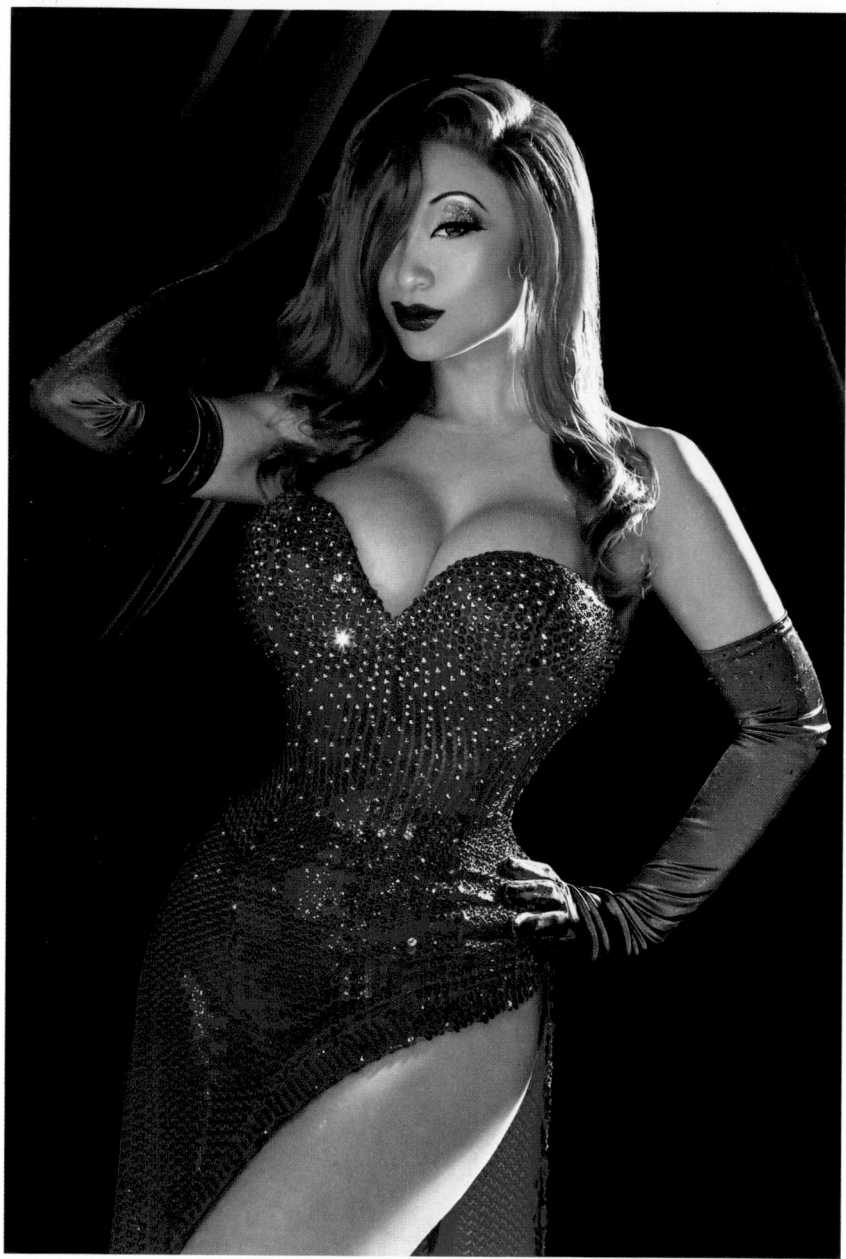

Posing in my Jessica Rabbit cosplay

Growing up, I always loved Jessica Rabbit. When I finally cosplayed her in 2012, when the movement to make Cosplay =/= Consent into official policy was the loudest, it was another way for me to deliver the movement's message. Just because I was wearing a sexy costume didn't mean I was bad.

Women don't dress up to please someone else. They do it for themselves. By dressing up as a character who you consider beautiful, confident, courageous, and, yes, sexy, you can find the strength to embrace those qualities within yourself. The first time I wore a revealing costume, I thought I would feel very self-conscious and uncomfortable in my crisscross bandage top, because it was something I never would have worn in everyday life. Instead, dressed as the character Mill from the anime *Maze*, who is a boisterous, upbeat, funny princess who doesn't take any shit from anyone, I felt a sense of confidence. For the first time in my life, I actually liked the way my body looked.

Cosplay can be incredibly empowering in unexpected ways. In my opinion, creating sexy cosplay content based on existing characters is no more scandalous than fan artists creating NSFW fan art or fan fiction writers creating explicit fanfics. If it makes someone happy, let them do it. That said, I do believe that proper supervision and guidance should be given to underage cosplayers and that the line must be drawn at pedophilic and extremely violent content.

Within sensible moral parameters, we should encourage as much diversity and creativity as possible.

— — —

After I was groped that evening, I immediately went back to my room and changed out of the bunny suit. I did not go back out that night or cosplay the next day. I never saw the perpetrator again. I did not report the incident to any security staff, partially because this was in the days before Cosplay =/= Consent and I didn't think of it as an option. I didn't even tell my friends after the con because in that time, we all knew that being touched inappropriately was a risk that came with the territory of dressing up in costume.

This is an incident I've never forgotten and probably never will, but it hasn't stopped me from cosplaying who I want and how I want. Looking back on it, I can say, without a shadow of a doubt, that being grabbed like that had *nothing* to do with the fact that I was in a costume. What I experienced is no different than the experiences of women who are catcalled, whispered about at work, touched in public, or followed around while trying to live their everyday lives. Sexual harassment is a global gender equality issue that permeates all facets of society, and only recently have we awoken to the fact that it is a daily reality for women (and men) working in the entertainment industry, in information technology, and even in politics. Movements like #MeToo and #TimesUp have exposed a lot of underlying abusive factors in society that, for so long, were normalized and brushed aside. It is important to recognize that body image issues and harassment affect not only women but men as well, so these movements are helpful to all parties.

There is still a long road ahead, but the added pressure to include more women in the entertainment industry has create more diverse characters and more forward-thinking stories. We finally have two top-grossing female superhero movies in *Wonder Woman* and *Captain Marvel*. *Black Panther* gave us an entire army of female warriors to admire—not to mention a black main cast. Women involved in the reboots of titles such as *She-Ra and the Princesses of Power* and *Batgirl* have redesigned their costumes in more realistic and functional ways. These examples of empowered females are inspirations for the cosplay community. They speak to us, and we are answering their calls.

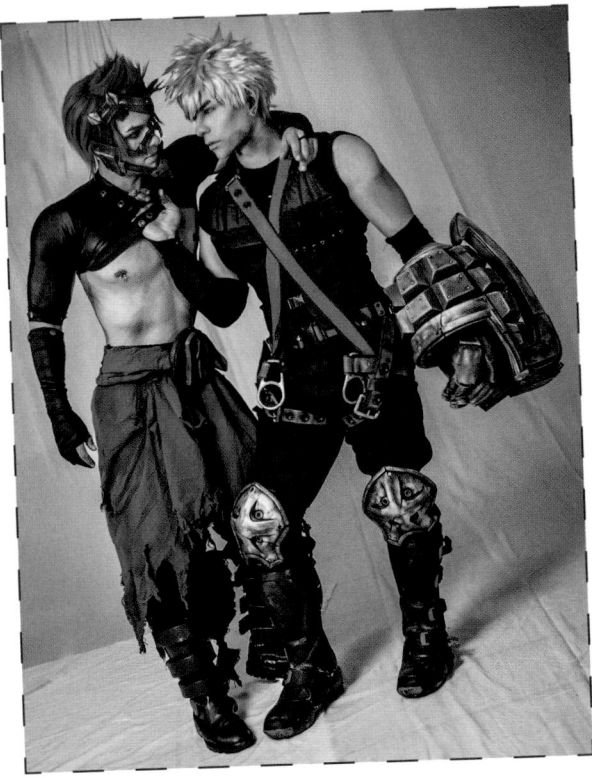

Two male cosplayers as characters from *My Hero Academia*.

Beyond large-scale movements such as Cosplay Is Not Consent and body positivity, the cosplay community comes together to vigilantly defend its members and shut down body shaming and sexist comments on a daily basis. I want every cosplayer to know: You are not alone. You can call out bad behavior when you see it. If a person makes you uncomfortable at an event, tell someone. Stay positive, and don't stop doing what makes you happy. The power of the cosplay community is that we all share the same passion. We all deserve the same freedom to enjoy this lifestyle.

CHAPTER 13

Racism and Blackface in Cosplay

The Things We Don't Want to Talk About

There is a big, ugly, and open wound on the face of cosplay. It oozes and stings and has never healed. As toxic as slut shaming, this wound is inflicted on a large and marginalized group that crosses all ages and genders.

I'm talking about racism and blackface in cosplay.

Cosplay is a global phenomenon, and as such, our community is populated by people of all ethnicities and skin colors living in all corners of the world. With cosplay becoming more and more popular, the issue of race has come to the forefront—specifically when it comes to the standards of accuracy some people hold others to when they portray characters through the art form. As we previously discussed, the mind-set of many fans is to idolize fictional characters, and so they feel protective of them. Unfortunately, the same prejudices that are applied against plus-size cosplayers can extend to POC (people of color) cosplayers as well.

I am not black, but I know the feeling of "otherness" all too well. I am Chinese, which is arguably the most stereotyped Asian minority, and I grew up amongst Europeans in a country with a 2-percent Asian population. On playgrounds, kids shouted "ching chang chong" at me. At school, classmates pulled their eyelids into slanted shapes and talked to me in a mock-Chinese accent. As an adult, I've had people catcall at me by saying, "Me love you long time" or "Two dolla make you holla!"

Much like every other form of discrimination I have faced, racism followed me into the cosplay community. I've gotten used to comments such as "Sorry [insert character] is not Asian." When I cosplayed Snow White, I was called "Snow Yellow." Once, someone even called me "sweet-and-sour chicken" from a passing truck while I was in full costume doing a photoshoot. After receiving so many stale comments, I couldn't help but laugh at that one. At least it was unique in its own terrible way.

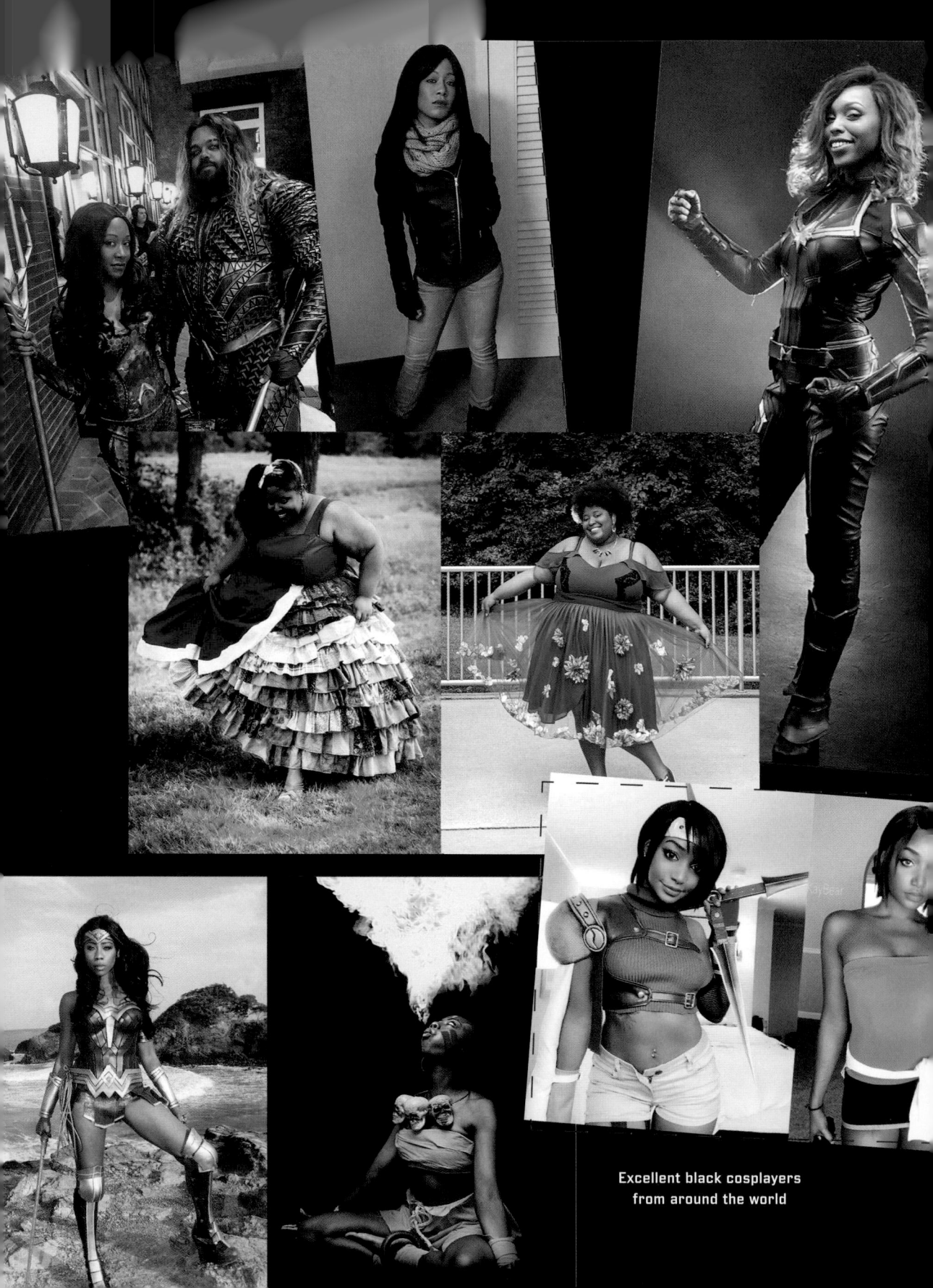

Excellent black cosplayers
from around the world

However, any racist remarks I have received are nothing compared to the vitriol that black cosplayers have to face on a daily basis. I get singled out for my ethnicity and cultural heritage but not for the color of my skin. Every single time a black cosplayer steps out onto a con floor or makes a post on social media, they must brace themselves against the most deplorable and horrible commentary imaginable.

As cosplayer Chaka Cumberbatch-Tinsley puts it, "When I cosplayed Sailor Venus from *Sailor Moon*, I received alternating slurs like 'N-word' and 'Ghetto Venus' for years." Writer and cosplayer Brichibi notes that black cosplayers are often called "monkey/ape/gorilla" version of the characters they portray or receive stereotypical comments about "eating watermelon or fried chicken." Kay Bear has posted screenshots of comments directed at her after her Jill Valentine cosplay blew up on Reddit. They included lines such as "How dirty" and "Hey look, it's Dark Jill."

The reason so many of us cosplay is that it gives us the freedom to be whoever we want while still feeling content in our own skin. Black cosplayers do not have that luxury, though. From the get-go they are out of their element, because they have to reach beyond their communities to socialize in a scene that is mainly inhabited by people with light skin. On top of that, the number of dark-skinned characters in entertainment is pitifully low. That means that black cosplayers often have to cosplay characters who do not share their ethnicity and take on costume projects while knowing they will be ridiculed for doing so.

On top of being a minority in the cosplay community, black cosplayers are also less visible—and I mean that in the literal sense. In recent years, the lack of representation of black cosplayers online has been especially noticeable. Whether it's in convention photo galleries, interview features with media outlets, or guest invitations to cons, most cosplayers highlighted in our community are not black. This does not suggest that the media consciously avoids black cosplayers. Rather, the invisibility of black cosplayers mirrors the experience of black people in the real world.

In a community that has always been a refuge for misfits, it seems insane to think that cosplayers are out there being racist toward one another, especially given the globality and diversity of the scene. However, extremist views exist in every corner of our society, and just because we cosplay does not mean there aren't those in the cosplay community who share such views. Some people do leave racially charged comments on cosplayers' posts, and when those obvious incidents of hate occur, we can confidently and loudly condemn them as morally wrong. Just as we shouldn't fat shame cosplayers, we should also not mock anyone for their race.

However, how should we handle racism that is born not of hate but of ignorance? What should we do when we encounter something that is done with good intentions but causes harm, such as blackface?

Blackface is the practice of using makeup or paint to darken one's skin tone in order to emulate another face. In the United States, it was historically used by slave owners and slave trade supporters to mock the black population. This practice persisted long past the Civil War into the twentieth century and has only become taboo in recent decades. Around the globe, blackface continues to show up in comedy shows in Asia and during the Dutch Krampus celebration in Europe each Christmas. The historical implications of blackface are severe enough to render the practice immoral and place it alongside the N-word and the Nazi salute as things you cannot do because they are considered morally wrong.

Today, whenever you hear about blackface in the media, the practitioners usually attribute its usage to racial ignorance. A celebrity might dress up as a black character for Halloween, or a major animation studio might license a mass-retail brown bodysuit kids' costume for release. Every once in a while, a politician's old blackface photos surface from past yearbooks. These incidents create public outrage, and in response, the brands or personalities getting called out usually apologize for their ignorance, pull down the products and photos in question, and denounce the act of blackface to the world.

However, in the cosplay community, the response to blackface is a bit more complicated.

You see, people from around the world use makeup or tanning products in order to cosplay dark-skinned characters from anime, video games, and comic books. Whether it's Anthy Himemiya from *Revolutionary Girl Utena*, Sombra from *Overwatch*, or Storm from *X-Men*, this type of blackface has been present in cosplay for decades, and it is one of the most incendiary topics discussed by the community. The rationalization behind darkening skin tones for cosplay is usually a variation of one or more of the following statements:

"I want to portray the character accurately."

"I think the character's dark skin is beautiful, and I want to pay homage to it."

"I mean no harm to others by darkening my skin tone."

"There is no difference between painting myself blue, green, or brown."

I have lost count of how many times I've heard these statements. The arguments for and against blackface are heated, the comment threads centered around the topic are lengthy, and at the end of the day everyone is left hurt and angry with no solution in sight. Every few months, a post of a cosplayer in dark makeup goes viral and the same vicious cycle repeats itself.

Why do we go through the same frustrating discussions over and over again? What is it about blackface that sets off such polarizing opinions within the cosplay community?

The main argument for the continued practice of blackface in cosplay is that if it is done for the sake of cosplaying a character, it is not a racist gesture. As a note, some cosplayers use the term *blackfacing* colloquially during discourse and arguments, as if to differentiate the act from the traditional, historical practice. I've seen cosplayers who were called out for blackface look visibly hurt and confused by the accusation. Others have responded with indignation and anger. Either way, they overwhelmingly insist that they had no intention to cause harm with their actions. They did not darken their skin to mock black people. On the contrary, they say that they chose to cosplay Michonne, the katana-wielding character from *The Walking Dead*, or Katara, the waterbender from *Avatar: The Last Airbender*, because they admire the chosen character and want to pay homage to them. They love these characters and want to do the best job possible in portraying them. To these cosplayers, the kind of blackface that white comedians practiced in the 1920s during minstrel shows in order to ridicule black people is the opposite of what they are doing by darkening their skin for a costume. These cosplayers' *intentions* are to celebrate POC characters and even to raise awareness for them.

Besides, such cosplayers argue, cosplay is about having fun. These characters are not real people, so no harm is inflicted on anyone, right?

Here's the problem with this argument: There are no real people with green skin on Earth, so painting yourself green to play an alien, such as Gamora from *Guardians of the Galaxy*, indeed does not hurt anyone. However, there are billions of dark-skinned people living in the world. Emulating a living race through cosplay does have real-world implications, regardless of whether or not the source material is fictional.

As progressive and diverse as our society may seem these days, the battle for racial equality is an ongoing one that has raged since the dawn of civilization. Human history has been shaped by prejudice against darker skin colors. Countries have been invaded. Wars have been waged. Genocide has been committed. Western colonialism has forever changed human history. Even though modern society has learned from the past and there are laws in place against outright racism, racial injustice still exists today.

Light skin is considered the norm in our society. When your identity exists within what is considered the norm, it's easy to think you don't see colors and to avoid being reminded of how far the gap is between yourself and those who fall outside society's standards. For a white or light-skinned person, the tone of their skin has no relevance on their quality of life because it is considered normal to be white. The concept of being discriminated against based on skin color is foreign to them. For a black person, though, their skin tone is their identity. They are acutely aware of it because it affects every day of their lives, often in negative ways. No amount of makeup or costuming will make them forget that they are black.

By darkening your skin tone to emulate another real human race, whether it is African, Native American, or Pacific Islander, you are pointing out to an entire marginalized group of your peers that for you, skin tone is interchangeable. It highlights the fact that you can choose to wear someone else's skin tone for one day to enjoy your cosplay without having to experience the negativity that marginalized people often have to live with. While you can take off the makeup at night, members of the group you are imitating cannot wash away their own skin tones. A white cosplayer might see dark makeup as no different than putting in colored contacts or using a wig to change their appearance, but it can come across as mockery to people of color.

Borrowing someone's skin tone is not only insensitive; it also diminishes the visibility of that person. Just look at Hollywood. For decades, white actors have played POC characters, severely limiting the opportunities for minority actors to build careers and to stretch beyond racially stereotyped supporting roles. Even though the entertainment industry has made strides toward inclusion, this disparity continues to this day.

As a member of the Asian minority community in America, I'm drawn toward Asian characters in mainstream media. When you see yourself represented in a public forum, you get to feel pride for and acceptance of who you are. I cosplayed Lady Deathstrike from *X2* and Gogo Yubari from *Kill Bill* not only because I loved the characters themselves but also because they were played by Asian actresses. For black cosplayers, a fictional character like Miles Morales from *Spider-Man: Into the Spider-Verse* is a representation of hope and greatness for black people in a world that has not always been kind to them. Seeing dark-skinned characters rise above age-old stereotypes, kick ass, and be celebrated as heroes gives people who look like them more strength to go out and face real-world challenges.

When someone darkens their skin to cosplay a POC character, can you blame a black cosplayer for wondering, "Why are you cosplaying this character when you already have so many options?" When a white cosplayer in dark makeup is praised for "perfectly pulling off" a character, can you imagine how insignificant a black cosplayer dressed as the same character must feel? This is why blackface is a double-whammy insult for so many people in our community. The practice not only borrows their skin color but also reminds them of their inability to fit in.

Representation matters. Just ask marginalized fandom groups such as plus-size cosplayers and LGBTQ+ cosplayers. Like them, black cosplayers are fighting for a safe and open space to express themselves. In an effort to raise awareness and to shine a positive light on the black cosplay community, people have started multiple movements that highlight cosplayers from this minority group. #28DaysOfBlackCosplay was created by Chaka Cumberbatch-Tinsley after she endured years of ridicule for her costumes. Every February,

Group photo of black cosplayers at Dragon Con; trio of *Black Panther* cosplayers; spear-holding cosplayers being filmed

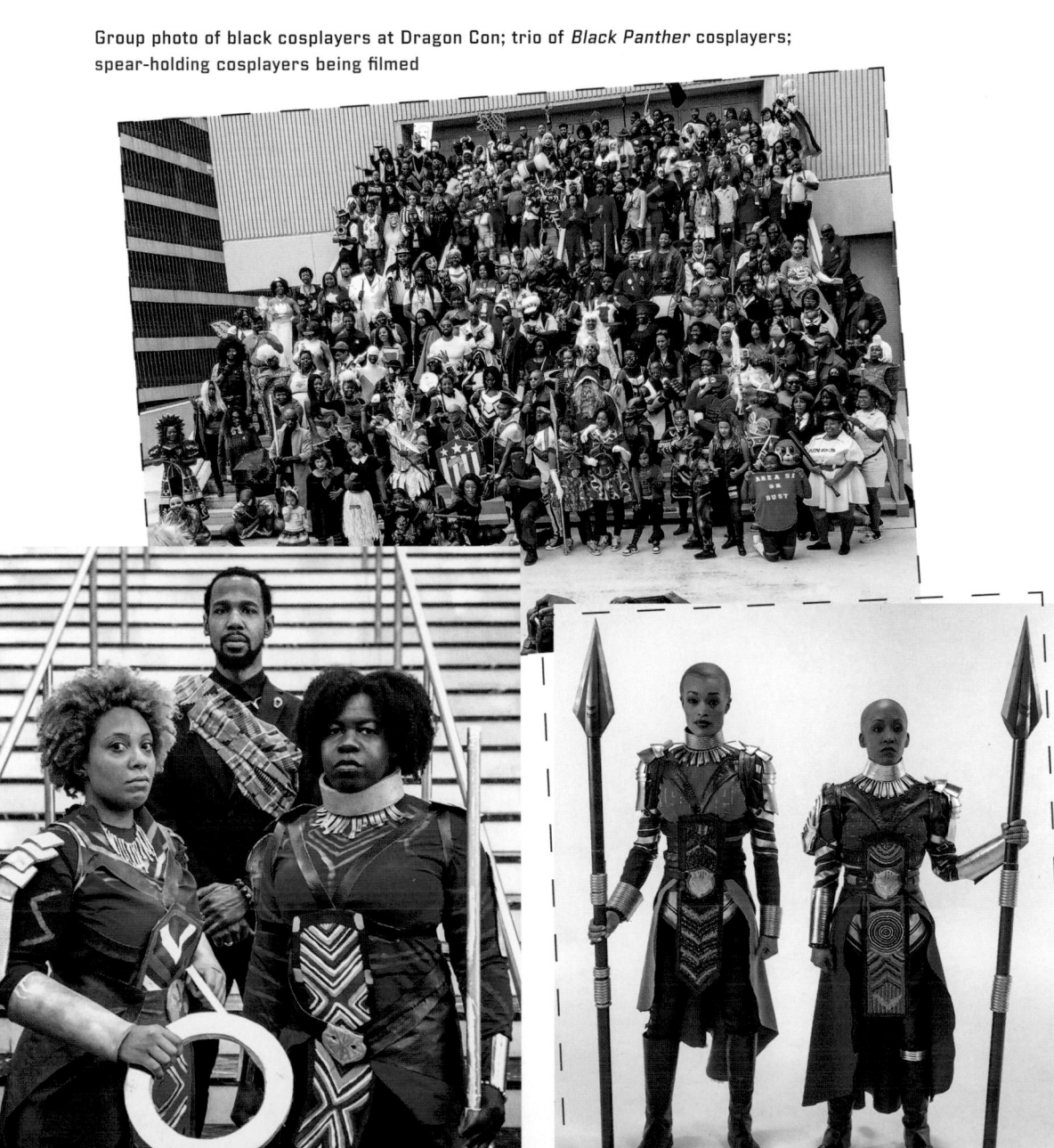

in celebration of Black History Month, the hashtag highlights black cosplayers and encourages the cosplay community at large to share, repost, and follow members of the group. The year 2019 marked the fifth anniversary for the hashtag. Meanwhile, #BlackCosplayerHere was started by Belema Boyle in 2018 in response to the idea that black cosplayers were a rarity in the community. Since then, cosplayers like Petite Ebby Cosplay have made entire databases of black cosplayers where people can find and follow their work.

These efforts move at a slow pace, and many black cosplayers feel hopeless about the situation, believing that the cosplay community will never become truly tolerant and welcoming toward them. But there has been progress. Movements like the ones described have led to more photographers making an effort to post black cosplayers in their galleries. They have also led to greater diversity in cosplay guests who get invited to cons. Together, we can continue to rally against exclusion and underrepresentation.

At the same time, it is so important for us to face more ambiguous and complicated issues such as blackface, even if they are unpleasant to deal with.

After years of observation and interactions with people in the cosplay community, I don't believe that cosplayers who darken their skin for cosplay are inherently racist. Rather, I think they don't understand what effects their actions have on others. It's ignorance. Racism is a nasty, ugly, and awful concept of which no one wants to be considered a proponent.

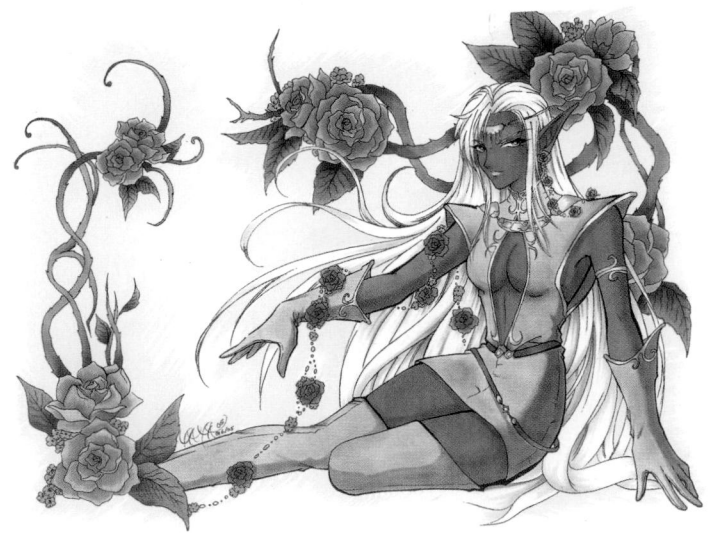

My colored pencil drawing of the character Pirotess

The most important thing I have learned about racism is that it is not a hard line but a gradient. There are degrees and tiers to racial bias, and most of the time the acts that stem from such bias are unintentional and invisible. The mind-set behind blackface, in cosplay specifically, resembles cultural ignorance more than outright racism, so we should not lump them together or condemn them at the same level.

There was a time when I did not understand the real-world implications of blackface, too. In 2002, I considered one of my dream costumes to be Pirotess from *Record of Lodoss War*. This character is a dark elf with brown skin and white-blond hair. I loved her fiercely and plotted out her costume in detail, even going as far as to buy boots and fabric for the project. For various reasons, I never got around to cosplaying Pirotess, but if I had made the costume . . . the Yaya back then would have been fully ready and prepared to darken her skin for it.

In the years following this, however, the more black cosplayers I befriended, the more I recognized the severity of their daily plight. I learned how naive I was to even consider emulating their skin tone. My friend Celia made her cosplay moniker "Blikku," as in black Rikku (her favorite character from *Final Fantasy X-2* and her first costume), as if to tell the world to stop making the same predictable comments every time she posted a photo. It was hard to watch Celia struggle with all the negativity thrown at her. At the same time, I was amazed at her strength to continue cosplaying whatever characters she wanted. In 2012, when we posed together as Snow White and Esmeralda in a Disney group, neither of us matched the characters' ethnicities, and both of us were made aware of that in the comments, but that didn't matter. We had fun together.

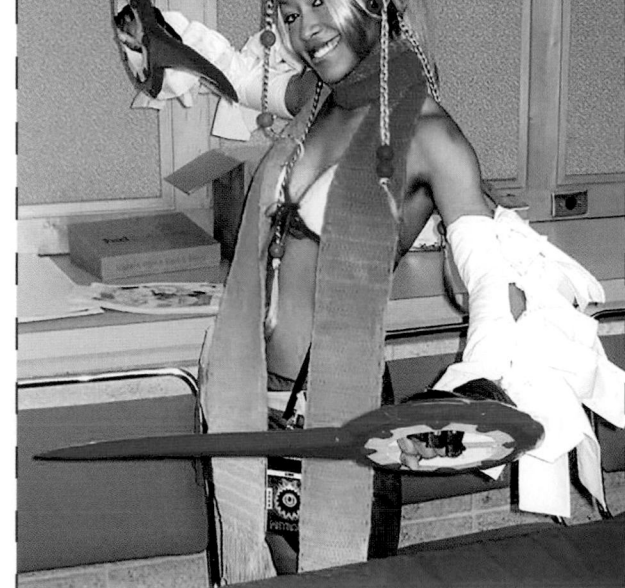

Blikku in her Rikku costume

I thank my lucky stars that I never made a dark elf Pirotess costume with the naive mind-set I once had. I daresay, most cosplayers who have darkened their skin in the past also never considered the message it sent. It takes time and effort to fully grasp the nuances of racial issues. It's even harder to differentiate between ignorance born out of privilege and deliberately hateful actions.

I think the reason why the topic of blackface catches cosplayers off guard is that cosplay is truly a global phenomenon. Social media platforms create the illusion that we cosplayers are all the same, no matter where in the world we live—we take the same selfies, we watch the same shows, and we cosplay the same characters. Everyone in cosplay has a global audience online, so no matter where a black cosplayer lives, their photos are seen everywhere in the world and are free to be commented on by anyone. A white cosplayer in one part of the world can post a photo of themselves with darkened skin and be seen by countless black cosplayers in another part of the world.

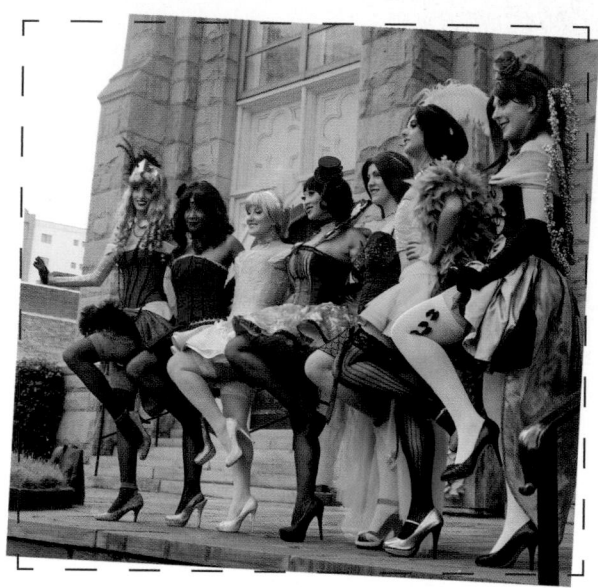

Celia and I in the Disney princess group

Just as you can experience culture shock when you visit another country, I think blackface in cosplay is so explosive because people with very different day-to-day lives are meeting in a virtual space and are not prepared for a "real-life issue" to collide with their recreational outlet.

As someone who grew up in three distinctly different countries, I know how much one's cultural environment can affect their view on the world. Each country and culture also has to deal with its own prejudices and marginalized groups, whether they are based on skin tone or otherwise. In all my years living as a minority in a predominantly white culture, I have learned that many privileged people do not see their lives as privileged because they have also experienced prejudice for things about their identities besides race. These can range from being bullied for being "scrawny" or "redneck" and extend all the way to outright hatred for their sexual orientation or religion. It can be hard to see beyond your own problems and relate to other people, especially when they are asking you to give up something that you see as harmless.

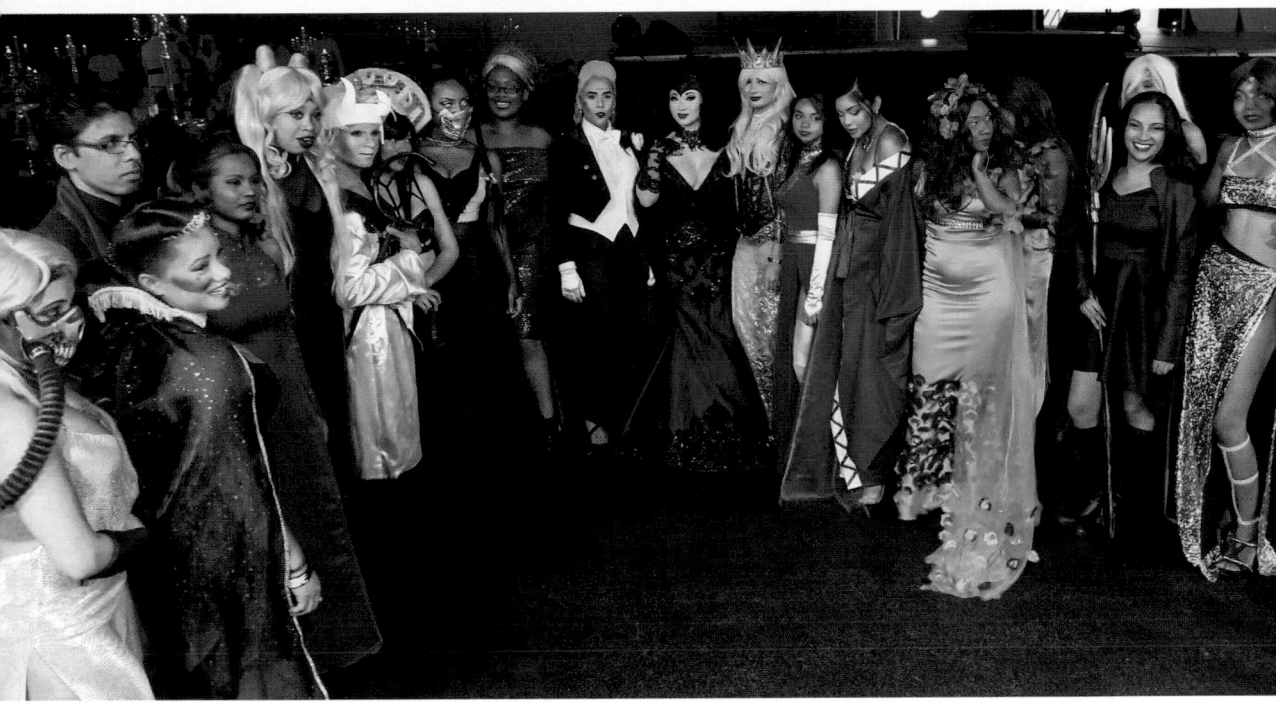

Posing with a group of cosplayers in Trinidad

Cosplay is a safe space for so many of us because we know what it's like to be judged. No matter where we live or the color of our skin, we each have faced hardships and tried to fit into a society with rigid ideas of right and wrong. This community is our weird and wonderful escape.

So let's make it a safe space for as many people as possible.

Let's approach the issue of blackface with compassion and understanding from both sides. Let's remind one another that we share more commonalities than differences. Instead of condemning someone outright, help them learn why something that they've done is hurtful to you, even if it was done with the best intentions. Let patience and empathy guide your conversations by considering that maybe the person you're talking to has never experienced racial injustice up close and personal. Alternatively, maybe they were never educated at length on the severity of race-related problems in all parts of the world. Use a conversation as a chance to share your experiences with them.

In my travels, I have had many conversations with cosplayers around the world on the topic of blackface. Despite the occasional language barrier or jet lag, these discussions were always engaging and passionate; they have gone long into the night at dinner tables. Some people I spoke to had never thought about darkening their skin for cosplay as a problem before or were completely misinformed on some facts regarding the practice and its implications. Even if we parted ways in disagreement, every cosplayer I spoke to appreciated the insight and walked away with a better understanding of the severity of the issue. Having a civil conversation will achieve more than an outright condemnation, because the goal doesn't have to be to change their opinion completely. Instead, make them aware of a problem, show them how much it means to you, and give them time to explore it on their own. For cosplayers who want to be on the international stage or turn their hobby into a career, it is prudent to stay up to date on complicated topics such as racism and cultural divisions. Then you should consider the implications of partaking in highly scrutinized practices such as blackfacing. I believe that with enough time, patience, and kindness, a greater number of our peers will be able to look past the superficial benefits of their actions and start considering the consequences of them as well.

In the end, the solution to blackface in cosplay is painfully simple: Cosplay whoever you want, but don't darken your skin. Cosplay Katara, Storm, or Pocahontas to your heart's content. Rock it out in their costumes, but do so in your own skin tone.

Or you can get creative, like I did when I dressed up as Storm but with the green skin of Skrull Invaders from *Secret Invasion*.

I have a message to cosplayers who have, once upon a time, darkened their skin: You're not a bad person, and your past actions do not define who you are now. We all learn and grow from our experiences, and we all have the ability to adapt and make changes. If, by reading this chapter, you were able to gain more understanding of the plight of POC cosplayers or of the consequences of blackface, then I will be ecstatic. If you choose to not do it again, that is wonderful. I hope you will pass your understanding on to others.

For cosplayers who still want to darken their skin tone for a costume, I ask you to take a step back and put yourself in the shoes of a fellow fan with dark skin. How would you feel in their place, knowing what you know now? Your good intentions are upsetting to a large portion of your peers who share your love for cosplay. It makes them feel bad.

Ask yourself the following: How much difference would it have on your happiness and quality of life if you did not darken your skin for this one costume? Is your love for a fictional character worth hurting a real-life group of people, and will your love for that character diminish if you don't alter your skin tone?

We each have a moral line that we won't cross. What is acceptable for you is up to you. This is a matter of empathy and abstaining from doing something out of consideration for someone else. For me, blackface is as immoral as cosplaying a Nazi officer or dressing as a burning World Trade Center tower (yes, that happened on Halloween one year). I won't cross that line.

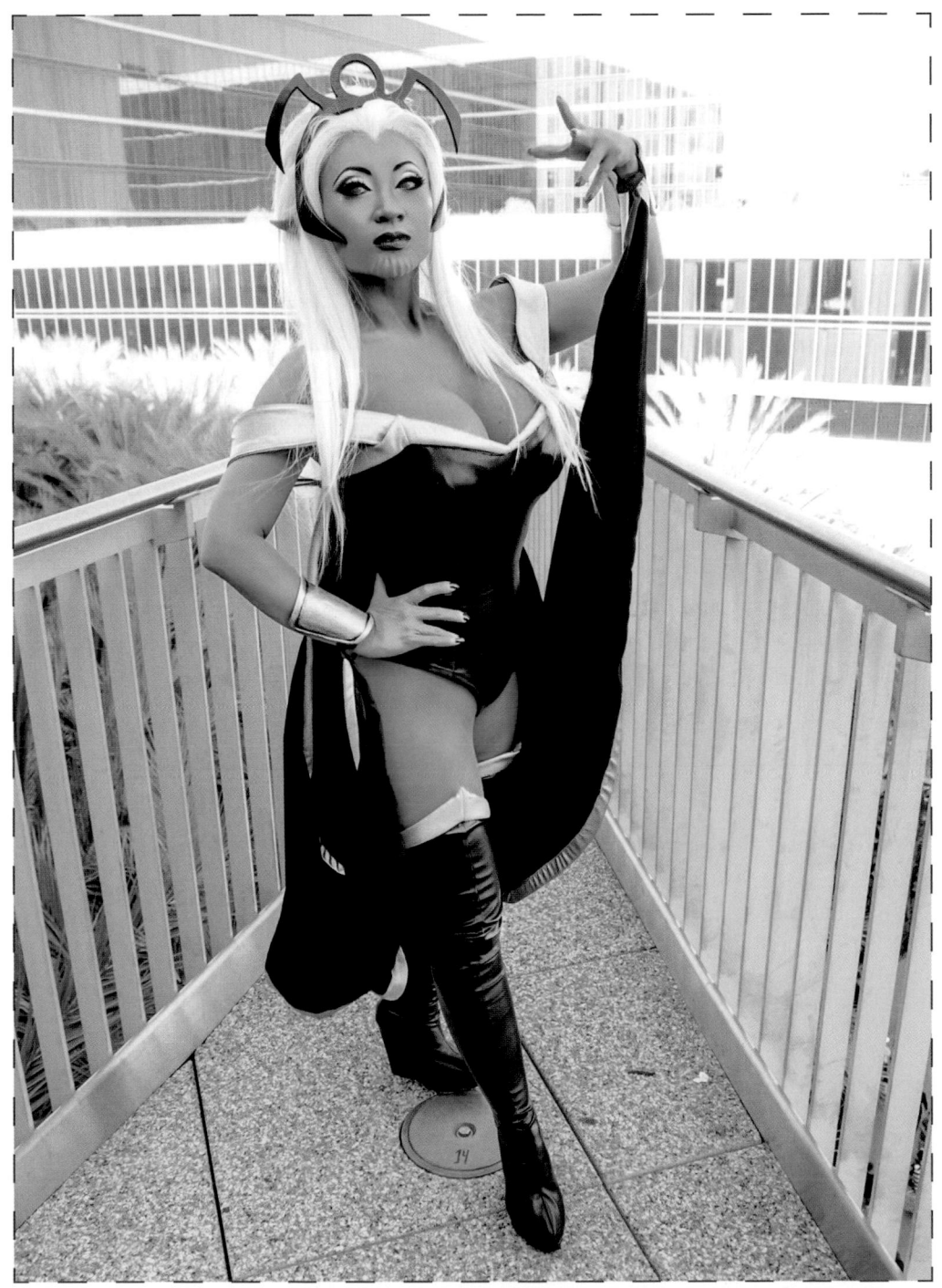

My Skrull Storm costume, for which I was painted green to emulate the Skrull Aliens.

TRANSFORMING NEGATIVITY
INTO POSITIVITY

After twenty years in the cosplay community, I can tell you it's an intense and highly charged environment that can bring out the best and worst in people. No matter what, though, I believe the positives of being in the community always outweigh the negatives. For the rest of this chapter, I will share advice on how to combat negativity and turn that bad energy into something positive.

PERSONAL SELF-CARE AND COMBATING NEGATIVITY

Let's first talk about self-care. What has helped me most on my journey to overcome negative thoughts is striving to actively understand the reasons behind them. I've also found it important to implement simple self-care methods that allow me to deal with issues in the moment. These are guidelines that I follow not only in cosplay but in everyday life as well.

Ignore, delete, ban. On my social media platforms, if I receive a comment that crosses the line for me, I ignore the commenter, delete the comment, and ban the poster from my page. I have a pretty high tolerance level, but there are still plenty of comments that veer into the range of hate speech, obscenities, and trolling. Regardless of where you decide to set your boundaries, when someone crosses them, do not respond to their words. This is your platform, and you don't have to leave their comment up if it upsets you or your audience. Delete the comment, ban the user, and move on.

It's not personal. One thing that's helped me a lot was coming to understand the psychology of online trolls. It's a power play for them, and usually, the goal is to get a reaction out of the cosplayer. The negative comments I receive say more about the commenters than about me. They highlight the commentor's own insecurities, prejudices, anger, and hurt. Remove yourself from their agendas. The comments are not personal, so don't give them the satisfaction of a response.

It's okay to be affected. Here's the truth: Even if you tell yourself that the negative comments are not personal, even after ignoring, deleting, and banning . . . sometimes the words you read leave a stinging impact. You can't unsee comments or unfeel emotions. I used to get upset at myself for taking a slight personally; I felt as though I was not strong enough to fight the negativity. But in truth, some comments do hit harder than others, and

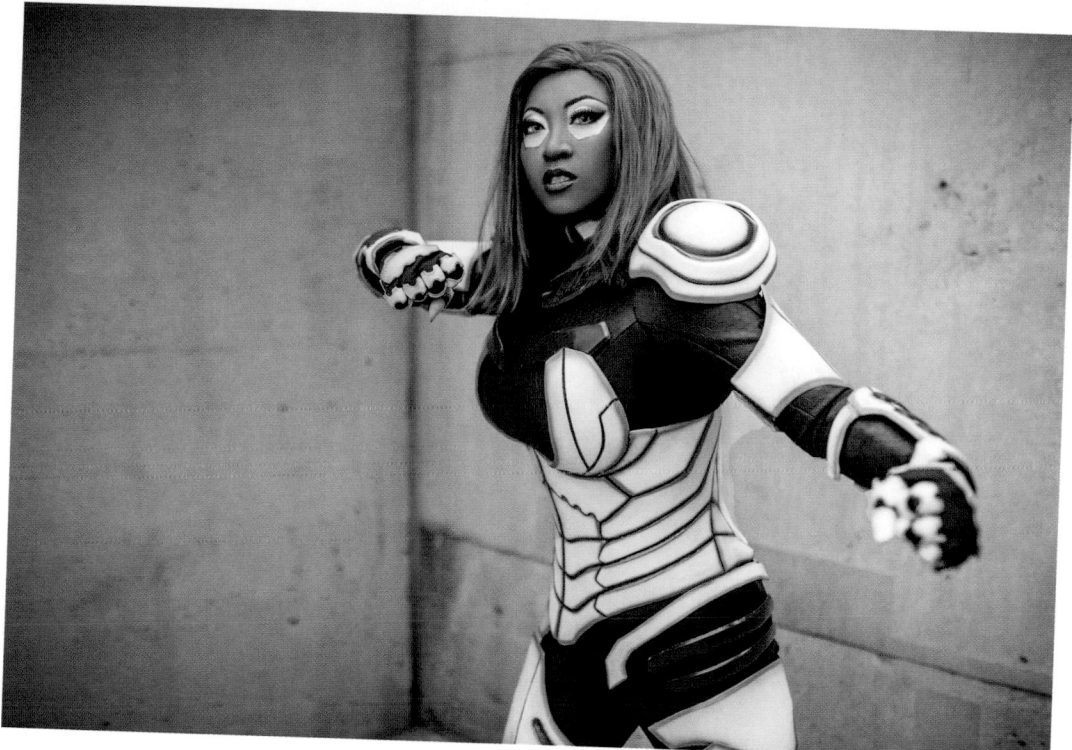

Cosplaying as Gamora

it's not a sign of weakness to feel affected. When I made Gamora's white armor from the *Guardians of the Galaxy* comic book series, I received a number of negative comments on the craftsmanship and look of the costume. It really bummed me out, because I worked super hard on it for five weeks. Only after acknowledging that I was affected and letting the emotions run their course was I able to move on. The great thing is that no matter how bad you feel, it will pass—I promise you that. Trust that your mind and body will feel better as you process your emotions and move on.

Don your imaginary armor. I learned that I have good days, when I feel confident and ready to take on anything, but I also have bad days, when I'm more susceptible to negativity. I do my best to look at comments and messages when I am mentally prepared. I suit up in my imaginary armor, so to speak. Before you do the same, make a mental list of all the things you are grateful for, think of the good things going on in your life, and remember why you love cosplay (or whatever else you're engaged in). These thoughts can give you more perspective and strength when you tackle a difficult subject or face some kind of setback during your day.

Take social media breaks. Especially after a situation where you get hit with negativity, it is important to take breaks from social media. This is something I personally still struggle with, but I do my best to get off the apps and websites and do something different instead. Watch a funny show, go for a walk, snuggle with your pet . . . whatever you do, just take some time for yourself. Come back when you're ready.

Reach out to your support network. Sometimes it really helps to vent to your loved ones, be it family or friends. In hard times, we can feel really alone in our thoughts. When you have a support network to reach out to, though, it can make a world of difference. I choose to do this in private, or at least in a closed setting, instead of venting in public, because my platforms are large enough that it can generate a lot of noise. I do not want to counter negativity with more negativity. On the other hand, serious incidents of abuse, stalking, doxing, and harassment should be reported to the appropriate authorities. Never stay quiet if you are afraid for your safety or well-being.

Dealing with negativity has strengthened me as a person and taught me how to navigate many challenges in my life outside of cosplay. I can look back and genuinely say that a lot of issues don't bother me anymore because I understand the reasoning behind them. It's freeing and allows me to have a more positive and happy life.

BUILDING A COMMUNITY OF POSITIVITY

Now let's look at how we can work together to make the cosplay community a more positive space. From interacting with one another to supporting initiatives, here are some ways for you to actively influence the climate of the cosplay community.

Inject critique with compassion. In a creative space such as cosplay, critique is inevitable and can be a great way to learn and improve your skills. However, when critical comments are left carelessly (as they often are) on something you've worked hard to create, they can be more demoralizing rather than motivational.

There is a way to critique compassionately—by pausing for a moment before commenting to consider how the critique could benefit the creator. Here are some factors to keep in mind when you look at a creator's post of their cosplay:

- Read the caption that goes along with the photo before commenting. Even better, look through the creator's timeline to see what else they've already said about the costume before adding your two cents.

- If something looks off, there is probably an explanation for it. You don't know the circumstances behind a project, so unless the creator asks for constructive criticism, it's probably not helpful to point out flaws or mistakes.

- Positive feedback is encouraging. Be it brief or detailed, writing something positive shows appreciation for the work done, perfect or otherwise.

- Do not try to compliment the cosplayer by comparing them to someone else and putting other cosplayers or actors down. "You look much better in this than . . ." is not a compliment. It just makes everyone you mentioned feel bad. Focus on what you like about the costume and the photo. And if you can't think of anything nice to say, sometimes it's better to smile and move on!

Support fellow creators. The best way you can create positivity in the community is to support your peers. Follow cosplayers, photographers, and other creators. Share those people with your network. Take time out of your day to like and comment on the posts you scroll past in your timeline. Giving someone a compliment, affirmation, or encouragement can make a big difference—and they might just reciprocate!

Embrace your online community. Join groups and communities with your interests, and share your knowledge and experiences in those areas. I know it can feel vulnerable to put yourself out there, but engaging actively rather than passively can help foster a deep and lasting connection with your passion and give meaning to your craft. You can choose the level of engagement you want to have and expand your circle at your comfort level. Being active in a community for the sake of the community (and not just yourself) will give you many layers of joy in return.

Engage at events. Another great way to spread positivity is to become actively engaged at events. Most conventions have volunteer programs, and it's also possible to apply as staff at your local con. If you have valuable knowledge and experience, consider teaching a panel or offering to host an event. Help out with the behind-the-scenes aspect of a cosplay contest, or suggest cosplay programming and accomplished cosplayers as guests to a con. You can even set up a local get-together or a cosplay photoshoot outside of a convention. Whatever you do, engage actively.

Support a charity or cause. Cosplay is a great way to participate in charitable efforts. Some cosplayers create solo charity campaigns and pledge to support causes that are important to them, and there are many great nonprofit organizations within the fandom community that you can join.

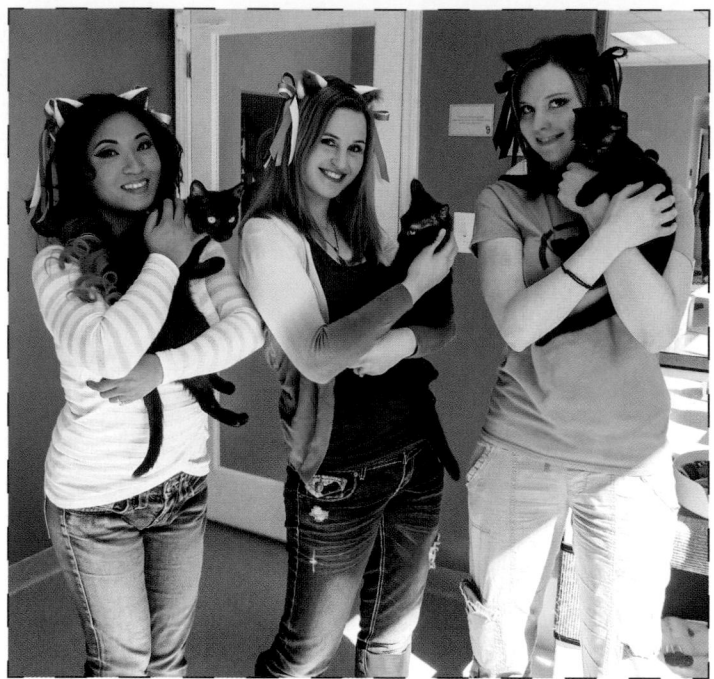

The 501st Legion and the Rebel Legion are long-standing volunteer organizations involved in many charitable efforts. They also have a mission to bring the *Star Wars* fandom together through costuming. They are officially endorsed by the creators at Lucasfilm, so memberships come with a certain amount of prestige and loyalty to local chapters, lovingly referred to as "bases" or "garrisons" by members.

Wearing cat ears and holding kitties at the Good Mews shelter!

All over the United States, fan-organized costuming charities, such as Costumers With A Cause and the Avengers Initiative, have formed. They and the Heroes Alliance, a charity organization with chapters around the world, organize for volunteer cosplayers to visit sick children in hospitals and to speak at schools.

Other initiatives, such as the Causeplay Shop and Cosplay for a Cure, raise money for worthwhile causes like breast cancer research.

If you don't have the money or time to support a charity at the moment, you can use hashtags on social media to highlight a topic you want to see more of and to raise awareness for a good cause or an underrepresented group.

Be the change you want to see. The goal for many of us is to foster a diverse and welcoming cosplay community, and the easiest way you can help is to share and highlight those people you want to see represented more. If you want to see more media features on male cosplayers, more interviews with plus-size cosplayers, more photos of black cosplayers, or more emphasis on craftsmanship-heavy costumes, share those cosplayers, leave positive comments on their posts, and encourage more people to follow them on social media. Help them become more visible and show your support for their efforts through active participation.

WHY COSPLAY IS WORTH IT

There are so many wonderful aspects of cosplay that it is worth dealing with the obstacles that come with engaging in the craft. I'd like to think that I have filled most of this book with the great parts of being in the cosplay community, but just in case, as we close out the topic of negativity, let's revisit the most incredible benefits of cosplaying.

Creative Fulfillment: Cosplay allows you to explore limitless creativity and learn a myriad of hands-on skills that you otherwise might never have been interested in. Learning is essential to the human experience, and there aren't many activities that give you as much opportunity to learn diverse, creative skills as cosplay.

Self-Improvement: The process of making a costume is a form of self-discovery in which you not only learn technical skills but also how to handle challenges.

Testing your skills, dedicating yourself to a project, overcoming practical obstacles, exceeding personal limitations, and, finally, holding something in your hands that you made yourself . . . Making a cosplay is a priceless experience and an overwhelming source of pride and satisfaction. As you settle into the cosplay routine, you will become more efficient and capable when handling all sorts of tasks and deadlines.

Socialization: Children and teenagers especially can benefit from cosplaying because it is an activity where they are encouraged to craft at home in a safe environment, use their imaginations, and then engage socially. In a day and age where playing video games reigns supreme on a child's list of hobbies, cosplay offers young people the chance to step out into the world and interact with one another in a fun and unconventional way. Costume making is a wonderful group activity, and there is nothing that breaks the ice or encourages conversation faster than cosplaying at an event.

Confidence: I can't overstate this benefit enough. We all have insecurities, but cosplay allows us to take strength from the larger-than-life characters we portray in order to overcome. I would never have been able to perform onstage in front of people or make public speeches at panels if I didn't first do it while dressed up as my favorite characters. Being in costume gave me the security of a disguise, even when I was standing in the public eye. It's a truly unique way to get over stage fright and, more importantly, to build confidence.

Joy and Happiness: At the heart of all of it, cosplay brings joy. It fills your life with exciting and stimulating experiences. I hope we can always remember that we're doing this for fun and to take the good and the bad in stride.

— — —

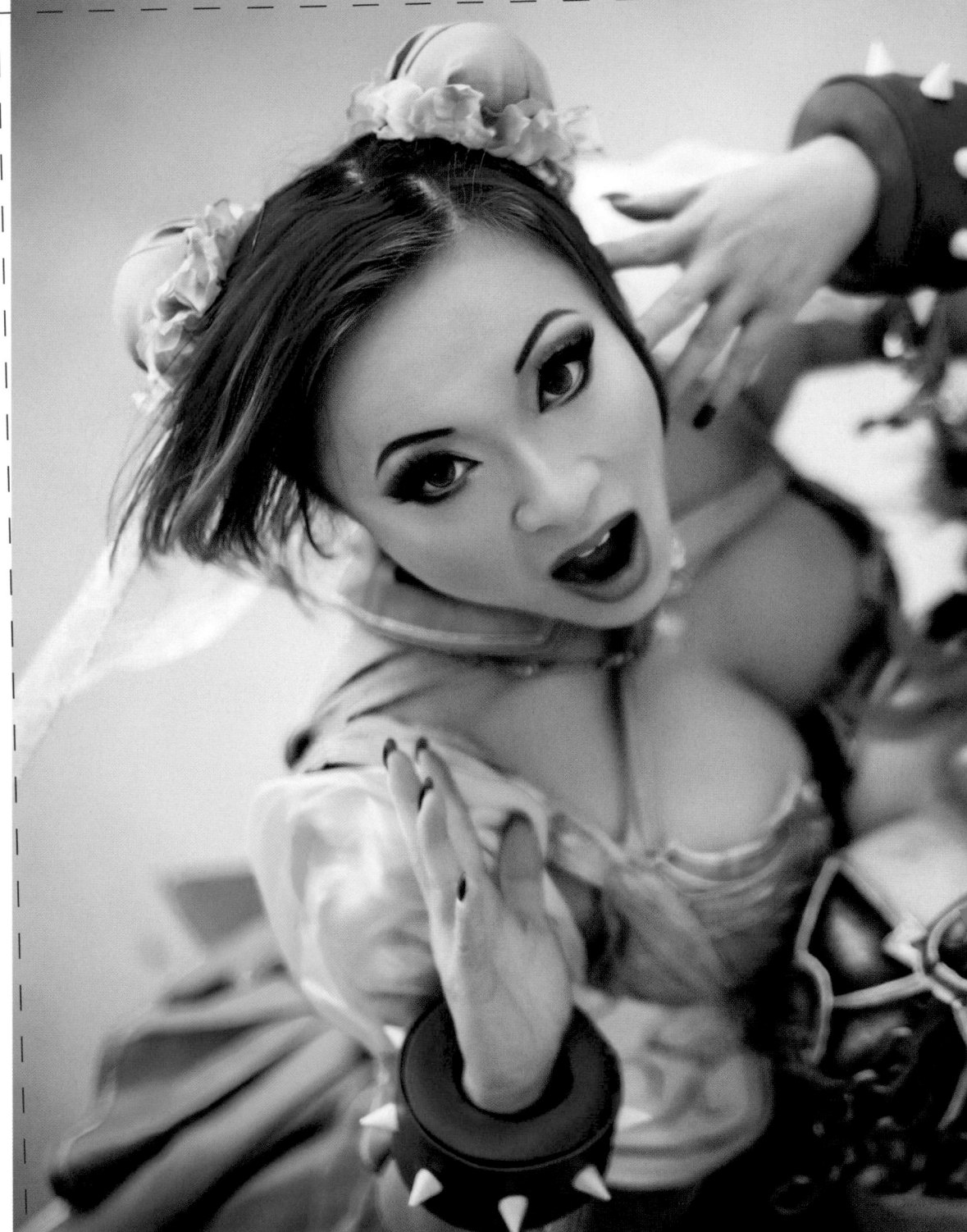

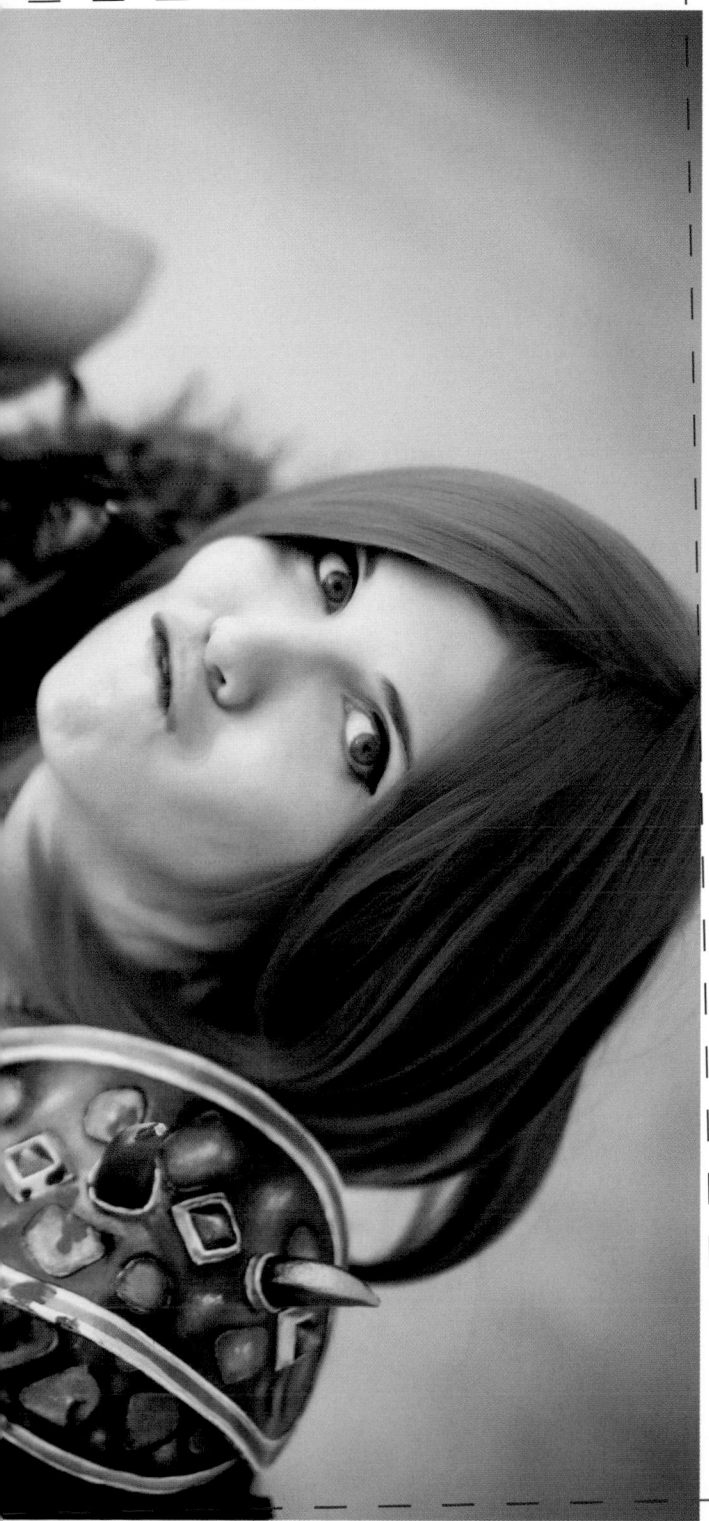

Looking at the cosplay community, it's been incredible to watch the significant social stigma once aimed at cosplay slowly change into acceptance. Cosplayers used to be considered outcasts, even amongst the geeks, but now we can freely enjoy dressing up. At one point in time, parents forbade their kids to cosplay, but now they support them and even make costumes with them.

I believe in the bright future of cosplay and will continue to build and grow a community that is positive, creative, and supportive of everyone within it. I hope you will join me.

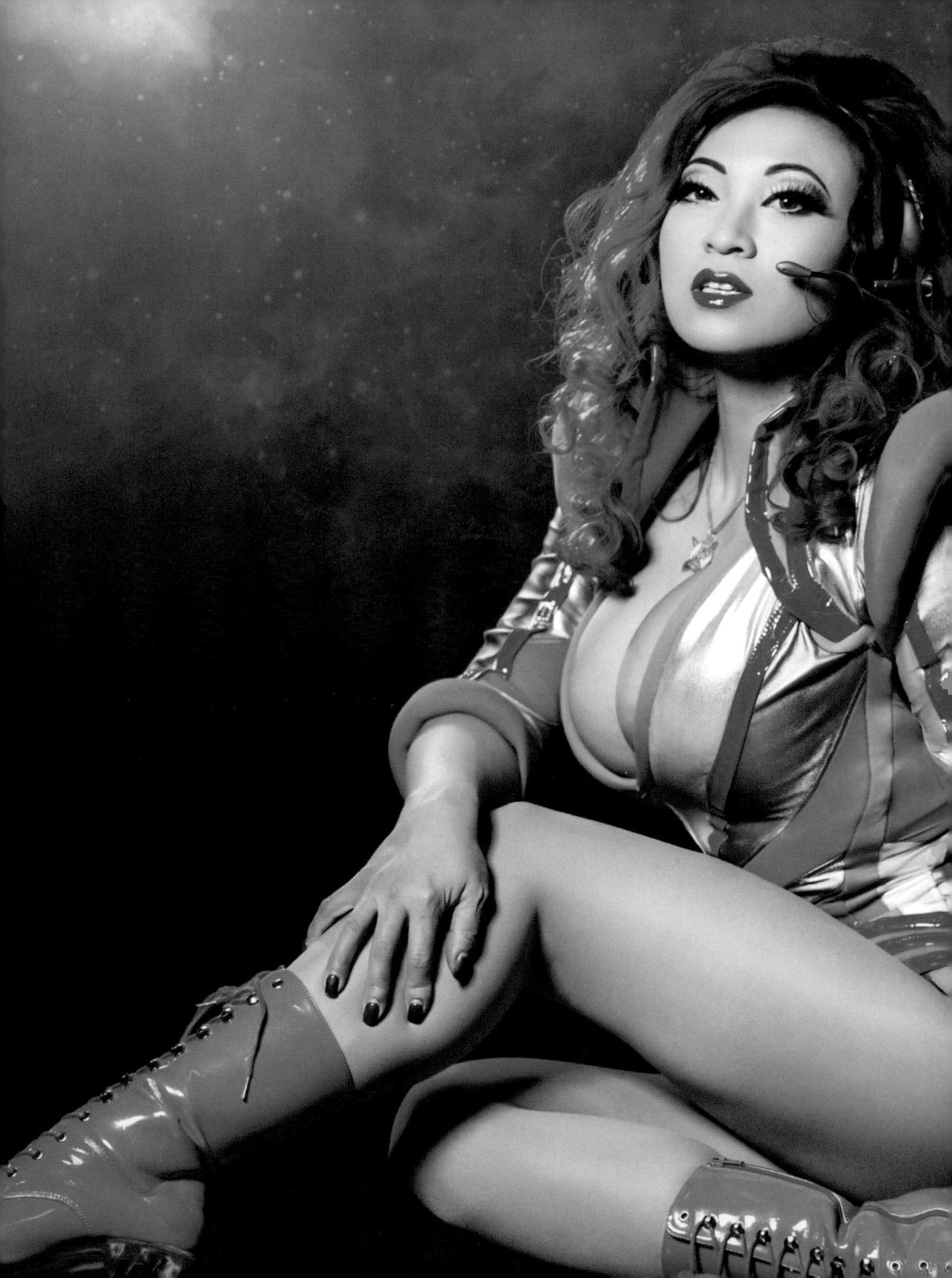

PART FIVE

The Industry
of Cosplay

CHAPTER 14

Becoming Yaya Han

The Long Road to Going Pro

For many years before I "made it big," I would get asked what my real job was. How could I afford a hobby as expensive as cosplay? When I said that cosplay *was* my job, it caused a lot of scoffing and noises of disbelief. Follow-up questions usually included "So . . . people just . . . pay you to dress up in costumes?" and "What do you actually do to make *money*?" These kinds of discussions exhausted me because it was very difficult to describe exactly what I did to make money. I'd have to spend fifteen minutes explaining the entire cultural structure of fandom first.

On the other hand, now that I am commercially successful, I get praised a lot for my entrepreneurial acumen and enterprising nature. People tell me all the time how much they respect my business sense. Now I'm asked how to attract prestigious sponsorships and convention invitations, how to build name recognition, and how to make it to the top. When people scroll through my Instagram and see travel photos from around the world, smiling selfies, and sleek cosplay photos, they probably think that being a career cosplayer looks like the dream life of a glamorous social media influencer who gets paid big bucks to look beautiful and wear cool outfits in exotic locations.

As an amateur cosplayer, I was criticized for my tenacity, but as a professional, I am admired for my hustle. Occasionally someone winks at me and says something like "You're so sly, you got in at the right time and knew what was going on!" Another person might lean in and ask in a low voice, "So how did you really do it?" as if I could reveal some hidden magic trick that would cause money to rain down on them.

If I sound cynical, that's because there is no secret to my success. I'm knowledgeable about business because I made a shit ton of mistakes and was burned more times than I can count. When I started cosplaying, it was impossible to do it for a living. I didn't even dream of it. There was no strategizing or planning, no preparation or anticipation, and I definitely didn't know what was going to happen. Even now, my dream life as a cosplayer is not as

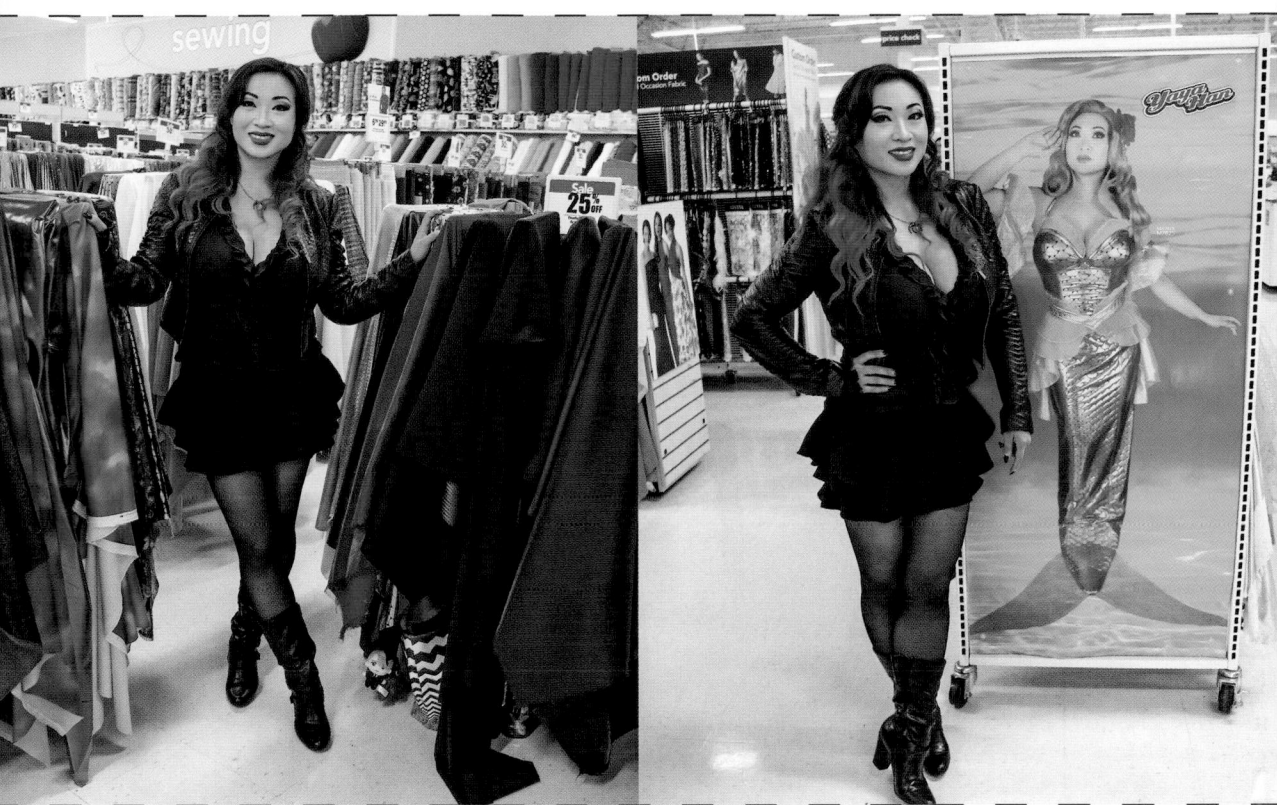

Standing by my fabric section and store display in JOANN

simple as getting paid to dress up in cool costumes. It still consists of juggling various jobs and fighting against deadlines. At times, it remains utter chaos.

That being said, cosplay is emerging as an industry you can enter into with a career in mind. In this section of the book, I will tell you how I made the jump from amateur to professional cosplayer, give you a well-rounded overview of the career opportunities available in cosplay, and share suggestions for those interested in going pro.

Well, technically it wasn't a jump. It wasn't even a steady rise. For me, going pro was a slow crawl in the dark.

By now, you're familiar with my awkward early years in cosplay. As I flitted from con to con in my homemade satin costumes, I never dreamed of making money with cosplay. It was purely a hobby. However, as time went on and I kept cosplaying, people saw pictures of my costumes and e-mailed me to ask if I could make something for them. In our budding community, people were not used to the concept of paying for custom-made cosplay costumes yet, but by 2003 I had started to accept some requests after repeated nudging from my friends. At the time, I still felt inexperienced in my crafting abilities, so I chose to focus on simpler accessories, such as sculpted cat ears, small pairs of angel wings, and fantasy hair-pieces. I also took commissions of costume parts that I had already made for myself at some other point, such as Lulu's hair sticks and jewelry from *Final Fantasy X*. I did this because I knew I wouldn't have to spend a lot of time researching and experimenting on these pieces before crafting them. On my Angelic Star cosplay website, I created a page with made-to-order products that generated enough sales to keep me busy each month.

I did all of this while working a full-time data entry job, which paid enough to cover the bills but was deeply unsatisfying to a creative person like me. The stale office environment and monotonous forty-hour workweek schedule made me feel apathetic and numb. There was no prospect for me to move up in the company because I didn't have enough education or work experience. My office kept hiring new and more qualified technicians; they even had me train them to use the in-house software system before moving them into better-paid departments. Whenever I asked for additional training or chances for advancement, I was brushed off.

At some point, sitting in the same cubicle, in the same office, with the same meager salary, I realized that this would be my life for the next twenty years unless I changed something. I stopped trying to impress my supervisors in any way and resorted to only doing the bare mini-mum required. My work performance dropped so low that I got negative performance reviews and was given an employment warning.

While my office life threatened to kill my spirit, I continued to thrive in cosplay. By 2005 I was being invited as a guest to conventions on a regular basis, was interviewed and featured in magazines often, and received steady commission requests and product orders. I became somewhat known for the life-size angel wings I made and was commissioned to build several pairs for nightclubs as well as for private clients. At over $1,000 per pair, these were the first big-ticket

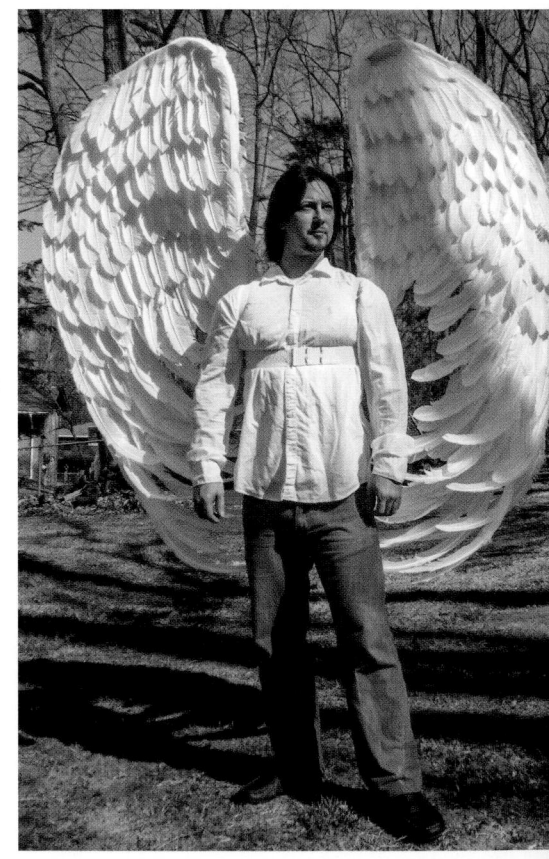

A pair of my life-size angel wings, modeled by Brian

items I sold through my cosplay commission store, and they gave me the confidence to continue pursuing custom-made work.

Eventually, I was working forty hours per week at my office job and then working another thirty to forty hours in my spare time and on weekends in order to fill cosplay commission orders. I became quite overwhelmed by the workload, but crafting was fun and fulfilling in all the ways that my day job wasn't. At that point, my biggest problem was my limited vacation time: My job gave me only fifteen days per year. I set aside every vacation day I had for conventions, but as more events invited me, it became more difficult to get time off for them. More than once, I called in sick from a convention. On those occasions, I felt guilty for lying to my supervisor and scared that I would get caught in one of those lies.

It couldn't go on this way. I had to make a choice: keep my salaried job and cut back on cosplay, or quit the office life and become a freelance artist. The desire to quit grew stronger by the day, but I had no business knowledge or experience. Plus the thought of losing my steady income and health insurance was mortifying. At the time I was contemplating this decision a whopping decade and a half ago, cosplay was still quite underground. I had no guarantee or security in going freelance.

Thankfully, though, I did not have to make my decision alone.

During those first few whirlwind years of adjusting to life in the United States, I met the one constant in my life: my partner, Brian Boling (who has popped up a couple of times throughout this book already). In the year 2000, we were introduced at Dragon Con, the legendary four-day costuming-focused convention in Atlanta. He was wearing a fantastic Boba Fett costume, and as soon as he took his helmet off, I was smitten. Brian was a self-taught prop maker in all the same ways that I was a self-taught sewer and crafter. It was obvious that we both loved costuming, and we had mutual respect for each other's unique skills.

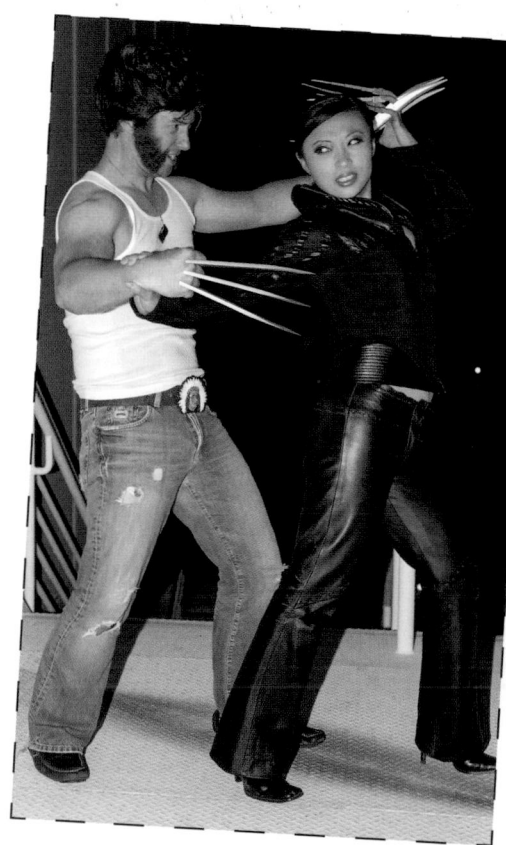

Brian and I cosplaying Wolverine
and Lady Deathstrike

It took a few years for us to move past being friends, but by 2005, we were in love and living together. Like me, Brian was also working a full-time job that made him unhappy. We both dreamed of a life where we could be more creative and free. Brian had started to take on some of the commission requests I received that required molding and casting. We really enjoyed combining our skills to make things together and often talked about creating a costume studio or moving to LA to work in the film industry.

One night, though, after receiving a horrible performance review and a warning from my supervisor, I was in tears. I'd been told that if my performance didn't improve soon, I would be fired.

Brian took my hand and said, "You hate this job anyway. Why don't you quit and make costumes?"

My pragmatic German upbringing started protesting. "I can't lose my paycheck. What if I can't make enough money with commissions?"

He tried a different approach. "Well, what would you want to do if you could do anything?"

I replied in earnest, "I want to make costumes. I want to travel. I want to spend more time with you."

Brian's reply left me slack-jawed: "Why don't I quit my job, too? Then we can do all of this together."

Before the summer was out, we'd both submitted our resignations. Over the next couple of months, we set the gears in motion for starting our business together. Knowing that I was going on this venture with Brian helped me push through the fears and doubts. I also took confidence in the fact that we could use both our skill sets to take on bigger and more lucrative costume commissions. I built us a website and wrote up detailed information regarding our crafting capabilities, such as sewn garments; full costumes including styled wigs; resin and wood props; jewelry and accessories, etc. I also set up a structure for clients to send in requests and I devised a payment system to help with the sticker shock of higher-priced projects. Lastly, I added my tried-and-true made-to-order products to our store as well.

It was like jumping off a cliff. We started getting orders right away but were soon caught up in the pitfalls that come with freelance work at equal speed. We thought that our experience making personal costumes would translate well into crafting commissions for clients, but there was a whole set of challenges for which we were unprepared. Communication, time management, and organization are all factors that have less to do with actually being creative and everything to do with running a business.

Out of all the commission requests that we received, only about 10 percent turned into real jobs. However, I still had to answer each potential client in detail. We quickly learned that people had unrealistic expectations of how much a custom-made costume or prop costs. My e-mails became increasingly longer because I had to explain our creative process as well as compile references, shopping lists, and cost breakdowns. Most people would never reply to my e-mails. Those who did would often try to argue over the "ridiculously high" price we quoted them.

In addition, we didn't think to accurately keep track of our expenses, so we consistently undercharged ourselves and underestimated the cost of materials and hours of labor we'd need for a given project. It was difficult to send progress photos in the age before smartphones, so I would frequently get stressed out over e-mails from clients asking for updates on their costumes at the same time as new commission requests were rolling in. While we had experience making costumes for ourselves and could cut corners here and there during a con crunch, there was added pressure to make every client piece as perfect as possible. Every commission required more research and creation time than we had anticipated, and sometimes we struggled to meet deadlines. More than once, we had to pay exorbitant overnight shipping fees to get a commissioned item delivered on time. While most of our clients were satisfied, every bit of unhappy feedback we received felt like a defeat and wracked me with guilt.

Brian and I had the commission business for less than a year before we gave up on it. The lifestyle was too stressful for me, Brian felt unappreciated by nitpicky clients, and overall, we didn't enjoy having to repeatedly justify the worth of our services. Looking back, we were not only inexperienced at handling clients; the cosplay market was too undeveloped at the time for our business model to flourish. Today, there is a huge demand for custom-made costumes, so if we had started our business a few years later, maybe it would have thrived.

Anyway, with full-costume commissions in the rearview mirror, we moved on to our next business idea: ready-to-wear cosplay accessories. Throughout the years, the accessory I sold most consistently was a pair of cartoony animal ears that I'd sculpted by hand with Model Magic and priced at $30. Each pair was hand-painted and decorated with ribbons and beaded dangles. They really appealed to people who attended renaissance faires, to fantasy lovers, and to hobbyist costumers. After watching me hand-sculpt cat ears in larger and larger batches over time, Brian suggested a change to the manufacturing process. Brian already had a lot of experience with molding and casting on costume projects and felt confident that we could make ears faster using those methods. Once the commission business shut down, I told Brian we'd give it a try.

To start, I made a master pair of animal ears out of clay and let him mold them. He showed me how to cast resin, and after that we even came up with color formulas for dyeing the material so I wouldn't have to paint each pair by hand. This process combined our skills in the best way possible and we quickly found a routine: Brian cast ears and drilled holes into them while I strung them on to elastic bands and added colorful fluff and embellishments. We sold the cat ears through my website online, and whenever I had an artist alley table at a convention, we laid them out right next to my art prints. To our delight, people loved our new refined-resin ears. We kept selling out, so we started investing more and more time into making them. Even with the molding and casting method, we struggled to keep up with demand whenever summer con season rolled around. Cat ears quickly took over our entire apartment.

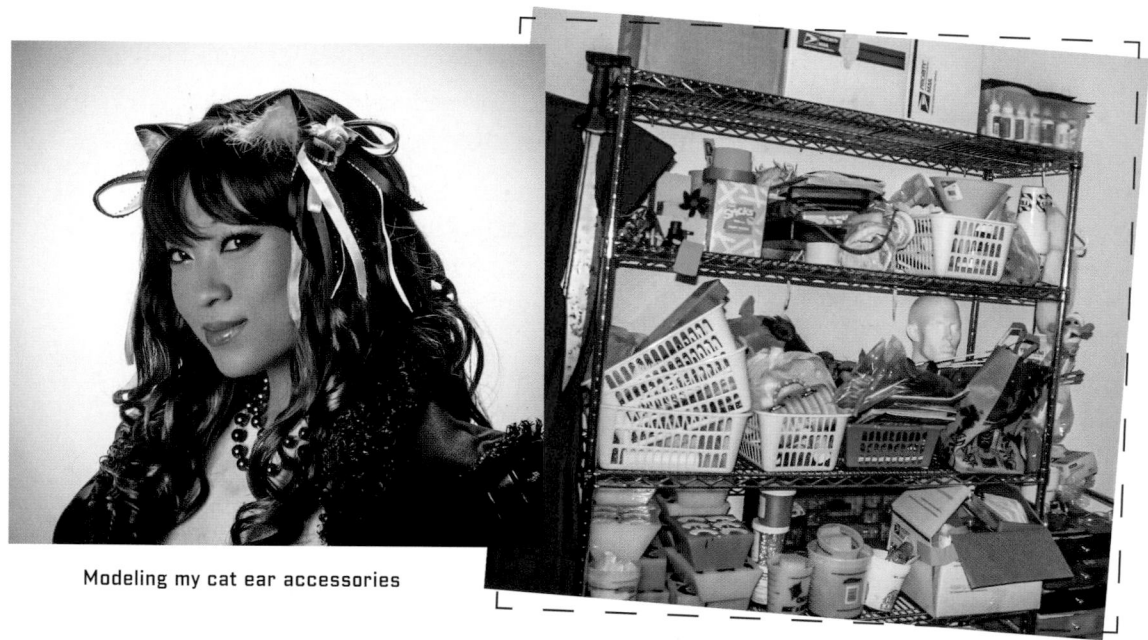

Modeling my cat ear accessories

Various molding and casting materials
needed to make our cat ears

After testing the waters by selling cosplay accessories at artist alley tables, we made the leap to buying vendor booths at shows. These spaces were a lot more expensive, but they also attracted more people. The first year we did this was really scary, because we spent almost every penny we had reserving exhibitor booths, booking travel, and paying for lodging at each convention we attended. We had no idea if our products would sell or if we had brought enough stock for any given event. Each day was a rush of nerves as we awaited the crowd that would burst through the exhibitor hall doors when the convention opened.

It was a trial by fire, but we passed. The Yaya Han cat ears consistently sold out at conventions, no matter how many we stocked. Until that point, I was used to living frugally and off money at hand, because my unusual immigration circumstances didn't allow me to take out credit. Sure, I had no debt, but I also worried about bills all the time and felt guilty for spending any bit of money. As the cosplay accessories took off and became more and more successful, we realized that after setting aside everything for bills and necessities, we had disposable income left over. Brian and I actually allowed ourselves to

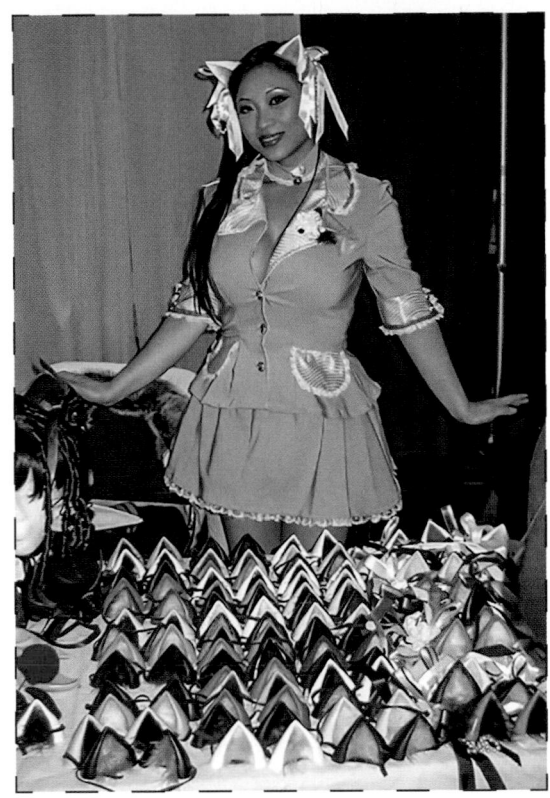

Merchandising our cosplay accessories at cons

splurge on nice dinners once in a while. I was able to buy quality silk for a costume. At one point, we even had savings. For the first time in my life, I felt successful.

Then we got ripped off.

Virtually identical copies of our cat ears began to show up at conventions around 2008. Vendors we were friendly with stopped talking to us as they laid out products on their tables that were identical to ours. Feeling sick to my stomach, I asked a friend to buy a few pairs of these ears so I could get a closer look at them. They were injection-molded plastic products and thus mass-produced with inferior materials, but the ears looked close enough to ours, so people didn't care. To add insult to injury, they were priced a third less than ours were. The message was clear: "Get out. This is our turf." Weekend by weekend, we watched people walk around wearing the knockoff ears while our sales plummeted. Out of options, we were forced to drop our prices to match the competition, which meant making a lot more product and bringing home less income.

The first few months after this started, I was utterly crushed. The truth was undeniable—a member of the anime vendor community bought our cat ears, had them copied en masse at a factory, and then wholesaled them to everyone else. Our colleagues were profiting from the knockoff cat ears even though they knew how much it hurt our business. These other vendors attended forty to fifty cons per year and were hawking copies of my cat ears as if they had come up with the newest, hottest anime merch. The aggressive price drop they made was meant to drive Brian and me out of business because they knew we couldn't keep up with the production rate of a factory, but it ultimately only served to undervalue the product itself. They flooded the market.

I started researching copyright law and counterfeit culture. I knew anime conventions generally had a clause against bootleg merchandise in their vendor agreements because they were trying to stop the rampant spread of knockoff anime DVDs and branded plushies. I looked over booth documents that I had signed and found that, indeed, all of them banned the sale of counterfeit merchandise. Since the Yaya Han cat ears were my copyrighted products, those other cat ears were technically counterfeit items. I just had to prove it.

A few months after the knockoff cat ears surfaced, a friend of ours recommended a patent attorney in Atlanta who was also a convention goer. He knew of me and understood my situation immediately. I took his advice and started gathering proof that we were the first to create the cat ears in order to begin the harrowing process of building a legal case against the bootleggers. Since my name was attached to the products, I had to take the lead in the legal proceedings. The next several months became a flurry of attorney meetings, research, and evidence collection. On top of all this, somehow, I continued to run our online store. I even kept cosplaying on the side.

When it came time to serve cease-and-desist letters, I couldn't afford to fly my attorney out to every con we attended, so I had to do it myself. In hindsight, that was a mistake. By not having a representative advocate on my behalf, I put myself in the line of fire. For a long, painful summer, every time we arrived at a show for booth setup, I had to plead my case to the dealer coordinators who managed that con's exhibitor hall. I gave them proof of my copyright over the cat ears and requested their assistance in asserting their own show's bootleg policy. Unfortunately, no one had ever dealt with a case like ours before, and the vendors accused of violating our copyright were some of the most prominent ones on the circuit. More often than not, I was met with hesitation, and my integrity was called into question. Even when dealer coordinators agreed to handle my request, I had to go around and serve the cease-and-desist letters to affected vendors myself. Brian would stay behind to set up the booth, so there I was, a little Asian girl walking up to seasoned anime vendors in order to hand them legal papers that told them to remove a super-popular product from their tables.

It did not go over well.

After I served them, some vendors became angry and threatening toward me. Others loudly complained to vendor staff. The death stares and derisive remarks I received drove me close to panic and left me shaken for hours afterward. Even now, recounting the scenes many years later, I feel queasy in my stomach. One vendor became so enraged, they started giving away cat ears for free outside of the vendor hall in hopes of diluting our sales that weekend. The worst moment was when someone posted the cease-and-desist letter on 4chan, an anonymous online forum. The letter included my home address at the time.

That year I learned another valuable lesson: When it comes to legal proceedings, employ a representative to handle confrontations. After the cease-and-desist letter was leaked, a huge discussion broke out about the copyright claim that spilled over into the cosplay community at large. All sorts of misinformation were spread about the claim. Rumors flew around that I was a horrible and greedy bitch who was trying to create a monopoly on all cat ears. At that point, I was used to being a subject of speculation in the cosplay community, but this situation had quickly became quite volatile. I received harassing messages and comments, as well as threats.

Me, a troublemaker? What else is new?

While all of this was going on, we continued to prepare the inevitable lawsuit against the maker of the knockoff Yaya cat ears. Shell-shocked by the public's reaction to learning about our cease-and-desist letters, I stopped handing them out and focused all of my energy on gathering evidence and strengthening our arguments. In August 2010, we officially filed our lawsuit, and after one year of relentless back-and-forth, the case was settled out of court. I can't say much about the settlement, but it included the other party's agreement to stop making and selling the cat ears in question. During the entirety of litigation, various anime vendors were still selling the copycat ears, but once news of the settlement spread in the community, the products started slowly disappearing from the marketplace.

As an inexperienced small business owner, this entire experience was terrifying. For one, it felt insane to go to court over cosplay cat ears. At times, there was so much negativity thrown our way that I felt crazy and doubted myself. However, at the end of the day, the ears were my design and they translated into real income for myself and Brian. I wanted to fight for them. The ordeal taught me the responsibility that comes with having your name attached to something but also how empowering it can be to build a brand. Brian really helped me stay strong through these difficult years, and we both felt incredible relief when the settlement was announced.

After regaining control of my cosplay products, I continued to think up new cosplay accessory designs, make costumes for myself, and travel to conventions as both a guest and a vendor. The market for cosplay convention guests was still in its nascent phase, so I was still years away from being able to ask for any kind of appearance fee. However, because I now had branded products, I could negotiate to have my vendor booth comped by the conventions. This was an easy request for the organizers to fulfill and saved me a lot of money. Having free booths meant I was able to go to more cons to sell cosplay accessories and, in doing so, expand the business. I registered my name as a trademark and revamped yayahan.com. I hired a few local cosplay friends as part-time employees to help us make products and therefore got to learn all about running payroll. Brian found us a warehouse to move the product production into. Slowly, with the help of our new employees, we grew into a proper small business.

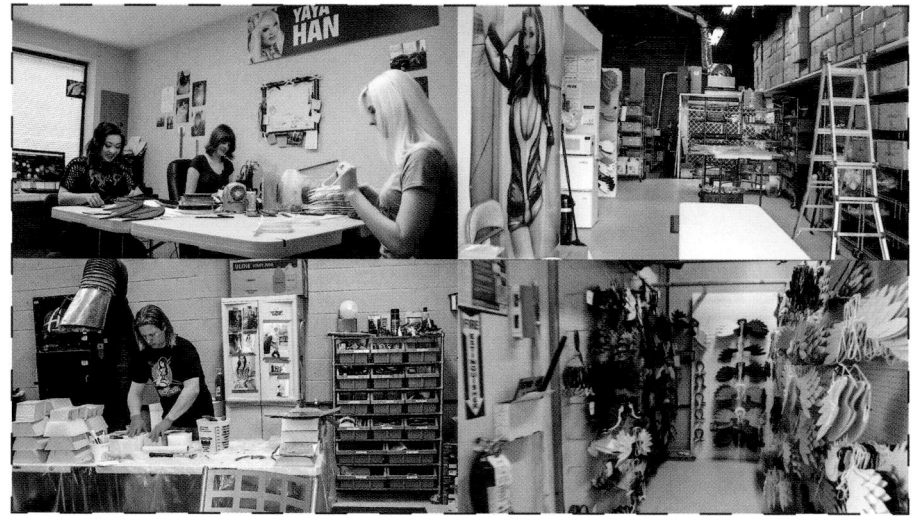

Our employees and warehouse where we create our cosplay magic

As we continued to sell cosplay products online and at conventions, I stopped managing the logistics of the store and let Brian handle merchandise production so I could focus on design, marketing, and brand building. After years of turmoil, I was able to devote more time to making costumes and creative content again. Around this same time, cosplay started booming on social media and my name recognition expanded even further. This created an increased demand for me to appear at events. Invitations flew in rapidly, and I filled up my calendar with twenty to twenty-five conventions each year. This new lifestyle was a hectic one, but now I got to travel and work with Brian all the time, just like we had dreamed about all those years ago. I started to fantasize about making costumes, going to cons, and selling my cat ears for the next ten or fifteen years.

Oh, sweet summer child. It was never going to be that easy.

---CHAPTER 15---

The Cost of Building
a Cosplay Empire

I thought that overcoming an intellectual property lawsuit would be the biggest hurdle in my career as a professional nerd. However, a few years after my case was settled, cosplay would teach me the most important and profound lesson of my life: an awful situation can leave a positive impact and create lasting change.

Let me tell you about that time I was on a reality TV show.

In 2012, the NBC offshoot network Syfy greenlit *Heroes of Cosplay*. This twelve-episode reality series followed cosplayers as we made costumes and competed at fandom conventions. Syfy aired the six-episode season one of *Heroes of Cosplay* in 2013 and concluded with another six-episode season in 2014.

While *Heroes of Cosplay* was the first network TV show dedicated to the art form, the show's producers were by no means the only ones trying to make a series like it. By 2011, cosplay had become such a hot topic that major networks were starting to consider it as viable for content production. I was contacted by several different producers around this time. The number of random e-mails I received with TV show ideas was almost hilarious; some of the proposals were wildly ridiculous. However, as a longtime member of the cosplay community, I felt incredibly conflicted. On one hand, I was proud that our little dress-up hobby had finally grown to the point that mainstream entertainment was paying attention. On the other hand, I was terrified of the possibility that a TV show centered on cosplay might portray our craft in a terrible and sensationalized way.

One day, after speaking to yet another hotshot producer about yet another show where the pitch was "*The Real Housewives* but cosplay," I realized the inevitable: One day soon, a cosplay show would be made, and there was no telling how good or bad it would be. I decided that, if possible, I wanted to be a part of the show that did get greenlit so that I could have some influence in how cosplay would be shown to the world.

The *Heroes of Cosplay* project (originally called *CosWorld*) was the most promising out of all the proposals I received, but even it required more than two years to get off the ground. The show went through multiple concepts and production companies before being greenlit, and all the lead time was incredibly nerve-wracking. Whenever a new producer came onboard, they filmed a different concept proof in hopes of securing a spot for the show on the network. Many of these included dramatic ambushes and manufactured fights between would-be cast members that clearly did not reflect who we were. I used to lie awake at night, agonizing over whether or not to walk away from the show, but the inevitability of it existing somewhere, in some form, hung over my head. This kind of show was going to get made no matter what, and I could only influence the series if I was on it.

After many months, the production team finally settled on a format for *Heroes of Cosplay*. The show would be competition-based, with a run time of one hour per episode and featuring contestants from Atlanta and Los Angeles. We started filming in early 2013. Each episode followed cosplayers as they made costumes, traveled to a con, and participated in a contest and would always show whether the cosplayers won or lost. Unlike the other cast members, who participated as contestants, I served as a judge on the show, providing the perspective of someone who cosplayed professionally. Every contest I judged on the show was at an established fandom convention and following that event's competition criteria, so my story line offered insights on real judging parameters and proceedings in the world of cosplay. On paper, all of this sounds not too far off from what cosplay is like in real life, but the way the show was filmed and edited deviated from reality in quite a few ways.

It's not easy to prepare for a contest, so most cosplayers take on only one or two a year. They devote months to preparing for each. However, due to the time restrictions imposed on the filming of seasonal television shows, the production team on *Heroes of Cosplay* required the cast to make new costumes for each convention with only two weeks of lead time. They also had to enter multiple contests back-to-back. Even in the role of a judge, the production team and I agreed that I should prepare new outfits for each episode. The filmmakers wanted to build up the stakes and payoffs in my story line, while I wanted to show that even as a professional cosplayer, I was still making all of my costumes by hand. After all, the foundation of my business was rooted in designing and creating. It turned out that having a film crew follow your entire costume-making process slows it down to a crawl. Not only did I (and the other cast members) have to wait to execute certain crucial tasks on our costumes until scheduled filming days, but having a dozen people take over your house with film and lighting equipment adds a whole lot of stress and chaos. Waiting for camera and sound setups, having

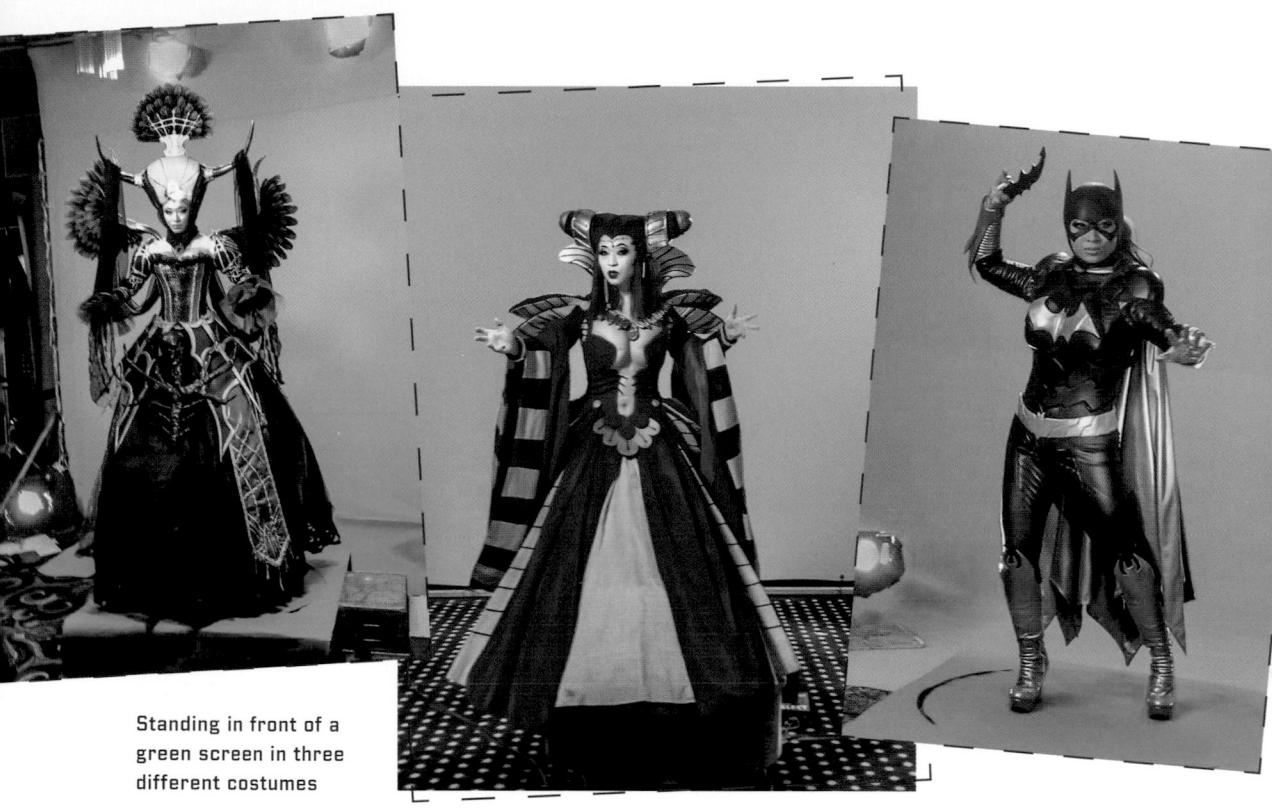

Standing in front of a green screen in three different costumes

to repeat one task for different takes, changing locations to grab all the shots needed on the list . . . and then you still have to finish making a costume in time for the convention. All these factors made an already daunting workload into an overwhelming challenge.

Logistical issues are understandable. Reality TV shows are not documentaries, in which the filmmakers can spend months—or even years—waiting for the real story to unfold. On network TV, you will always have to fudge some details to move the story along. The really unfortunate part about *Heroes of Cosplay*, however, was the way the story format pigeonholed its cast members into certain roles.

Some of the other cast members were accomplished cosplayers in their own rights. In addition to myself, several of them had also appeared at cons as guests and cosplay judges. For the sake of storytelling, however, the show downplayed these cosplayers' accomplishments and dialed up the authoritative side of my role as a judge. Each cosplayer became a character known for both their specialties and shortcomings, which were reiterated throughout the series. To the audience, I was the stern judge who presided over everyone and nitpicked flaws in every costume. However, what the viewers didn't know was that before the show started, some of the other cast members were my friends from the cosplay community.

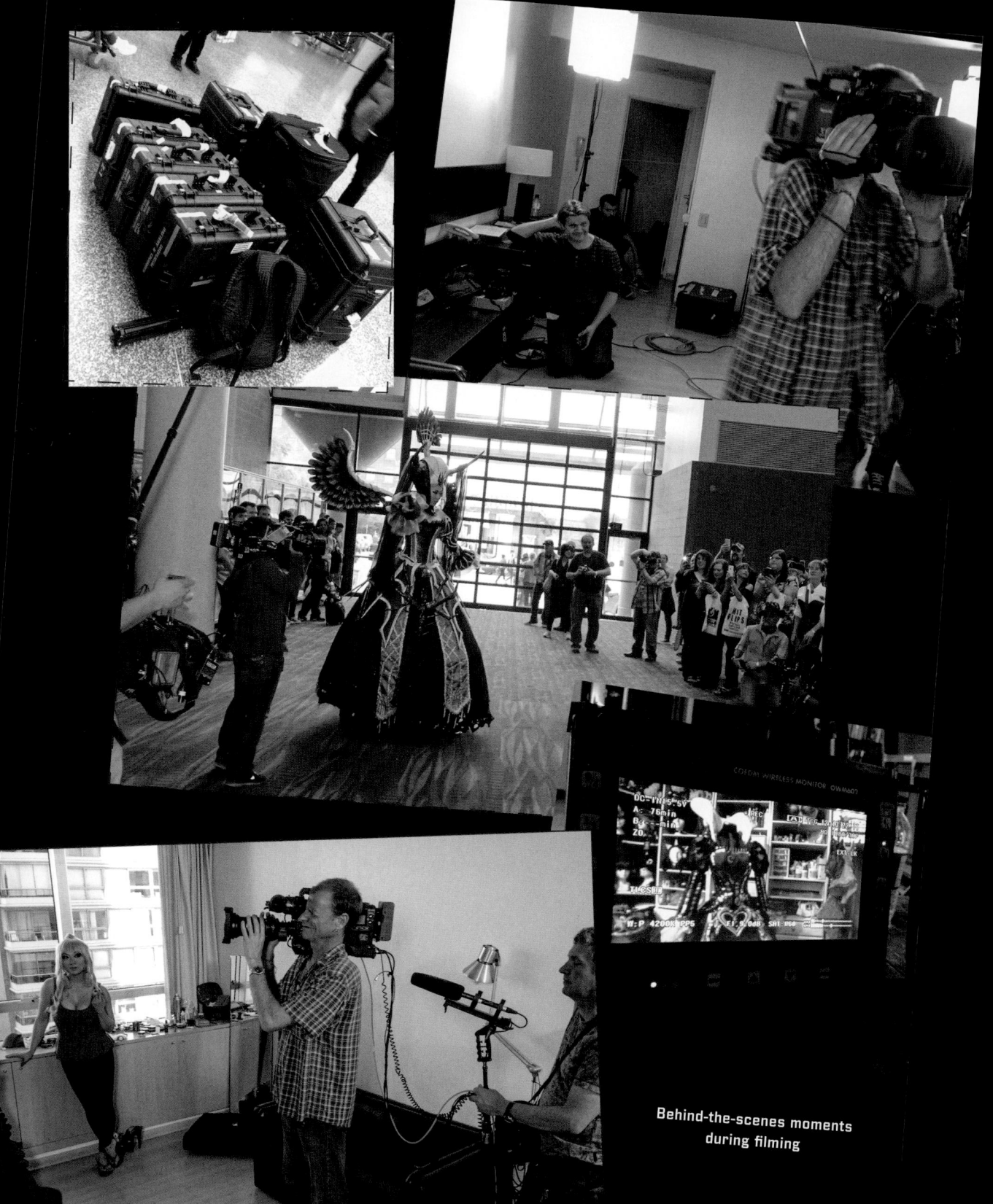

Behind-the-scenes moments
during filming

In addition to having to be critical of them on camera, I was separated from them while we weren't filming in order to preserve the integrity of the competitions. That meant that I couldn't visit them in their rooms, talk to them during filming unless we actually had a scene together, or see their costumes before judging. Filming the show in this way made me feel very isolated and really put a strain on our friendships.

Immediately after the first episode debuted and throughout its run, *Heroes of Cosplay* caused a lot of controversy within the cosplay community. In general, there was an outcry against how the show used manufactured drama to portray cosplay as a hypercompetitive and catty environment. Cosplay fans were convinced that we had ruined the hobby for the rest of the world. Syfy was criticized for sensationalizing cosplay in order to get higher ratings for its channel without understanding what cosplay culture was really like. The cast was accused of selling the cosplay community out for its own personal gain.

And then there was the editing. Editing is notoriously deceptive in reality TV. Good editing is so natural, you can't tell what has been injected and what has been cut. A sentiment can sound completely different if you just remove a couple of words from it. For example: "I don't like hot dogs with mustard" versus "I don't like hot dogs." That's a cut. Throughout *Heroes of Cosplay*, interviews with the cast were filmed in a confessional style, where the person being interviewed speaks directly to the camera. These confessions were often scheduled after long days of costume making or traveling, so I found it difficult to stay eloquent while recording them in my sleep-deprived state. Ultimately, because the show was generally unscripted, it was up to the editing to make a cohesive story out of all the footage.

On the night the second episode of *Heroes of Cosplay* aired, I was shocked to watch a scene where a comment I made was edited to sound as if I was telling plus-size cosplayers to be aware of how they looked, when actually, I was talking about myself: Sharing how I take a moment to get into the right mind-set before walking out into a crowded con hall in a costume. I had been cosplaying for almost fifteen years at that point and always spoke out on issues like inclusion and body positivity. Making disparaging comments against plus-size cosplayers is something I would never, ever do. I understood the production was just creating conflict to move the story line along, but that one little scene decimated me.

Within minutes, my Twitter and Facebook blew up. Seemingly endless comments appeared on my feed. They all condemned me as a fat shaming bitch. I received e-mails, tweets, and direct messages that told me what a horrible person I was. My follower count dropped. Several people said they threw away my signed merchandise.

In short, I got cancelled.

It was like getting punched in the gut. I couldn't believe how easily people accepted what they saw on TV as fact and how quickly they disregarded everything I'd stood for before that moment. Self-righteous gloating radiated from comment to comment, as if the show had indubitably confirmed all the awful things that people had always suspected of me.

I had tough skin and was used to being criticized, but the fallout I received from this moment on *Heroes of Cosplay* was unlike anything I'd ever experienced in the past. I really had no idea how to handle it. It felt like irreparable damage had been done to my image. The show's cast members, including myself, were still under contract, so I couldn't openly talk about what happened behind the scenes. I made a statement on my Facebook page that reiterated my belief that all people of all sizes and skin tones could, and should, cosplay. Beyond that, though, the only thing I could do was shut myself off from comments. However, despite doing so, the incident was brought up in professional settings and in my personal life again and again, well beyond the time when the show ended more than a year later. To this day, the same fat shaming rumors still pop up every once in a while.

Syfy didn't renew *Heroes of Cosplay* after the twelfth episode aired. Going into the show, I knew the process of being on reality TV was not going to be easy. However, I thought I'd done plenty of research on the format and had mentally prepared myself for the production. Before filming, everyone on the cast vowed to do everything we could to shift the focus of the show away from manufactured drama in order to reflect the real, diverse, and beautiful world of cosplay. However, once we had signed our contracts, with all their fine print and conditions, we found that we had very little influence on the outcome of the show. Still, when I look back on everything related to *Heroes of Cosplay* and compare it to all the outlandish concepts and pitches that I received before the show began production, I think the other cast members and myself did our best under the given circumstances.

The truth is that *Heroes of Cosplay* was not made for cosplayers but rather to introduce the world of cosplay to a mainstream audience. I believe that, no matter what, any first effort to make a series about cosplay would've caused controversy, because it's such a unique and complicated phenomenon that has too many facets to accurately showcase in just one season of television. Even though *Heroes of Cosplay* drew criticism for focusing too much on competition, it also provided audiences with the opportunity to see every step of a costume's creation. It showed people what it's like to debut a costume at an event and the excitement of entering a competition. The DIY, "can-do" spirit of cosplay came through in the tension-filled episodes and made the activity relatable to people who'd never considered dressing up before. The show even excited many viewers enough that they looked for their own conventions to attend, because *Heroes of Cosplay* was not shot on a soundstage—it took place in the real world.

Even though cosplayers hated *Heroes of Cosplay*, the positive impact it had on the community was felt right away. The cosplayers featured on the show were able to use their experiences to move on to new projects, and the public's greater interest in our community opened a lot of doors for other cosplayers on the scene as well. More eyes on us meant that big companies and conglomerates were more compelled to get in on the cosplay phenomenon. It also meant that there was more demand for cosplay-centric crafting materials, because an influx of cosplayers went from buying costumes to making them. In addition, a slew of new cosplayers joined the community thanks to the show. To this day, people come up to me at conventions and tell me they found cosplay through *Heroes of Cosplay*.

When I think back on my experience of being on the cosplay show, it was one of the hardest things I've ever done. However, I don't regret participating because the project did what I hoped it would: It brought new people into the world of cosplay. It expanded the commercial opportunities for people in cosplay and opened

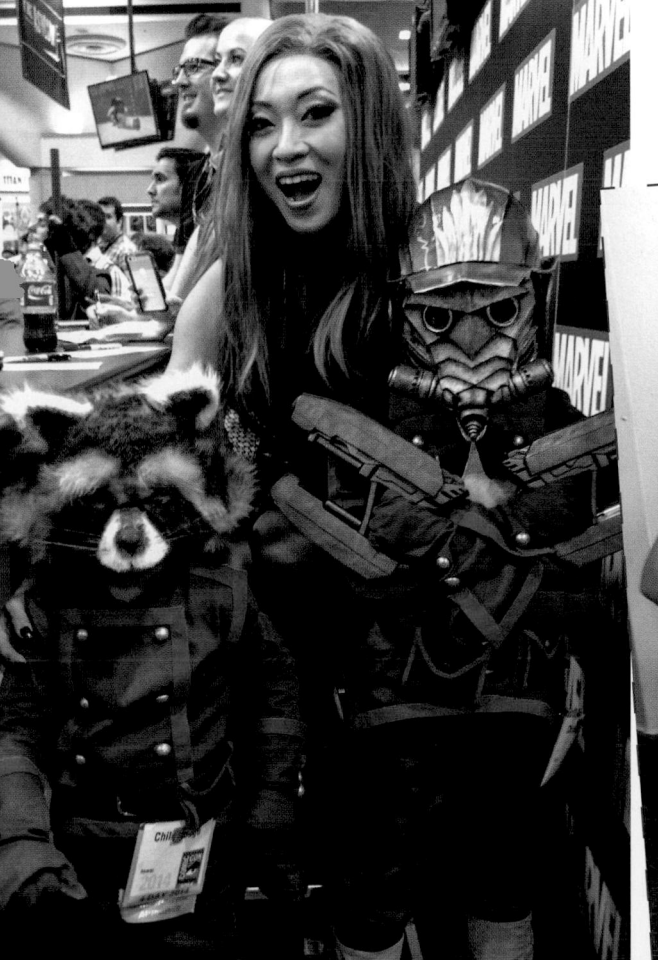

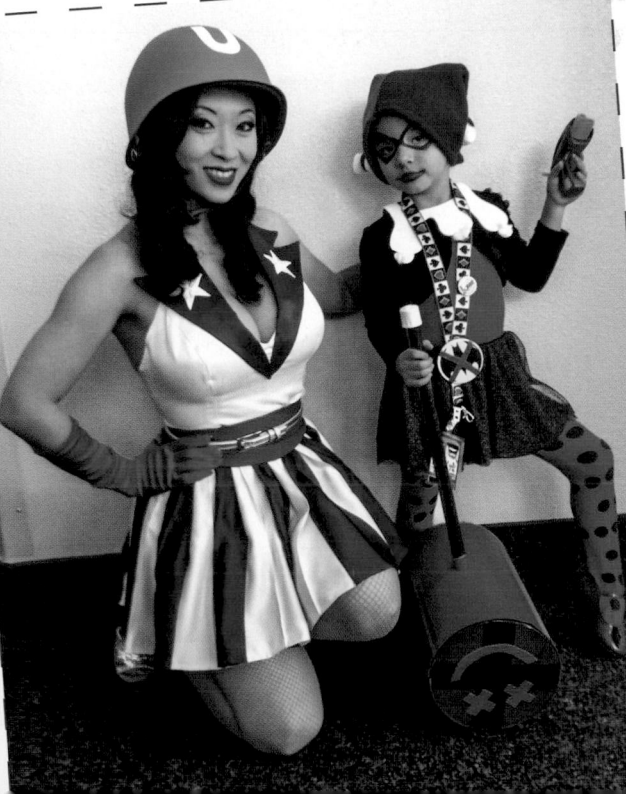

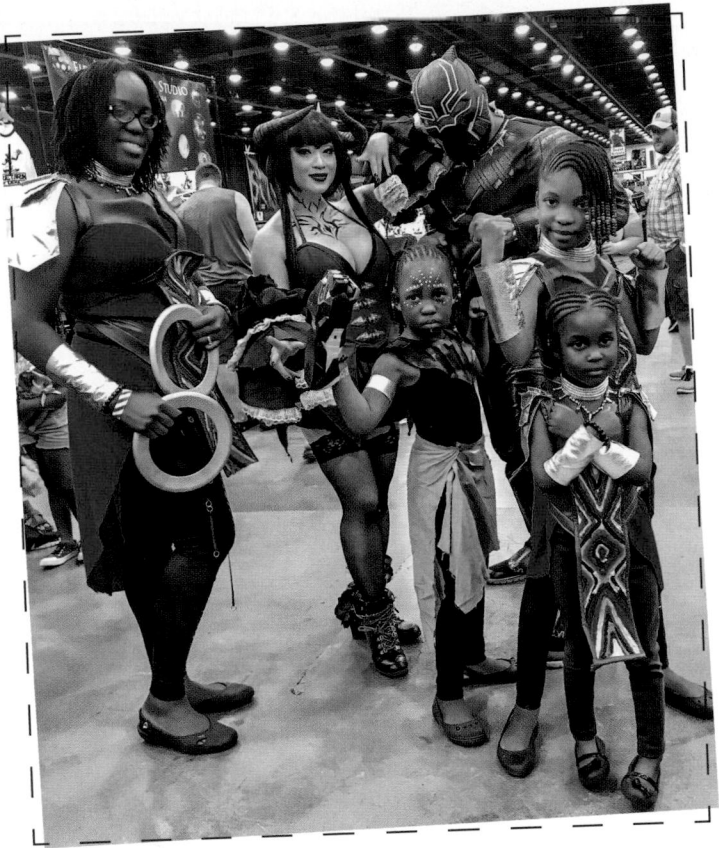
A cosplaying family!

the public's mind about how much fun the make-it-yourself aspect of the hobby could be. For every negative comment that was sent to me by people on the Internet, I met an excited new cosplayer who was inspired by *Heroes of Cosplay*. Kids would run up to me while calling out my name as if I was a family friend . . . or a Disney princess. They'd break into huge smiles when I asked them about their costumes, and sometimes they insisted on coming back to every day of a con to visit me. I've lost count of how many multigenerational families introduced themselves to me during events, all of them excited to have watched the show and found a joint hobby for the entire family to enjoy.

As I said earlier, the most valuable lesson I learned from my stint in reality TV is that even the most negative experiences can have positive outcomes. With time and understanding, the worst moments will pass, and you will be wiser for having weathered the storm. I definitely gained a lot of perspective (and patience) during the years I worked on *Heroes of Cosplay*. And at the end of the journey, I found that my name recognition and brand ultimately benefited from being on the show.

After all, being on *Heroes of Cosplay* was how the McCall Pattern Company found me and, how together, we jumpstarted a new market for cosplay in the sewing and crafting industry.

In 2014, the same year that *Heroes of Cosplay* finished airing, one of the directors at McCall approached me at New York Comic Con and asked if I'd like to design a pattern for them. As a longtime user of their sewing instructionals, I was beyond thrilled. Sewing was an area I was intricately familiar with thanks to fifteen years of cosplaying, and this

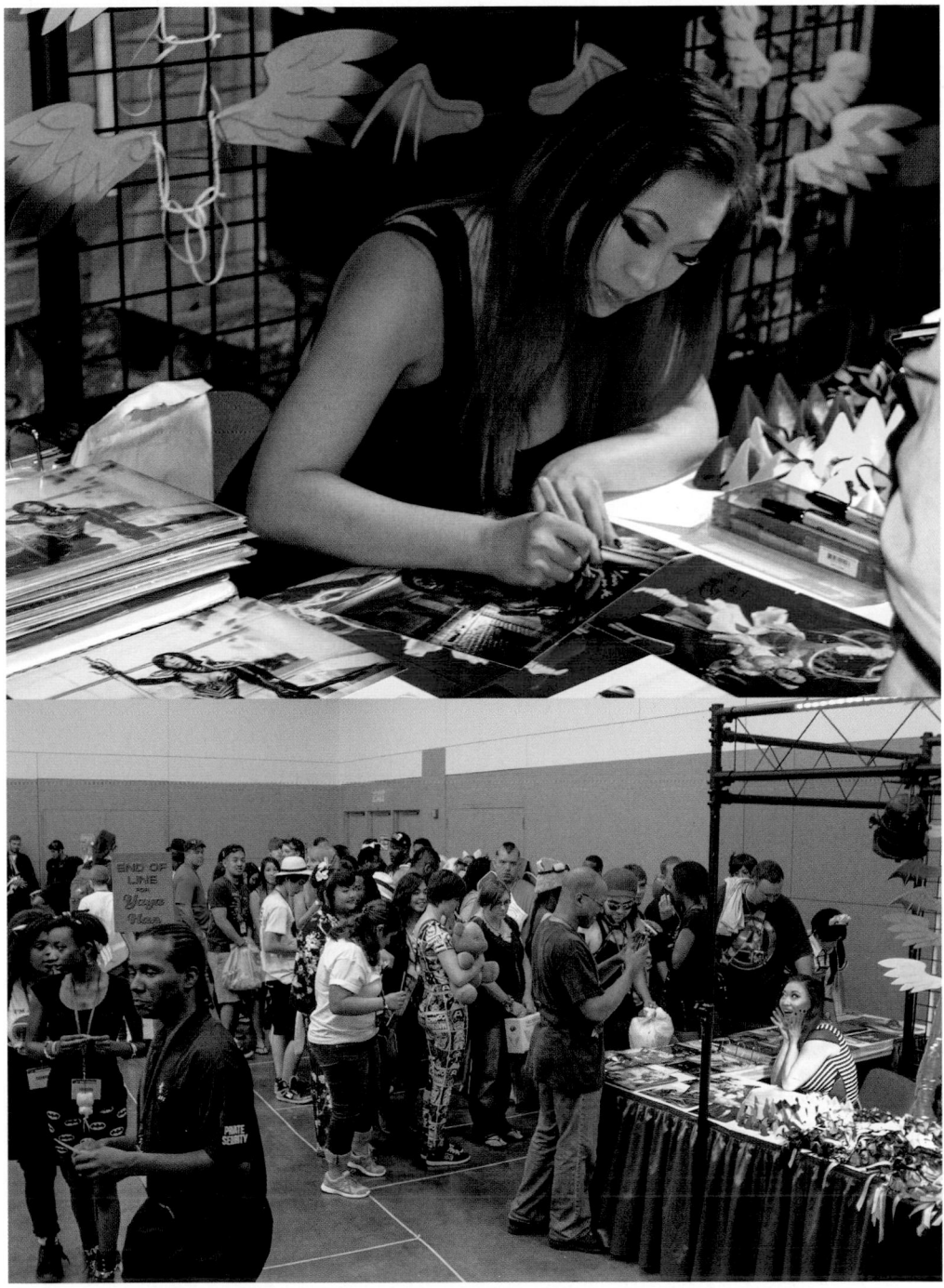

Signing prints and greeting fans at my booth at a con

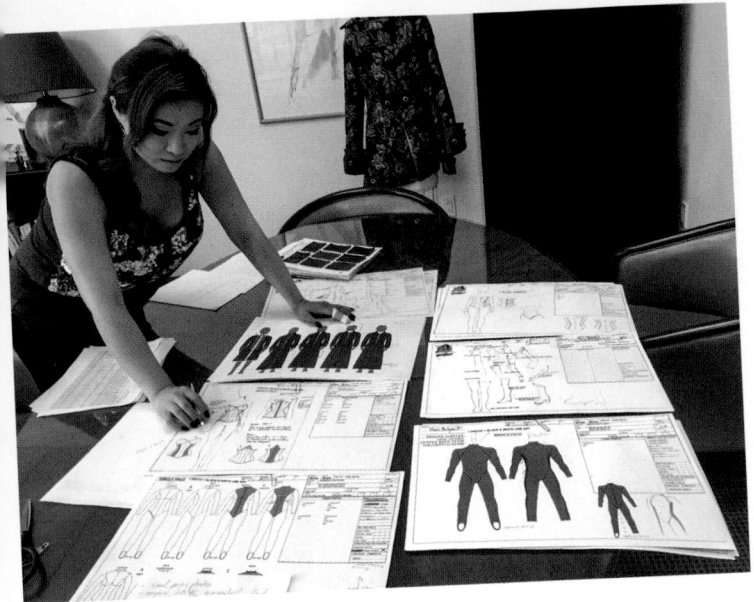
Reviewing pattern croquis in development

opportunity caused me to feel a type of excitement that I'd never known before. One five-minute conversation opened a door in my mind: The sewing industry wanted to get into cosplay, and I knew exactly what was missing from the market. All the memories I had of patterns I desperately needed for costumes but that didn't exist for purchase at the time came flooding through my brain. These would be the patterns I would create. My excitement must have been palpable, because the McCall team invited me to a meeting in their New York headquarters soon after the convention ended. During that discussion, I spent hours talking the team members' ears off about the cosplay community, how cosplayers like me shop, what kinds of costumes we make, and what patterns we need. In one day, we established a mutual vision for a partnership, and shortly thereafter, I signed a design license agreement. This is where I have to thank *Heroes of Cosplay*, because not only was it the reason McCall reached out to me; the show also served as a multi-year bootcamp in business negotiations.

The first pattern I designed for McCall was the Ultimate Bodysuit Pattern. This was a tight-fitting one-piece with strategic seam placements that allowed each buyer to alter the suit to their specific body shape. It was easy to sew, looked flattering, and was versatile. I knew without a doubt that this was going to be the first product in my collection because a custom-fitted bodysuit was the one pattern I'd wished for most throughout the years. Working closely with McCall's pattern-drafting team, we finalized the croquis drawings of the bodysuit and made mock-ups of the design. After those were complete, I sewed a black bodysuit based on the sample pattern and Brian took photos of me for the packaging.

I announced the McCall × Yaya Han collaboration on my birthday: April 10, 2015. It was an instant hit. In fact, the reaction to my first pattern was so positive that I didn't know what to do with myself—I'd gotten used to receiving criticism for so long. People were incredibly excited and thankful for patterns made by a cosplayer, and I lost count of how many

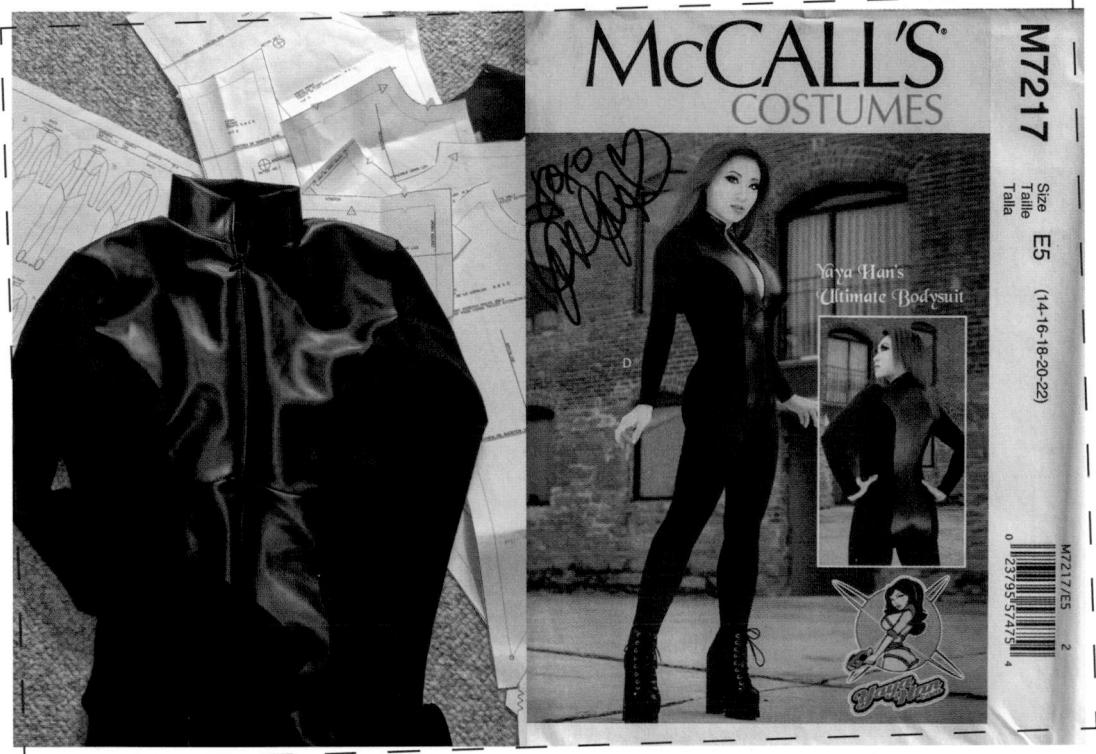

Mock up bodysuit and finished pattern side by side

commented that they couldn't wait to make something with the bodysuit pattern. In the first week it hit shelves, it sold out at just about every JOANN and Hancock store. McCall had to scramble to ship stock to replenish the in-store pattern drawers. I designed a plus-size version of the pattern, and that was released a couple of months later. From that point on, I developed a workflow with the McCall team that allowed me to freely explore new pattern ideas and designs. As of today, we have released more than forty patterns as part of the Yaya Han collection. Thanks to McCall's global distribution network, these instructional materials are sold worldwide.

Working with McCall was a new type of experience for me because we were making products for mass retail. I could walk into a store anywhere in America, touch my patterns, and see my picture inside catalogues. Best of all, my products were helping cosplayers around the world to learn and improve their costume-making skills in a manner that I never could when I was taking commissions or making cosplay accessories. Having a step-by-step instructional pattern taught me how to sew all those years ago, and I could see that same excitement in cosplayers using my McCall products. Even now, every time someone tags me in a progress post or walks up to me at a con wearing a costume made with my patterns, my heart does a flip.

After my relationship with McCall was established and we had successfully tested out the market, McCall's merchandising director introduced me to Wyla, Inc., the fabric manufacturing company with whom McCall collaborates. The people at Wyla hit me with a whammy: They wanted to explore the possibility of creating a line of cosplay-centric fabrics with me. Just as with the patterns, all the fabrics I wished for during my years of cosplay came flowing through my mind until I felt about ready to burst. What followed our first conversation were months of exciting creative talks and brainstorming sessions, as well as the satisfying feeling of validation that all my years of fabric hoarding had been worth it. Even though I had never gone to school for fashion design or textile design, the fifteen years I spent making costumes gave me excellent experience in understanding how fabrics can be used in different ways, how they go through wear and tear, and how to tell if a fabric is of high quality. I knew exactly what kind of features and finishes I wanted in my fabrics, and often my partners (who had been in the textile business for decades) seemed surprised by my choices. Cosplay is, if anything, unconventional, and I wanted unconventional fabrics.

At first we were just going to release my line of cosplay fabrics on the Internet. However, one day Wyla told me that JOANN was interested in carrying it instead. I was stunned. It was already hard to believe that the few sewing patterns I'd designed were available in stores, but an entire fabric aisle with the fabrics I wanted to make? They were quite unusual after all—stretch pearlescent pleather, peacock-patterned brocade, metallic spandex—and nothing like what I had seen in JOANN stores before. It seemed completely outside of the realm of possibility. JOANN was the biggest fabric and craft chain in the US, and every cosplayer shopped there; I practically lived in my local franchise during con crunch time. I didn't believe the deal was real for months, even when I got updates on negotiations, signed off on sample fabrics, or was asked to provide images for signage and labels. The entire time, I thought, *Sure, whatever. This is not happening.*

In February 2016, the first Cosplay by Yaya fabric collection arrived in JOANN stores across the nation . . . and it almost made me quit cosplay.

Within the first couple of days of the collection's release, the online cosplay community went off the rails over the fabric line. People became hung up on the term *cosplay fabrics*. They argued that all fabrics are cosplay fabrics and that by branding mine with the word *cosplay*, I was trying to monopolize the market.

It was the damn cat ears situation all over again.

A huge number of complaints centered around the pricing on the fabrics: It was too high. Even though I had no control over distribution or pricing as the licensor, I was accused of unfairly capitalizing on cosplay.

On top of all this, someone made a post about how they used some of the Yaya fabrics to make a costume and broke out in horrible hives after they wore it. The post went viral in the cosplay community, sparking rumors about my fabrics being toxic. The accusations spiraled out of control into a full-out smear campaign that accused me of deliberately creating poisonous fabrics with the intention of hurting people. Even if I had done such a thing, those fabrics would not have passed the stringent examinations all imported textiles have to pass before going to market in America. The charge was ludicrous.

Once again, my social media was flooded with outcries and demands for a statement. Caught between disbelief, hurt, and anger, I scrolled through my feed and felt heat rising to the back of my neck. I desperately wanted to reply to my critics and defend myself, but the whole situation was so ridiculously fabricated that I couldn't formulate the words with which to do so.

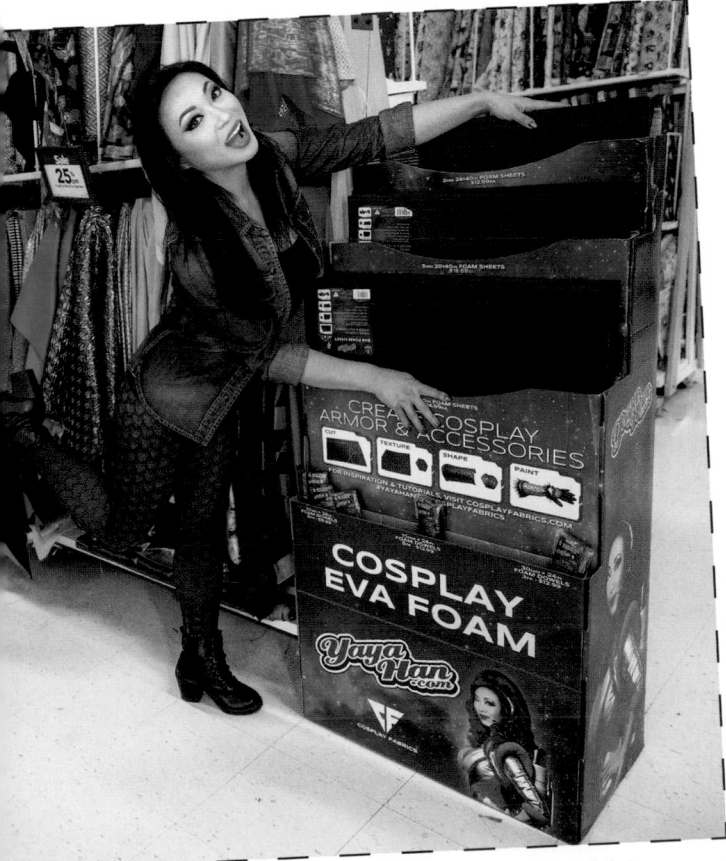

While I had been attacked before, matters felt different this time. In the past I was criticized over my costumes or how I looked in them. In this situation, even the specific attack on my character as a poison-mixing witch didn't bother me that much. What hurt me most was the fact that I had worked incredibly hard on a fabric line with the cosplay community in mind the entire time. Finally, a fabric manufacturer listened to my ideas and actually

Visiting my in-store EVA foam display for the first time.

created hard-to-find and unique materials for cosplayers, and I was so excited to share the news with my community, knowing that others would find them useful. But when I proudly presented it to my peers, they completely rejected it. Upon the announcement of the up-coming release, people immediately misconstrued my intentions as selfish and conniving. For the first time in many years, I daydreamed about doing something other than cosplay. I thought about moving to Africa and working on a conservation project. What would it be like to devote my life to saving endangered animals instead of trudging through a hostile environment where everything I did was misunderstood?

However, as always, Brian calmed me down. I deleted every social media app from my phone and didn't look at any of them for a few days. Then I got an e-mail from a Good Samaritan cosplayer. She told me that she found the toxic fabric post fishy and had taken the time to investigate it. She'd called multiple JOANN stores to verify when the fabrics were stocked and that those dates did not match the date when the viral post was originally uploaded. My fabrics arrived in stores an entire week later than the post's date stamp, so there was no way some-one could have already made a costume with them. I logged on to Facebook and discovered that tons of people, including some of my friends, had been coming to my defense by refuting the negative claims with facts and writing supportive comments and posts regarding my new cosplay fabric initiative. Counterarguments were being shared and others were posting about how much they liked the fabrics from my collection when they saw them in their local stores. It was truly heartwarming.

The rumors died down quickly within a couple of weeks, and after a few months I started spotting my fabrics in people's costumes. Since then, response to my fabric line has been overwhelmingly positive, giving me the chance to create two seasonal collections with new textiles each year (Spring and Fall). I've also added a Basics collection with the most popular fabric styles and colors that's available year-round. The continued success of the fabric line has opened the doors for other cosplay categories in JOANN as well. In February 2019, I launched the Cosplay by Yaya Han trims and embellishments collection in all 800+ JOANN stores, followed up by a cosplay EVA foam collection a few months later. I also recently con-tributed to the launch of Dremel rotary tools and accessories.

One of my proudest life's accomplishments is having helped the sewing and crafting industry understand cosplay and the immense potential of that market, both in creative innovation and market growth. I love bragging about the exceptional creators in our com-munity and convincing companies to invest in cosplay-centric products. It is a win for everyone. The easier it is for people to make costumes, the more they will be tempted to join in on the fun. In turn, expanding the audience for cosplay provides its community members with more opportunities to realize their personal dream cosplays, to show their dedication to the characters these artists created, to be featured in books and magazines, or even to make cosplay their livelihood.

The release of the cosplay EVA foam coincided with my twentieth anniversary of cosplaying in July 2019, and to my unfettered surprise, the cosplay community exploded with positive sentiments. Hundreds of tweets, posts, and comments tagged me in messages of thanks not just for the easier accessibility to armor-making foam but also for all the contributions I had made to the cosplay community. It felt so good to be recognized by my peers, and to know that my products helped them finish a project in a pinch or made it easier for them to learn a new skill. It has given me more confidence to design and develop new materials and really cherish this new avenue in my career. Creating supplies that people deem worthy enough to include in their costumes has been a deeply satisfying experience, and I hope to continue innovating in this field for a long time to come.

My journey from amateur to professional was no walk in the park. The road to entrepreneurship was even bumpier. There is a great cost to building empires—even small ones. However, if you can withstand the challenges, building something can lead to great rewards as well. I am incredibly grateful for the opportunities the cosplay community has given me, and I wouldn't trade them for the world (even if I still dream about taking care of lion cubs sometimes).

CHAPTER 16

Cosplay as a Career

Forging Your Own Path

The cosplay community used to laugh at the idea that their hobby could ever become a commercial industry. However, that was before the unstoppable juggernaut of geek culture changed the world forever. Fandom brought cosplay into the mainstream, and the increased awareness of this craft meant a never-before-seen market demand for everything related to cosplay. In recent years, a growing percentage of cosplayers have successfully made the jump from hobbyists to relying solely on cosplay for their income. Newcomers routinely enter the cosplay scene with the goal of eventually turning their hobby into a business.

That being said, any career in cosplay requires a lot of hard work, determination, and patience. Pop culture is established, but the cosplay industry is still in its infancy. It is an emerging market with fast changes, unforeseen shifts, and few statistics on which to rely on. I can't share a step-by-step plan to making guaranteed money with cosplay simply because there hasn't yet been a proven formula. That is what makes the business so exciting, though—what we don't know can't hold us back.

In this section of the book, I will help you understand cosplay as a commercial industry and give you an overview of the basic skills needed to enter this field in a professional capacity if you so choose. I will also cover the wide range of work that professional cosplayers have been known to take on. Then I will give you general business advice and share the lessons that I have learned from my own experiences and observations over the years.

Let's get started.

TYPES OF PROFESSIONAL COSPLAYERS

The term *professional cosplayer* can be misleading because it conjures up the image of someone who gets paid to just dress up in costumes. It's not that simple. A career as a cosplayer is comparable to the experience of being a commercial artist. There is no bar exam to pass or certification to acquire. Both are highly individualized and skill-driven fields that can be pursued as full-time jobs. Alternatively, they can be done part-time. Many artists with industry credits also have supplemental jobs or additional avenues of income that do not invalidate them as professionals. The same goes for cosplayers. Just like artists can work on many different types of projects, from comics to technical drawings, and have them all fall under the realm of commercial art, cosplayers can do many different activities with their skills as well. There is no universal formula to becoming a professional artist. The same applies to becoming a pro cosplayer.

Cosplay is a unique industry because it combines art, fandom, entertainment, and merchandising. Just as hobbyists are often drawn to cosplay for multiple different reasons, the people who cosplay for a living tend to gravitate to more than one area in the industry and combine various revenue streams into individualized business models. To "make it in the biz," you need out-of-the-box thinking, patience, and—of course—a little bit of luck.

Let's take a look at the three overarching career paths in cosplay, starting with . . .

THE COSPLAY ENTERTAINER

The social media boom has created a slew of self-made celebrities and Internet personalities. In this new career field, the persona is the product, and a large-enough fanbase can

Picture of cosplayer Meg Turney with a bunch of fans

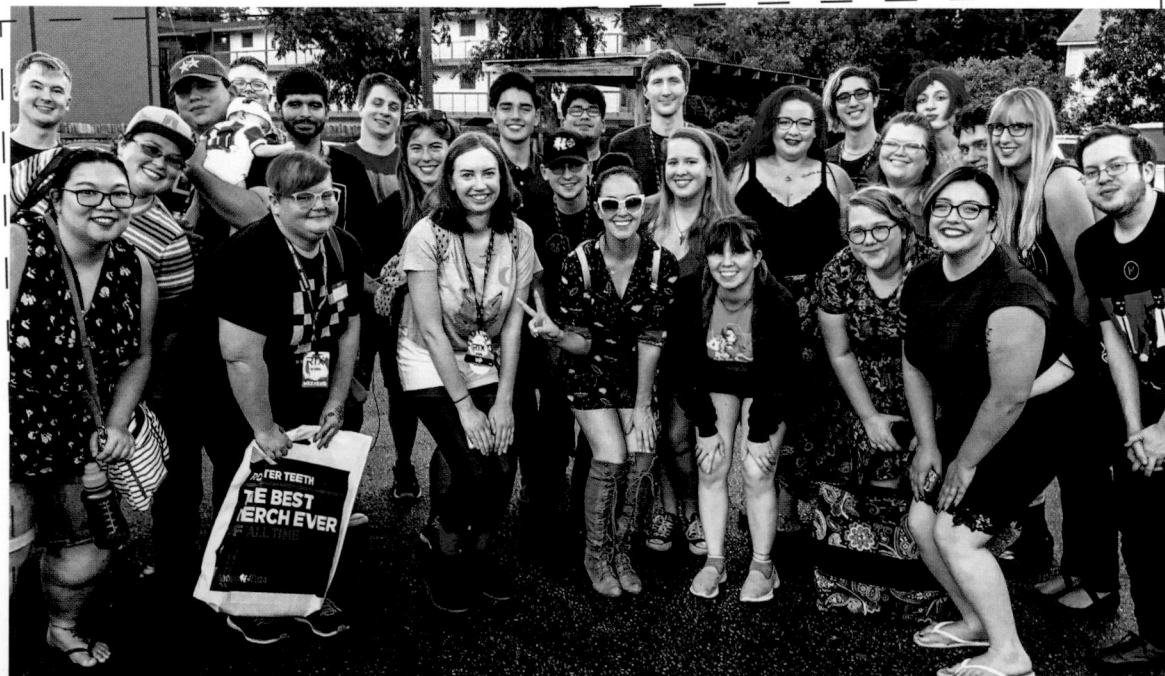

translate into financial income. Some cosplayers have tapped into this personality-driven market and become what I like to call cosplay entertainers. They not only captivate an audience with their ability to transform into other characters; they also create lasting fan interest by branding themselves as artists, models, or a combination thereof.

While cosplay entertainers may often be known for their sexy images, their personalities are the true keys to their success. They are charming and personable, and they engage with their followers on a daily basis. To succeed as a cosplay entertainer, you have to be willing to share a lot of yourself in order to create meaningful relationships with fans.

Top cosplay entertainers can earn more than six figures per year, but it usually means combining several avenues of income. Here are some of them.

Cosplay Prints: Cosplay prints are the most common merchandise that cosplayers offer. They range from 4×6–inch postcard-size to 8×10–inch and 11×17–inch sizes. They are usually printed on cardstock or photo paper. Much like fan art prints, cosplayers offer their prints for sale at conventions and online. Many people who buy prints are fans of the cosplayer and want their autograph. Other buyers like the images and collect cosplay prints in a similar manner to which they collect fan art. For many, prints are souvenirs and a way to support the cosplayers they like.

Advantages: Cardstock prints cost less than one dollar per piece to produce, and a signed print can be sold for as much as twenty dollars. You can also create printed products such as photo books and calendars that have a collectible quality to them.

Disadvantages: Consumer interest in prints varies greatly. It is mostly determined by the popularity of the cosplayer and the appeal of the photos. More often than not, the best-selling prints are sexually provocative in nature. To produce quality prints, you have to do regular photoshoots, which can be quite involved.

Cosplay Guest Work: Going to a convention as an invited guest is a dream shared by many cosplayers because it means getting paid to do what we already do for fun. It is often the first milestone goal that cosplayers set for themselves in the quest to become a professional. Guest appearances can entail tasks like partaking in convention programming as a panelist, host, or judge. Other potential activities include autograph sessions, photo ops, Q and As, interviews, fan meet and greets, and more.

Advantages: Besides income from merchandise sales and appearance fees, guest appearances can really help with brand building. An invitation is a tangible credit on a résumé, and cons are a great forum for networking.

Disadvantages: A con invitation doesn't necessarily mean payment in hand. Appearance fees have to be negotiated, and they all depend on what the organizers deem worthy—the cosplayer's popularity, as well as the programming content they provide, are all part of the negotiations. Con guesting can involve long and exhausting days in addition to all the pitfalls that come with vending at a trade show.

Vlogging and Streaming: A lot of cosplay entertainers create YouTube videos that generate ad revenue. The video content can range from travel vlogs and convention reports to unboxings and, well, anything their fans want to see. Cosplayers can also make money by streaming on platforms such as Twitch or Caffeine. There are paid subscription options and incentives for viewers to donate during streams.

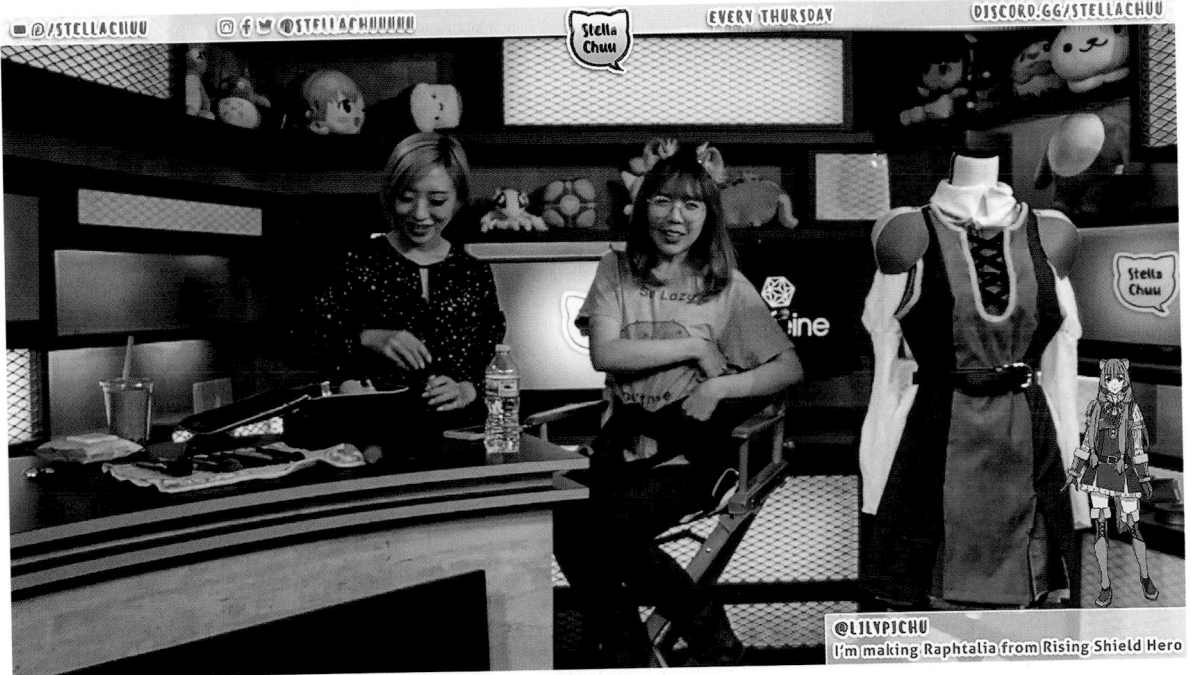

Stella Chuu (left) with a cosplayer (right) on the set of her streaming show *Stella Transforms.*

Advantages: Video is the fastest-growing media form on social media and often yields more engagement than other types of content. More importantly, it is a great way for creators to connect with their fans and show more of their personalities and what makes them uniquely entertaining.

Disadvantages: The time commitment for recording and editing can be daunting. Building an audience also requires a regular schedule and consistency. Lastly, anything can happen during a livestream, so a lot of streamers have to implement added helpers in the form of moderators for their sessions.

Sponsorships: Sponsorships mostly pertain to free products sent to cosplayers. These products can range from costume-making materials and accessories, such as wigs and contacts, to just about anything else social media influencers get offered. Some cosplayers with a sizable following are able to negotiate paid promotional posts. A company might also provide an affiliate code that allows a cosplayer to earn a percentage of sales generated through posts.

Advantages: Free stuff! Most influencers in cosplay are compensated with free products, while some personalities get paid on top of swag. Unpaid sponsorships become available quite early on in a cosplayer's career, so give it a try.

Disadvantages: You need some social media presence before these opportunities arise, and once the offers come in, you may have to deal with a lot of dubious sellers and products. There are no industry standards for cosplay-related influencer work yet, so everything is up for negotiation. Do not agree to purchase a product at a discount in exchange for a promotion, and make sure the products are in line with how you present yourself as a cosplayer.

Ambassadorships and Endorsements: These are more prestigious agreements than sponsorships in which a cosplayer becomes a representative for a product and/or a company.

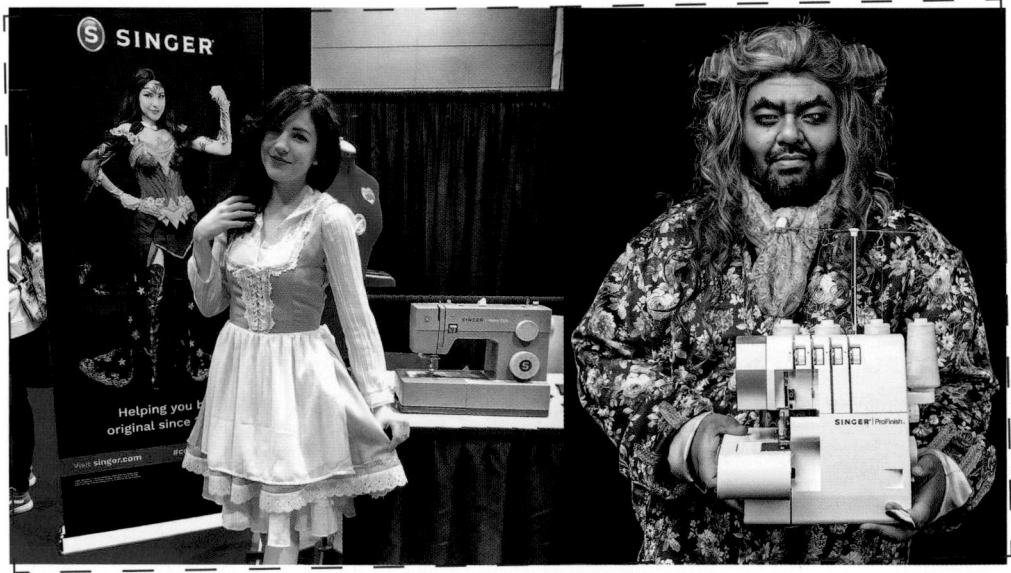

Cosplay brand ambassadors AvantGeek and Canvas Cosplay

Sewing machine manufacturers such as SINGER sewing machine brand and BERNINA have ambassadorship agreements with cosplayers, as do some companies that produce crafting material. I predict a lot of growth and new opportunities in this area in the future.

Advantages: The exposure and association with a bigger brand can help legitimize you and/or increase your social media following. The pay can also be lucrative, depending on what you're able to negotiate.

Disadvantages: Ambassadorships entail more responsibilities and can mean a lot more work. Also, as a representative of a brand, your actions and words can reflect negatively on the company you're working for, so you have to be aware of your conduct during and outside of active campaigns—we've all seen brands drop celebrity endorsers over a scandal. There is also usually an exclusivity clause, so you cannot work with competing brands.

Spokesmodel Work: One of the most coveted jobs in cosplay is spokesmodel work for gaming companies, comic book studios, and anime distributors. In the past, studios hired models and actors for event promotion, but there are multiple advantages to hiring cosplayers instead. By nature, cosplayers are more likely to have a vested interest in the properties they're hired to promote, especially when the product is a video game or new comic book series. Cosplayers can also create the costume they'll be wearing.

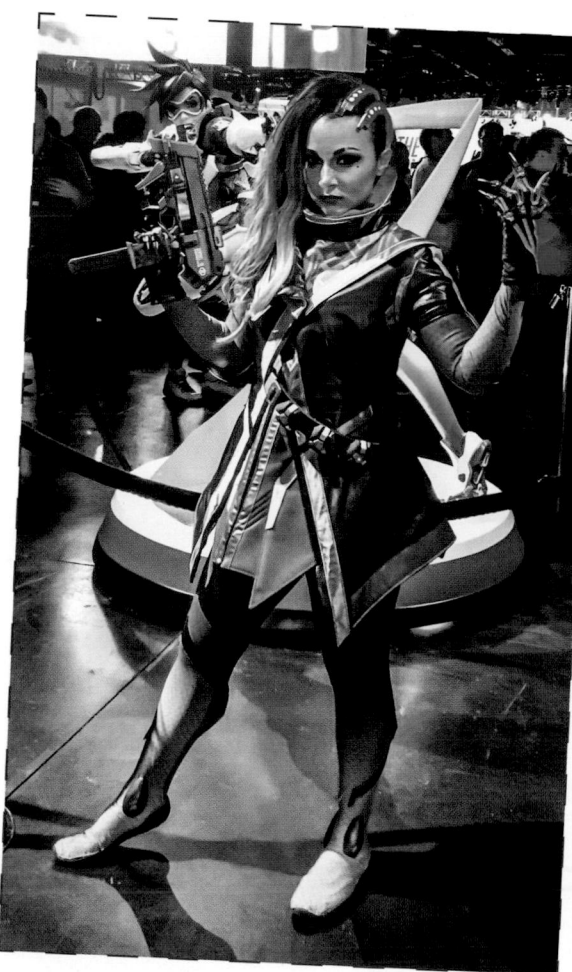

Cosplaying spokesmodels can be hired for individual events or for entire promotional campaigns. Some of these spokesmodels even ultimately become the official real-life version of a character. Most of the time, this type of work is offered to photogenic cosplayers with big name recognition or a proven track record. The pay scale for this type of job can

Soni Aralynn as the official Sombra from *Overwatch* for the character debut at BlizzCon.

range from a few hundred dollars for a day's work all the way up to five figures for a full campaign that includes costume creation and promotion.

Advantages: The biggest advantage here is probably the prestige and joy of working in a field in which you are personally invested. A good spokesmodel campaign can provide exposure and monetary income as well as give you fulfillment as a fan.

Disadvantages: This type of work is often accompanied by last-minute requests and tight deadlines. There is also the added stress of handling a costume commission as well as acting as a spokesmodel; you will likely be wearing multiple hats and managing a lot of expectations. Event workdays can be long and exhausting. They also often involve a hectic travel schedule. Usually the costume belongs to the company after the project is wrapped unless otherwise negotiated.

Patreon and Fan Clubs: Patreon is a monthly subscription website through which people can pay what they want in order to support artists, musicians, YouTube creators, podcasters, and other creatives. Cosplayers have been using Patreon since 2015 to create exclusive content for paying subscribers, and the practice has grown into a type of idol fan club. Until Patreon, hypersexual cosplay (called "lewds") was quite stigmatized in the fandom community, and there weren't many ways to consistently monetize it. Patreon turned out to be the perfect platform for cosplayers to create sexy content and market it directly to paying customers. While there are non-lewd cosplay Patreon accounts, the highest-earning cosplayers on the platform are women who offer sexually appealing content. This material can include

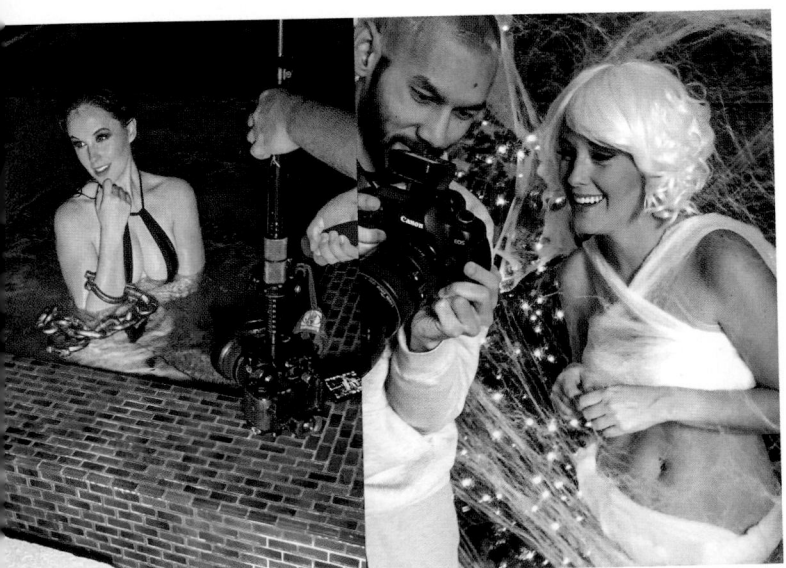

themed photo sets, Polaroids, signed prints, video content, Google Hangouts sessions, and more. All of these can be provided as monthly rewards to subscribers who pay varying amounts to subscribe to different tiers of a Patreon account.

Advantages: Since Patreon is an Internet platform, this route can give you creative

Meg Turney shooting for a Patreon set

freedom and a flexible schedule as well as the ability to work from the comfort of your home. There are a lot of people who are willing to pay for sexy content, so the potential for substantial income is quite good.

Disadvantages: Mature or adult content tends to be a slope where you have to increase the tease to hold your customers' attention, so in order to keep subscribers paying each month, you have to be extra creative in keeping your content fresh and interesting. Lewds can also affect your chances to partner with some global companies or brands with more family-friendly reputations. Lastly, social media platforms are increasingly becoming stricter about hosting adult content. Instagram, Facebook, and Tumblr all have enforced guidelines that limit inappropriate content from appearing on their platforms. Even Patreon has imposed tighter restrictions on adult content.

COSPLAY EDUCATORS

Another viable career path in cosplay is to build your brand around creating educational content. The explosive growth of cosplay's visibility in the world, as well as the influx of new cosplayers to the community, has made educational content incredibly valuable. Unlike the entertainer career paths I outlined before, as an educator your audience is made up of other cosplayers and crafters. Although you might experience slower growth than entertainers do, your audience is composed of dedicated people whose needs are similar to yours.

Tutorials and Educational Content: The first cosplayers to find commercial success with tutorial books were American prop maker Bill Doran of Punished Props Academy and German cosplayer Kamui Cosplay. Both of them have written multiple books on armor making, painting, and other cosplay crafting techniques. These books are available in printed form and as digital downloads. Nowadays many other people are self-publishing crafting books and tutorial pamphlets, giving creators who want to focus on process a financial avenue to pursue their passion.

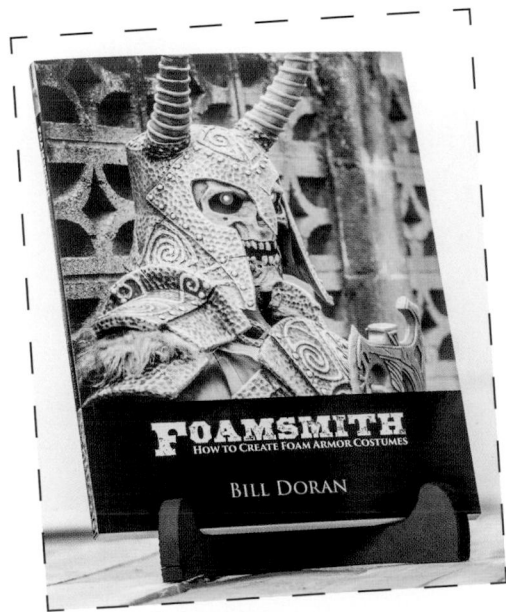

Bill Doran's *Foamsmith* book

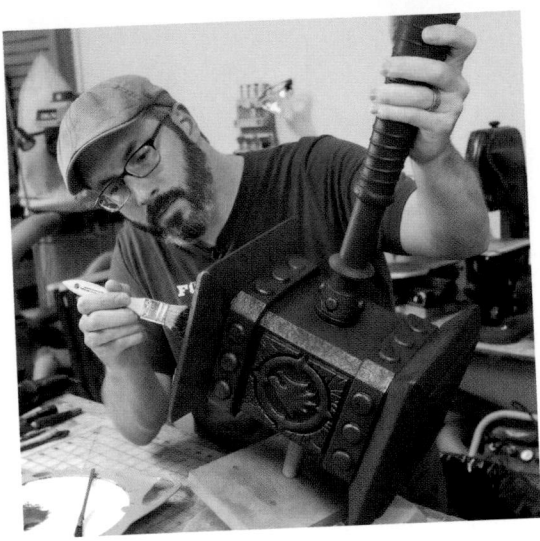
Bill painting a hammer for a tutorial

Advantages: Tutorial books are a valuable commodity that can generate continued income. By teaching someone to make something, you inspire loyalty and trust. Cosplay educators who post a lot of progress content may attract sponsorships and commercial work from crafting material companies and gaming companies.

Disadvantages: Creating educational content requires a lot of work and dedication. You have to first establish yourself as an expert in a field before people will consider you a teacher. Not only do cosplay educators have to hone their skills; they also have to constantly innovate and learn new techniques. To self-publish a book, you have to consider the initial cost of printing, and you might also have to hire a graphic designer, a photographer, and a copy editor. If you choose to go down this route, you should strive to develop a teaching style that works for your content and audience. Additionally, be sure not to neglect branding, marketing, and regular use of social media.

Patterns, Templates, and Build Kits: A lot of cosplayers make downloadable PDF patterns and printable blueprints of costumes and props. These are great products because they give cosplayers starting points for their projects. While generally inexpensive, pattern sales can add up over time and provide supplemental income. Nowadays people also offer ready-to-print 3-D models.

Build kits include raw casts of gems, buckles, and accessories, as well as other parts that cosplayers can purchase and finish on their own. A lot of build kits consist of 3-D-printed, resin-cast, or laser-cut pieces.

Advantages: It is easier to crank out raw and unfinished pieces than it is to produce polished items. Raw kits are cheaper and allow the buyer to customize the finish—it's a win-win for both parties. You can make patterns while you're working on a new costume, and once the digital file is done, it can continuously generate sales for you.

Disadvantages: It is time-consuming to prototype build kits and draft pattern templates, especially if you supplement them with instructions or tutorials on how to craft a finished showcase piece. Digital downloads are small-ticket items, so you have to rely on sales volume for any significant income. The success of these products also depends on what is popular in cosplay at any given moment, so many creators work under pressure to make templates and kits in time to hit new trends in cosplay.

Streaming and Subscriptions: Live crafting sessions on Twitch, YouTube, Facebook, or Caffeine can be very entertaining and interesting for viewers. They also provide learning possibilities. Subscribers will sometimes donate to funds that allow you to purchase more materials. Livestreams can build a fanbase interested in buying your other offerings, such as tutorial books or prop templates.

Patreon is another platform where you can build an audience for educational content. You can post tutorials, let people follow your costume builds in detail, and share other educational content. As mentioned previously, the growth rate for this type of Patreon might be slower than that of a cosplay entertainer's Patreon, but a number of cosplay educators such as Kinpatsu Cosplay have successful accounts. The rewards for supporting Kinpatsu Cosplay include progress on builds, templates, instructional booklets, and prints.

Advantages: By focusing on streaming, you can work from home, set your own schedule, and get paid to craft. Once you have established a following, the income can be somewhat reliable. However, the best thing about this line of work is probably the dedicated fan base you'll build. For people who love to craft, this is a great way to immerse yourself in a community of like-minded people.

Disadvantages: As with any type of streaming or video content, there is an initial set-up cost for equipment, and you will probably need a dedicated crafting space in which to film or stream. The process for building an audience can be slow, and there is a learning curve to creating crafting content that is also entertaining to viewers. As with any type of subscription service, you enter an agreement with your paying subscribers and therefore have to fulfill rewards on time and release promised content consistently.

Prop and Costume Commissions: If the commission business Brian and I had in 2005 had started ten years later, it might not have failed. After all, today cosplay commissions are in high demand. The market is big enough now that people understand the value of a custom-made costume compared to the value of a mass-produced costume made in China. A commissioned costume is like a wedding dress—it's a high-quality and one-of-a-kind tailored piece worth investing in.

Let's break down what it takes to run a commission business today.

Commissioners usually have an area of expertise, whether it is sewing, sculpting, or 3-D printing. They are also confidently able to gauge the time and effort required for a project, which is a skill you can build only through experience and repetition. Commissioners who actively learn new skills are able to expand their capabilities and take on new types of projects, but there are plenty who stick with what they know best.

If you take on commissions, you don't have to make every part of a person's project yourself. Some cosplayers take on only wig commissions. Others specialize in leather and corsets. Sometimes commissioners will work with other crafters who have skill sets they don't in order to complete a project together.

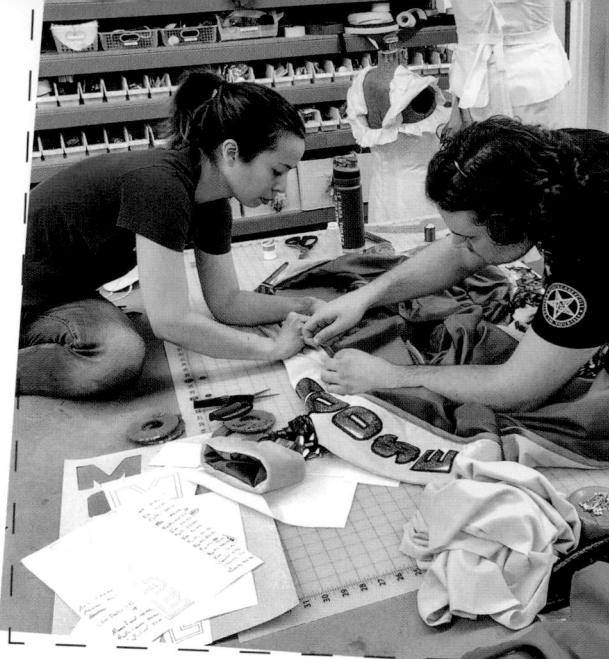

Catherine Jones and an assistant adding details to a green garment

Besides craftsmanship skills, commissioners have to stay organized and maintain communication with their customers. I know a number of cosplay commissioners who hire assistants to help answer e-mails and perform administrative tasks. As a commission business grows, it is not uncommon for the owner to hire employees for the sewing and crafting work as well.

The top commissioners in cosplay usually also do commercial work for the film or video game industry. Examples of success stories include Volpin Props, Henchmen Studios, God Save the Queen Fashions, and

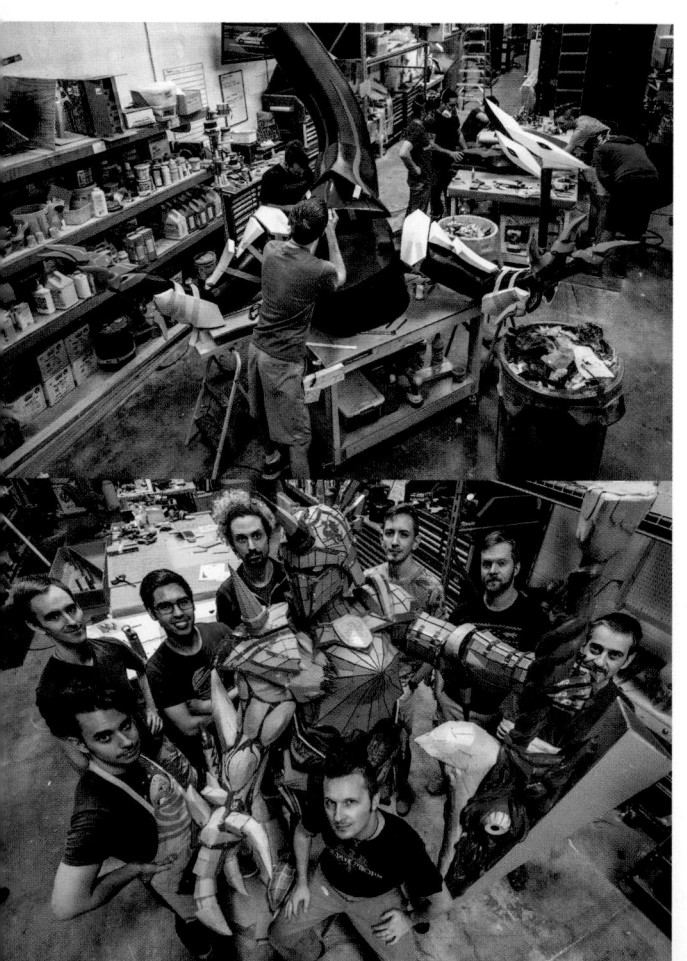

Volpin Props team standing with a big commission they finished

AmazonMandy. It's really exciting to think about where the high-end commission-based business model might expand in the future.

Advantages: There are few things that feel as rewarding as owning your own business and using your creative skills to make a living. You can work on your own schedule and, to an extent, specialize in what you want to make. There is also the excitement of taking on cool and challenging projects that you would have never tackled otherwise. Commissioners are in demand, and depending on your skills and reputation, you can generate lucrative income with this business model.

Disadvantages: It can be easy to take on more projects than you can manage; even the most experienced commissioners can get overwhelmed. Learn to gauge your time and costs, and keep your clients updated with honest info. Start small and build up your project roster with time and experience. To take on commissions, you have to be not only skilled in crafting but also efficient and organized. A client-based business inadvertently means customer service. That includes the active exchange of information, up-to-date communication, and knowing how to occasionally deal with demanding individuals.

COSPLAY MERCHANDISER

It is also possible to make money in the cosplay industry without being a cosplayer at all. The demand for materials that are suitable for cosplay is steadily rising. A fairly new but fast-growing market exists for cosplay-specific materials.

Materials and Supplies: A number of cosplayers have become retailers for cosplay materials and supplies in recent years. They saw a need for materials and entered the business of sourcing—manufacturing in order to directly sell key crafting materials and costume-related products to the public through online shops and at conventions. Other companies started off as theatrical costuming suppliers and expanded into the cosplay market after realizing their products were being used by cosplayers. An example of a company that did this is the Canadian corporation cosplaysupplies.com, which continues to expand its long roster of crafting materials year by year.

Another example of a key cosplay product now sold by cosplayers themselves is wigs. Arda Wigs is a prominent wig company that was created by a pair of American cosplayers, Crystina and Amy. They saw a lack of wig variety and quality as far back as 2008 and decided to fix the situation. When they started, the two of them had to learn how to get into the manufacturing industry and create a distribution network. Since then they have grown into an international company with more than eighty-five styles of wigs. They even have a

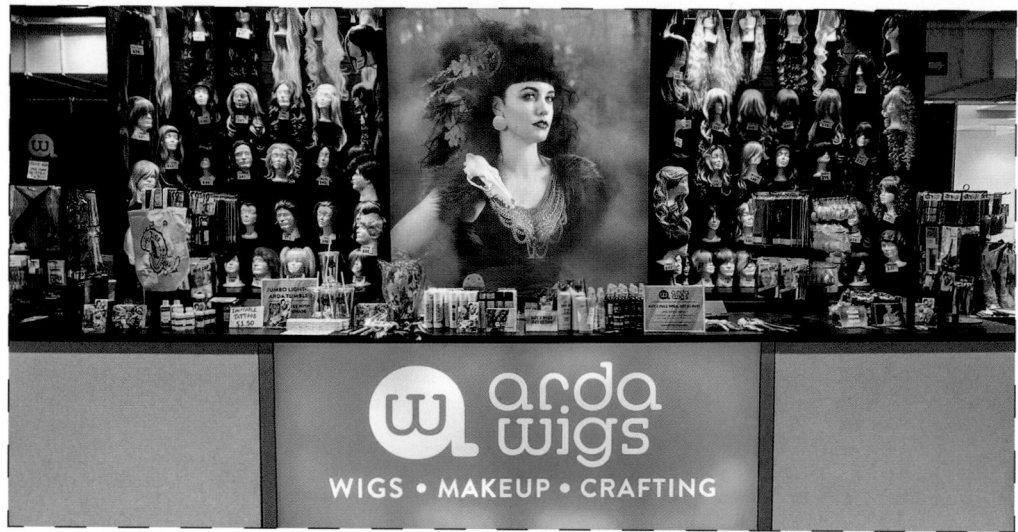

Arda Wigs booth at a con

franchise branch in Canada. Because of their own experiences as cosplayers, they were able to develop products with the features and quality they felt cosplayers needed. There are multiple wig companies that cater to cosplayers these days, such as Epic Cosplay Wigs and Purple Plum.

Beyond wigs and raw materials, there are ready-to-use cosplay products such as my cat ears, horns, wings, and other types of finished accessories. Colored contacts, fascinator hats, and even corsets can be worthwhile specializations for cosplay-related businesses to explore.

Advantages: A specialized business focused on one or two types of products is more manageable than, say, a full-on Halloween costume store. By finding your niche, you can focus your company's efforts on unique, high-quality items that will help you build a brand. My cosplay accessories are known as the Yaya Han® brand, and people can buy them with confidence because the quality of my products has not wavered throughout the years. As you build and expand your brand over time, you can develop relationships with reliable vendors who will source raw materials to you at wholesale prices, which cuts down on production costs. This is something that has helped my business sustain itself.

Since you are offering useful items, your customer base will be very dedicated to you, especially if your products helped them make a costume. Good-quality items inspire good word of mouth, so set a high standard for your wares and do right by your customers. As long as your production process, from sourcing to shipping, is smooth, you could be surprised at how quickly things can take off.

Disadvantages: Getting into sourcing, manufacturing, and distribution is a serious business decision. It requires not only monetary capital but also dedication. You have to be willing to learn about many areas of business, including the manufacturing industry, import taxes, and import procedures. You also have to implement sales strategies to move stock and recoup your costs, just as you would with any other type of product. I don't want to get into manufacturing and sales tips too much, as they would require a lot more words to explain. Instead, I want to give you this advice: Believe in your product and the demand for it. Let that passion guide you in your quest to bring your works to the market.

Convention Sales: Since cosplay is still a niche industry, it doesn't make much sense to open a storefront. Instead, most business owners choose to set up vendor booths at conventions. I talked extensively about my own experience selling at cons in the previous two chapters, and to this day I still offer merchandise in convention exhibit halls around the country.

Vendor booths can range from $150 for a small local event all the way up to $2,000 (or more) for a booth at a big, prestigious pop culture expo. If you want to apply for a booth, you usually have to fill out an application form on the convention's website. Beyond that, however, each con's sign-up process is different.

Do a lot of research and start with one con that is close to you and easy to manage. If you handmade your products, you can also sell them in an artist alley, where the tables are smaller and less expensive. This could be a way to test the market and learn the ropes of convention sales before investing in a proper exhibitor booth. Beware that artist alley tables are in high demand, so you have to sign up for them early.

Once you've decided to do regular convention sales, make a spreadsheet of the cons you are interested in vending at in order to help you stay organized.

This is the type of business that can't be scaled up without hiring employees and managing payroll. Moreover, the nomadic convention vendor life, in which you go from city to city to set up, sell, and tear down, is not for everyone. If you enjoy it, though, it can be incredibly lucrative and exciting.

Advantages: Convention sales have the potential to generate high income. By bringing your products to the perfect target audience at each event, you can make a lot of sales in a short amount of time. Vending at a booth is also a great opportunity to market your brand directly to customers and to find out which products work and which don't. I often display prototype products at my booth and ask people what they like about them. It's free market research. Finally, it is very fulfilling to make a product and see it make someone happy in person.

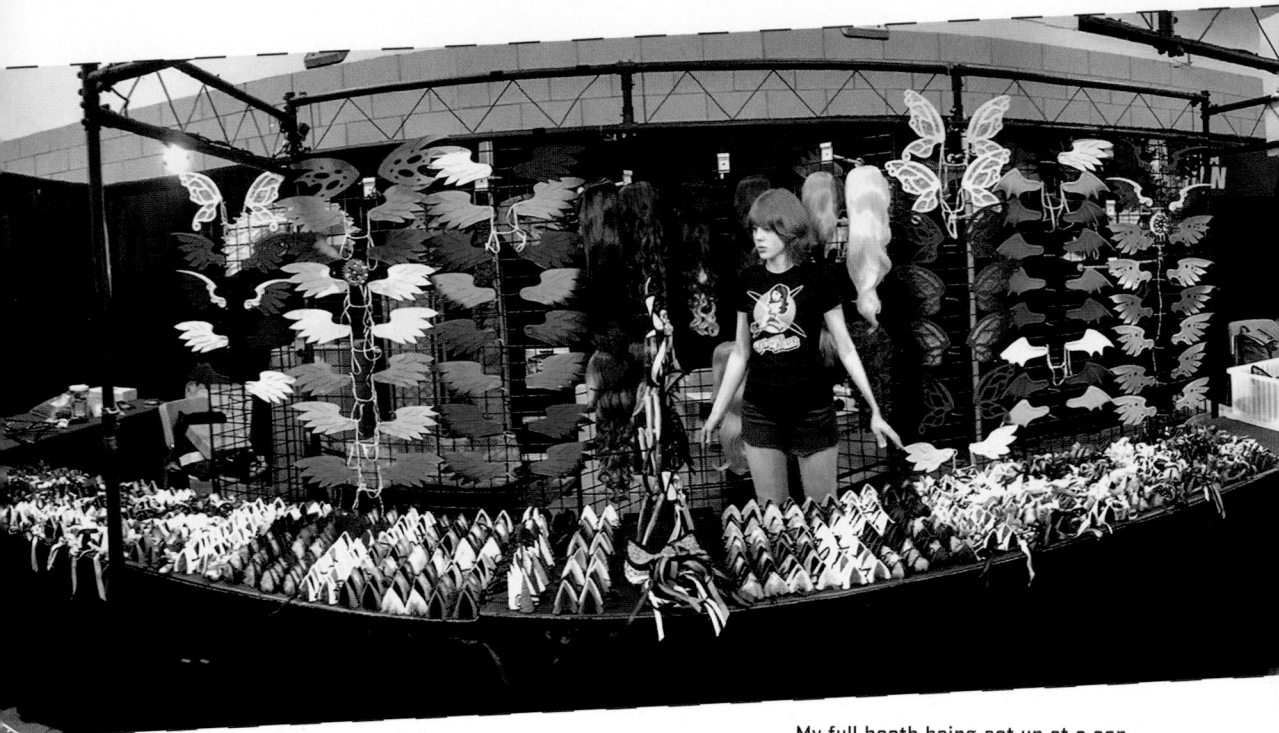

My full booth being set up at a con

Disadvantages: Direct sales is not an easy area to get into. Con booths can be expensive, some cons are hard to get into (with long waitlists), and you have to figure out how to transport your products. The first year of applying and paying for booths can suck your funding dry, fast. Once you've vended at a con, use part of your profits to sign up for the next year in advance.

On-site at a convention, you have to set up your booth, endure the long hours of selling for two, three, or even four days, and then tear down everything at the end. You have to find somewhere to sleep as well. It's physically and mentally draining, so add events only when you feel confident in doing so and consider hiring someone trustworthy to help you during cons. Keep your cash safe and deposit it as quickly as possible. Lastly, each state has its own tax requirements, so as a retailer, you have to get the right permits and file the appropriate tax reports after each show.

Working for a Cosplay Company: You don't have to form a business to join the industry. With more cosplay-centric companies starting up, growing, and thriving, there are more job openings for cosplayers than ever before. These opportunities can be rare and the competition for spots can be tough, but those who are selected to join a team as interns, part-timers, or full-time employees have the great benefit of not only receiving a paycheck but also the opportunity to gain invaluable knowledge and experience.

Advantages: Honestly, if you want to start your own business, one of the best ways to learn how to do so is to work for an established and successful company first. Nothing beats first-hand lessons on business affairs, especially when they pertain to a niche industry such as cosplay. Working for another company also means a steady paycheck in the field in which you are interested (cosplay). You may also feel so happy and fulfilled in your position as a part of a bigger studio or store that you can devote your life to building it and growing with it.

Disadvantages: Working for someone else leaves you susceptible to all the issues that may develop in joint workplaces. You may not get to work on a project that you really like. You may wish your skills were put to better use. When we work in an area in which we are personally invested, it can become a matter of not just getting paid but also doing something worthwhile. Do your best, make the greater good of the company your priority, and ask your employer to utilize you to your full potential.

If you ever decide to pursue your own business endeavors after your time with another company, talk it over with your boss and see if there is a way for your new company to complement your old employer's business. Basically, leave on good terms. We're all in this industry together.

— — —

Compared to my agonizingly slow crawl in the mid-2000s, the prospects for cosplay-related jobs are so promising these days that you can create sustainable income through cosplay in a relatively short time span if you work hard and stay focused. I've seen cosplay entrepreneurs who started their business as a side hustle, eventually quit their day job, and then made enough money to support themselves and even hire employees within three years or less.

Since cosplay is an evolving industry, these are just some of the exciting possibilities awaiting those who want to pursue cosplay as a career—and there are surely more to come.

YAYA'S ADVICE
WHAT YOU NEED TO KNOW IF YOU WANT TO GO PRO

Now that we have looked at a slew of different business formats and the many types of work that professional cosplayers do, the burning question remains: How do *you* get started if you want to go pro? What steps do you have to take to acquire these opportunities? In this last chapter, let's look at what you need to take cosplay to the next level.

First things first.

Find your passion. Whether you want to write a tutorial book on how to make costumes or become a spokesmodel for your favorite gaming franchise, you have to ask yourself: Do I love cosplay enough to dedicate my livelihood to it?

Cosplay is fueled by creative passion, so to make it into a job you have to do something you are passionate about. Think about the tasks you enjoy most while cosplaying and imagine yourself doing them as a full-time job. How does crafting for eight hours (or more) every day sound compared to the tasks you currently perform for work? Can you see yourself performing your chosen task for the next five or ten years?

Did you identify the thing you love the most? I want you to write it down on a sheet of paper. That is your DREAM.

Next, it's important to talk about . . .

Weigh goals versus benefits. Keeping your dream in mind, it is imperative to distinguish between goals and benefits.

Goals are tangible targets you can set. They can include big tasks, like starting a costume commission business and completing twenty cosplay projects in the first year. Alternatively, you can set smaller goals, such as creating two costumes per month and doing one photoshoot every two weeks. The point is to set short-term and long-term goals that are concrete so that you can implement strategies and follow steps to reach them.

By comparison, signing autographs and taking photos with fans are benefits of success. Getting hundreds of compliments on each of your Instagram photos is a benefit of having built an audience; it is a testament to the quality of work you've produced and the goals you've achieved.

If you view superficial benefits such as "getting people to fawn over me so I feel good" as goals, then know that they can distract you from reaching the long-term targets you set for yourself—the targets that actually result in financial returns. Instead, realize that these benefits will come naturally with enough achievements under your belt.

Go back to your sheet of paper and write down potential GOALS under your DREAM. These goals give you a better idea of what you have to do to turn your dream into reality.

Now, it's time to research and implement the steps needed to reach your goals. Consider the following points as guidelines on how to run a business with integrity.

Hone your craft. Cosplay is an artistic freelance industry. It is essential to hone your skills and learn new ones on a regular basis. Even if you already know how to do something well, such as perform a specific crafting technique, you should strive to do it faster, better,

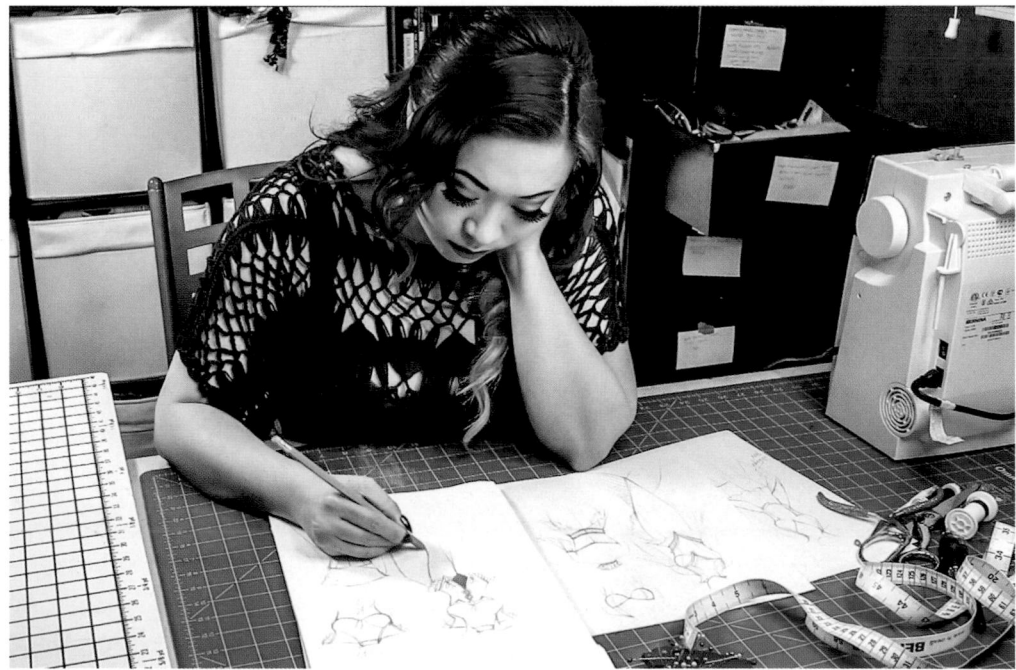

Sketching new designs

and more efficiently. Market demands change, and so do popular techniques and materials that people like to see employed in their costumes. Continue to innovate in order to avoid becoming stagnant.

Embrace time management and discipline. Creative people tend to become engrossed in the artistic aspects of their work and have trouble following a set schedule. Think of time management as another skill to hone, and create a workflow that gives you some form of daily routine. Just as you would while making a costume, keep your business ventures organized and manage your time and workload efficiently. Block out time each day to work on client orders or to curate your social media, but don't mix these activities. Stay focused, and log your time. It will help you manage expectations of what you can achieve, and it's essential to quote realistic prices for your services to your clients.

Build trust and understand the responsibility of transaction. Whatever route you choose to pursue in professional cosplay, you will be offering a product or a service for sale in some form. It is essential to build trust with your customers and collaborators; you need to recognize the responsibility of asking for a monetary transaction. Trust is best built by creating the best products or content that you can, as well as by communicating openly with your customers.

When something doesn't turn out the way you wanted, deal with it in a professional manner. Be honest, and own up to your mistakes. It's easy to have your customers' support in sunny times, but it's how you navigate the storms that sets you apart from other service providers.

Pace yourself. Sometimes businesses expand too fast or are not prepared to deal with sudden success. There is a feast or famine aspect to the cosplay industry, so when something good happens, matters can snowball. This is why you should work on your time management skills. They will give you an understanding of how much work you can handle and what type of work you can take on. Don't be afraid to say no to a project or to hire help if your workload is too big.

Take time off. As a self-employed entrepreneur, it can be really hard to separate work from free time. This is especially true if you work from home. I know it's hard to believe at first, but you will get tired of the constant hustle, and eventually your body will just shut down. Your mental and physical health are the basis of your livelihood as a solopreneur, so take care of yourself. Get used to scheduling time for yourself and for your loved ones where you do not answer business e-mails or think about anything related to cosplay.

Diversify. Every professional cosplayer combines different types of work to generate a sustainable income. Even the most successful cosplayers have multiple revenue strategies.

Keeping your goals in mind, try performing different tasks, coming up with various product ideas, and experimenting with sales routes. The key is to diversify. The cosplay industry is still developing, so you never know what might work for you. That might sound scary to some people, but the possibilities are quite exciting, in my opinion.

> **Every business has to perform administrative tasks. They are not always fun, but they are an important part of pursuing your creative endeavors. You don't have to become a business expert, but I do recommend educating yourself on the basics of running a company, either on your own or through learning platforms or classes. You'll reap the benefits once your business takes off and you have no time left to lose!**

Set up your business. A career in cosplay almost certainly means running your own business, either as a sole proprietor or as the owner of a company with employees. Take the appropriate steps to register your business and secure the necessary licenses. My company is registered as an LLC, or limited liability company. For you, though, it might make more sense to file under a sole proprietorship or to become a C corporation. Study the various types of businesses and choose the structure that best suits your needs.

Even though the process of registering your business might appear tedious or daunting, it is necessary and will protect you down the road. You can do a lot of the work involved on your own—information about establishing your company is freely available on official government websites, after all. That said, it may be worth it to hire a legal professional and/or a tax advisor to facilitate the steps.

It goes without saying that you should file taxes properly and keep track of your earnings and expenditures. As your business grows, you might want to consider hiring or outsourcing work to a bookkeeper who can help sort through the administrative tasks involved with running your business. There are plenty of computer programs out there to help with these responsibilities as well. Keeping track of your finances will give you more confidence as a business owner.

Form a brand. Whether you create physical products or sell your unique image, make sure the name, logo, and design aesthetic of your company are cohesive and identifiable as a brand. In cosplay, it does help to associate a specific person with a brand, since the industry is built around creativity and fandom, so consider clearly making yourself the face of your company.

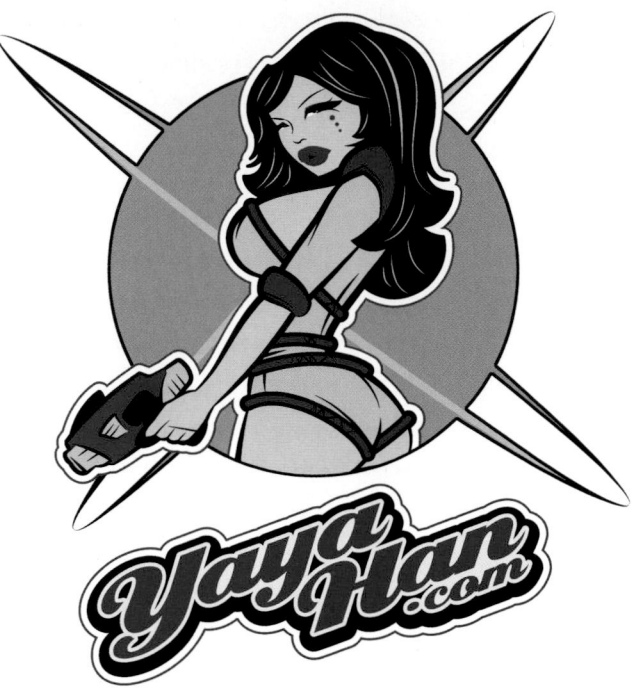

My Retro Space Girl logo

Think about registering your brand name and trademarking your logo as well. I did this with my Retro Space Girl character years ago, and these legal protections have always given me peace of mind and the confidence to continue building on that image.

Create a web presence. Buy a website domain and create your own little corner of the Internet. It can be a super simple website hosted with Wix.com or it can be a more involved blog on WordPress, but no matter what you do, make sure you have a place where all of your best work is gathered and showcased outside of social media platforms. You do not own your social media pages, so your following and the content you put out on a daily basis could all amount to nothing if trends and algorithms change (anyone remember Myspace?) or if you lose access to your account.

That said, besides owning your own website, I suggest choosing two or three social media platforms that suit your brand and the style of online content you like to produce. Then focus on posting your content on those platforms as well. Have a unique and consistent username across all platforms so that people can easily find and follow you.

Connect and communicate. No matter how great your products or services are, the way you market them to the public will strongly influence your success. People are invested in the brands they buy and the public figures they follow, so use your chosen communication channel to connect with your customers in a genuinely heartfelt manner. You can, of course, learn and follow traditional marketing strategies, but from my experience, cosplay is an industry all about personal connections and shared passions. I'm not saying that you have to share every aspect of your life with your fans, but your enthusiasm and excitement about your products or services could make a bigger impression on an audience than generic slogans.

Hopefully, by now your sheet of paper is full of dreams, goals, and ideas. I will leave you with two more thoughts to keep with you throughout your new journey. I use them as mantras to help me conquer hard workdays as well as to stay on track with my long-term goals.

Presenting my trims at the JOANN headquarters

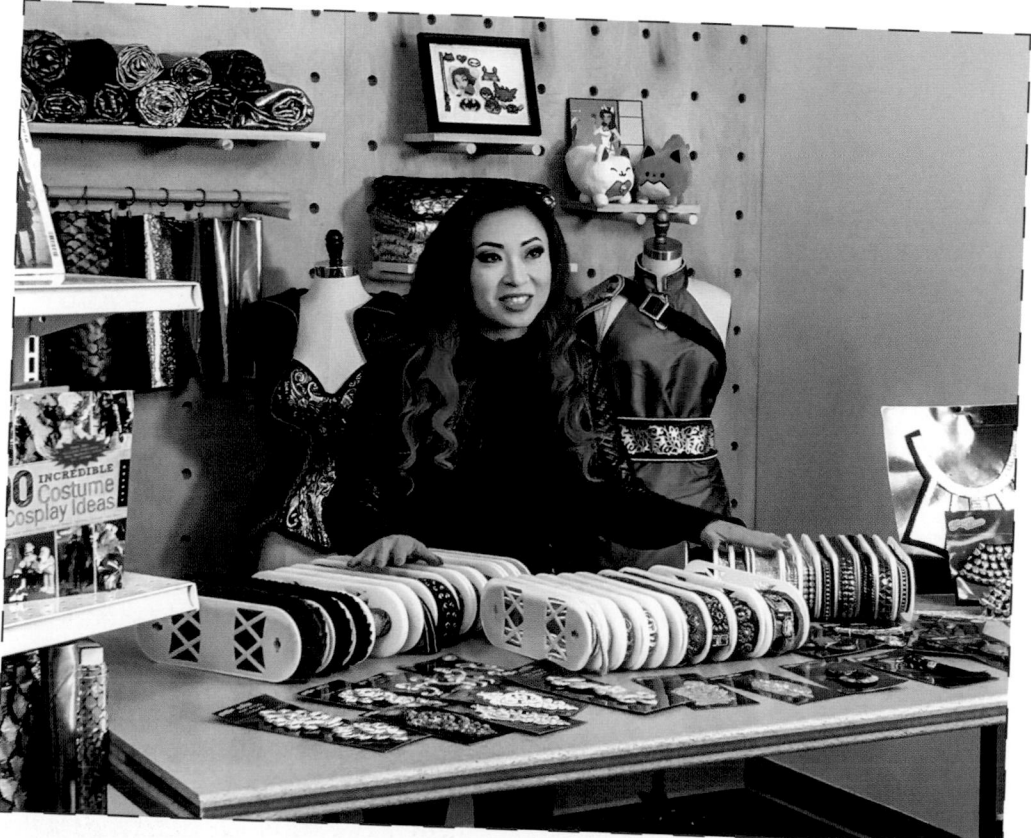

Be patient and consistent. No matter what you set out to do, be consistent with your content and be patient, even if you don't see immediate success. With social media posts, for example—you never know who will see your content and what it might lead to, so don't be discouraged if a post doesn't receive a ton of likes or comments. When it comes to selling products at conventions, don't give up if your first vendor table doesn't generate as much income as you had expected. Instead, view the event as an opportunity to tell people about your brand.

Some businesses and brands take off immediately, but most require time and nurturing to grow. This is another reason why you should choose to do something about which you are genuinely passionate. That passion will help you be more consistent in creating content and more patient in your endeavors.

Contribute and share. Becoming a professional cosplayer is not about putting yourself on a pedestal and letting people admire you. Rather, ask yourself some questions: How can you contribute to the community? What value does your work bring to the public?

From a marketing perspective, ask yourself: Who are my ideal customers (and who are not)? How can I help them? What problem do I solve for them?

When you put something out, think about how it might influence the people who see it and about what kind of message you want to send. Hopefully your work empowers your audience and fellow creators.

Success doesn't get smaller by sharing it. Rather, it grows and gives back. Take care of your community and it will take care of you.

— — —

I got into cosplay before there was a market for it, so I was able to take a lot of time to try different things, make mistakes, and really figure out, in my heart, what I wanted to do. Now that cosplay is such a fast-developing industry, though, if you are a new cosplayer, there is pressure to succeed from the get-go. The emphasis is now placed on avoiding mistakes rather than learning from them. Also, with so many success stories, it's easy to get swept up by the glamorous lifestyle of top cosplayers and emulate their business models without taking enough time to figure out what you really like to do as a cosplayer. What works for another creator may not work for you, so if you go down a road without enough consideration, you might discover challenges and drawbacks that were not so apparent at the beginning.

That's why I want you to write your dream down on paper and use it as a beacon to guide you through the process of becoming an independent businessperson. It will keep you motivated during good times and help you weather bad times.

Going pro as a cosplayer is not for everyone, and it shouldn't have to be, but for those who dream of owning their own businesses or who wish to do something creative for a living, I hope that my tips are able to give you confidence and make those dreams seem a little more real.

My last advice is this: Don't be afraid to give your dreams a shot. If you can envision your place in the cosplay industry (or any industry, for that matter), go for it! Like me, you can try, fail, and try again. Your cosplay career might lead you to a completely unexpected path. Who knows?

Cosplay is an exciting industry. It can become an amazing springboard into other fields and careers such as acting, modeling, design, marketing, and publishing. When I started down my road in this crazy pastime more than twenty years ago, no one could have imagined the career paths that would open up for creative entrepreneurs and professional nerds.

Get ready for your level-up, cosplayers, because the future belongs to you!

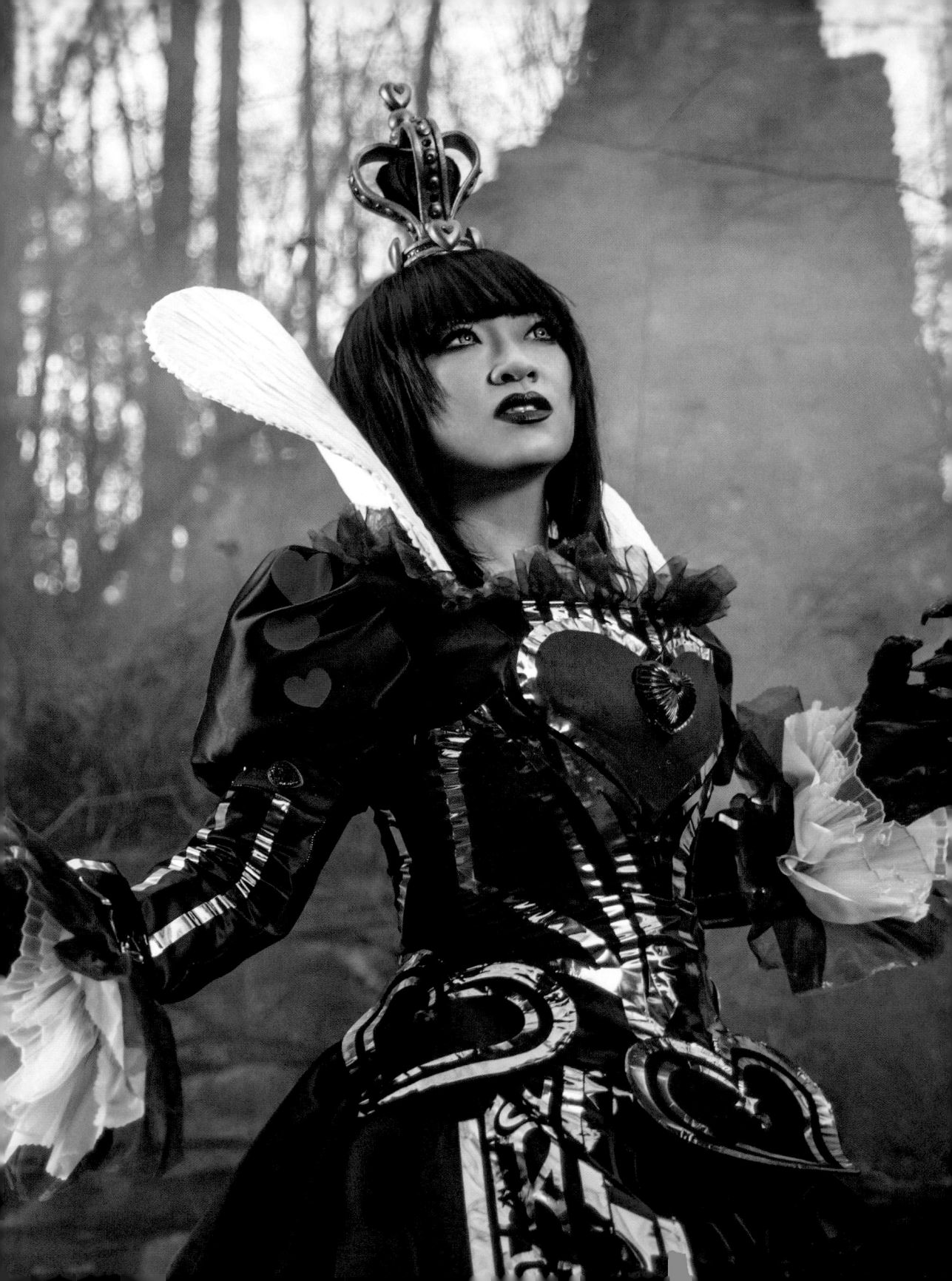

The Dream of Cosplay

On a sunny September day, I sat in a small Volkswagen that wove through the narrow streets of the historic city of Kassel, Germany. Next to me, my mom was engrossed in driving, listening intently to GPS instructions.

Our destination was the anime convention Connichi. We had driven three hours from Wiesbaden, my parents' home in Germany, in order for me to appear as the convention's first-ever cosplay guest. The year was 2012, and I was already a well-established name in the cosplay community. Back in the United States, my cosplay business was thriving. We had just moved into a shiny new warehouse, I was recognized in and out of costume at every fandom event in the country, and I was in the midst of preparing for my upcoming network TV show on Syfy.

However, at that moment, as I looked out into the passing streets, I felt more like a rookie than a pro. This weekend would mark my very first convention appearance in Germany and, more importantly, would be the first time my mom came to a convention and saw me cosplay. I tensed up with nervousness.

Cosplay was a sore topic in our family. Ever since I'd left Germany for the United States thirteen years prior, the relationship between my mom and I had been strained. Coming from an Asian family, it would have been hard enough to embark on a creative career even if I had stayed put in Germany—moving to America only increased the distance and disconnect between us. My German upbringing further multiplied the pressure to succeed and hammered in the importance of achieving stability in life.

By choosing to move so far away at such a young age, I didn't just veer from the path that was laid out for me—I abandoned it. For a long time, my mom could not come to grips with my decision. Whenever we talked on the phone, she alternated between scolding me for not staying in school and pleading with me to find a real job. In the first six years, we visited each other only once, and sometimes we would go for months without contact. Things got especially bad after I quit my first job to start a cosplay commission business, and for a couple of years, I really felt estranged from my family. Years later, even after I found success and told my mom about all the exciting things I got to do and places I was able to travel, she continued to be suspicious of my cosplay lifestyle.

The concept of dressing up as fictional characters was completely foreign to her. While she appreciated my intricate costume-making skills, she scoffed at the exaggerated makeup and excessive cleavage in my photos. She'd ask, "*Warum so ein Schwachsinn?*" which translates to "Why this ridiculousness?" No matter how much time I spent explaining the world of cosplay to her or how many photos and videos I showed her, I could not get her to understand the value of the activity. Once I even did a presentation for her on my business structure and showed her my banking info so she would not worry so much. Despite that, she always fretted over my future and wondered when this "thing" would go away. I realized that my only option was to drag my mom to a con and show her the fandom world firsthand.

When Connichi expressed interest in having me as their first cosplay guest in 2012, I jumped at the opportunity. Not only was this a great honor from a convention I respected, but I also saw it as a way to go back to my roots. As a teen, I left Germany to pursue my creative dreams, and now I was going to return as an accomplished professional with a purpose. I was going to teach panels, do interviews, and judge the prestigious World Cosplay Summit German Preliminaries. Finally, my parents would have the chance to come to a convention with me and see me in my full glory.

We pulled up to the Stadthalle Kassel, a large neoclassical city hall with a colonnade entrance in an open plaza. It was already bustling with attendees, many of whom were dressed in costume.

My mom stopped the car, leaned past me to look at the colorful crowd outside the window, and said, "Look at these crazy people."

I whipped around and hissed at her, "Don't say that, Mama! I am one of these crazy people!"

She seemed taken aback by my outburst but only made a sheepish face and said, "Sorry, okay." We went off to check into our hotel near the convention hall, and the whole time I reminded her to not say anything weird during the show. Dear goodness, please.

To my surprise, my mom turned out to be the best assistant I ever had. She offered to iron my costumes and brush out my wigs, which were tasks that no one had ever done for me before. She helped me get into costume every morning and made sure I drank water and took breaks during the day. More than once, she peeled a banana and shoved it in my face after she recognized my habit of forgetting to eat at conventions.

I had a little table with autographed cosplay prints and cat ears laid out at the show. My mom seemed to really enjoy getting people to try on the ears, and she enthusiastically chatted with attendees who waited in line to see me. My stepdad, Robert, made the drive to Connichi in order to see me on the Saturday of the convention, which was another big surprise to me. He had never come out for anything I was interested in before. Soon he was put to work as well, mostly to take cellphone photos of people with me. At one point, I remember looking over at my parents in mild disbelief, because they were both sporting cat ears on their heads and laughing with cosplayers. Then I was pulled back into the frenzy of the con.

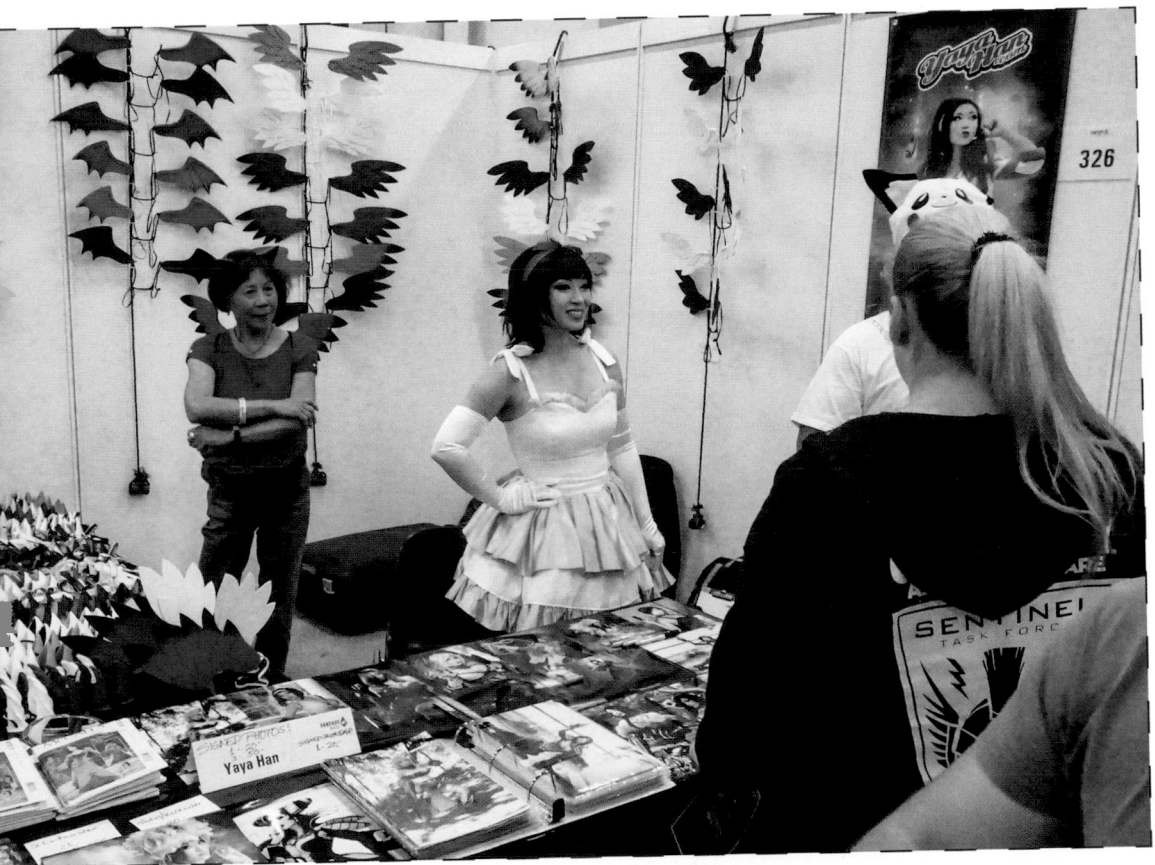

My mom (wearing cat ears!) and I at a con

Connichi was a whirlwind. My costumes were well received. My panels and contests went swimmingly. Most of the time I had long lines of attendees waiting to see me at my table, and I received endless photo requests. A lot of the cosplayers who I met were extremely excited to ask me questions and tell stories about how they had found cosplay. Some even said they were inspired to cosplay because of my pictures. I was very amused by the fact that I could make people's jaws drop by speaking German to them. Most show attendees only had an inkling that I had once lived in Germany, so they did not expect me to speak the language fluently. It was so nice to connect with people on so many levels, and I ended the event with a profound feeling of having come full circle.

Despite how well the con went, though, I kept wondering what my mom really thought of the geeky environment I had brought her to. Was it still *Schwachsinn* to her?

After Connichi, I had a few more days left to spend in Germany, so I went home with my parents to decompress and rest. On the first night after the event, my mom cooked a hearty dinner for the three of us. Sitting at the table together as a family, in between bites, my mom suddenly paused and looked up at me with a serious expression.

"Yaya," she said, "do you know that these people idolize you?"

I blinked.

"All the stories they told . . . how you inspired them. I had no idea."

I put down my utensils and replied, "Yes. I know, Mama. That's why I take this so seriously. I feel responsible."

I saw in her eyes that she finally understood my love for cosplay. All the things I tried to explain to her for so many years had finally clicked. I recalled all the times I had asked her to trust me and let me explore this path, as well as all the ways in which I wanted her to accept me for who I was, but in the end, it was the power of the cosplay community that convinced her of the validity of this art form. In that moment, my mom and I formed a bond we had never shared before.

From that point on, my mom and Robert embraced cosplay and became my biggest supporters. Whenever I was invited to a convention in Europe, they took time off from work and met me at the event to help out (or, if they couldn't come to a show, I would extend my trip abroad to visit them in Germany). We spent time together in Switzerland, France, Spain, and Sweden, all because of cosplay. My parents even came to China and India to assist me during cons and to travel around with me afterward.

For the first time ever, I felt as if my interests were genuinely important to them. We saw one another every few months, and I even bought a sewing machine in Germany so I could visit them for weeks at a time and work on costumes. My mom always wanted to know what I was making. I showed both my parents clips from *Heroes of Cosplay* after it aired. Whenever a new opportunity arose, such as the chance to make cosplay fabrics for JOANN stores, I shared the news with them. My mom seemed especially impressed with the McCall

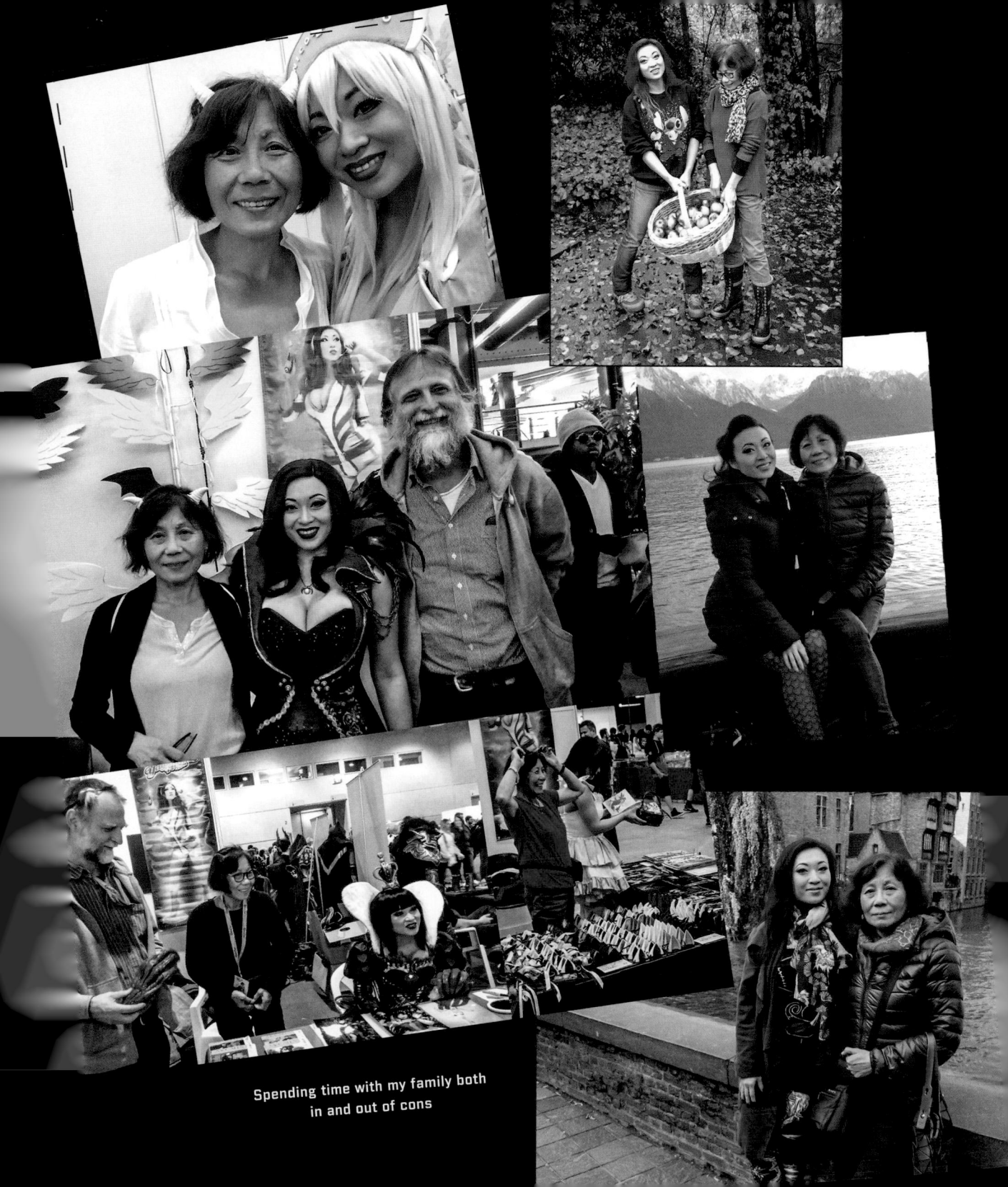

Spending time with my family both
in and out of cons

patterns. Maybe that was because she could hold the envelopes that contained those patterns in her hands and look at my picture on them. Recently she has even started learning English so that she can come visit me in the United States and help me here.

Of all the incredible accomplishments and huge changes that cosplay has brought to my life, I never expected that it would also repair my estranged relationship with my family. For the better part of my youth, I thought of my family as broken and of myself as an outcast. When I ran away to America, I didn't think about how my decision would affect everyone I left behind. In the many conversations I've had with my mom since Connichi 2012, I learned just how terrified she was for me and how helpless she felt as a parent after I moved. I always knew that her worry came from a place of wanting the best for me, but I never knew how many tearful and sleepless nights she went through, thinking of her only child surviving in a foreign country that was thousands of miles away. We talked out many of our problems, going all the way back to my childhood, and I have never felt closer to my mom than I do now.

It's amazing how many parallels my journey to the United States has to my mom's own journey from China to Germany. Like me, she felt suffocated in her life and was compelled to break free so she could try something new. We both even crossed an ocean to do just that. Neither of us knew what was going to happen to us, and each of us found love and a new life on a different continent.

Meeting Brian and building a life together with him helped me understand how much Robert must have sacrificed for my mom. It also helped me see how hard he must have tried to be a good dad to me. We get along wonderfully now—especially through our shared passion for exotic foods.

My father is still back in China. I don't see him as much as I'd like, but he did come to Beijing Comic Con one year and saw me in full action for two days. Still a man of few words, he preferred to take a ton of photos and keep a stack of my cosplay prints at the end of

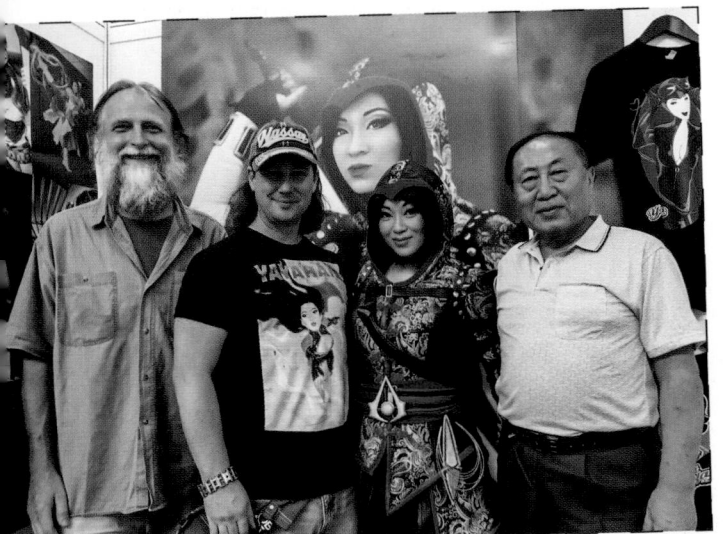

Robert, Brian, Dad, and I posing at a con in China.

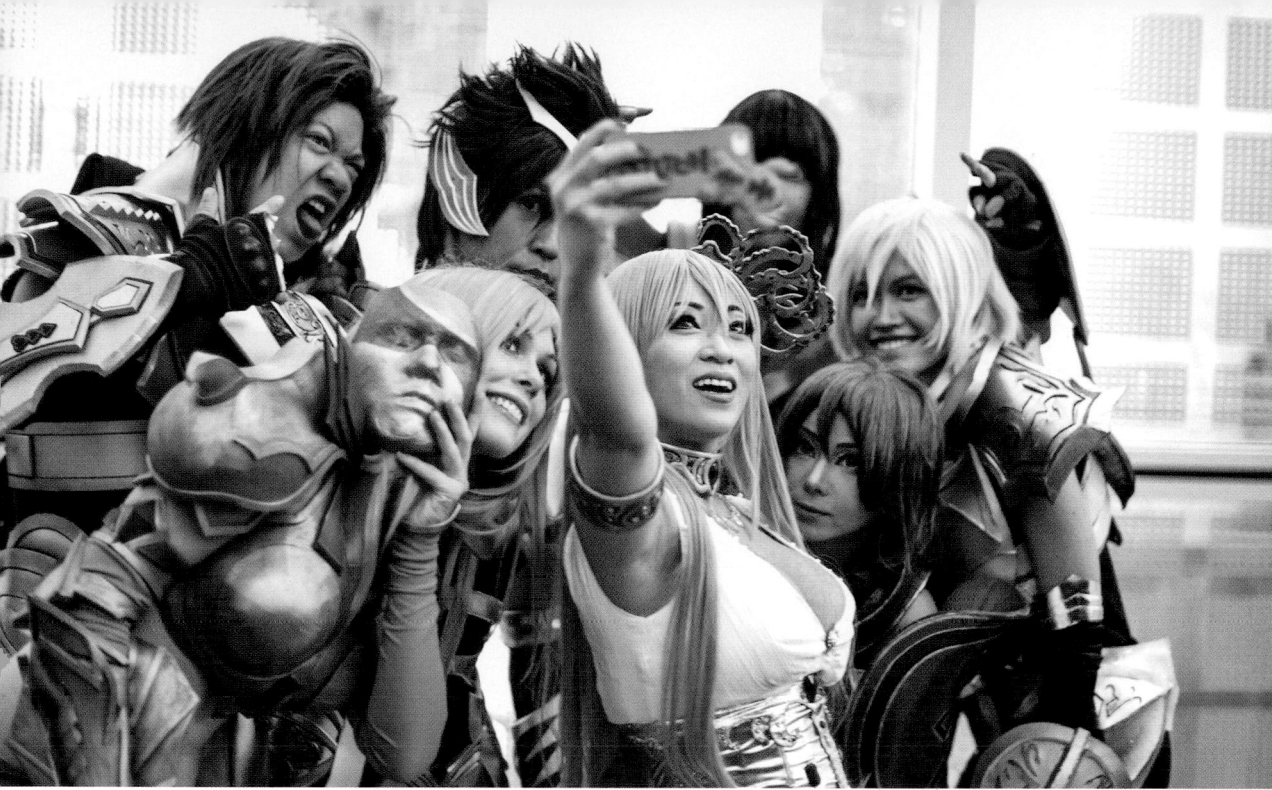

My friends and I taking a selfie together

the weekend to show friends and family back home. If there was ever a photo to sum up my crazy life, it is the one of me (cosplaying, of course) with the three men in my life: my Chinese father, my German stepdad, and my American fiancé.

I used to think it was cliché to call my journey the pursuit of an "American dream" because I wasn't escaping extreme poverty or persecution. But most people don't just leave their entire existence behind to move to another country unless there are strong enough reasons that drive them to do so. America beckoned, with promises of opportunity and the freedom to pursue whatever career I wanted. I thought I wanted to become a Disney animator, but I was really looking for purpose and kinship. In the most pivotal moment of my life, when I was utterly lost and alone in the world, I discovered cosplay. It lit a fire in me. The joy this craft brought me helped me push myself through the hardest of times, kept me looking ahead during long stretches of uncertainty, and gave me confidence in all my endeavors.

I never became an animator, but my American dream did come true. Cosplay gave me all I ever wanted, plus things I never considered possible. It continues to dazzle me and surprise me, and I can't wait to see what's on the horizon for the world of cosplay.

I hope that after reading this book, you feel fired up to begin your own cosplay journey! May it give you as much happiness as it's given me.

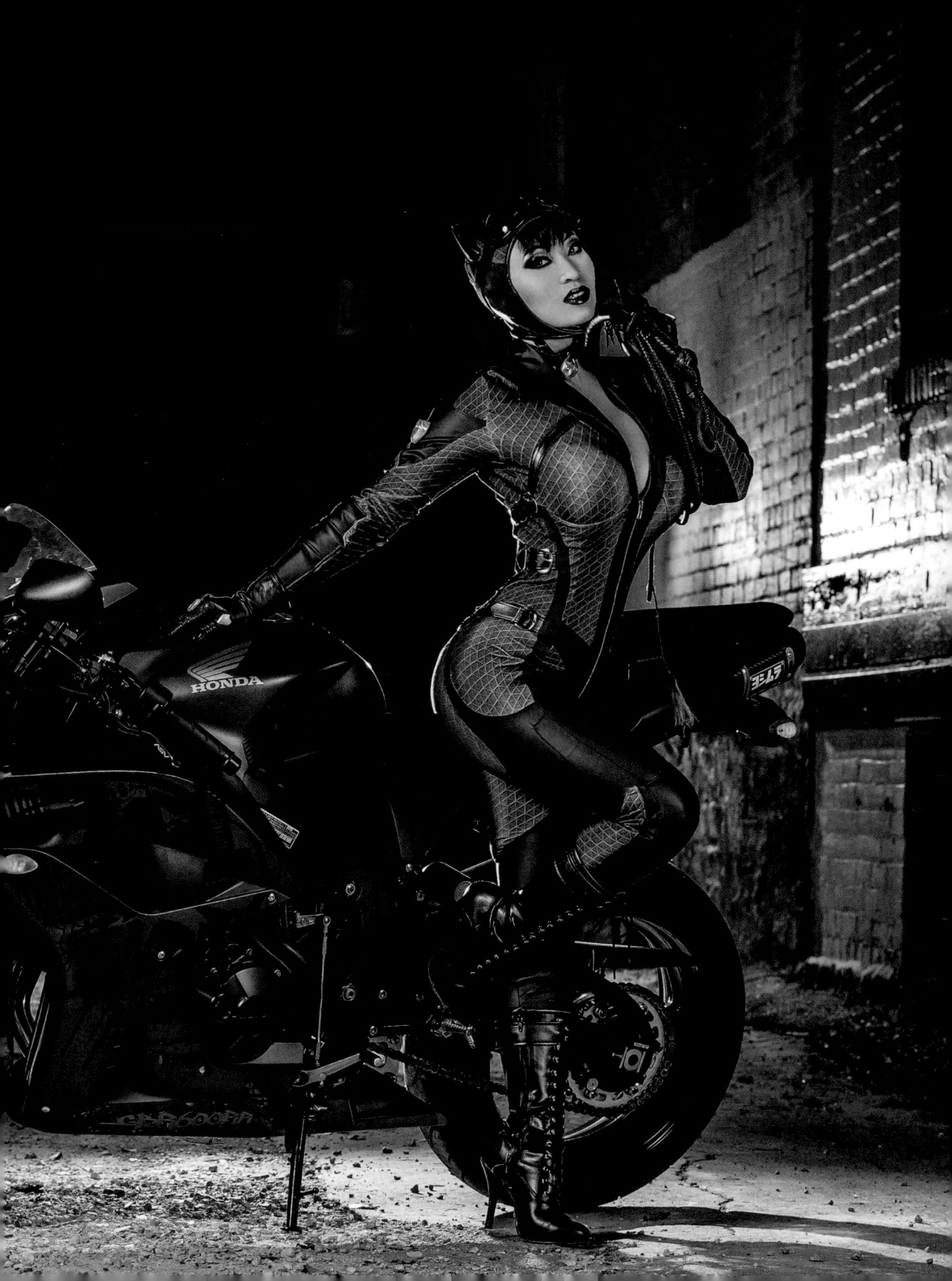

ACKNOWLEDGMENTS

This book would not have been possible without the following incredible human beings.

My editor Kate Zimmermann, who openly welcomed my ideas, reassured me during moments of uncertainty, spurred me on, and taught me so much about the world of book publishing. Everyone at Sterling Publishing, from the editing team to layout, design, sales, and marketing, thank you for supporting this book and making it look so wonderful and so "Yaya." I give thank-yous to Colette Bennett, for being so enthusiastic and helpful throughout the entire writing process. You kept me going when I was stuck, and you were so invested in this story that I felt obligated to tell it in full, even when I felt scared at times. I could not have asked for a better content editor and appreciated our video chats and in-person café meet-ups immensely. Karen Heinrich, for your wealth of knowledge and shared love of cosplay that helped me organize my thoughts on so many of the chapters. Briana Lawrence, for helping me find the right tone when talking about some of the more difficult topics in our community. Matt Munson, for recommending me to Kate and leading me to the hardest assignment I have ever been given, lol.

A million thank-yous to all my amazing friends, photographers, cosplayers, artists, and everyone who so kindly donated their photographs for usage in this book—your images were vital in illustrating the vibrant cosplay scene and I appreciate your many hours of digging through archives, scanning in of images, and uploading of files. And to my dear patient friends on Facebook who answered my polls and research questions with such enthusiasm, as well as cheered me on during those super tough writing days, thank you so much.

Lastly, I want to acknowledge my three wonderful parents who support everything I do and whom I hope to have made proud with this book. And to Brian Boling, my partner in life, best travel buddy ever, and big damn super hero, thank you for loving me and for being on this journey with me (and for making delicious breakfast every morning while I wrote).

RESOURCES

EDUCATIONAL RESOURCES FOR COSPLAY

The following list of educators, community sites, and tutorial channels will help you get started in your costume-making quest. Happy crafting!

GENERAL COSPLAY TUTORIAL OUTLETS

INSTRUCTABLES

instructables.com

Website featuring all kinds of subjects—not just costuming; allows access to project tutorials and workshops

ADAM SAVAGE'S TESTED

tested.com

Videos, podcasts, and articles on pop culture, art, how-tos, and many other subjects

COSPLAY TUTORIAL

cosplaytutorial.com

Costuming tutorials on a wide variety of subjects and projects

KAMUI COSPLAY

kamuicosplay.com

https://www.youtube.com/user/Mogrymillian

Tons of cosplay tutorials, digital and print crafting books, and free and affordable downloadable patterns

KINPATSU COSPLAY

kinpatsucosplay.com

Monthly cosplay tutorials, walk-throughs, plus digital crafting books and patterns for a variety of topics ranging from sewing to wig styling to armor making and makeup

LEARN TO SEW

SO SEW EASY

so-sew-easy.com
Website featuring basic sewing tutorials and techniques; mostly geared toward average clothing projects but includes good instructions for beginners and also offers a selection of free patterns

ALL FREE SEWING

allfreesewing.com
Another good website for beginners; tutorials range from pattern making to threading a sewing machine; offers free ebooks and a selection of sewing materials

MELLY SEWS

mellysews.com
Large selection of basic clothing sewing tutorials, from modifying patterns to taking measurements; not really geared toward costuming but offers a good place for beginners to start; also offers a selection of free patterns

FOUNDATIONS REVEALED

foundationsrevealed.com
Fantastic learning community for corset makers

SEWING FOR BEGINNERS BY NARAKU BROCK

narakubrock.storenvy.com
Straightforward and easy-to-read sewing book, available in digital download and paperback

LEARN TO MAKE ARMOR AND PROPS

PUNISHED PROPS ACADEMY

punishedprops.com
https://www.youtube.com/user/punishedprops
Huge selection of tutorials on foam-smithing, 3-D printing, and painting; offers digital and paperback armor and prop-making books; lists free prop blueprints with instructions for how to download and print out the files; also includes other resources, tools, and supplies you might need, at punishedprops.com/bills-tools/

SKS PROPS

sksprops.com
Extensive armor and prop walk-throughs and build-documentation, as well as video tutorials

EVIL TED SMITH

eviltedsmith.com
https://www.youtube.com/user/evilted40
Maker of armor patterns and another resource for foam tutorials

VOLPIN PROPS

volpinprops.com
https://www.youtube.com/user/volpin
Offers project walk-throughs and PDF or vector file illustrations of a variety of creations

LIGHTNING COSPLAY

lightningcosplay.com
Supplies costume walk-throughs and mold making and casting books

STELLA CHUU

stellachuu.com
Selection of cosplay prop patterns such as Overwatch's *Mercy wings and Doomfist gauntlets and* Boku no Hero Academia's *Bakugou grenade gauntlets*

SMOOTH-ON

smooth-on.com
The leader in molding and casting materials with an ever-expanding selection of products. Includes extensive how-to videos and instructional content

LEARN OTHER SPECIALITY SKILLS

ARDA WIGS

arda-wigs.com
Great selection of wig styling tutorials to accompany a trusted cosplay wig brand

WIGS101

wigs101.com
Easy to follow, free wig styling, dyeing, and cutting tutorials by German cosplayer Kukkii-san; digital and paperback wig styling book available in English and German

KLEINER PIXEL MAKEUP

https://m.youtube.com/user/KleinerPixel
Simple, easy-to-follow cosplay makeup tutorials for specific characters, mostly anime and video games

DREMEL MAKER STUDIO

dremelmakerstudio.chaordix.com
Great online learning community for Dremel users with educational content and challenges for DIY projects spanning beyond armor making

ADAFRUIT

adafruit.com
Offers a large selection of LEDs and LED accessories as well as extensive tutorials on how to work with electronics

HATS BY LEKO

hatsupply.com/tutorials
Free PDF tutorials for hat-making projects and beginner millinery techniques

PHOTOGRAPHY CREDITS

Courtesy Yaya Han: 1, 5, 6, 8, 9, 10, 11, 12, 13, 18 (bottom), 20, 21, 22, 27, 35 (top, lower right), 36, 37 (bottom), 38, 39, 41 (both), 46, 47, 49 (top), 51, 54, 55, 56, 59 (bottom), 60, 62, 63, 64, 67, 68, 76 (all), 80, 85 (bottom), 86 (both), 89, 92, 99, 152, 162, 170, 174, 175, 178, 181, 182, 185 (both), 186, 187 (both),188, 189 (courtesy McCalls), 208, 211, 214, 221, 223 (all), 224

Affliction Media Productions: 128-129, 218; Hannah Alexander/Alexandra Lee Studio: 112 (center and bottom); Hannah Alexander/Brian Bolling: 17; Vicky Bunny Angel: 59 (top); Soni Aralynn: 199; Arda Wigs: 206; Avant Geek: 113 (lower right); Avant Geek (left) and courtesy of Canvas Cosplay and Singer® (right): 198; Tayla Barter: 65 (bottom), 81, 83; Blikku: 146 (upper left 2), 153; Brian Boling: x, xii-xiii, xiv, 18 (top), 69, 70-71, 82 (right), 85 (top), 90, 94, 96, 97, 103, 114, 124, 127, 137, 139 (bottom), 142, 155, 169, 191; Brichibi (Elyse Lavonne / Tyrine C of Musetap Studios): 146 (center 2); Fernando Brischetto: 225; Mark Caldarola, donated to the International Costumers Guild: 30 (top); Jason Chau: 159; Ejen Chung: 16, 57; Stella Chuu: 197; Nicole Ciaramella: 146 (upper right); CoolADN: 82 (lower left); Ted Cornell, personal collection of Nora Mai, donated to the International Costumers Guild: 30 (lower left); Kim Razvan Courtney: 107; Ginny Di/Anne Barhyte: 111 (bottom); Zach Fischer / Dave Yang: 114 (bottom); Kevin Green: 44, 73 (all), 122, 157; Paul Hillier: 151 (top); Sherry Jackson: 30 (bottom right), 33 (lower right); KayBear: 146 (lower right); Kayhettin: ii-iii; Gladzy Kei/Dave Yang: 116; Josh Kent: 154; Harrison Krix: 65 (top); Heather Laude: 215; Ackson Lee: 120; Benny Lee: 108 (lower right), 133; Leonard Lee: 52, 82 (top), 108 (upper left and center); Kevin Lillard: 42 (right), 79 (bottom two), 95 (top); Adrian Lozano: 28 (both); Lionel Lum: 26, 35 (lower left), 79 (top two), 109; Damien Martinet: 88; Brandon Isaacson (McThor): 113 (top); MLZ Studios: 121; Micah Moore: 204 (both); Jennifer Newman: 37 (top), 42 (left); Geoffrey Nicholson: 135; Jessica Nigri/Martin Wong, Tayla Barter, Kay Bear, Vivi Vision: 102; Jessica Nigri: 100; Kyle O'neal/Elemental Photography: 117; Panterona Cosplay/GK Studios: 146 (bottom left 2); Phaced Photography: 98 (left); Pink Elephant Photography: 226; Pixelette Photography: 166-167; Punished Props: 105, 201, 202; Svetlana Quindt: 111 (top), 164-165; Sarcasm-hime: 45; Judith Stephens: ix, 74-75, 123, 132, 134, 151 (bottom 2); Kevin Stewart: 95 (bottom); Sunset Dragon: 115 (top); Alyson Tabbitha: 118; Jay Tablante: 98 (right); 108 (upper right); Nobuyuki Takahashi: 31; Paul Tien: 49 (bottom), 171; Meg Turney: 195, 200; TWIIN Cosplay: 139 (top), 144; Jacqueline Ward: 33 (left, upper right); Martin Wong: 24-25, 61, 108 (lower left), 125; Colin Young-Wolff for Riot Games: 4

INDEX

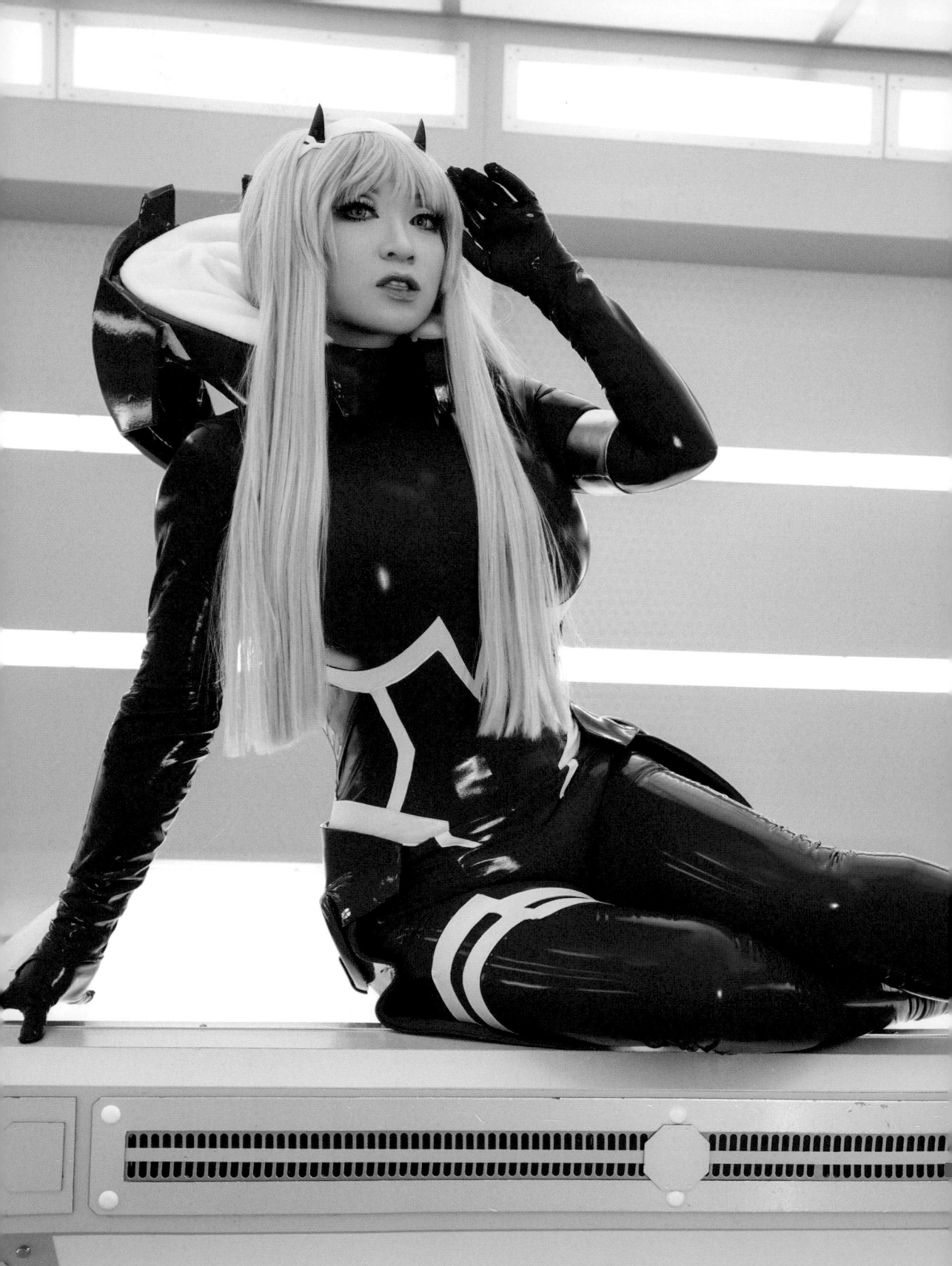

ABOUT THE AUTHOR

YAYA HAN is an award-winning cosplayer, costume designer, and TV personality. She is considered a leader and pioneer in the fan costuming industry, who played a pivotal role in introducing cosplay to the global mainstream audience. Yaya has been a guest judge on three seasons of TBS's *King of the Nerds* competition show, starred in Syfy's docu-series *Heroes of Cosplay*, and coproduced the feature documentary film *Cosplay Universe*. She has graced the covers of magazines, been quoted in books, and been interviewed countless times by print and internet media outlets. She has also lent her image to the comic book series *Wonderous 2: The Yaya Han Saga*, produced by Lion Forge Comics, becoming a legitimate superhero in the comic book world.

Starting out as a young cosplaying fan in 1999, Yaya gained notoriety through her prolific award-winning costume creations. With close to four hundred intricate and lavish costumes to date, Yaya is a craftsmanship icon in the fandom world and has inspired countless people to get into cosplay. She has appeared as a guest, panelist, judge, performer, and host at hundreds of conventions and events all over the world. Her unmatched knowledge of the cosplay world eventually led her to focus on product design and development of cosplay-centric materials and tools. As the first cosplayer to successfully enter mass retail, Yaya has been designing cosplay-specific sewing patterns with the McCall Pattern Company since 2015. She helped launch the B590 sewing machine model for BERNINA International AG. In 2016, US crafting giant JOANN Fabric and Craft released the Cosplay by Yaya Han fabric line nationwide, making high-quality cosplay-centric materials easily accessible to professionals and amateur users in North America. With Yaya's guidance, JOANN has since expanded the Cosplay by Yaya Han collections into trims, embellishments, and armor-making materials, creating a game-changing cosplay store within a store.

Through hard work, unmatched passion, and infectious enthusiasm, Yaya has helped cosplay gain respect and integrity as an art form. Everyday, Yaya continues to pave the path for the beloved art and lifestyle we know as Costume Play.

Where to find Yaya Han: yayahan.com; instagram.com/yayahan; facebook.com/yayacosplay; twitter.com/yayahan; youtube.com/user/yayacosplay; deviantart.com/yayacosplay

Where to purchase Yaya Han branded products: yayahan.com (Cosplay cat ears, wings, demon horns, elf ears and more. Also offers a selection of autographed prints, posters, and other Yaya merchandise); **joann.com** (Cosplay by Yaya Han fabrics, trims and embellishments, EVA foam, Dremel rotary tools and more. Frequent sales and every day coupons, as well as free shipping on some products.); **Cosplay.mccall.com** (Cosplay patterns in various sizes); **cosplayfabrics.com** (Yaya's creative partner in cosplay materials); **spotlightstores.com** (Cosplay by Yaya Han fabrics in Australia).